A Biographical Dictionary of

English Women Writers
1580–1720

A Biographical Dictionary of

English Women Writers 1580–1720

Maureen Bell
George Parfitt
Simon Shepherd

G.K.HALL&CO.
70 LINCOLN STREET, BOSTON, MASS.

First published in the United States of America by
G.K. Hall & Co., 70 Lincoln Street, Boston, Mass.

First published in Great Britain in 1990 by
Harvester Wheatsheaf,
66 Wood Lane End, Hemel Hempstead,
Hertfordshire, HP2 4RG
A division of
Simon & Schuster International Group

© Maureen Bell, George Parfitt, Simon Shepherd 1990

Printed and bound in Great Britain.

Library of Congress Cataloging-in-Publication Data

Bell, Maureen
   A biographical dictionary of English women writers, 1580–1720 /
Maureen Bell, George Parfitt, Simon Shepherd.
      p.   cm.
   Includes bibliographical references.
   ISBN 0–8161–1806–X
   1. Women authors. English — Early modern, 1500–1700 — Biography —
Dictionaries.   2. Women authors, English — 18th century — Biography —
Dictionaries.   3. English literature — Early modern, 1500–1700 — Bio
bibliography.   4. English literature — Women authors — Bio
bibliography.   5. English literature — 18th century — Bio
bibliography.   6. Women — Great Britain — Biography — Dictionaries.
7. Women — Ireland — Biography — Dictionaries.   I. Parfitt, George A.
E.   II. Shepherd, Simon.   III. Title.
PR113.B46 1990
820.9'9287'03 — dc20
[B]   89–26844
                                                                  CIP

---

1 2 3 4 5   94 93 92 91 90

For Elaine Hobby with our love and thanks

Contents

Contents

Acknowledgements

We should like to thank the staff of Friends House for their hospitality and help; Dr Hector MacDonald and Maureen Townley of the National Library of Scotland for help with Mother Greg; the staffs of the Bodleian Library and the British Library; Deborah Bragan-Turner, David Young and the inter-library loan department of Nottingham University Library. Also, the staff at the National Library of Ireland; the National Library of Scotland; the Houghton Library, Harvard University; the Royal Irish Academy; the library of Lincoln's Inn; the library of Christ Church College, Oxford; J. Samuel Hammond at William R. Perkins Library, Duke University; Thomas V. Lange at the Huntington Library; Robert Karrow at the Newberry Library; Clare Brind at Woodhead-Faulkner Publishers, and our editor at Harvester Wheatsheaf, Jackie Jones: all for their patience and interest in the project.

We owe much to Elaine Hobby, whose pioneering work and friendship have inspired us. And without the love and support of Mick Wallis and Jessica Parfitt, the task would have been much harder.

Introduction

In 1983 we worked together to produce an exhibition for the Department of English Studies at the University of Nottingham. The exhibition was designed to draw the attention of students and staff to the existence of women writers in the seventeenth century, and to suggest too the ways in which women were involved in the material production and distribution of printed texts. Under the title 'Have we not an equal interest with the men of this nation . . . ?' we included the names of all the women writers we then knew of: a total of seventy-seven names. We knew then that there must have been many more women writers, and our enthusiasm for finding them and their writing generated the project which has resulted in this book.

Finding women writers and recording the facts of their existence are not, of course, ends in themselves. Grasping the very numbers of women involved and the extraordinary range of their writing raises questions about the processes of cultural production and the meanings of history, and has implications for our critical practice as teachers of literature. The chances of readers being able to read for themselves what most of these women wrote are slim, though the situation is better than it was five years ago: there has been some reprinting of women's plays, and there have been some performances of Restoration plays by women. A few anthologies of women's writing have appeared, which means that if personal (or library) finances permit some students can now read the work of some women. It is now possible to include a token woman or two in courses on seventeenth-century English literature. Our point is not, however, that there should be enough published material available for us to include five or six (as opposed to one or two) token women; but that reading these women, even being aware of their numbers, leads to a fundamental questioning of the dominant literary canon and the men who have constructed it.

Publishers are beginning to realise that there is a market for work on these writers, but there is still a greater readiness to commission books *about* women writers than reprints of the works themselves. The marketing strategies of publishers, tied to this process of commodification, mean that when reprints do appear the same handful of women is repeatedly reprinted. The tercentenary of Aphra Behn in 1989, for example, has led to more publishers printing the same plays of Aphra Behn, whose writing is now recognised as commodity, rather than publishing the work of her contemporaries, which is not. As it is, Behn remains largely isolated from other women writers of her time.

In this book we have attempted to widen the picture and to show not only how many women were writing in this period, but also the broad range of social backgrounds they came from, the variety of forms their writing took, and the many concerns they expressed. If we succeed in our purpose, this book should soon be superseded, for what we aim to do is both to compel an interest by making visible what has hitherto been unseen, and to provide a starting point for further reading and research.

THE DICTIONARY

In choosing the form of a biographical dictionary as a convenient way of presenting information, we have developed a number of criticisms of the form itself. Consequently the book as a whole is constructed so as to problematise the dictionary section which forms part of it. The reader can, of course, use the dictionary in isolation, as a reference work which we hope is readable and informative on its own terms; ideally, however, it should be read alongside the introduction and the critical appendices which frame it. Our argument with the generic form of biographical dictionary is that it rests on precisely the same critical assumptions as the literary canon which has obscured the women writers presented here.

The very format, focusing on the individual named author as entry point and elevating a particular kind of writing – that which is valued as the signed product of an individual author – conceals the ways in which texts were produced and used. It makes difficult, for example, the inclusion of texts produced jointly by several authors or texts by authors with no known name. It has therefore been our intention to create a book which self-consciously undermines its own authority: by making the dictionary section only part of the whole; and by adopting a policy of inclusiveness across the *whole* volume, refusing to exclude writing by women which does not fit with the approved generic classifications of literary criticism. In the appendices we have included information on women (such as printers and booksellers) who were not themselves writers but who were instrumental in seeing women's writing into print. Appendices also provide information additional to what is presented in the dictionary: on, for example, texts which are anonymous, those written pseudonymously by women, and those written by men using women's names. We have also, in brief essays, pulled together some material dispersed across the dictionary entries in order to raise specific questions about the forms and practices of women's writing in the period. We have chosen to write on half a dozen topics which strike us as being of particular interest: prophetic writing, Quaker women, petitions, letters, the role of men as 'gatekeepers', women and publishing. Others would no doubt have chosen different areas, such as conduct books, cookery books, sexuality, mothers and daughters, and we hope that the models we provide will indeed lead others to use the dictionary to generate material on other topics in these ways. The critical appendices are offered, then, as a corrective to some of the limitations of the generic form of the biographical dictionary, and the dictionary section is both expanded and placed in perspective by the rest of the text.

SCOPE

We chose to work on seventeenth-century women because our own interest as teachers and as readers is in that period and because researchers, writers and publishers have overwhelmingly concentrated on women's writing of the nineteenth and twentieth centuries. We wanted, though, to include two women we have worked on who are not seventeenth-century writers: Jane Anger and Susanna Centlivre. Conscious that the world did not change dramatically either in 1600 or in 1700, we have extended our boundaries by twenty years at either end of the period, and thus include some women who wrote before 1600 and after 1700. This means that we have been able to suggest, by inclusion, continuities across the limits of the century. Our concern with the *writing* within those time-limits leads to some entries which seem odd, dealing as they do with only one or two texts from a much longer writing career.

The women who appear in the dictionary and the critical appendices are those whose writing was published between 1580 and 1720, whether during their lifetimes or posthumously, those whose writing has since been published from surviving manuscript copies and some of those whose writing survives only in manuscript form. As far as the first category is concerned, we have tried to be comprehensive: to include every woman whose writing was printed between 1580 and 1700, and many (though probably not all) who wrote in the following twenty years. The coverage of women in the last two categories is partial, and here we cannot claim to have attempted comprehensiveness. For both these categories our research has been more serendipitous than systematic, and is discussed in 'Methodology' below. In researching the first category, and in our general reading over the last five years, we have come across seventeenth-century women writers in many unlikely places and have noted post-1720 publications of diaries, letters and account-books, often by local history societies. They are included here as particularly useful (since in most cases these publications are more access- ible to readers than seventeenth-century manuscripts); but the hit-and-miss way in which we have found them suggests that there are many we have missed. The third category, women whose writing remains in manuscript, is included more as a reminder of what still exists unread than as a major part of our project. To trawl all the public (let alone private) libraries in search of manuscripts by women would be a mammoth task and is beyond our capabilities and resources. We are thus aware of a contradiction: that our work has itself been shaped by what in part is the object of its study: the precedence of print. Our aim is to open up an area of study; to exclude information about manuscript material simply because we could not hope to be comprehensive would be against the spirit of our work. So we have included manuscript writings we happen to know about as 'extra' informa- tion indicative of a wide and as yet largely unexplored area of women's writing, to give the reader a glimpse of what must be only the tip of a very large iceberg, in the hope of encouraging more work. Our work is only part of a process, generated by and feeding back into the political as well as the academic imperatives of the growth area – women's studies – of which this volume is part.

In our definition of 'writing' we have been unashamedly and consistently inclusive. *Any* writing by a woman merits her entry in the dictionary or appendices. This means, in some cases, the inclusion of a woman whose only known writing is a single surviving manuscript letter. Raymond Williams has identified the shift from writing to literature (from literature to 'Literature') as happening in the eighteenth century (see, for example, *Keywords*); in refusing to include only women who wrote in genres recog- nised as 'literary' we are refusing a modern (capitalist) definition of the literary commodity which is inapplicable to this period. If we are to read women's writing of the seventeenth century, then we should start by look- ing at what women actually wrote, rather than at what they did not. Some of the women here *did* write in 'literary' forms – novels, poems, plays – but many more wrote otherwise: letters, petitions, appeals, polemics, propa- ganda, prophecies, practical handbooks, spiritual autobiographies, philo- sophy, biography, translations, diaries, journals.

It would be premature to select only the 'literary' forms as of particular importance for women's writing. It should be noted, in passing, that the majority of men did not write in these 'literary' forms either: the con- struction of 'Literature' is not only of relevance for women's writing, though that is our concern here.

Longer entries could have been written for a number of the women we in- clude, providing the reader with more information. Longer entries, however, would have meant fewer entries overall, and selection (or exclusion) would be unacceptable given our concern to record as wide a range of writers and writing as we could find. The prescription of a canon of 'great' women writers is not our business; that would be to replicate the value systems of literary criticism which the commodification of women's studies produces and we prefer to resist. While it may be argued that the longer entries in, for example, Janet Todd's welcome *A Dictionary of British and American Women Writers 1660–1800* are more informative and readable than ours, the kind of selection which such a project necessitates (covering as it does *two* countries) obscures important features of the ways in which writing was produced, such as the connections between Quakerism and women's writing, which our more inclusive project can identify. And if we are to understand how women came to write, and how they came to be published (as well as reading what they produced) then we have to attend not only to the commodity 'writing' but also to the modes of its production.

The geographical scope of the dictionary is confined to the British Isles. Specifically, entries are given for women born in the British Isles and for those born elsewhere who became naturalised and who wrote in English. We therefore exclude, reluctantly, Mary Macleod (Mairi nighean Alasdair Ruaidh), a bard whose work, not printed until after her death, was in Gaelic. Mary Macleod has been confused with another Gaelic woman poet, Flora Macleod (Finnghal nighean Alasdair Ruaidh): a reminder that there may be many more women bards, singers and writers who wrote in the Scots, Welsh and Irish vernaculars, whose work, beyond our competence to read, may be in just as urgent need of research as that of the writers in English. It is a symptom of the dominance of English-centredness that all foreign women writers merge into one.

We have included a number of authors living in 'the New World', but we tried to observe a rule that the authors should be English in origin. It may be that some women about whom we know very little, for example the correspondents of Alice Curwen, originated in the New World, but we have listed them anyway. It is difficult to trace the histories of emigrants to the New World at this period, since records were haphazard. *The New England Historical and Genealogical Register*, published by the New England Historical Genealogy Society (Boston, 1847–), 50 vols., is useful.

METHODOLOGY

Our major sources of writing published in the seventeenth century were the short-title catalogues of Pollard and Redgrave (for the period to 1640) and Wing (1641–1700). Smith's *A Descriptive Catalogue of Friends' Books* . . . and *Bibliotheca anti-Quakeriana* . . . provided a useful supplement. All titles have been checked against the British Museum Catalogue and, in difficult cases, against the National Union Catalogue and those of other libraries. We have not seen a copy of every publication we have identified: while we have found more than 400 women writers whose work was published in the period, examining their every printed text was beyond our resources of time, energy and money. Regular trips to libraries holding texts, especially the Bodleian, the British Library and Friends House, have enabled us to see and check a proportion, and to clear up some problematic ascriptions. For a full list of sources, see pp. xxi–xxvi.

We have included about 150 women whose texts were not published during the period: some have had their texts printed subsequently, while the texts of others remain in manuscript. The only systematic searching undertaken in relation to manuscripts was the use of W. Matthews' *British Diaries Between 1442 and 1942*, and we have incorporated information picked up from a search through the *Calendar of State Papers: Domestic series* for the years 1640–90, which provides a sample of the kinds of material by women contained in the Public Record Office. Our 'serendipitous' sources are listed on p. xxvi.

Biographical information has been accumulated in several ways: by reading the texts themselves; by the systematic use of the *Dictionary of National Biography* and other standard biographical dictionaries; and by a less systematic following of hunches leading us to specialist works on religious groupings, political histories, local history publications, the *Mormon Index*, and to other researchers. To all the people who have shared information with us we are especially indebted. Despite all our searching, there are still far too many women about whom we know nothing beyond their name and the title of their writing; we would be grateful to anyone who can shed light on any of the women who have so far remained elusive.

It has not been possible, in terms of space, to list our sources for each entry. It may, however, help future researchers if we note the basic procedure we followed in the case of the more 'obscure' authors. For Quakers, we used first the (unpublished) loose-leaf 'Dictionary of Quaker Biography' held (in Britain) at Friends House (although there are errors in some of the entries); then we used the digests of the registers of Quaker Monthly Meetings, also in Friends House. (We did not use the registers themselves, at the Public Record Office, nor the manuscript archives of Devonshire House, held in Friends.) For non-Quakers we looked up surnames in Marshall's *Genealogist's Guide* and Whitmore's supplement to it (see Secondary sources, p. xxi). Then we consulted the relevant sources, such as a) volumes on the peerage: e.g. Betham's Baronetage, Wood's Douglas's Scottish Peerage, Wotton's Baronetage; b) journals: e.g. *The Genealogist, Notes & Queries*; c) county histories and genealogies: e.g. Baker's Northampton, Berry's Sussex, Hants, Berks, Clutterbuck's Hertford, Morant's Essex, Surtees's Durham, Vivian's

Cornwall, Devon, Harleian Society publications of county visitations. We have not consulted manuscript archives in county record offices nor parish registers. We would suggest that anyone researching any of the authors looks again at these materials, since we have probably missed a great deal of information.

Finally, we add a note of caution about the sources we have used. The construction of library catalogues and short-title catalogues is such that women are often submerged: the single-author entries such catalogues provide can easily hide writing by a woman which forms *part* of a printed text, and such writing remains hidden from view, embedded as it is in a multiple-authored text which is entered as the work of a man (see Elaine Hobby, *Virtue of Necessity*, final chapter). We have no doubt missed many such 'hidden' texts by women which exist as prefaces to and testimonies within works by men, or within collections such as those made of deathbed testimonies and records of spiritual experiences. Many texts in the period were published with only the author's initials (a glance through the short-title catalogues will show how common a practice this was) and many of these, to us anonymous, must have been written by women. Thus possibly hundreds of pieces of writing by women survive, but are unrecognisable or are inaccessible via the catalogues which exist. The male-centredness which affects orthodox cataloguing and indexing practices is even more readily apparent in standard works of biography. The *Dictionary of National Biography* is not alone in the way it treats women: they are rarely given entries to themselves and the details of their lives are spread across the entries of their fathers, husbands, brothers and sons. The fragments of the history of women are strewn across the parentheses, margins and footnotes of a history written with man as its centre. While we cannot hope to make a whole of this jigsaw (too many pieces are lost or broken) we hope to have collected enough fragments to offer a glimpse, at least, of women who lived and acted. One of the most remarkable things about these women is that they *did*, and it is out of their doing – their agency in religion, politics, trade, skilled work of all kinds – that their writing came.

There is one last source to mention: the best of them all. We are fortunate that Elaine Hobby, whose knowledge and reading of women's writing in the later part of the period is unparalleled, allowed us to use her listing of women's writing 1649–88 as a final check on our own. Her book, *Virtue of Necessity*, and her thesis which preceded it, are monumental works of scholarship, and she has shared her knowledge from the early days of our project with generosity and enthusiasm. That our information on the period 1649–88 has stood the test of comparison with her own extensive research gives us some confidence that the information we present here on the period as a whole is reliable. What errors and omissions remain are entirely our own.

FORMAT OF ENTRIES

Consistent with the principle of inclusiveness we have worked to in compiling the dictionary, we have adopted a 'levelling' principle for the entries themselves. Each woman has been notionally allocated the same length of entry (about 200 words) and where an entry is shorter it reflects our lack of information about that particular woman. The dictionary section consists of more than 550 entries, written to a standard format to facilitate comparison across the book as a whole. Where possible, within entries we point to specific sources of further information for the individual woman concerned, and we indicate modern reprints of texts where known.

Entries are made throughout under the names of individual women. Where a woman was known by more than one name we have made the main entry under the name which she most frequently used when writing; where such a preference on the part of the woman could not be established, we have had to choose. In all cases, cross-references from other names used by the woman are supplied. The one exception to entry by name is our creation of an entry headed 'Petitions'. While such works might more properly be described as anonymous, we felt that it would be useful to provide a chronological listing of petitions made by groups of women. 'Anonymous' was indeed sometimes a woman, and we have provided a list of anonymous works by women separate from the main body of the dictionary (Appendix I); this list is probably much shorter than it would be if only we could fill out the initials with which so many writers, female and male, signed their work in this period. Appendix II is a list of pseudonymous and possibly pseudonymous texts and pseudonyms. Appendix III lists women whose authorship has been doubted.

After the woman's name we give, where possible, birth and death dates or dates when the woman is known to have been active (fl. = *floruit/* flourished). Each entry consists of two parts. The first is a summary of biographical information, keyed by number as follows:

1. Patronym (where different from entry heading)
2. Areas and places with which she was connected (e.g. birthplace, later places of residence)
3. Social status or occupation
4. Religion
5. Husband's name (with date of marriage [m.] indicated where no birth date is available)
6. Husband's social status or occupation.

The second part of each entry is a passage giving further biographical information but concentrating on the woman's writing. Exhaustive listing of all works by prolific authors is not attempted: in these cases an indication of total output and sample titles is given. The titles of seventeenth-century books and pamphlets are often very long, descriptive and detailed; we have used full titles only where little biographical information is available, in order to give the reader an indication of the writer's style and subject matter. Elsewhere, and most often, we have abbreviated titles, providing (at the minimum) the same length title as will be found in the short-title catalogues covering the period, but more often expanding on the minimum so as to be more informative. Titles are otherwise unchanged except by the removal of capitalisation, which can be distracting to readers unfamiliar with seventeenth-century practice; spelling and punctuation are given as in the original. Throughout the book, quotations are reproduced exactly from their source. At the end of an entry, where relevant, a note of modern reprints and of selected secondary sources is given, but for a fuller list of secondary sources see pp. xxi–xxv. Particular mention is made of a woman's association with other writers, and with other women. Women's names are given throughout in small capitals, and an asterisk following the name of a female associate indicates that there is an entry for that associate in the dictionary. Printers' and publishers' names are given where they are known to have been women.

The spelling of surnames in the seventeenth century tended to be flexible. We have tried to spell women's names as they appeared on their publications. These may differ from modern versions of the name, or from husbands' spellings; registers of births and deaths will spell the same family name in a variety of ways. So in some entries we have preserved an inconsistency in the spelling of the surname.

Tempting as it was to exclude men from entries, our main purpose is to assist the reader in following up women writers and in many cases women can only be traced in records and in secondary sources via the men with whom they were associated. Information about husbands, sons, fathers and male friends and colleagues is therefore given (grudgingly) where this may facilitate further research on the women themselves.

Very few entries are complete. We remain unrepentant of the many gaps that exist: more work by more people will undoubtedly fill at least some of them. We are hopeful that this dictionary will quickly be superseded, as more of these texts are read and as more women are researched. In the words of Joanna Russ, whose book *How to Suppress Women's Writing* shows us how women's writing has been made to disappear: 'Clearly it's not finished. *You* finish it.'

Secondary sources

Many of these works are mentioned with some frequency in the text; they are referred to by initials (e.g. *DNB*), by the author's name (e.g. Besse) or by author's name and short title (e.g. Hobby, thesis; Hobby, *Virtue*).

Banks, T. C., *The Dormant and Extinct Baronage of England*, London: J. White, 1807, 4 vols.

Barbour, H. and Roberts, A., *Early Quaker Writings 1650–1700*, Grand Rapids, Michigan: Eerdman's Publishing, 1973.

Bell, M., 'A dictionary of women in the London book trade, 1540–1730', Master of Library Studies dissertation, Loughborough University of Technology, 1983.

Bell, M., 'Women publishers of puritan literature in the mid-seventeenth century: three case studies', Ph.D. thesis, Loughborough University of Technology, 1987.

Belsey, C., *The Subject of Tragedy: Identity and difference in Renaissance drama*, London: Methuen, 1985.

Besse, J., *A Collection of the Sufferings of the People called Quakers*, London, 1753, 2 vols.

Brailsford, M. R., *Quaker Women 1650–90*, London: Duckworth, 1915.

Braithwaite, W. C., *The Beginnings of Quakerism*, London: Macmillan, 1912.

Brown, L. F., *The Political Activities of the Baptists and Fifth Monarchy Men in England During the Interregnum*, Washington: Oxford University Press, 1912.

Burke, John, *A Genealogical and Heraldic History of the Commoners of Great Britain and Ireland*, London: Henry Colburn, 1833, 4 vols.

Burke, John and Burke, John Bernard, *A Genealogical and Heraldic History of the Extinct and Dormant Baronetcies of England*, London: Scott, Webster & Geary, 1841.

Capp, B. S., *Astrology and the Popular Press*, London: Faber, 1979.

Capp, B. S., *The Fifth Monarchy Men: A study in seventeenth-century English millenarianism*, Totowa: Rowman & Littlefield, 1972.

Cotton, N., *Women Playwrights in England, c. 1363–1750*, Lewisburg: Bucknell University Press; London: Associated University Presses, 1980.

Crawford, P., 'Women's published writings 1600–1700' in Prior, M. (ed.), *Women in English Society 1500–1800*, London: Methuen, 1985.

Cross, C., ' "He-goats before the flocks": A note on the part played by women in the founding of some civil war churches', *Studies in Church History*, vol. 8, 1972.

Dunton, J., *The Life and Errors of John Dunton, Citizen of London*, London, 1818.

Edwards, T., *Gangraena*, London, 1646, 3 vols.; repr. Exeter: The Rota, 1977.

Ferguson, M. (ed.), *First Feminists: British women writers 1578–1799*, Indiana: The Feminist Press, 1985.

Foster, J., *Alumni Oxonienses: The members of the University of Oxford 1500–1714*, Oxford: James Palmer & Co., 1891, 4 vols.

Fraser, A., *The Weaker Vessel: Woman's lot in seventeenth-century England*, London: Weidenfeld & Nicolson, 1984.

Friends House, 'Dictionary of Quaker Biography' (*DQB*).

Friends House, 'Digest of Registers of Quaker Monthly Meetings'.

Gibbs, V., *The Complete Peerage of England, Scotland, Ireland, Great Britain and the United Kingdom*, London: The St. Catherine's Press, 1916, 13 vols.

Gillow, J., *A Literary and Biographical History, or Bibliographical Dictionary of the English Catholics*, New York and London: Burns & Oates, 1885–1902, 5 vols.

Graham, E., Hinds, H., Hobby, E. and Wilcox, H., *Her Own Life: Autobiographical writings by seventeenth-century English women*, London: Routledge, 1989.

Greaves, R. L. and Zaller, R. (eds), *A Biographical Dictionary of British Radicals in the Seventeenth Century*, Brighton: Harvester, 1982–84, 3 vols.

Greer, G., Medoff, J., Sansone, M. and Hastings, S. (eds), *Kissing the Rod: An anthology of 17th century women's verse*, London: Virago, 1988.

Harleian Society Publications, London.

Higgins, P., 'The reactions of women, with special reference to women petitioners', in Manning, B. (ed.), *Politics, Religion, and the English Civil War*, London: Edward Arnold, 1973.

Hill, C., Reay, B. and Lamont, W., *The World of the Muggletonians*, London: Temple Smith, 1983.

Hobby, E., 'English women's writing 1649–1688', Ph.D. thesis, University of Birmingham, 1984.

Hobby, E., *Virtue of Necessity: English women's writing 1649–88*, London: Virago, 1988.

Houlbrooke, R., *English Family Life 1576–1716*, Oxford: Blackwell, 1988.

Hunt, M., 'Hawkers, bawlers and mercuries: women and the London press in the early enlightenment', *Women and History*, vol. 9, 1984, pp. 41–68.

International Genealogical Index, Salt Lake City: The Church of Jesus Christ of the Latter Day Saints, 1981– .

Journal of the Friends' Historical Society (JFHS).

Kendell (ed.), *Love and Thunder: Plays by women in the age of Queen Anne*, London: Methuen, 1988.

Marshall, G. W., *A Genealogist's Guide*, Guildford: Billing & Sons, 1903.

Matthews, A. G., *Calamy Revised: Being a revision of Edmund Calamy's Account of the ministers and others ejected and silenced, 1660–2*, Oxford: Oxford University Press, 1934.

Matthews, W., *British Diaries: An annotated bibliography of British diaries written between 1442 and 1942*, Berkeley: University of California Press, 1950.

Montgomery Massingberd, H. (ed.), *Burke's Family Index*, London: Burke's Peerage Ltd., 1976.

Morgan, F., *The Female Wits: Women playwrights of the Restoration*, London: Virago, 1981.

Nichols, J., *Literary Anecdotes of the Eighteenth Century*, 2nd ed. revised, London, 1812–15, 9 vols.

O'Malley, T. P., ' "Defying the powers and tempering the spirit." A review of Quaker control over their publications 1672–1689', *Journal of Ecclesiastical History*, vol. 33, 1982, pp. 72–88.

O'Malley, T. P., 'The press and Quakerism 1653–1659', *JFHS*, vol. 54, 1979, pp. 169–84.

Ormerod, G., *Index to the Pedigrees in Burke's Commoners*, Oxford: Queen's College, 1907.

Partnow, E. (comp./ed.), *The Quotable Woman: From Eve to 1799*, New York: Facts on File, 1986.

Pearson, J., *The Prostituted Muse: Images of women and women dramatists 1642–1737*, Brighton: Harvester, 1988.

Penney, N. (ed.), *The Journal of George Fox*, Cambridge: Cambridge University Press, 1911, 2 vols.

Pirie-Gordon, H. (ed.), *Burke's Genealogical and Heraldic History of the Landed Gentry*, London: Shaw Publishing Co., 1937.

Pollock, L., *A Lasting Relationship: Parents and children over three centuries*, London: Fourth Estate, 1987.

Prior, M. (ed.), *Women in English Society 1500–1800*, London: Methuen, 1985.

Public Record Office, *Calendar of State Papers: Domestic series, 1547–1704*, London: HMSO, 1856–1972 (*CSPD*).

Reynolds, M., *The Learned Lady in England 1650–1760* (1920), repr. New York: Peter Smith, 1964.

Roberts, D., *The Ladies: Female patronage of Restoration drama*, Oxford: Clarendon Press, 1989.

Rothstein, E., *Restoration and Eighteenth-century Poetry, 1660–1780*, Boston and London: Routledge, 1981.

Russ, J., *How to Suppress Women's Writing*, London: Women's Press, 1984.

Salzman, P., *English Prose Fiction 1558–1700: A critical history*, Oxford: Clarendon Press, 1985.

Siebert, F. S., *Freedom of the Press in England 1476–1776: The rise and decline of government control*, Urbana: University of Illinois Press, 1965.

Shepherd, S. (ed.), *The Women's Sharp Revenge*, London: Fourth Estate, 1985.

Smith, N., *Perfection Proclaimed: Language and literature in English radical religion 1640–1660*, Oxford: Clarendon Press, 1989.

Spencer, J., *The Rise of the Woman Novelist from Aphra Behn to Jane Austen*, Oxford: Blackwell, 1986.

Spender, L., *Intruders on the Rights of Men*, London and Boston: Pandora, 1983.

Stenton, D. M., *The English Woman in History*, London: Allen & Unwin, 1957.

Stephen, L. and Lee, S. (eds), *Dictionary of National Biography*, Oxford: Oxford University Press, 1921–2, 21 vols. and suppl. (*DNB*).

Thomas, K., *Religion and the Decline of Magic*, Harmondsworth: Penguin, 1978.

Todd, J. (ed.), *A Dictionary of British and American Women Writers 1660–1800*, London: Methuen, 1987.

Townend, Peter (ed.), *Burke's Genealogical and Heraldic History of the Peerage, Baronetage and Knightage*, London: Burke's Peerage Ltd., 1970.

Travitsky, B. (ed.), *The Paradise of Women: Writings by Englishwomen of the Renaissance*, Westport, Connecticut; London: Greenwood Press, 1981.

Vann, R. T., *The Social Development of English Quakerism 1655–1755*, Cambridge, Mass.: Harvard University Press, 1969.

Venn, J. and Venn, J. A., *Alumni Cantabrigienses: A biographical list of all known students, graduates and holders of office at the University of Cambridge, from the earliest times to 1900, Part 1*, Cambridge: Cambridge University Press, 1922, 4 vols.

Wallas, A., *Before the Bluestockings*, London: Allen & Unwin, 1929.

Whitmore, J. B., *A Genealogist's Guide*, London: Walford Bros., 1953.

Williams, E. M., 'Women preachers in the civil war', *Journal of Modern History*, vol. 1, 1929, pp. 561–9.

Woodbridge, L., *Women and the English Renaissance: Literature and the nature of womankind 1540–1620*, Brighton: Harvester, 1987.

Principal libraries, manuscript collections and catalogues used

Bodleian Library.

British Museum, Department of Manuscripts.

British Museum, Department of Printed Books, *General Catalogue of Printed Books* (*BMC*).

Friends House, London.

Pollard, A. W. and Redgrave, G. R. (comp.), *A Short-title Catalogue of Books Printed in England, Scotland and Ireland and of English Books Printed Abroad 1475–1640*, London: Bibliographical Society, 1926, 2 vols.; vol. 2, 2nd ed., 1976.

Public Record Office, London, State Papers.

Smith, J., *Bibliotheca Anti-Quakeriana; Or, a catalogue of books adverse to the Society of Friends*, London, 1873.

Smith, J., *A Descriptive Catalogue of Friends' Books*, London: Smith, 1867, 2 vols.; repr. New York: Kraus, 1970.

Swarthmore MSS, Friends House.

Whitley, W. A., *A Baptist Bibliography: Being a register of the chief materials for Baptist history, whether in manuscript or print, preserved in Great Britain, Ireland, and the Colonies*, London: Kingsgate Press, 1916, 2 vols.

Wing, D. (comp.), *Short Title Catalogue of Books, Printed in England, Scotland, Ireland, Wales and British America and of English Books Printed in Other Countries, 1641–1700*, New York: Modern Language Association of America, 1945–51; vols. 1 and 2, 2nd ed., 1972–82.

A Biographical Dictionary of

English Women Writers
1580–1720

A

ABBOTT, Margaret, *fl.* ?1629–59

Author of *A testimony against the false teachers of this generation by one who is come from under them, unto the true teacher and shepherd of the soul* (?1659). She says she was 'Thirty years (or more) . . . a hearer of the Priests' and left them when she saw them 'turn their coats' on seeing that they might lose their tithes. When she 'came to be lighted with the light of Jesus Christ' she realised 'that Priests and people were professing the Saints words, & out of the life and power of the Saints' (by which she means that people say holy things but are 'outside', deviating from, real godly lives): 'all sects and judgments of men, all out of [outside] the life and power of God', 'Anabaptists, and others, a teaching people, and need to be taught themselves . . .'.

The text offers too little to identify her: there were several radical men called Abbot: among them, Daniel Abbot, a colonel in the Parliamentary army (he went to Ireland in 1649, was arrested in 1660 but later escaped); Robert Abbot, vicar of Cranbrook, Kent (1616–43), then Southwick, Hampshire, a pro-Presbyterian, anti-Brownist (which might connect with her position).

ABERGAVENNY, Lady Frances, –1576

1. Manners; 2. Birling (Kent); 3. genteel; 5. Henry Nevill, Lord Bergavenny; 6. genteel.

Also known as Elizabeth FANE, Frances MANNERS.

Cited by Partnow as a poet (pp. 133, 457), but she quotes prose extracts from 'The precious perles of perfect Godliness' (in *The monument of matrones conteining seven severall lamps of virginitie, or distinct treatises*, ed. T. Bentley, 1582).

ADAMS, Alice, *fl.* 1674

1. Simmons; 2. Bristol, St Nevis; 4. Baptist.

Wrote a letter to the Broadmead Baptist church in Bristol, probably in response to a letter sent out by the church in 1672 asking for information about members who had moved away. Her letter is dated 12 February 1674 from St Nevis, and it speaks of her religious isolation. It is quoted in R. Hayden, *The records of a church of Christ in Bristol (1640–87)*, Bristol Records Society, vol. 27 (1974), p. 10.

ADAMS, Mary, *fl.* 1676

A warning to the inhabitants of England and London in particular by M.A. (1676, 1678). There is too little in the text to identify her. She may possibly be connected with Richard Adams, a Baptist minister (licensed 1672) from Leicester, who was at Shad Thames, Bermondsey in 1689.

Advice to the women . . .

See Appendix I.

ALBEMARLE, Elizabeth, Duchess of, 1654–1734

1. Cavendish; 2. London; 3. gentry; 5(a) Christopher Monck, Duke of Albemarle (m. 1669), (b) Ralph, 1st Duke of Montagu (m. 1692); 6. gentry.

The case of Elizabeth Dutchess of Albemarle, and Christopher Monke Esquire, Appellants (1688): the text concerns the inheritance of the previous Duke of Albemarle, which was contested by the Earl of Bath on the basis that Charles II had decreed in 1661 that in the event of failure of the male issue of General Monck the family estates should pass to the Earl of Bath. In 1688 this was apparent, but the decree had died with Charles in 1685. The appellants want to insist that, despite a previous will and legal wrangles, the final will of July 1687 be honoured. The Duchess was the daughter of Henry, Duke of Newcastle.

ALDRIDGE, Susanna, *fl.* 1676–85

1. Salter; 2. Buckinghamshire; 4. Quaker (disunited); 5. Robert Aldridge (m. 1676).

Her text, *Abominations in Jerusalem discovered* (1685), does not survive and the only evidence for its title comes from the reply to it by Mary ELL-WOOD* and Margery CLIPSHAM/CLIPSON* (written for the benefit of Quaker readers). Apparently Aldridge had been raised as a Quaker by her father (this was perhaps the George Salter who had been imprisoned in 1660); her mother had died soon after childbirth. She was married at the famous Quaker meeting-house, Jordans, and her career is represented as alternations between loyalty to and rebellion against Quaker meetings. Her first son was born in 1677; the second in 1679 died after a year. ELLWOOD and CLIPSHAM say that at the time of her lying-in she 'came forth again with a pretence of Visions and Revelations, wherewith Friends were greatly dissatisfied, and burthened' (her religious 'visions' may connect, as in several cases, with states of pregnancy). Her husband was imprisoned in 1683. She travelled to meetings in High Wycombe, London and Bristol; it is particularly noted that she went to men's meetings and argued with them. Spiritually she is said to have been a follower of 'C.H.' (presumably Charles Harris of High Wycombe, a Quaker dissident who in 1691 was to publish, with John Raunce, *A memorial for the present generation*, a text attacked by Thomas Ellwood). The text of Aldridge's pamphlet formed the substance of a speech or reading she made at the meeting at Jordans (accompanied by Harris's wife) where she claimed C.H. as a 'true Prophet' and that there was 'great deadness and dryness over the Assemblies of God's People'.

ALKIN, Elizabeth, *fl*. 1651–4

2. Portsmouth, London; 3. polemical journalist, newspaper 'spy', nurse.

See Critical Appendix 7.

Elizabeth Alkin was known as 'Parliament Joan'. She nursed the wounded in the Civil War and is often mentioned in *CSPD* between 1651 and 1654, where she is seen seeking payment for 'spying' and nursing services, petitioning for the position of nurse to maimed seamen at Dover and for the release of one Thomas Budd from Newgate. She published two government newspapers and the pseudo-royalist *Mercurius Scotius*.

See Isabel Macdonald, *Elizabeth Alkin* (Keighley: Wadsworth & Co., 1934).

ALLEINE, Theodosia, *fl*. 1653–77

1. Alleine; 2. Ditcheat, Taunton; 3. schoolteacher; 4. Presbyterian, Calvinist; 5(a) Joseph Alleine, (b) Robert Taylor (?of Herefs.); 6(a) minister and scholar, (b) ?minister.

Daughter of the ejected minister Richard Alleine; she felt pressurised to marry (in 1659) before she was ready: it was 'contrary to our purpose, we resolving to have lived much longer single'. They had no children; but she set up a school of 50–60 pupils, in which she taught. After Joseph Alleine's death in 1668, she married again, possibly to another ejected minister.

She was still alive in 1677. Her 'A full narrative of his life (from his silencing to his death)', in *The life and death of that excellent minister of Christ Mr Joseph Alleine* (1671) had several editions by 1693: 'she not imagining it should be put forth in her own words'. This text tells of their persecution under the Act of Uniformity and the Five Mile Act, and of how she visited her husband in prison and nursed him (assisted by ten other women) until he died. When he was sick she dealt with his correspondence.

ALLEN, Hannah, *fl.* before 1670–83

1. Archer; 2. Derbyshire, Warwickshire; 4. Independent; 5(a) Hannibal Allen, (b) Charles Hatt; 6(a) merchant.

Satan his methods and malice baffled. A narrative of God's gracious dealings with that choice Christian Mrs Hannah Allen, afterwards married to Mr Hatt (1683) tells of her depression and suicide attempts. She mentions the counsel of her minister, Mr Shorthose. This is perhaps John Shorthose who became rector of Edlington, Yorkshire (died 1670); he was a cousin of Richard Archer, clerk of Pesone, Derbys. (died 1659). We have not found a connection between Richard and Hannah Allen. Extracts in Graham.

ALLEN, Martha, *fl.* 1673–80

1. Gibson; 2. Colchester, Earls Colne (Essex); 4. Quaker; 5. William Allen (m. 1673); 6. minister.

'The testimony of Martha Allen concerning her deceased husband, William Allen' in *The last words of . . . William Allen* (1680). This also includes testimonies by Stephen Crisp, Elizabeth FRYET,* Anna FURLY,* Martha KING,* Susanna POTTER.*

ANDERDON, Jane, –1693

1. Bicknell; 2. Bridgwater (Somerset); 4. Quaker; 5. John Anderdon (m. 1660); 6. lawyer.

Wrote a testimony, with her husband John (the Quaker lawyer of Bridgwater) concerning Jane WHITEHEAD (WAUGH*) in Theophila TOWNSEND's* *A testimony concerning . . . J. Whitehead* (1676). The Anderdon testimony was written from Ilchester prison (1675).

ANDERDON, Mary, 1635–

2. Bradford (Devon); 3. trade; 4. Quaker; 5. John Bellamy (m. 1663).

She was the sister of John Anderdon (see above). In 1662, she and John Bellamy were taken out of a meeting in Okehampton and imprisoned.

A word to the world. From the spirit of truth as a tender visitation of my father's love etc. From Exon. gaol, the 23rd of the 9th month, 1662, where I am a prisoner for truth's sake . . . (1662): 'Therefore haste, haste, haste out of Babylon at God's call, before a day of bitter howling overtake you, which you shall not escape except you repent, the Lord hath spoken it.'

ANDREWS, Elizabeth, *c.* 1628–1718

1. Farmer; 2. Malpas (Cheshire), Broseley (Shrops.); 3. shopkeeper; 4. Quaker; 5(a) John Yardley (m. 1659), (b) Roger Andrews; 6(a) mercer.

She kept a draper's shop, but her goods were distrained because she opened on Christmas Day and refused to pay 'Sunday shillings' (tithes); a minister threatened to excommunicate those who traded with her and her husband. In 1708 money was paid from the London meeting to relieve the Andrews' poverty; the same year her 'still' was sold. In 1711, after her husband's death (in 1709), she sought a certificate to travel as a Quaker minister.

'An account of the birth, education and sufferings for the truth's sake of that faithful Friend Elizabeth Andrews' (MS; printed in *JFHS*, vol. 26: 1929).

ANGER, Jane, *fl.* 1589

See Critical Appendix 6.

Although this name is readily assumed to be pseudonymous, it is worth remembering that the family name Anger or Ongar was fairly common in some counties bordering London (Berkshire, Essex). Further, the formation of a female pseudonym is usually at this time either 'comically' obvious (Mary Tattlewell) or focused on a specific, known male (Ester Sowernam, Elizabeth Cromwell).

Anger's book is *Jane Anger; her protection for women to defend them against the scandalous reports of a late surfeiting lover, and all other like Venerians that complaine so to bee overcloyed with women's kindness* (1589). This is a reply to *Book: his surfeit in love* of the previous year. Both were printed by Thomas Orwin, who seems to have organised a 'gender debate'. It is reprinted in Shepherd and Ferguson.

ANNE OF DENMARK, Queen, 1574–1619

1. Oldenburg; 2. Denmark, Scotland, England; 3. queen; 4. Protestant, Catholic; 5. James I/VI; 6. king.

Queen Anne converted to Catholicism in the 1590s. She is best remembered for her interest in court masques: Jonson speaks of her as 'Oriana' and 'Bel-Anna'. She and James lived apart from *c.* 1606; Anne CLIFFORD* tells of a visit to court when Anne advised her not to trust the king as a fair adjudicator in her inheritance dispute (see extract in Graham). Anne died of dropsy, from which she suffered from 1612.

Letters by her are to be found in *Letters to King James*, printed for the Maitland Club (1835) from originals in the Library of the Faculty of Advocates.

ANNE, Queen of England, 1665–1714

1. Stuart; 2. London, Richmond; 3. queen; 4. Anglican; 5. Prince George of Denmark; 6. prince.

MARY II*

Her marriage took place in 1683; she succeeded to the throne in 1702. Two daughters died 1686–7. Traditionally known to be lesbian.

The Princess Anne of Denmark's letter (1688). *Her majesty's most gracious letter to the Parliament of Scotland* (1706). *Three letters sent . . .* (1712). *Queen Anne's reason for her conduct . . .* (1715). *Her majesty's reasons for creating the Electoral Prince of Hanover a peer of this realm* (Somers Tracts, 13, 1809).

Also *Letters of two queens*, ed. B. Bathurst (London: Holden & Co., 1925); *Letters and diplomatic instructions*, ed. B. Brown (London: Cassell, 1935). See E. Gregg, *Queen Anne* (London: Routledge & Kegan Paul, 1980).

'Anonymous business diary of a midwife'

See Appendix I.

'Aphra Behn's circle'

See Appendix I.

ARESKINE, Dame Margaret, Lady Castlehaven, *fl.* 1661–90

2. Scotland; 5(a) Sir John Mackenzie, (b) Sir James Foulis (m. 1661); 6(a)/(b) genteel.

She accused her second husband of illegally taking £59,904 from her (from an income accumulated before the marriage from rents on her own property); she wants this money back from his son. Her husband had been in debt at the time of marriage and had brought her no money; in the marriage contract he had relinquished all claims to his wife's property and her inheritance was specifically defined. Sir James

Foulis the younger fought the case through a series of courts and won. The pamphlet he had published to celebrate the justice of his case includes her own texts: a summons 'Dame Margaret Areskine against Sir James Foulis', 'The ladies appeal and protestation', and her petition 'Unto his grace his majesties high commissioner', all in *An exact and faithful relation of the process pursued by Dame Margaret Areskine, Lady Castlehaven* (1690). The court decided that she had no legal right to monies from rent on her own property and that the husband had the right to use the interest from her estate to pay off his debts.

ARIADNE

See Appendix II.

ARNOLD, Elizabeth, *fl.* 1616
3. translator.

Translated Thomas Tuke's *A treatise against painting* (1616). Perhaps connected with the Arnold family of Cromer, Norfolk.

ARUNDEL, Anne, Countess of, ?1577–?1630
1. ?Dacre; 2. ?Carlisle, Shropshire; 3. genteel; 5. ?Philip Howard, Earl of Arundel; 6. genteel.

Pollock (pp. 22, 62, 72, 107) quotes from manuscript letters (1606–8) by her about aspects of the birth and upbringing of children.

ARUNDELL, Dorothy, *fl.* 1587–97
2. Cornwall, Brussels; 3. genteel, nun; 4. Catholic.

Great-niece of Mary ARUNDELL* (below), she was the daughter of (another) Sir John Arundell, of Lanherne. She and her sister Gertrude are mentioned in their uncle Edward's will in 1587; they professed at the Benedictine convent in Brussels in 1597. Her 'Life of Fr. Cornelius, the martyr' survives in manuscript (Gillow).

ARUNDELL, Mary, *fl.* 1540s
2. Cornwall; 3. genteel; 5(a) Robert Ratcliffe, Earl of Sussex, (b) Henry Fitz-Alan, Earl of Arundel (m. after 1542); 6(a)/(b) genteel.

DNB claims she died in 1691, which is impossible. She was the only daughter of the second marriage of Sir John Arundell of Lanherne, Cornwall, who died 1545. She was Ratcliffe's third wife and he died

1542. She was the second wife of Fitz-Alan (died 1580) who was president of the Council under Mary and Elizabeth. She bore one son in her first marriage; the second marriage was childless. She translated *The sayings and doings of the emperor Severus* and *Select sentences of the seven wise men of Greece*, both from Latin and both unpublished. There are also manuscripts in the royal collections at Windsor. (We include her here on the basis that her texts might conceivably have been written post-1580.)

ASHFIELD, Patience, 1627–1708

1. Hart; 2. Staines (Middx.); 4. Quaker; 5. Richard Ashfield (m. 1660); 6. soldier.

The second wife of Colonel Ashfield, an important figure in Army politics in the late 1650s, she bore a son Richard in 1662. She wrote accounts of her husband, who died in Newgate in 1677 (imprisoned for refusal to pay tithes), and of her sufferings at the hands of William Field, a constable (Besse 1.440). She was fined £10 for meetings at Longford (1682) and goods worth £26 were taken from her, when she was very weak. In 1686 she signed the general testimony for Anne WHITEHEAD* in *Piety Promoted* (henceforward referred to as *Piety* . . .).

ASHTON, Elizabeth, *fl.* 1630s–62

1. Harrington; 2. Rutland, Lancashire; 3. genteel; 5. Sir Ralph Ashton; 6. genteel.

Daughter of Sir Sapcote Harrington and sister of the political philosopher, James Harrington (born 1611). James supervised the education of his sisters in the 1630s, and she wrote an unpublished memoir of his life; this is used by John Toland (a radical Whig) in his 'Life of Harrington' which is prefixed to a reprint of Harrington's *Oceana* (1700). When James was imprisoned in 1661, his sisters petitioned on his behalf and Elizabeth tried to persuade MPs to obtain a trial for him. She travelled to Plymouth to see and care for him. Her husband was from Lever and Whalley, Lancashire; there were no children.

ASTELL, Mary, 1666–1731

2. Newcastle, London; 3. trade, writer; 4. Anglican.

Mary Astell was the author of some dozen works between 1694 and 1730. She wrote about marriage (*Some reflections upon marriage*, 1700), and Anglicanism (*The Christian religion as professed by a daughter of the Church of England*, 1705). Some of her writings were published anonymously. She corresponded with John Norris and worked with John Walker on *The sufferings of the clergy* (1714). Steele used some 100 pages of her *A serious proposal to the ladies* (1694) in *The ladies library* (1714), but without attribution. *An essay in defence of the female sex* (1696), published anonymously, is now usually attributed to Judith DRAKE.* See Mary CHUDLEIGH* and Damaris CUDWORTH* for defences of women.

See extracts in Ferguson, p. 181 f. and Florence Smith, *Mary Astell* (New York; Columbia University Studies, 1916). Also Greer, p. 333 f., which includes verse extracts.

ASTON, Gertrude, *fl.* 1630s–90
2. Tixall (Staffs.), Louvain; 3. genteel, nun; 4. Catholic; 5. Henry Thimelby.

Daughter of Sir Walter Aston (who died in 1639) and sister of Constance FOWLER*. She bore one child and her husband died young. She then became a nun at Louvain, where her sister-in-law, Winefrid THIMELBY,* was abbess (1668–90). She wrote verses, including an epitaph on a son of Sir William Persall.

ASTON, Mary, *fl.* 1690
2. Tixall (Staffs.); 3. genteel.

Daughter of Walter, 2nd Lord Aston (died 1678), and sister of Eliza SOUTHCOTE*. She wrote a letter to Gertrude ASTON* in Louvain on the death of her aunt Winefrid THIMELBY* (1690). She died unmarried.

ASTRY, Diana, 1679–1716
2. Gloucestershire, Bedfordshire, Northamptonshire; 3. genteel; 5. Richard Orlebar (m. 1708); 6. genteel.

Also known as Mrs ORLEBAR.

She was the daughter of Sir Samuel Astry of Henbury (Gloucestershire/Avon), clerk of the Privy Council to James II; her husband built Hinwick House, Podington, Beds. Frederica Orlebar makes use of her 'Social Diary 1701–8' in *The Orlebar Chronicles in Bedfordshire and Northamptonshire 1553–1733* (1930).

ATKINSON, Elizabeth, *fl.* 1660–75
2. Somerset; 4. Quaker, Muggletonian; 5. — Henn.

Muggleton tried to dissuade her from making a marriage, for which she was cursed by her mother (1671). She attacked Quakers in two pamphlets:

A breif and plain discovery of the labourers in mistery Babylon, called Quakers, with a description how the subtile serpent deceived them (1669) and *Weapons of the people called Quakers* (1669). Elizabeth COLEMAN,* Ann TRAVERS* and Rebeckah TRAVERS* wrote replies. Atkinson had been a Quaker for nine years; Rebeckah Travers associates her dissident position with that of Robert Cobbet, a follower of Jacob Bœhme.

AUBERT, Isabella, *fl.* 1715–19

2. London; 3. singer.

She appeared in Mancini's opera *Hydaspes* in 1715; her parody of it was the mock-opera, *Harlequin-Hydaspes: or the Greshamite*, in which she performed at Lincoln's Inn Fields in 1719. It was published, anonymously, in the same year. (*BMC* queries authorship, and the play's preface speaks of the author as 'he'.) The Aubert family came from Montpelier: a Nicholas Aubert was born in 1726 (and naturalised in 1758), but we are not able to connect him definitely with Isabella Aubert.

AUBIN, Penelope, 1679–1731

2. South-West England, ?Wales, London; 3. novelist, playwright, translator, poet, preacher.

Todd (p. 34) says that Aubin was 'probably of French émigré parents'. Her seven novels were published after 1720, as was her single play. She produced four translations from French and at least three poems in our period ('The Stuarts', 1707; 'The Extasy', 1708; 'The Welcome', 1708). She was preaching near Charing Cross by 1729.

AUDLAND, Anne, 1627–1705

1. Newby; 2. Kendal (Westmorland), London; 3. preacher; 4. Seeker, Quaker; 5(a) John Audland (m. 1650), (b) Thomas Camm (m. 1666); 6 (b) preacher.

Also known as Anne CAMM.

Travelled to London aged 13, returned to Westmorland, joined the Seekers, met her first husband and bore a son. Convinced in 1652, she was imprisoned in Auckland for preaching (1654), then travelled with Mabel BENSON* through Yorkshire, Derbyshire, Leicestershire and Oxfordshire. She was arrested for blasphemy in Banbury (1655) and imprisoned for eight months (although the jury acquitted her of the charge). Her first husband died in 1664.

The saints testimony finishing through suffering (1655) is a collective text to which she contributed. It relates to the debate about women speaking (see also Mary COLE,* Priscilla COTTON,* Margaret FELL*): she disliked addressing meetings where qualified male speakers were present, and disapproved of women who were 'too hasty, forward, or unseasonable'. Other pamphlets include *The admirable and glorious appearance of the eternal God* (1684; with Thomas Camm) and *A true declaration* (1655; with Jane WAUGH*). 'Anne Camm, her testimony concerning John Audland' (1681) appeared as part of *The memory of the righteous revived* (1689). She wrote a testimony (1687) in *The Life and Death of Robert Widders* (1688).

AUDLEY, Eleanor

Eleanor DAVIES*

AUDLEY, Lucy, –before 1610

1. Mervyn; 2. Fonthill (Wilts.); 3. genteel; 5. George Touchet, Lord Audley and later Earl of Castlehaven; 6. genteel.

Mother of Amie/Anne BLOUNT,* Eleanor DAVIES* (1590) and Maria THYNNE* (*c.* 1578). She was said to be still alive in 1608/9. Her letters are reprinted in *Two Elizabethan women: correspondence of Joan and Maria Thynne 1575–1611*, ed. A. Wall, Devizes: Wiltshire Record Society, vol. 38, 1983.

AUSTEN, Katherine, 1629–83

1. Wilson; 5. Thomas Austen.

A diary for *c.* 1664–8 survives, but is unpublished (BL, Add. MS 4454). It consists largely of 'memoranda, reflections and meditations' (Houlbrooke, p. 242, who also prints extracts).

AUSTILL, Bridget, 1637–93

2. Tottenham; 3. schoolmistress; 4. Quaker.

Author of a testimony in Anne WHITEHEAD,* *Piety* . . . (1686): Whitehead died in Austill's house.

AVERY, Elizabeth, 1595–1677

1. Parker; 2. Wiltshire, Newbury (Berks.), Ireland; 4. millenarian, Baptist; 5. ?Henry Avery; 6. soldier.

Daughter of the religious radical and separatist, Robert Parker (author of *De politeia ecclesiastica Christi*, 1616) who was prebendary at Stanton St

Bernard, Wilts. 1594–1607, then in exile in Holland. Elizabeth developed as a millenarian as seen in *Scripture-prophecies opened, which are to be accomplished in these last times, which do attend the second coming of Christ; in seven letters written to Christian friends* (1647): 'though I may be accounted mad to the world, I shall speak the words of soberness and if I am mad . . . it is to God.' This produced opposition from several quarters, including her brother Thomas Parker (born 1593) who published a letter to her (1648), saying she claimed to be 'above Ordinances, above the Word and Sacraments, ye above the Blood of Christ himself, living as a glorified Saint, and taught immediately by the Spirit'; 'your printing of a Book, beyond the custom of your Sex, doth rankly smell.' Major General Lambert apparently summoned her to Oxford, where she heard religious debates, and he censured her beliefs: she was told 'I was under the opening of the fifth seal, and very near the sixth, in the condition which I was in.' She travelled with her husband, who was sent as commissary to Ireland, and there she associated herself with the new Baptist church of John Rogers, who printed her 'experiences' in *Ohel or Beth-Shemesh* (1653) (henceforward referred to as *Ohel* . . .): 'In the times of the Wars in England, I was brought out of Egypt into the Wilderness.'

Avery was a common name in Berkshire. We conjecture Henry Avery to be her husband, since he was serving as a soldier in Ireland (Youghal) from 1649 until at least 1654. The entry for Parker in Greaves and Zaller suggests she became a Quaker: this may be confusing her with Elizabeth, wife of Reynold Avery of Berkshire who died in 1697/8.

B

B—, M—
See Appendix I.

BABTHORPE, Lady Grace, 1573–1635
1. ? Bernard; 2. York, Louvain; 3. genteel, nun; 4. Catholic; 5. Sir Ralph Babthorpe.

Her father was Recorder of York. She was imprisoned for nearly two years at Sheriff Hutton (Yorkshire) for refusing to conform to Protestantism: she and her husband seem to have gone abroad to avoid persecution. When widowed she entered the convent of St Monica, Louvain (1621).
'Lady Babthorpe's recollections' has not survived. 'Another narrative of the Lady Babthorpe' is apparently a manuscript continuation of her notes (Gillow).

BACON, Lady Ann, 1528–1610
1. Coke; 3. genteel, ?governess; 5. Nicholas Bacon; 6. government official.

Ann Bacon read Latin, Greek, Italian and French; and was the mother of Anthony and Francis Bacon. She translated *Fourteene sermons of Barnardine Ochyne . . .* (1550) from Italian and Bishop Jewel's *Apologie of the Church of England* (1564, 1600) from Latin. Correspondence with her sons is in J. Spedding, R. Ellis, D. Heath (eds), *Works of Francis Bacon*, vol. 8 (London: Longman, 1858–74).

BAILLIE, Lady Grissel, 1665–1746
1. Hume; 2. Berwickshire, Holland, London; 3. deaconess, genteel; 4. Presbyterian, Church of Scotland; 5. George Baillie (m. 1692); 6. genteel.

When she was still a child, Grissel Baillie's father (Sir Patrick Hume) apparently used her to carry messages to the imprisoned Jacobite,

Robert Baillie, father of her future husband. As eldest daughter she ran the family while her father was in exile in Utrecht. In 1688, when she returned to Scotland, she was invited to become a Maid of Honour to the Princess of Orange and refused. She seems to have become the first deaconess of the Church of Scotland.

Poems by Grissel Baillie were published anonymously in such collections as Ramsay's *Tea-Table Miscellany* (1723–40), while many memoranda, account books, recipes, etc. survive from the years of her marriage, 1692–1733. A selection was published as *The Household Book* (Edinburgh: Scottish Historical Society Publications, series 2, vol. 1, 1911). Greer (p. 342) says that Grissel's daughter, in her manuscript life of her mother, mentions a lost 'book of songs of her writing'.

Details partly from Greer, p. 342 f. which includes a poem.

BAKER, Mary, ?1649–?1743
2. ?Aylesbury (Bucks.); 4. Quaker; 5. Richard Baker.

Wrote a testimony for her husband (1697) in Richard Baker, *A testimony to the power of God, being greater than the power of Satan* (1699; printed by Tace SOWLE). She says here that she married her husband (who was imprisoned) in the 'latter part' of his days. She signed the general testimony from the Reading Women's Meeting for Joan VOKINS* in 1691 and wrote with Mary LARCUM* and Mary WHARLEY* 'A Testimony from the Women's Meeting, concerning Thomas Ellwood' (1713; the meeting was Hunger-Hill, Bedfordshire), in *The history of the life of Thomas Ellwood* (1714).

BANKS, Hannah, *fl.* 1696–1711
2. Meare, Street (Somerset), Cumberland; 4. Quaker; 5(a) — Champion, (b) John Banks (m. 1696).

Her 'Account and testimony concerning her dear and tender husband' (1711) appears in John Banks, *Journal and Works* (1712).

BARBAR, Anne, –1688
2. Falmouth (Cornwall); 4. Quaker.

Author of a letter (1678) with Stephen Richards to Thomas and Alice CURWEN* in *A relation* (1680). The register of her death says 'Our ancient and truly faithfull friend who had travelled through many discouragements and inward exercises through all which she was reserved faithful to the Lord.' Her daughter, Anne, died in 1689.

BARKER, Jane, 1660–1723
2. Lincolnshire, France, London; 3. genteel, poet, novelist; 4. Catholic convert.

Jane Barker was of a Royalist family and seems to have left England for a time at the fall of James II. She went blind in later life. She formed close female friendships and was well aware of male dominance: 'Suffer me not to fall into the Pow'rs of Men's almost Omnipotent Amours' ('A virgin life').

Poetical recreations: consisting of original poems, odes etc. (1688; a book in two parts, the first by her, the second by various Cambridge students; some of the poems were later worked into the novels). *Love's intrigues . . . a novel* (1713). *Exilius . . . a new romance* (1715). *The entertaining novels of Jane Barker* (1715, 1716, 1719, 1736).

Other novels by her are post-1720, while a manuscript collection of her poems exists (BL, Add. MS 21.621). She also translated Fénelon's *The Christian Pilgrimage* (1718): Fénelon's quietist philosophy seems to have appealed to Jacobites (see F. McLynn, *The Jacobites,* London: Routledge, 1985).

See Ferguson, p. 172 f. for extracts and Greer, p. 354 f. (including poems). For her relationship with her publisher Edmund Curll see William H. Burney, 'Edmund Curll, Mrs Jane Barker and the English novel', *Philological Quarterly,* vol. 37, no. 4 (1958), pp. 385–99.

BARKER, Mary, *fl.* **1652–3**
2. Dublin; 4. Baptist.

Her 'experiences' are in Rogers, *Ohel . . .* (1653) (see Elizabeth AVERY* for details). She says she has been much afflicted for many years by the loss of her relations (this may refer to deaths in the Irish rebellion which started *c.* 1641); but that John Rogers's ministry has spiritually helped her. Rogers was sent to Ireland in 1651, but returned in March 1652. We suspect that many of the women associated with his new Baptist or Fifth Monarchist congregation in Dublin (which is propagandised for in *Ohel . . .*) were connected with the English army. Some links are certain; others more vague. A Captain Edward Barker served in a regiment originally destined for Ireland, but it seems to have stayed in Scotland; also a Captain John Barker served in the New Model horse regiments.

BARNWELL, Sarah, *fl.* **1652–3**
2. Dublin; 4. Baptist; 5. ?Robert Barnwell.

Her 'experiences' are in Rogers, *Ohel . . .* (1653) (see also Mary BARKER*). She speaks of moving from works and duties to 'spirituall holinesse', praying, preaching, etc.; and says that she had heard 'Mr Dunstable' preach. This may be a reference to Dunstal of Staffordshire (1655), which gives us some clue to her identity. She also refers to plague in the city (presumably Dublin).

BARROW, Deborah, –1692

1. Briggs; 2. Great Sankey (Cheshire); 4. Quaker; 5. Samuel Barrow (m. 1667).

Daughter of Thomas Briggs, she bore five children between 1668 and 1678. Wrote a testimony in *An account of some of the travels and sufferings of . . . Thomas Briggs* (1685).

BARWICK, Grace, *c.* 1618–1701

2. Kelk (Yorkshire); 4. Quaker; 5(a) Robert Barwick, (b) Joseph Helmsley (m. 1664); 6(a) soldier.

See Critical Appendix 4.

She had twin daughters in 1657 (one died that year). In the autumn of 1659 she travelled to London to deliver a message from God, which was published by Mary WESTWOOD* as *To all present rulers, whether Parliament, or whom-soever of England* (1659). The pamphlet contains an address to Lambert and the officers, arguing for the abolition of tithes and pressing them to act while they have the power. In 1660 she gave birth to a son, and suffered distraint for non-payment of tithes. Her first husband, a cornet in Lambert's Yorkshire regiment, died in 1661 in gaol; her son died the same year. She was imprisoned in York castle in 1662. George Fox is known to have held a meeting in her Yorkshire house in 1666 and there is a letter from her to him in Swarthmore MSS iv.174. She signed the general epistle from the York Women's Meeting in 1692.

BASTWICK, Susanna, *fl.* 1634–54

2. Colchester, London; 4. Presbyterian; 5. John Bastwick; 6. physician, religious controversialist.

See Critical Appendix 4 for analysis of this sort of text.

She petitioned for her husband in 1634, at which time she was said to be pregnant; she made a deposition on his behalf in February 1635 (which was dismissed as frivolous). A son John was born in 1636 in Essex. Her husband was again in prison, after a Star Chamber trial, 1637–40: she had access to him in 1637, but he was moved to the Scilly Isles, and in 1640 she again petitioned, claiming she had many small children and had not seen him for three years. Her petition *To the high court of Parliament of the Commonwealth of England, Scotland, and Ireland. The remonstrance and humble petition of Susanna Bastwick (the distressed widow of John Bastwick, Doctor in Physick) and her children* (1654) dates from the year her husband died. Hobby says that she had petitioned the Commons on eight previous occasions (*Virtue*, p. 14).

BATEMAN, Phoebe, 1675–

1. Gratton; 2. Chesterfield (Derbys.); 4. Quaker.

Her 'Testimony concerning her late father and mother' (1712) is in John Gratton, *Journal and Works* (1720). She may be connected to John Bateman of Oxfordshire, whose death in 1748 was recorded by the Mansfield meeting.

BATEMAN, Susanna, *fl.* 1656

4. Quaker.

She is author of an untitled writing which begins with ten lines of verse ('I matter not how I appear to man/A witness in my soul there lives that can/Bear record to the Father this . . .') (1656). It attacks religious backsliders and priests: 'many of you have turned like the Dog to his vomit, and like the Sow washed to the wallowing in the mire.' The common surname makes her difficult to trace: a Susannah Bateman married Jacob Scarth in Yorkshire in 1664; another Susannah Bateman of London married John Yarnton in 1672.

BATHURST, Anne, ?1656–82

2. Bishopsgate (London); 4. Quaker; 5. William Kent (m. 1679); 6. cheesemonger.

A daughter was born in 1680, but two sons (born 1681–82) died within a few weeks, the second one of the 'consumption' which killed his mother.

Memoirs, and spiritual diary for 1679. Also the postscript for Elizabeth BATHURST's* *Truth's vindication* (1679) and the last part of Elizabeth's *An expostulatory appeal* (?1679).

BATHURST, Elizabeth, ?1655–85

2. London; 4. Presbyterian, Quaker.

She was imprisoned in the Marshalsea, after being thrown out of a service being conducted by Samuel Annesley (1678). In 1682 she went on a preaching tour, with her father, to Windsor, Reading, Newbury, Oxford and Bristol. Grace BATHURST* was her stepmother.

Author of *Truth's vindication, or, a gentle stroke to wipe off the foul aspersions, false accusations and misrepresentations cast upon the people of God, called, Quakers* (1679, 1683, 1695). The last of these impressions was printed for Tace SOWLE, as *Truth vindicated by the faithful testimony and writings of the innocent servant and hand-maid of the Lord.* There were several further editions to 1788. Elizabeth Bathurst also wrote/compiled *The sayings of women, which were spoken upon sundry occasions, in several places of the Scriptures, etc.* (1683) and *An expostulatory appeal to the professors of Christianity joyned in community with Samuel Annesley* (?1679, of which the last part was written by Anne BATHURST*). She defended women's preaching: 'Yea, though we have not all the Gift of Prophecying (vocally) bestowed on us, yet by our upright Carriage, we shall every one become Preachers of Righteousness amongst our Neighbours, whereby we shall reach to the Witness, they hath slain in their Consciences, and shall cause it to arise and stand upon its Feet, and Prophesie in their Streets.'

BATHURST, Grace, 1634–1703

2. London; 4. Quaker; 5(a) Richard Hubbard, (b) Charles Bathurst (m. 1676); 6(b) confectioner.

Her daughter by her first marriage was born 1669. Her 'Testimony concerning Elizabeth Bathurst' (1691) is in Elizabeth BATHURST's* *Truth's vindication* (Elizabeth was a stepdaughter). There is also a testimony in Anne WHITEHEAD,* *Piety* . . . (1686). She signed *A tender and Christian testimony* (1685; see Mary ELSON* for details).

BATTEN, Joan, *fl.* 1643–64

2. Bristol.

She was one of the women who led the organisation of the fortification of Bristol, by women, in the Civil War. Her deposition is in W. Prynne and C. Walker, *A true and full relation of the prosecution . . . of Nathaneal Fiennes* (1664): she describes how she offered to Fiennes to work on the fortification, how he told them to use earth to fortify with and how the women held the Frome gate against the Royalists; she also laments his capitulation. See Dorothy HAZZARD.*

BAXTER, Margaret, 1636–81

1. Charlton; 2. nr. Wellington (Shropshire), Oxford, Kidderminster; 5. Richard Baxter; 6. minister, writer.

Diary, in Richard Baxter, *Breviate of the life of Mrs Margaret Baxter* (1681).

In his autobiography, Baxter speaks of Margaret as 'a woman of extraordinary acuteness of wit, solidity of judgment, incredible prudence and sagacity.' (Everyman abridgement of *Reliquiae Baxterianae*, ed. J. M. Lloyd Thomas, 1931, p. 249.) Thomas (Appendix 2, p. 267 ff.) speaks of 'Her secret confessions' as showing 'how dependent she had become on his private and public spiritual direction'. He adds 'These documents . . . give us also her personal examination of her own soul, self-questioned with . . . ruthless realism.' This appendix includes quotations from her papers.

BAYLY, Mary

Mary FISHER*

BEALE, Mary/Martha, 1632–97

1. Craddock; 2. London, Buckinghamshire; 3. artist; 5. Charles Beale; 6. genteel.

There are portraits by her in the National Portrait Gallery, etc., and she also left water-colours and crayon drawings. She may have been a pupil of Lely and she taught Sarah CURTIS to paint portraits. According to Fraser, Mary Beale earned £429 for eighty-three commissions in 1677. *The Woodforde Diaries and Papers* (ed. Dorothy Woodforde, London: Peter Davies, 1932) refers to two psalms by her in Samuel Woodforde's *Paraphrase of the Psalms*. Harriet Sampson's edition of John Evelyn, *The life of Mrs Godolphin* (1939, p. 273) refers to Beale's manuscript 'Discourse on friendship' (Harleian MS. 6828 ff.).

See Fraser, p. 342 and Greer, *The Obstacle Race* (London: Secker & Warburg, 1979), pp. 255–7.

BEAUMONT, Agnes, 1652–1720

2. Bedfordshire, Hertfordshire; 3. trade; 4. Baptist; 4. — Storey (second husband); 6. merchant.

The narrative of the persecution of Agnes Beaumont in 1674 (1760) is a brief and moving account of her trouble with her father over her efforts to follow her religious convictions.

See G. B. Harrison (ed.) in Constable's *Miscellany of Original and Selected Publications in Literature* (1929) and the extract in William Myers (ed.), *Restoration and Revolution* (Beckenham, Kent: Croom Helm, 1986).

BECK, Margaret, *fl.* **1655**
3. genteel; 5. Nevill Beck.

She is the author of *The reward of oppression, tyranny and injustice, com-mitted by the late kings and queens of England, and others; by the unlawful entry, and unlawful deteiner of the dutchie lands of Lancaster. Declared in the case of Samuel Beck, an infant . . . Margaret Beck . . . mother and guardian to the infant* (1655). This is an address to Cromwell (who, she says, knew her husband) and the Privy Council, claiming that the duchy is her son's rightful inheritance (traced through the husband's link with the Neville family).

BECK, Sarah

See Appendix III.

BECKWITH, Elizabeth, –1720
1. Theakston; 2. Audbrough, nr. Masham (Yorks.); 4. Quaker; 5. Mar-maduke Beckwith (m. 1666).

Signed epistles from the Women's Meeting in York in 1688 (see Mary WAITE* for details) and 1692. Mother of Hannah and Sarah (see next entry).

BECKWITH, Hannah, 1667–
2. Audbrough, nr. Masham and Nosterfield (Yorks.); 4. Quaker; 5. Joseph Wynn (m. 1692).

She bore eight children between 1693 and 1710, and wrote *A true relation of the life and death of Sarah Beckwith [1671–91], daughter of Marmaduke and Elizabeth Beckwith, who in about the 20th. year of her age departed this life* (1692). Hannah was Sarah's sister. The text is commonly attributed to Sarah's parents, while Wing gives it to Marmaduke Beckwith alone.

BEHN, Aphra, ?1640–?89
1. ?Johnson, ?Cooper, ?Amis; 2. Surinam, London, Holland; 3. writer and spy.

Aphra Behn's life is surrounded by legend and ambiguity, but early life in Surinam and a period as a government spy in Holland seem established. She was imprisoned in London and is buried in Westminster Abbey.

Behn is one of the first English professional woman writers: there was an enormous output of plays, poems, novels and stories from 1670. Her plays, which include *Abdelazar* (1676), *The feign'd curtizans* (1679) and *The widow Ranter* (1690), held the stage for many years, and several have had successful recent revivals. Similarly, a number of her fictions have been recently reprinted.

The plays, histories and novels, ed. J. Pearson (London, 1871). *The works*, ed. M. Summers (London: Heinemann, 1915). *Loveletters from a nobleman to his sister*, ed. M. Duffy (London: Virago, 1987). *The lucky chance*, ed. F. Morgan (London: Methuen, 1984). *The rover*, ed. F. Link (Nebraska: Nebraska University Press, 1967). Also: M. Duffy, *The passionate shepherdess* (New York: Discus Books, 1977); A. Goreau, *Reconstructing Aphra* (Oxford: Oxford University Press, 1980).

BELL, Deborah, 1686–1738

1. Wynn; 2. Bradford (Yorks.), London; 4. Quaker; 5. John Bell (m. 1710).

'The testimony of Deborah Bell concerning her dear father John Wynn' (1715) appears in *The memory of the just reviv'd: in divers testimonies concerning John Wynn*. There is also a diary for 1707–37: *A short journal of the labours and travels in the work of the ministry of that faithful servant of Christ* . . . (1762). Daughter of Deborah WYNN,* she moved to London at her marriage.

BELL, Susanna, –1672

2. Roxbury (New England), London; 4. Independent; 5. Thomas Bell; 6. merchant.

Brought up in a family 'that feared the Lord'; after her marriage her husband wanted to join the puritan emigration to New England (presumably in the 1620s); she resisted because she had one young child and was pregnant. When her child died, she asked God why: 'it was given in to me, that it was because I would not go to New England.' Her narrative of New England consists mainly of her attempts to join the 'people of God', which were blocked because she had no 'particular promise' from God, and she entered a period of spiritual distress (after which she was accepted into Cotton's congregation). Her husband made trips to and from England (the first during the 1640s), during which she looked after the business, then she returned with him (letters of 'dismission' are sent from Roxbury to England in 1654). In England 'I was much troubled that there was no better observation of the Lords day'; she tells of the threat to them of 'publick dangers' (presumably after 1660), of her daughter's sickness and their survival of both the Plague and the Fire of London (1665–6). She was sole executrix of her husband, who died at Barking in 1671. In his dedicatory epistle (twice the length of Bell's text), Thomas Brookes addresses her children: four are specified in the *Legacy* and in her husband's will (and they too have children), and are themselves, or are married to, merchants. Brookes celebrates their parents' charity (money left for schools, etc.). Bell's experiences 'were taken from her by one of you, when she was in a very weakly condition': she died a widow after a period of sickness.

The legacy of a dying mother to her mourning children, being the experiences of Mrs Susanna Bell, who died March 13. 1672 (1673).

BENNET, Dorcas, *fl. c.* 1660–70
2. ?Dublin; 4. ?Congregationalist.

The epistle to her book describes her as not being a learned woman like 'great ones' but 'one who must work for her bread, please her husband, take care for her children, and guide the house'. She tells of a dream in which she heard Mr M[ather] preach, and makes reference to a congregation in 'Christ-Church': this may be the Congregationalist Samuel Mather who was in Dublin in the 1660s (though ordered to stop preaching in 1660); Dublin cathedral is Christ Church.

Good and seasonable counsel for women, from a woman, advising and reproving her sisters, for their frowardness, pride, and disobedience to their husbands. With many other things worthy to be noted in these licentious times (1670). The text attacks female failings: 'for our attire how unjust is it, that we should inject hellish thoughts into the minds of men by our immodest dress?'; 'The woman was first in the transgression.'

BENSON, Mabel, ?1605–92
2. Westmorland; 4. Quaker; 5(a) John Camm, (b) Gervase Benson (m. 1660).

Mabel Benson travelled as a minister with Anne AUDLAND* in 1655: they were assaulted in Banbury. In 1660 she was imprisoned over tithes. Her 'The testimony of Mabel Benson concerning her late husband, deceased' is in John Camm, *Memory . . .* (1689).

BENTLEY, Magdalene Augustine (baptised Catharine), *fl.* 1635
3. nun; 4. Catholic.

She translated Luke Wadding's *The history of the angellicall virgin glorious S. Clare* (Douai, 1635). Wadding was an Irish historian and theologian (1588–1657) who edited Duns Scotus.

BERGAVENNY, Frances

Frances ABERGAVENNY*

BERRY, Dorothy

She is the author of a commendatory poem in Diana PRIMROSE's* volume *A chain of pearl* (1630), but nothing else is known of her.
    See Greer, p. 83.

BERTIE, Lady Mary, 1655–1709

2. Norfolk; 3. genteel; 5. Charles Dormer, Earl of Caernarvon (m. after 1678); 6. genteel.

Daughter of Montagu Bertie, Earl of Lindsey, she was Dormer's second wife. Roberts (p. 82) cites letters by her in 1671–2 to 'her niece Kathern Noel' at Exton (his source is Historical Manuscripts Commission Rutland II. 22, 23). Katherine NOEL (1657–1732) married the Earl of Rutland in 1673/4; she was the granddaughter of Montagu Bertie.

BETTRIS, Jone/Jane, *fl.* 1657–69

2. Oxfordshire; 4. Quaker.

She wrote *A lamentation for the deceived people of the world. But in particular to them of Aylesbury* (1657) and *A short discovery of His Highness the Lord Protectors intentions touching the Anabaptists in the Army, and all such as are against his reforming things in the church* (1657). Hobby (*Virtue*, p. 232) lists *Spiritual discoveries . . .*, but has found no copy. In 1669 Jane Bettris and her daughter were fined for holding a Quaker meeting; she was apparently so poor that the law officer paid her fine. Besse mentions a Quaker activist in Oxfordshire called Richard Bettris, but we can find no link with Jane.

BIDDLE, Hester, 1629–96

2. Oxford, London; 4. Anglican, Quaker; 5(a) Thomas Biddle, ?(b) Christopher White (m. 1668); 6(a) shoemaker.

She was raised an Anglican; she came to despise the Oxford University scholars. In 1655 she was one of the first Quakers in Amsterdam, with Anne GARGIL* and Elizabeth HENDRICKS.* In 1659 George Fox advised her to be cautious about her prophecy of the restoration of Charles II, which advice she ignored (N. Penney, ed., *The journal of George Fox*, Cambridge, 1911). In *c.* 1664 she was seized at the Bull and Mouth;

punched, kicked, and imprisoned in Bridewell (*CSPD* 1664/5, 103: 75). She was also imprisoned in Newgate for speaking in the street. These events may be connected with her trial (as reported in Besse), during which the judge and jury expressed surprise about a woman preaching: 'she told them, Phoebe was a Prophetess, and Phillip had four Daughters that had prophesied, and Paul wrote to his Brethren that they should take care of the women that were fellow labourers with him in the Gospel. The Judge said, That was a great while ago; she told him, It was when the Church was in her Beauty and Glory.' Later in the same trial she was accused of leaving her husband for two years and travelling with a 'young man': 'she told him, That was not his business to judge at this time, nor was it fit for him to accuse her, but she went with three Women as she was moved of the Lord.' Between *c.* 1659 and 1662 she published eight broadsides and pamphlets, such as *Wo to thee city of Oxford, thy wickedness surmounteth the wickedness of Sodome* and *Oh! wo, wo, from the Lord* (1659). Between 1663 and 1668 she had three sons.

There is a problem over her possible remarriage: her death is recorded as Hester Biddle of St Sepulchre's parish; the Hester Biddle who married White in 1668 was from Stepney. She may have been known by, or reverted to, the name Biddle after White's death (it sometimes happens that women continued to use or were referred to by the name by which they were famous; e.g. Theophila TOWNSEND*). Death of a Thomas Biddle is recorded in 1682 (aged 70).

BINNS, Grace, –1729

1. Goldsbrough; 2. High Burton, Masham (Yorks.); 4. Quaker; 5. John Binns (m. 1676).

She bore five children between 1677 and 1688 (the last two being twins). Wrote 'A few words in testimony concerning the life and death of Sarah Beckwith' in *A true relation* (1692) (see Hannah BECKWITH*). She was one of the group of Quakers in Masham, being married in Anne BLACK-BURNE's* house at High Ellington.

BIRKHEAD, Anne, *fl.* 1680

2. Herring Creek (Maryland) 4. Quaker; 5. Christopher Birkhead.

Her husband worked with Fox in England, and they became major figures among Herring Creek Quakers (owning about 600 acres). She was with William Coale when he died: see her testimony (1680) in *A testimony concerning . . . William Coale* (1682).

BISHOP, Anne, *fl.* **1652–3**
2. Dublin; 4. Baptist; 5. ?George Bishop; 6. soldier.

'Experiences' in Rogers, *Ohel* . . . (1653) (see also Mary BARKER*). She speaks of learning to part with her parents for Christ. If the guess is correct, her husband commanded an English troop in Ireland, disbanding in 1653.

BLACKBERRY/BLACKBOROW, Sarah, –1665
2. Hammersmith (London); 3. preacher; 4. Quaker; 5. William Blackberry/Blackborow.

Mary ELSON*

One of the first London women Quaker ministers and a friend of Nayler, Sarah Blackberry set up the Hammersmith Quaker meeting, called a meeting of women to help poor Friends (1659), and signed the women's tithing petition. She produced some half-dozen tracts between 1657 and 1663, including *A visit to the spirit in prison* (1658), *The oppressed prisoners complaint of their great oppression* (1662) and *The just and equal balance discovered: with a true measure whereby the inhabitants of Sion doth fathom and compasse all false worships and their ground* . . . (1660; published by Mary WESTWOOD*). This includes the statement 'Christ was one in the Male and in the Female; and as he arises in both' (see Smith, p. 12).

BLACKBURNE, Anne, –1700
2. High Ellington, Masham (Yorks.); 4. Quaker; 5. Christopher Blackburne.

Her husband died the same year that her son was born, 1663. As a widow she seems to have been an important figure in the Masham area. She was fined £20 on six occasions in 1670–1 for being at Quaker meetings.
   Testimony in *Several living testimonies given forth by divers Friends to the faithful labours and travels of* . . . *Robert Lodge* (1691; printed and sold by Tace SOWLE).

BLACKBURNE, Rebecka, 1661–
2. High Ellington, Masham (Yorks.); 4. Quaker.

Daughter of Anne BLACKBURNE;* testimony in *Several living testimonies* . . . (1691), as above.

BLAGGE, Margaret, 1652–78
2. France, London; 3. Maid of Honour; 5. Sidney Godolphin; 6. MP, government servant.

Margaret Blagge married Godolphin secretly in 1675, after a nine year engagement: she was nervous about marrying because she thought she would die in childbirth, as she did. John Evelyn called her 'my dear friend' and claimed that he esteemed her 'infinitely' for her 'many and extraordinary virtues'. She acted in John Crowne's court play *Calisto* (1674), as did Henrietta Maria WENTWORTH.* She wrote a diary ('An account of her actions, failings and other particulars and infirmitys'). Her justified fears of childbirth were shared by, among others, Anne HALKET* and Elizabeth JOSCELINE.*

See Evelyn's *Life of Mrs Godolphin*, which begins with a reference to 'that Blessed Saint now in Heaven'. Evelyn quotes extensively from her letters. Her portrait was painted by Mary BEALE.*

BLAITHWAITE, Mary, *fl.* 1644–54

2. Cumberland; 5. Henry Blaithwaite; 6. ?farmer.

See Critical Appendix 4.

Mary Blaithwaite's text tells of political opposition from local Royalist officials, including attorneys, Commissioners of Array and a constable. This led to numerous arrests and mistreatment. She was arrested in 1644 for distributing pro-Parliament pamphlets: she was dragged through Cockermouth on market day; then she was arrested at a religious service and put in Carlisle castle: 'they caused me to be bound in [the cart] on my back with my face upwards under the horse's tail, and in a most inhumane manner caused the horses to gallop the more to torment me, and under pretence of searching for Parliament papers, stripped my husband to his shirt and me to my smock, which they tore in an uncivil manner, and gave direction to lay me in irons, and both my husband and myself were put amongst the common rogues and thieves.' Later she was forced to travel to Oxford to answer a subpoena; the attorneys made people frightened of being employed by her and her husband. He became sick and died (prior to 1647) as a result of this pressure.

The complaint of Mary Blaithwaite widdow; setting forth her sad condition, occasioned by the late dissolution of the Parliament, and neglect of justice ever since (1654). Her plea is based on an ordinance of 1642 that made reparations from the estates of delinquent gentry to those in the North who supported Parliament. She has been pursuing her case for seven years, and waiting 18 weeks to have her petition heard.

BLAND, Elizabeth, *fl.* 1681–1712

1. Fisher; 2. Leeds, London; 4. Quaker; 5. Nathaniel Bland (m. 1681); 6. linen-draper.

Elizabeth was a Hebrew scholar who wrote a phylactery ('four sentences on a scroll presented to the Royal Society') and a 'Turkish Commission'. These objects are 'listed as curiosities from the area of Leeds by Thoresby', in his *Ducatus Leodiensis* (1715). Information from Todd, pp. 50–1. She bore at least three children; her son Nathaniel died in 1684, aged 3 months.

BLANDFORD, Susannah, *fl.* 1658–1700

2. Northamptonshire; 4. Quaker.

A follower of William Rogers, she wrote *A small account given forth by one that hath been a traveller for these 40 years in the good old way* (1698) and *A small treatise writ by one of the true Christian faith; who believes in God and in his son Jesus Christ . . .* (1700).

BLAUGDONE, Barbara, 1609–1704

1. Brock; 2. Bristol; 3. landowner and schoolmistress; 4. Quaker.

Converted to Quakerism in 1654, she was soon imprisoned for preaching and went on hunger strike. Her life was full of missionary travels and violent persecution. Leaving a Quaker meeting in Bristol with Mary PRINCE* she was stabbed, but proceeded on to Marlborough (Wilts.) and then (after six weeks' imprisonment) to various places in Devon (where she also tried to convert the Countess of Bath). She was whipped and imprisoned in Exeter, began preaching on her release and went to Basingstoke to obtain the freedom of imprisoned Quakers (1655). From here she went to Ireland, where she complained to Henry Cromwell about the mistreatment of Quakers; she was accused of witchcraft in Cork, robbed by pirates on a return journey to Bristol, imprisoned in Dublin and Limerick, and banished with other Quakers from Ireland in 1664. (When she wrote to Fox in October 1656 of her plans for going to Jerusalem she received no support.) In Bristol in 1681 she was imprisoned (she was working as a schoolmistress at this period), fined in 1683 for refusing to attend church and imprisoned in Ilchester the same year for illegal assembly.

Her *Account of the travels, sufferings and persecutions of Barbara Blaugdone. Given forth as a testimony to the Lords power, and for the encouragement of Friends* (1691) was printed and published by Tace SOWLE.

BLEMING, Jone

See Appendix III.

BLOUNT, Lady Amie/Anne, *fl.* 1616–21
1. Touchet; 2. Harlaston (Derbys.); 3. genteel; 5. Edward Blount; 6. genteel.

Daughter of George Touchet, Earl of Castlehaven (died 1616) and Lucy AUDLEY.* The name on her petition is Amie, presumably a misprint for Anne. Since at least January 1617 she obtained legal judgements against William Holt, demanding payment of debts. He tried to use legal means to delay payment. She says she fears she will lose the money owed. *To the honorable assembly of the Commons House. The humble complaint of the ladie Amie Blount daughter of George late Earl of Castle-Haven* (?1621).

BLOW, Anne, *fl.* ?1664–6
2. London; 4. ?Quaker.

CSPD for 18 October 1666 refers to a 'seditious' letter she sent to the mayor of Chester, advising him and the aldermen to repent. She apparently walked 150 miles to declare this to them. A letter of 3 December 1666 (*CSPD*) probably refers to her: she should be imprisoned pending orders from London. Besse (1.404) refers to an Anne Blow sentenced (with nine others) to transportation to Jamaica in 1664/5. This may not be the same woman, although Besse's dates are sometimes inaccurate. There are records from the London meetings of two children of Nicholas Blow who died of plague in 1665, but again there is no definite link with Anne Blow.

BODELY, Elizabeth, *fl.* 1671

4. ?Quaker.

CSPD for 19 April 1671 refers to 'a very scandalous and rebellious paper' addressed to the King: 'It is subscribed by one Elizabeth Bodely, & justified by the Quaker to be delivered to His Majesty's own hand.' The paper is described as 'full of venom' and the author should be punished.

BOOTH, Mary, *fl.* 1650–61
2. London; 4. Quaker.

Described as 'sister' to Rebeckah TRAVERS,* though no family relationship has been established, and the term may be one of religious solidarity. She was friend to James Nayler and, later, to John Perrot, who refers to her as 'sister and mother', and who left her a gift in his will. Her name occurs often as a correspondent of Perrot in the early 1650s (K. L. Carroll, *John Perrot*, London: Friends Historical Society, 1971). She was imprisoned; signed the women's tithing petition; and wrote a preface to Nayler's *Milk for babes* (1661; signed M.B.). Carroll (p. 45) cites the manuscript volume by Edmund Crosse (Friends House Library) as including letters by her.

BOOTHBY, Frances, *fl.* 1669–70
2. ?Derbyshire; 4. ?Catholic.

She claimed to be related to Lady YATE of Worcestershire (this may be Mary, daughter of Humphrey Pakington of Worcester, who married Sir John Yate). Her tragicomedy, *Marcelia: Or the treacherous friend* (1670), was performed at Drury Lane in June/July 1669. The dedication to Lady Yate contains an appeal to her to 'appose the Censuring World, upon this uncommon action in my Sex'. She addressed a poem to her cousin, Mrs SOMERSET, about the 'Unjust Censure' of her play. She may perhaps be identified as Frances, daughter of John Milward, who married Sir William Boothby (of an Oxfordshire branch of the Derbyshire Boothbys).

See extracts in Greer, p. 233 f.

BOREMAN, Mary, 1631–1701
1. Bond; 2. London; 4. Quaker; 5(a) Henry Boreman, (b) John Pennyman; 6(a) oilman, (b) draper and businessman.

Three children were born between 1657 and 1661. After Henry Boreman's death Mary lived at Tottenham with other widows and dissociated herself from the Quakers, developing views similar to those of Jane LEAD.* Her 'wedding' to Pennyman scandalised Quakers, 250 guests (including Elizabeth CALVERT*) having been invited from all the sects: it was lampooned in a ballad, 'Ye Quakers wedding'.

Mary Boreman's works were considered unsound by the Quakers. They include *The ark is begun to be opened* (1671; with Pennyman), part of Pennyman's *Instruction to his children* (1674), *Something formerly writ . . .* (1696) and *Some of the letters and papers which were written by Mrs Mary Pennyman* (1701).

BOULBIE, Judith, –1706
2. Skipwith (Yorks.); 4. Quaker.

See Critical Appendix 6.

She wrote five pamphlets, including *A testimony for truth against all hireling priests and deceivers: with a cry to the inhabitants of this nation, to turn to the*

Lord, before his dreadful judgments overtake them (1665) and *A warning and lamentation over England.* (Hobby, *Virtue*, p. 232, doubts this latter ascription, having found no copy.) Judith Boulbie's goods were distrained in 1671 and she was imprisoned over tithes in 1688. She is a signatory to Epistles from the York Women's Meetings in 1688 (Mary WAITE*) and 1692. Although a member of this Meeting, she seems at some time to have been considered unsound by Friends. (The Rebecca Boulbie who was married in 1682 may be a daughter.)

BRABAZON, Juliana, –1692

1. Chaworth; 2. Nottinghamshire; 3. genteel; 5. Chambre Brabazon, Earl of Meath (m. in or before 1682).

Daughter of Patrick Chaworth, 3rd Viscount Chaworth of Armagh, she bore six children and was buried in Nottingham. Roberts (p. 121, n. 88) cites a letter in 1682 to the Countess of Rutland (to whom she may have been connected through her mother).

BRACKLEY, Lady Elizabeth, 1626–63

1. Cavendish; 2. Welbeck Abbey (Notts.); 3. genteel; 5. John Egerton, Viscount Brackley (later Earl of Bridgwater); 6. genteel.

Elizabeth was the sister of Jane CAVENDISH* and stepdaughter of Margaret CAVENDISH.* She wrote (unpublished) songs and poems, and a play, *The concealed fansyes* (*c.* 1646) in collaboration with her sister. This has been edited by N. Starr (*Proceedings of the Modern Languages Association of America*, vol. 46, 1931). There is also 'Loose papers left by y. Right hobl. Elizabeth Countess of Bridgwater', which consists of a poem and prose meditations on pregnancies, childbed, etc. (BL, MS Egerton 607; extracts in Houlbrooke). She was imprisoned with her husband as a result of his involvement in a duel. Welbeck, where the Cavendish sisters seem to have collaborated, was first a Royalist garrison in the Civil War and later captured by Parliament. She died in childbirth.

BRADMORE, Sarah

See Appendix III.

BRADSTREET, Anne, 1613–72

1. Dudley; 2. Northamptonshire, Lincolnshire, Massachusetts; 3. poet; 4. puritan; 5. Simon Bradstreet; 6. estate steward, colonist.

She was educated in a staunchly puritan household, but also read poetry when young. She and her husband lived at the estate of the Countess of Warwick (where he was employed) until they emigrated with her parents in 1630. She bore eight children between 1634 and 1652, and wrote poetry during this time: *The tenth Muse lately sprung up in America* (1650). *Several poems compiled with great variety of wit and learning, full of delight* (Boston, 1678) reprinted (with changes) the poems in *Tenth Muse* and added new poems.

BRAIDLEY, Margaret, –1692

2. Knipe (Westmorland); 4. Quaker; 5. ?Thomas Braidley.

Her text *Written from the spirit of the living God, Margaret Braidley, one, whom the world calls a Quaker* is bound with Christopher Taylor's *Certain papers which is the word of the Lord* (?1655). It consists of a series of accusatory letters to the town of Appleby, local ministers and John Lowther of Lowther Hall: 'The word of the Lord came unto me the twelf day of the nineth moneth, saying, write, woe unto thee that hath lost the key of knowledge, that calls good evil, and evil good.' The birth of Thomas Braidley's daughter Ester is recorded in 1654; we assume Margaret Braidley was the mother.

BRAYTHWAITE, Elizabeth, *c.* 1667–84

2. Westmorland; 4. Quaker.

Daughter of Richard and Anne Braythwaite (see Anne GARDNER*) of the Kendal meeting, Westmorland. She worked as a housekeeper for her brother and authored a passage in the volume which commemorates her death: T.C., *A brief relation* (1684; information from Hobby manuscript notes).

BRIDGWATER, Elizabeth Egerton, Countess of

Elizabeth BRACKLEY*

BROCKMAN, Ann, –1660

1. Bunce; 2. Linstead Parva (Suffolk), Beachborough (Kent); 3. genteel; 4. William Brockman (m. 1616); 6. gentry (knighted 1633).

Author of an unprinted medical book (1638), which is quoted by Pollock (p. 100); her source is the Drake-Brockman papers (BL, Add. MSS 42586–710, 45193–220). Ann Brockman bore seven children to this Royalist family.

BROOKE, Lady Elizabeth, 1601–83

1. Colepepper; 2. London, Hertfordshire, Suffolk; 3. genteel; 5. Sir Robert Brooke; 6. genteel.

Her large manuscript volume 'Observations, Rules for practice' was begun in 1631. Selections appeared in *The Lady's Monitor* for 1828.

BROOKES, Martha, –1676

2. London; 4. Congregationalist; 5. Thomas Brookes; 6. minister.

A few religious quotations from her (such as 'Though I grone, yet I bless God I do not grumble') are included in her husband's spiritual biography of her: 'A short account of some of the choice experiences, blessed discoveries, and gracious evidences of Mrs. Martha Brooks, who fell asleep in Jesus, June 20 1676. Drawn up by a near relation, that best understood her spiritual estate and condition.' It is in J. C. (John Collins), *Strength in weakness. A sermon preached at the funeral of Mrs Martha Brooks* (1676). The suffering religious woman was often used by ministers as spiritual example and exhortation: see Calamy's use of Elizabeth MOORE.*

BROOKSOP, Joan, –1680/1

2. Chesterfield (Derbys.); 4. Quaker; 5. Thomas Brooksop.

Four children were born between 1641 and 1653. In 1661 she travelled with Elizabeth HOOTON* to New England. They were imprisoned in Boston (Massachusetts) and then driven into the woods without food. They survived, travelled to Providence, Rhode Island (a refuge for Quakers) and Barbados, before returning to Boston, where they were arrested and shipped to Virginia. Another visit to New England took place in 1676.

An invitation of love unto the seed of God, throughout the world. With a word to the wise at heart. And a lamentation for New England (1662).

BROWN, Ellin, *fl.* 1688

5. Henry Brown.

The case of Ellin Brown widow of Henry Brown who in 1688 was executed for pretended high treason against the late King James (?1700).

BROWNE, Sarah

Sarah FEATHERSTONE*

BULL, Katharine, –1666
2. King's Lynn (Norfolk); 4. Quaker; 5. George Bull.

She signed the 1659 tithing petition and speaks of having been instructed by William Dewsbury (in *Letters to William Dewsbury and others*, ed.
H. Cadbury, Friends Historical Society, 1948).

BULSTRODE, Cecelea, –c. 1609
2. ?Buckinghamshire, London.

She was Lady in Waiting to ANNE OF DENMARK* and was called 'the
pucelle [whore] of the Court Mistris Bulstrode'. She was attacked by Ben
Jonson, whom she had censured, but he and Donne both wrote sympathetic poems on her death (she died after illness). She may be the
daughter of Cecily and Edward Bulstrode of Buckinghamshire, being
born 1583. 'Newes of my morning worke, by Mist. B.' is in the ninth
edition of *The conceited news of Thomas Overbury*, ed. J. E. Savage (New
York: Scholars Facsimiles and Reprints, 1968): 'honesty in the Court
lives in persecution, like protestants in Spain.'

BURCH, Dorothy, *fl.* 1646
2. Strood (Kent); 3. ?genteel; 4. Calvinist.

Author of *A catechism of several heads of the Christian religion, gathered
together in question and answer, it being intended onely for private use, but now
published for the good and benefit of others; by the importunitie of some friends*
(1646). The epistle to the reader speaks of her parish priest seeking to
make her and others 'odious' in people's eyes because they will not
honour him. She describes those vilified by the priest as 'a knowing
people, and precious in the sight of God'. Her text uses the language of
election and rebirth.

BURGHOPE, Maria, *fl.* 1699
2. Ashridge.

Daughter of the Earl of Bridgwater's chaplain at Ashridge, and author of
a manuscript celebration of Ashridge, 'A Vision', dedicated to Mary
EGERTON (1699). This is in the Huntington Library. In the dedication,
Burghope speaks of her devotion to poetry as being as 'sure as lawfull
and laudable, as our ordinary chatt, telling of news, and backbiteing,
dressing up, patching, painting, putting ourselves into a posture of talk-
ing nonsence in the mode, and other the admired qualifications of our
sex.' (Greer, p. 21.)

BURGIS, Hannah, 1646–1704

1. Vokins; 2. West Challow (Berks.), London; 4. Quaker; 5. Samuel Burgis (m. 1689); 6. haberdasher.

Daughter of Joan VOKINS,* with her sisters Sarah LAWRENCE,* Mary LOCKEY* and Elizabeth VOKINS* she signed a testimony 'concerning our dear and tender mother, Joan Vokins' in 1691. The second wife of Burgis, she bore four children (the first two twins) between 1691 and 1699 (three died in infancy).

BURNET, Elizabeth, 1661–?1709/?1712

1. Blake; 2. Hampshire, Holland, Worcestershire, London; 3. genteel; 5(a) Robert Berkeley, (b) Gilbert Burnet; 6(b) bishop and historian.

The anonymous *Method of devotion; or rules for holy and devout loving . . .* (1709-second edition; 1713, 1730, 1738) includes prayers by her. She was a great reader of the scriptures and a supporter of William of Orange.

BURRILL, Mary, *fl.* 1652–3

2. Dublin; 4. Baptist; 5. ?Thomas Burrell.

'Experiences' in Rogers, *Ohel . . .* (1653) (see also Mary BARKER*). She tells of being spiritually troubled, but is comforted by the arrival in Dublin of the Baptist minister John Rogers. She says she has been married twice. Captain Thomas Burrell is listed as a soldier of the Commonwealth in Ireland.

BURTON, Sarah, *fl.* 1636–52

2. London; 4. ?Presbyterian; 5. Henry Burton; 6. minister and writer.

Second wife of Henry Burton, who was rector of St Matthew, Friday Street, London, 1621–37: his political career (and thus hers) may be compared to that of Susanna BASTWICK's* husband. Both women regularly petitioned to visit their husbands in prison or to reside on the islands of their imprisonment. Sarah Burton was apparently imprisoned for presenting her husband's sermons (from *c.* 1636) to certain lords in Parliament. She petitioned the Commons in 1640 for her husband's release from prison (first in Lancaster, then Guernsey), and in 1652 for maintenance from delinquents' lands. She was granted £100 a year. Sarah Burton is representative of the hundreds of unpublished female petitioners whose cases are documented in *CSPD*; we take her as our single example of this writing because her case is relatively well-known.

BURY, Elizabeth, 1644–1720
1. Lawrence; 2. Suffolk, Cambridgeshire, Norfolk, Bristol; 4. Anglican,
?Quaker; 5(a) Griffith Lloyd, (b) Samuel Bury; 6(b) minister.

Elizabeth Bury was a polymath, learned in medicine, philology, heraldry,
French and Hebrew, and author of a puritan religious diary for 1693–
1720. An abridgment of this was published in Bristol in 1720 as *An
account of the life and death of Mrs Elizabeth Bury* . . . . She also left manuscript materials: Reynolds refers to a 'mass of manuscripts' (pp. 99–100).

BUTLER, Mrs A.

Milesian tales: mentioned on the back pages of HEARNE's* *Female deserters*
(1719).

C

'Experiences of E.C.' in Henry Walker, *Spirituall Experiences, of sundry believers* (1653; Smith, p. 80).

CSPD

See Appendix I.

CALDWELL, Elizabeth, –1603
1. Duncalffe; 2. Chester; 5. Thomas Caldwell.

Elizabeth Caldwell took Jeffrey Bownd as her lover, after her husband's travelling caused dissent in their marriage. Lady Mary CHOLMSLY tried, unsuccessfully, to have her reprieved for the crime for which she was executed (see below).

She is author of a letter in *A true discourse of the practises of Elizabeth Caldwell (and others) on the person of Ma. T. Caldwell in the county of Chester, to have murdered and poysoned him, with divers others. Together with her maner of godly life during her imprisonment, her arrainement and execution, with Isabell Hall widdow. Lastly a most excellent exhortatorie letter, written by her own selfe out of the prison to her husband, to cause him to fall into consideration of his sinnes etc. Serving likewise for the use of every good Christian. Being executed the 18 of June 1603* (1603). This text is a compendium moral volume compiled by Gilbert Dugdale, framing the criminal woman's penitent letter in a man's moralising text.

CALVERT, Elizabeth, ?1620–75
2. London; 3. bookseller and publisher; 4. ?Baptist; 5. Giles Calvert; 6. bookseller and publisher.

See Critical Appendices 5, 7.

Elizabeth Calvert was, with her husband, a publisher of radical and sectarian literature throughout the 1640s and 1650s. After the deaths of her husband and her son, Nathaniel, she continued the business until her own death. Between 1661 and 1664 she was arrested four times and spent at least seven months in prison. After the death of Giles she was in debt from legal expenses relating to his imprisonment, had her shop and stock destroyed in the Great Fire, but continued trading. She was arrested three more times, had books seized, had a secret press in Southwark (at Elizabeth POOLE's* house) which was dismantled by the Stationers' Company, and was eventually brought to trial in 1671. Letters of hers are collected in *CSPD* (including one to Jane WOODCOCK,* a Quaker supporter of John Nayler). Her sister-in-law was Martha SIMMONDS.* The Calvert shop, at the Black Spread Eagle, was a centre for radicals: Mary WESTWOOD* sold the 1659 tithing petition from that address. A Quaker description of Elizabeth Calvert as 'Jesebell' for attending Mary BOREMAN's* wedding suggests that she was on the extreme wing of those disaffected with Quakerism; she was buried with the Baptists.

CAMFIELD, Elizabeth, 1632–1716
2. Cheshunt (Herts.); 4. Quaker; 5. Francis Camfield.

A daughter was married in 1672, a son in 1677. She wrote 'Many are the testimonies', in Anne WHITEHEAD,* *Piety . . .* (1686).

CAMM, Anne

Anne AUDLAND*

CAMM, Mabel

Mabel BENSON*

CAREW/CAREY, Clementine (baptised Anne), 1615–71
2. Cambrai; 3. genteel, nun; 4. Catholic.

She was the eldest daughter of Elizabeth CAREW/CAREY.* All five daughters became Benedictine nuns at Cambrai, and Clementine may be the author of the manuscript 'The Lady Falkland; her life'.

CAREW/CAREY, Lady Elizabeth, Viscountess Falkland, 1585–1639
1. Tanfield; 2. Ireland, London; 3. professional, genteel; 4. Catholic convert; 5. Sir Henry Carey; 6. genteel.

Elizabeth Carew learnt French, Spanish, Italian and Hebrew. She separated from her husband in 1625, when she announced her conversion to Catholicism (which had actually happened many years earlier). She is generally assumed to be the author of *The tragedie of Mariam* (1613). In addition, she wrote a translation from Seneca, a 'Life of Tamerlane', and lives of SS Mary Magdalene, Agnes and Elizabeth of Portugal (all in verse and lost), as well as a translation of *The reply of the most illustrious cardinal of Perron* (Douai, 1630). This, done in a month, was suppressed, and her translations of the rest of Perron's writings were not printed. The translation of Ortelius' *Miroir du monde* (manuscript) and the blank verse *History of the life, reign and death of Edward II* (1627) have also been attributed to her. Her version of Perron's *The reply* . . . includes her statement 'I will not make vse of that worne-out forme of saying, I printed it against my will, mooued by the importunitie of Friends: I was mooued to it by my beleefe, that it might make those English that understand not French, whereof there are maine, euen in our universities, reade Perron.'

See Greer, p. 54 f. *The Lady Falkland her life*, written by one of her daughters, was published in London in 1861 from a manuscript of the English Benedictine nuns of Cambrai, now in the archives of Lille.

CAREY, Mary, *fl.* 1643–80

1. Jackson; 2. Berwick, London, Kent; 3. genteel; 5(a) Pelham Carey, (b) George Payler (m. *c.* 1643); 6(a) genteel, (b) Parliamentary soldier.

Daughter of Sir John Jackson of Berwick, her autobiography is in 'my Lady Carey's Meditation, & Poetry' (manuscript in possession of the Meynell family). She travelled widely, from one military garrison to another, with her second husband; two children survived of this marriage, one from the first, and a number died in infancy. She wrote the 'Meditation' when she was 45 and regrets the social pleasures ('Dancing, Masquing') of her early life. She never used her second husband's name. He died before 1680 and she acted as executor. Greer prints extracts from her poetry (p. 155 f.).

CARLETON, Mary, ?1634/?1642–73

1. ?Moders, ?van Wolway, ?Oundenia; 2. ?Cologne, ?Canterbury, ?Holland, London, Jamaica; 5. John Carleton; 6. student of law.

Mary Carleton, the so-called German Princess, was tried in 1663 for bigamy. This was probably a trumped-up charge designed to separate her from John Carleton (as an 'unsuitable' wife): Thomas Stedman, a shoemaker, testified to her being his wife, but was unable to identify her. She was found not guilty. She may have acted in Thomas Parker's play about her life-story (*A witty combat*, 1664). She was transported for theft in 1671, returned to England, and was hanged for theft in 1673. *BMC* has a number of entries for writings about Mary Carleton and her career, the authorship of these being uncertain or disputed in most cases. These include *An historical narrative of the German princess* and *The case of Mary Carleton . . . truly stated . . . by the said Mary Carleton* (both 1663; both accepted by Hobby as probably by her, *Virtue*, pp. 92–6); *A true account of the tryal of . . .* (1663) and *The memoirs of . . .* (1673). (Extracts in Graham.)

See C. F. Main, 'The German Princess', in *Harvard Library Bulletin*, vol. 10 (1956) and E. Bernbaum, *The Mary Carleton Narratives* (London: Arnold, 1914). Both of these oppose the idea of Carleton as a writer.

CARTER, Dorothy, *fl.* 1666
2. Derbyshire; 3. teacher; 4. Muggletonian.

Her correspondence with Muggleton includes accounts of her dreams, while Hill, Reay, and Lamont refer to a Muggletonian meeting in her home in 1666 (pp. 116, 150–2). Their references, however, do not give specific details as to where Carter's letters are.

CARTWRIGHT, Johanna, *fl.* 1649
2. Amsterdam.

See Critical Appendix 4.

The petition of the Jewes for the repealing of the Act of Parliament for their banishment out of England . . . (1649). This is bound with a petition about releasing debtors from prison and is co-authored by her son Ebenezer. Mother and son describe themselves as authors, now living in Amsterdam. Their petition was presented to Fairfax at Whitehall and 'favourably received'. 'This Nation of England, with the Inhabitants of the Netherlands, shall be the first and readiest to transport Izraels Sons and Daughters in their Ships to the land promised to their fore-Fathers.'

CARTWRIGHT, Ursula, 1647–1702
1. Fairfax; 2. Aynho (Northants.), Bloxham (Oxon.); 5. William Cartwright (m. 1669); 6. MP for East Retford.

Daughter of Ferdinando, 2nd Baron Fairfax, by his second wife Rhoda Chapman, whom he married in 1646 (he died 1648). She was stepsister to Thomas Fairfax, Commander-in-Chief of the Parliamentary army. Second wife of William Cartwright of Bloxham, she bore five children, three of whom died young: Thomas (1671) and Rhoda (1674) survived; her husband died 1676.

The case of Ursula Cartwright, widow, and of Thomas and Roda Cartwright the children of William Cartwright Esq; deceas'd, by the said Ursula his second wife, defendants, to the appeal of Fulk Grosvenor Esq; and Mary his wife, and Dorothy Cartwright, against a decree and dismission and several orders made in the Court of Chancery (?1680; Hobby, *Virtue,* p. 233): the law case contests the different entitlements to the estate of William Cartwright as between Ursula and the two daughters of his first marriage (Mary born 1654, Grosvenor was her second husband; Dorothy born 1657).

CARY, Mary, *c.* 1621–
4. Presbyterian, Fifth Monarchist.

In 1651 she writes of her change of name: 'In my former book, which I published in April, 1648, I subscribed my name Cary, for that was then my name; . . . but let the Reader know, That (having since changed my name) I am now known by the name of Mary Rande.' She does not explain the change and she continued to use both names together (writing under Cary, to help the reader, in the very book she says she is Rande). She tells us she began studying Scripture in 1636 and describes herself as 'a minister of the Gospel' in *The glorious excellencie of the Spirit* (1645). She was a Fifth Monarchist by 1648.

A word in season to the kingdom of England (1647) speaks of the right of all saints to preach, and says that 'Oppression of the poor, & suffering the violent man to afflict the needy . . . is not the way to happiness.'

The resurrection of the witnesses; and England's fall from (the mystical Babylon) Rome (1648, 1653), her first Fifth Monarchist tract.

The little horns doom and downfall; or, a Scripture prophesie of King James, and King Charles, and of the present parliament, unfolded (1651) with *A new and more exact mappe or, description of New Ierusalems glory.* This was dedicated to the wives of Cromwell, Ireton and Role. The first of these ranges across social and political issues: 'that which is given to the Husband, the wife must partake of: for there is nothing that he possesses that she hath not a right unto'; 'some shall not labour and toyl day and night . . . to maintain others that live vitiously in idleness, drunkenness, and other evil practices'; 'not onely men, but women shall prophesie'.

[Twelve humble] proposals to the supreme governours of the three nations now assembled at Westminster (1653).

CAVENDISH, Lady Elizabeth

Elizabeth BRACKLEY*

CAVENDISH, Lady Jane, 1621–69

2. Welbeck Abbey (Notts.), London; 3. genteel; 5. Charles Cheyne; 6. genteel, Royalist captain, MP.

Elizabeth BRACKLEY*

Greer refers to Jane Cavendish as leaving an account-book and letters (which are held by Nottingham University Library). She seems to have gone on writing after leaving Welbeck, but only one additional poem has been identified.

Extracts in Greer, p. 106 ff.

CAVENDISH, Margaret, Duchess of Newcastle, 1623–73

1. Lucas; 2. Colchester, France, Antwerp, London; 3. genteel; 4. Anglican; 5. William Cavendish, Duke of Newcastle; 6. genteel, landowner, writer, soldier.

Margaret Cavendish was a Maid of Honour to Henrietta Maria and met her future husband in France. In 1667 she was invited to the Royal Society (uniquely for a woman) and she was commonly regarded as an eccentric because of her independence and literary interests. She was a very prolific writer of plays, poems *(Poems and Fancies,* 1653), letters (*CCXI Sociable Letters,* 1664), essays, scientific and philosophical tracts and *The Life of William Cavendish* (1667). She is buried in Westminster Abbey.

Poems and Fancies was reprinted in facsimile (Scolar, 1972) and has important remarks about being a woman writer. *CCXI Sociable Letters* was also reprinted by Scolar (1969), while the *Life . . .* has been republished several times (e.g. ed. C. H. Firth, 1886). There are extracts from her work in Ferguson (p. 84 ff.) and Greer (p. 163 ff.), while Graham has extracts from her brief autobiography. There is an unsatisfactory biography by D. Grant (*Margaret the First,* London: Rupert Hart-Davis, 1957).

CELLIER, Elizabeth, *fl.* 1670–80

1. ?Marshall; 2. ?Kent, London; 3. midwife and pamphleteer; 4. Catholic; 5(a) an English merchant, (b) a man who had five children by her, before abandoning her, (c) Peter Cellier; 6(c) French merchant.

She was tried for High Treason in 1680, acquitted, and then tried for malicious slander in the same year. These trials relate to the so-called Meal-tub Plot. *Malice defeated* (1680) is Cellier's account of this affair (she arranged for the printing herself). She used one Dangerfield as an informant about the treatment of gaoled Catholics, and he claimed that there was a Protestant plot to replace Charles II with the Duke of Monmouth. She was later accused of being involved in a plan to burn ships at Chatham. Although she presented herself at her trial as 'a foolish vain woman', Cellier complained to the king about how her trial was rushed, allowing no time for her defence, and again about how she was pilloried for an hour longer than the time to which she was sentenced. She was physically maltreated: first ill with convulsive fits, then stoned in the pillory (where she was placed three times). She was fined £1000.

She took both her politics and her profession seriously: she wrote about her legal difficulties and about her project for a royal hospital for midwives. 'A scheme for the foundation of a royal hospital' is in the Harleian Miscellany for 1745. Cellier herself was midwife to Mary of Modena and other Catholic aristocrats.

CENTLIVRE, Susanna, ?c. 1670/?1677/?1680–1723

1. ?Freeman; 2. Ireland, London, Holbeach; 3. actor and author; 4. Anglican; 5(a) — Carroll (alias Rawkins), (b) Joseph Centlivre; 6(a) army officer, (b) court chef.

Susanna Centlivre was a prolific dramatist (tragedies, comedies, farces) between 1702 and 1723. Several of her plays held the stage for two centuries. *The wonder* (1714; reprinted in Morgan) was translated into German and Polish, and was chosen both by Kitty Clive and by Garrick for their farewell performances. The preface to *Perplexed lovers* got her into trouble because of its pro-Whig political stance, while *The Gotham election*, which was never acted, is an explicitly political play. *The platonick lady* is dedicated to 'All the Generous Encouragers of Female Ingenuity' and speaks of some women as being 'often backward to encourage a Female Pen'.

There are stories that Anthony Hammond dressed her as a boy and slipped her into Cambridge as his cousin Jack and that she joined a band of strolling players. Her early plays were either printed as anonymous or as by 'S. Carroll'.

A bold stroke for a wife has been edited by T. Stathas (Nebraska: University of Nebraska Press, 1968), and *The adventures of Venice* is in Kendell (1988). A 3 vol. edition of her *Works* was published in 1761 and reprinted 1872. See J. W. Bowyer, *The celebrated Mrs Centlivre* (Durham: Duke University Press, 1952).

CHAMBERS, Elizabeth, *fl.* ?1641–53

2. Dublin; 4. Baptist; 5. William Chambers; 6. soldier.

'Experiences' in Rogers, *Ohel* . . . (1653) (see also Mary BARKER*). She says that she had a dream of Rogers before hearing him in Dublin. 'Yea, the more the Lord hath taken away from me, as my Husband, Father, Friends, Sister, Children and 3 the more have I made Christ in me, in the room and stead of all these to me.' Her husband travelled to Ireland in 1647 as a captain in the English army, and was dead by November 1648 when she petitioned as a widow for 'relief'. She says that during the rebellion in Ireland (which may refer to any time between 1641 and 1649) she went to Bristol.

CHANNEL, Elinor, *fl.* 1653–4
2. Cranleigh (Surrey); 3. prophet; 4. Anglican.

Autobiographical details and her prophecies are contained in *A message from God – by a dumb woman – to his highness the Lord Protector. Together with a word of advice to the Commons of England and Wales for the electing of a Parliament* (1664). She says she has a poor husband and many children and that, having been struck a blow on the heart while sleeping, she heard a voice telling her that she was to be sent as a messenger to London. When her husband opposed this journey she was struck dumb, and remained silent until he agreed to it. (This may have happened soon after having given birth to another child: a Thomas Channel was baptised in Cranleigh in 1653.) When she arrived in London she looked for someone to publish her prophecy, went to Court (April 1654) and wandered around London. Beadles arrested her and dragged her to Bridewell while the crowd apparently tormented her.

Some of these details are supplied by Arise Evans, who published her prophecies. He was a Royalist and he annotated Channel's text in order to make propaganda for his own position. (It is likely that another woman prophet, Katherine JOHNSON,* had her text 'edited' in a similar way.)

CHEESEMAN, Elizabeth, *fl.* 1674–6
1. Userly; 2. Mortlake, Ludgate (London); 4. Quaker; 5. Christopher Cheeseman (m. 1674); 6. basket maker.

Author, with her husband, of a testimony in Francis Patchet, *Living words through a dying man* (1676): they visited Patchet in his final imprisonment in the Fleet, London.

CHEEVERS, Sarah, –1664
2. Wiltshire, Malta; 4. Quaker; 5. Henry Cheevers.

She travelled and collaborated with Katherine EVANS.* They visited Scotland in 1654, Salisbury (where they were whipped) and the Isle of Wight in 1657; in 1658 they intended to travel to Jerusalem but were imprisoned by the Inquisition in Malta.

Besse (2.399–406) has letters written during her imprisonment in Malta to Friends, a kinswoman, her husband, etc. She co-authored with EVANS, 'To all people upon the face of the earth. A sweet salutation, and a clear manifestation' (printed as part of *A true account*, 1663) and *This is a short relation* (1662). She wrote a letter to Deborah SANDHAM in Ireland (1664).

CHESTER, Elizabeth, ?1637–1719
1. Robins; 2. Dunstable (Beds.); 4. Quaker; 5. Edward Chester; 6. minister.

She was convinced by John Askew in London in 1655: 'I could read the Holy Scriptures and was pretty well acquainted with the literal Sense thereof; yet I found I wanted the Knowledge of that, which could give me Power, and strength to fulfill them'; 'the Lord was graciously pleased to hear the Cry, and regard the Panting of my poor Soul, which had breathed after him, even in my tender years.' She speaks of meetings at Market Street and Dunstable. 'Now after we had thus walked together, for several years, in the Profession of the Blessed Truth, my dear Husband and I took Each other in Marriage.' Theirs was the first Bedford Quaker marriage (1663): 'we had no Track to follow', 'Wherefore we took each other in a publick Meeting and had a Certificate thereof, signed by about seven Friends of the Meeting.' She and her husband were two of an original twelve Quakers in the area, but now she says she is the only one still alive. Her biography appears in her *A narrative of the life and death of Edward Chester* (1709; printed for Jane SOWLE*). *DQB* also mentions 'Our love increased to the last' (untraced).

CHESTERFIELD, Elizabeth, Countess of, –1666
1. Butler; 2. Bratby, London; 3. genteel; 5. Philip, 2nd Earl of Chesterfield.

Martha GIFFARD*

Five letters by her (1664–5) are in Julia Longe, *Martha Lady Giffard . . .* (London: George Allen & Sons, 1911).

CHEW, Anne, *fl.* 1679
2. Herring Creek (Maryland); 3. minister; 4. Quaker; 5. Samuel Chew; 6. merchant.

Testimony (1679) in *A testimony concerning . . . William Coale* (1682).

CHIDLEY, Katherine, *fl.* 1626–53

2. Shrewsbury, London; 3. preacher; 4. Brownist, Baptist; 5. Daniel Chidley; 6. tailor.

Mother of the Leveller Samuel Chidley and herself a Leveller, Katherine Chidley was 'the first woman openly to defend religious Independency in print'. She joined 'other women of St Chad's parish [Shrewsbury] in refusing to be churched following childbirth' (1626), then moved to London, where (1645) she evangelised at William Greenhill's Independent church (Stepney). She probably had a hand in the women's petition of 1649, and, in 1651–2 'supplied the government's troops in Ireland with 5,000 pairs of stockings'. In 1653 she led a deputation to present a petition of 6,000 signatures to the Commons for the release of John Lilburne from prison. PETITIONS.* (Quotations above from Greaves and Zaller.)

 The justification of the Independent churches of Christ . . . being an answer to Mr Edwards his book . . . (1641; the book being *Reasons against Independent government of particular congregations*, 1641). *A new yeares gift, or a brief exhortation to Mr Thomas Edwards* (1645). *Good counsell, to the petitioners for Presbyterian government* (1645). *Launsters launce* (n.d.; probably with Samuel Chidley).

CHOLMLEY, Elisabeth and Margaret, *fl.* 1669–73

The case of Elisabeth and Margaret Cholmley, Sarah Smith, and Sir Kingsmill Lucy Bart. Humbly presented to the consideration of the right honourable the Lords spiritual and temporal in Parliament assembled (1673). This is part of an attempt by creditors of the Grocers' Company to obtain repayment of and interest on a loan made *c.* 1660. The creditors had petitioned the Commons in 1669 but members of the Grocers' Company had used their contacts in Parliament to block the petition. In 1672, after more legal manoeuvres, the case went against the Company but they still refused to pay. The petition reveals a great deal of legal trickery on the part of the Company.

   Note that in general we have not included multiple-authored 'cases', since these are even more distant from female 'authorship'. We include this one since the women's names are mentioned first.

CHUDLEIGH, Lady Mary, 1656–1710

1. Lee; 2. Devon; 3. genteel; 4. Anglican; 5. Sir George Chudleigh; 6. genteel.

Mary Chudleigh (who used the pseudonym 'Eugenia') knew Mary ASTELL* and John Norris. She was a Royalist.

The female advocate (1700). *The ladies defence: or the bride-woman's counsellor answered*. . . (1699, 1701, 1709: an anonymous verse answer to John Sprint's sermon of 1699 advocating female subjugation to husbands). *Poems upon several occasions* (1703, 1709, 1713, 1722). *Essays upon several occasions* (1710).

Chudleigh may also be the author of *The female preacher* (1695), and Ballard (*Memoirs*, 1752) says that she wrote tragedies, a masque and translation from Lucian. Her poem 'To the ladies' begins 'Wife and servant are the same,/But only differ in the name' and ends 'Value yourselves, and men despise:/You must be proud, if you'll be wise.'

See extracts in Ferguson, p. 213 ff.

CHURCHMAN, Mary, *fl.* 1672
2. ?Cambridgeshire; 4. ?Congregationalist.

She wrote an account in 1672 of Francis Holcroft's preaching; see *Gospel Tidings* 5.276–82, 294–9 (reference in Greaves and Zaller, vol. 2, 100).

CLABIN, Anne, *fl.* 1665
4. Quaker.

A relation in part of what passed through a true and faithful servant and handmaid of the Lord, M. Page, when she lay upon her bed of sickness (*c.* 1665): written with Elizabeth NICHOLLS,* Bridget NICHOLS,* Anne WHITEHEAD.* Mary Page of Wellingborough, Northants., died in 1665; the text is also signed by Daniel Wills, a Quaker minister of Northants. Apart from the famous Anne Whitehead, we have been unable to trace the authors (they are not recorded in Northamptonshire or neighbouring counties).

CLARK, Frances, *fl.* 1653
1. Greenway; 2. Berkshire.

A brief reply to the narration of Don Pantaleon Sa. (1653) is a petition asking for justice against the murderer of her brother, Harcourt Greenway, of Leckhampstead, Berkshire. He was shot in the head in the New Exchange, London, by the brother of the Portuguese ambassador. She asks that he be prosecuted and that the family obtain financial relief (the trial took place in 1654). Although the title-page credits Frances Clark alone with authorship, the text speaks of the 'disconsolate sisters' Frances Clark and Elizabeth WORSOPP* as co-authors.

CLARK, Margaret, –1680

2. Southwark (London); 3. servant; 4. ?Catholic.

The true confession of Margaret Clark, who consented to the burning of her masters Mr Peter Delanoy's house in Southwark (1680).

A warning for servants; and a caution to Protestants. Or, the case of Margret Clark, lately executed for firing her master's house in Southwark. Faithfully relating the manner (as she affirmed to the last moment of her life) how she was drawn into that wicked act; set forth under her own hand after condemnation. Her penitent behaviour in prison. Her Christian advice to visitors, discourses with several ministers, and last words at execution (1680).

The latter text speaks of how Irish people 'frequently endeavoured to debauch servants, and with promises of large sums of money tempt them to set fire to their masters houses'. This can be linked with a spate of house burnings in Southwark which were attributed to Jesuits. Margaret Clark's own statement tells of how she was set up and warns people to 'be content with the places that God by his providence places them in, and not covet after great things (as I have done)'.

This is another in the genre of female confessions (e.g. Elizabeth CALDWELL*). Interestingly, the account by Nathaniel Thompson which adds to the 'official' record the claim that, on the gallows, Clark's resolution faltered, says that she wanted to marry the man beneath the gallows who offered to save her through marriage. This is said to be a 'malicious' story: it clearly changes the status of the moral, confessional, mouthpiece. We do not know whether such texts as these were written by, or merely signed by, the women concerned.

CLARK, Mary, *fl.* 1664–94

2. London; 3. physician; 5. Henry Clark; 6. physician.

The great and wonderful success and virtue of Clark's compound spirits of scurvy-grass (both golden and plain) in curing many languishing and grievous distempers. Faithfully prepared (by his widow) according to his own directions (post-1694) [scurvy-grass is a purgative]. The text advertises the authenticity of her cures, which were developed by her husband 30 years ago, against counterfeits by 'divers upstarts'; they are available from her house in the Strand. She lists successful cures around the country, one taking place in 1694. There is a number of such advertising broadsides, in formulaic language. They present similar problems of 'authorship' to the legal petitions and 'cases'.

CLARKE, Alice, –1706

2. Bedall (Yorks.); 4. Quaker.

Fined for meeting 1670/1. Testimonial in *Living testimonies . . . Robert Lodge* (1691); see Anne BLACKBURNE* for full title.

CLARKSON, Bessie, –1625

2. Lanark.

The conflict in conscience of a deare Christian named Bessie Clarkson in the parish of Lanark, which she lay under three year and an half. With the conference that past between her pastor and her at diverse times . . . (Edinburgh, 1632, 1664). The pastor was William Livingstone, who in the preface refers to the text as 'an uncorrect coppie, wherein my words are made hers at sometimes, and hers mine'. The text is written as a dialogue.

CLAYTON, Anne, *fl.* 1652–72

2. Suffolk, Swarthmore, Barbados; 3. genteel; 4. Quaker; 5. Nicholas Easton (m. before 1671); 6. governor of Rhode Island.

Born of Suffolk gentry, she and her brother Richard were members of the household at Swarthmore Hall and she was convinced when Fox visited the hall. She was imprisoned in Lancaster in 1654–6, travelled to Barbados in 1657 and 1659, was in England in 1658 (she was whipped in Marlborough, Wiltshire for preaching in the streets) and in 1660, before going overseas again in 1669. Anne was married and in Rhode Island before 1671.

A letter to the king (1660). This text welcomes Charles II at his restoration, calling him 'dear Friend'. Part of it reads 'I saw and felt in the Spirit that reacheth over Sea and Land, your Coming before you came, and my spirit breathed to the Lord for you; and I felt three, and one was a Woman, and that I spoke of then, that my spirit reached forth unto three; and they said you were three Brethren, but I said that one of the three that I felt was a woman, and still that did abide with me; and now that you are come, my spirit breaths to the Lord, desiring him to subdue that in you, that will not glorifie him, that the kingdoms may not be rent from you.' A letter from Barbados to Margaret FELL* is in Swarthmore MSS i.76.

CLEVELAND, Barbara Palmer, Countess of

See Appendix III.

CLIFFORD, Anne, Countess of Dorset, Pembroke and Montgomery, 1590–1676

2. Yorkshire, Kent, Wiltshire, London; 3. genteel; 5(a) Richard Sackville,

Earl of Dorset, (b) Philip Herbert, Earl of Pembroke and Montgomery; 6(a)/(b) genteel.

Anne Clifford spent many years fighting a legal battle to be allowed to inherit her father's property. She was opposed by the king, her husband and family. She was supported by her mother, and she won the battle. *The diary of the Lady Anne Clifford* was edited by V. Sackville-West (London: Heinemann, 1923) and *The lives of Lady Anne Clifford . . . and of her parents, summarized by herself* was published by the Roxburgh Club (1916; with introduction by J. P. Gibson). There is also a version of her autobiography in *Proceedings of the Archaeological Institute at York* (1846). The diary covers 1616–17 and 1619: extracts are in Houlbrooke and Graham.

See G. C. Williamson, *Lady Anne Clifford* (Kendal: T. Wilson & Son, 1922) and R. Spence, *Northern History*, vol. 15 (1979).

CLINTON, Elizabeth, ?1574–?1630
1. Knyvett; 3. genteel; 5. Thomas, Earl of Clinton; 6. genteel.

Elizabeth Clinton's *The countess of Lincoln's nursery* (which Fraser calls 'a defiant plea that the mother should suckle her own child', p. 79) was published in 1622 and reprinted in 1628, 1744 and 1809 (twice). See also *Knyvett Letters 1620–1644* (Norfolk Records Society, 1949).

CLIPSHAM/CLIPSON, Margery, –1693
2. Chalfont St Giles (Bucks.); 4. Quaker; 5. Richard Clipsham; 6. tailor.

She wrote *The spirit that works abomination and its abominable work discovered; and a faithful testimony born against it* (1685) with Mary ELLWOOD,* as a reply to Susanna ALDRIDGE.* The text was addressed to other Quakers rather than to the world in general.

COALE, Elizabeth, *fl.* 1682
2. West River (Maryland); 4. Quaker; 5. William Coale.

Testimony in *A testimony concerning . . . William Coale* (1682).

COBB, Alice, *fl.* 1673–82
1. Curwen; 2. London; 4. Quaker; 5. Thomas Cobb (m. 1673); 6. cordwainer.

Daughter of Alice CURWEN,* she bore four children between 1677 and 1682. She was present at her mother's death (as was Anne MARTINDALL*). Wrote 'Alice Cobb's testimony concerning her mother

Alice Curwen' in Alice CURWEN, *A relation . . .* (1680; in the two copies of this text in Friends House, this testimony is only in the unbound copy).

COCKBURN, Catherine, 1679–1749

1. Trotter; 2. Northumberland, London; 3. dramatist and philosophical writer; 4. Anglican, Catholic, again Anglican; 5. Patrick Cockburn; 6. cleric and teacher.

Sarah PIERS*

After the death of her father, a sea captain, the family was poor, and she began writing for publication at the age of 14. She wrote five plays:

Agnes de Castro (as anonymous; Drury Lane; published 1696; tragedy). *Fatal friendship* (Lincoln's Inn Fields; published 1698; tragedy; reprinted in Morgan). *Love at a loss, or most votes carry it* (Drury Lane; published ?1701; reprinted in Kendell). *The revolution of Sweden* (Lincoln's Inn Fields; published 1706). *The unhappy penitent* (Drury Lane; published 1701).

In addition, Catherine Cockburn published (as anonymous) the epistolary novel, *Olinda's adventures* (1693) and contributed to *Poems . . . upon the death . . . of John Dryden* (1700). She also wrote on philosophical and religious issues, notably in defence of John Locke (see *Collected Prose,* ed. T. Birch, 1751) and corresponded with Congreve, Locke and Leibnitz. According to Pearson, there is a lively correspondence with her niece Ann Arbuthnot, on topics such as playwrights, the nature of drama, philosophy, Homer.

Brief extracts in Greer, p. 406 f. *Olinda's adventures* has been edited by R. Day (Augustan Reprint Society, vol. 138, 1969).

COLE, Mary

2. Plymouth; 4. Quaker; 5. Nicholas Cole; 6. shopkeeper.

She wrote with Priscilla COTTON* *To the priests and people of England, we discharge our consciences, and give them warning* (1655): the text is written from Exeter gaol where the two women were placed after being railed at by priests 'who could not bear sound reproof'; they say priests 'kill, and persecute, pursue, and imprison the substance and life of what they speak' and attack those who elevate themselves with 'arts and learning'. The major importance of this text is its contribution to the debate around women speaking; for quotations see Priscilla COTTON,* and also Anne AUDLAND* and Margaret FELL.* Sarah HAYWARD* seems to have used Cole's name.

COLE, Sarah

Her poem, 'The Telescope Glass', appeared in *The Ladies Diary* (1711).

COLEMAN, Elizabeth, *fl.* 1669–75
1. Wills; 2. Somerset, Southwark; 4. Quaker; 5(a) — Coleman, (b) William Peachey (m. 1671).

She moved from Bristol to London, which is perhaps why she was still known as Coleman in Somerset after her second marriage: Besse records an Elizabeth Coleman imprisoned in Bath in 1675 (and later discharged) for attending a meeting. With Ann TRAVERS* she wrote *The harlots vail rent and her impudency rebuked* (1669; an answer to Elizabeth ATKINSON's* *A breif and plain discovery . . .*).

COLLINS, An, *fl.* 1653
4. Calvinist.

Author of *Divine songs and meditations composed by An Collins* (1653). This includes prose meditations which, like the prefatory material, stress chronic illness since childhood. Collins uses various verse forms and the preface is in rime royal.

Extracts from *Divine songs* were reprinted in the Augustan Reprint Society, vol. 94 (1961) (ed. S. Stewart); there are extracts in Greer, p. 148 f. and in Graham.

COLVILLE, Lady Elizabeth

Elizabeth MELVILL*

COMBERFORD, Mary, –1700
2. Stafford; 4. Quaker.

She may be connected to the genteel Comberford family of Staffordshire (Robert Comberford, who died 1671, had a daughter Mary). Her *A short testimony concerning that faithful servant of the Lord, Thomas Taylor* appeared in his *Collected works* (1681, printed by Tace SOWLE).

COMPTON, Elizabeth, –1632
1. Spenser; 2. London; 3. Maid of Honour to Elizabeth I; 5. William, 2nd Lord Compton (later Earl of Northampton); 6. genteel.

Partnow quotes from a letter to her husband (p. 140). William married her against her father's wishes, and tradition has it that she eloped in a baker's basket. Her father was Lord Mayor of London 1594–5. Chamberlain (*Chamberlain's Letters Temp Eliz*, Camden Society, 1861, pp. 43, 50, 109) gives some detail about the marriage.

CONSTANTIA MUNDA

See Appendix II.

CONWAY, Lady Anne, –1679

1. Finch; 2. London, Wales; 3. genteel; 4. Quaker; 5. Edward, Earl of Conway (m. 1651); 6. genteel.

Daughter of Sir Heneage Finch, Recorder of London, she was a linguist and friend of Henry More. Despite her ill health she wrote numerous works. *Opuscula philosophica* (Amsterdam, 1690) was published anonymously and attributed to her by Leibnitz. It appeared in English in 1692 as *The principles of the most ancient and modern philosophy concerning God, Christ and the creation*. Letters by Anne Conway appear in *Conway Letters*, ed. M. H. Nicolson (1930).

COOK, Frances, *fl.* ?1646–60

2. London, Ireland; 4. Independent; 5. John Cook; 6. Solicitor of the Commonwealth and pamphleteer.

Her husband not only defended John Lilburne before the House of Lords, but prepared the case against and prosecuted Charles I. Frances Cook is possibly the Frances Cutler who married John Cook in 1646; they had one daughter, Freelove. They resided in Ireland from 1650 onwards, owning a house at Waterford from 1653 (John Cook was Chief Justice of Munster till 1654). On the way to Ireland they were nearly shipwrecked. Wife and husband write about this event in separate pamphlets and clearly it had major significance for them, not only in terms of physical danger, but as a sort of spiritual testing both of their personal partnership and of the righteousness of the Parliamentary cause in the face of adversity, both of which God blesses by saving them. Frances Cook thus concludes with the wish that 'all we Sea-partners may obtain with Elisha a double portion of the Spirit of God, and with Solomon understanding hearts, that we may understand the Scriptures.' Her husband was executed as a regicide in 1660; in his final letters and prayers he recalls their leave-taking in 'the Storm' and pays tribute to his wife's continuing support: 'I bless God my poor wife does much encourage me to be faithfull to the Death, and she is a meet Helper indeed who helps her husband so to Heaven, as in a fiery Chariot; she is one who bears an unfeigned love to Christ and all the Saints' (quoted in *A complete collection of the lives and speeches of those persons lately executed*, 1661).

Mris Cooke's meditations. Being a humble thanksgiving to her heavenly father, for granting her a new life, having concluded her selfe dead, and her grave made in the bottome of the sea, in the great storme Jan 5 1649 Composed by her selfe at her unexpected safe arrivall at Corcke (1650). (Her husband's account is *A true relation of Mr Justice Cooke's passage by sea from Wexford to Kinsale*, 1650, 1652.)

COOK, Lucretia, 1606–94

2. London; 4. Quaker; 5. Richard Cook.

She had a daughter and a son, born 1639 and 1640. She was imprisoned in Kinsale, County Cork, for preaching in 1656, and again in Cork in 1662 and 1669 (it is possible that this may be another Lucretia Cook, connected with an Edward Cook). She claims to have known Anne WHITEHEAD* since 1660, and is mentioned (by Besse) as a 'sufferer' in 1686.

'A short testimony', in Ann WHITEHEAD,* *Piety* . . . (1686). A signatory of *A tender and Christian testimony* (1685; see Mary ELSON* for details).

CORNWALLIS, Lady Jane, 1581–1659

1. Meautys; 2. Essex, Suffolk; 3. genteel; 5(a) Sir William Cornwallis, (b) Sir Nicholas Bacon; 6(a)/(b) genteel.

The Private Correspondence of Lady Jane Cornwallis; 1613–1644 (ed. Lord Braybrooke, 1842).

COTTINGTON, Angela, *fl.* 1664–80

1. Gallina; 2. Turin, France, England; 5. Charles Cottington (m. 1671); 6. genteel.

The case of Angela Margarita Cottington, the lawful wife of Charles Cottington Esq; humbly offered to the consideration of the honourable the Commons, in Parliament assembled (1680). This is her response to her husband's attempt to annull their marriage (Charles Cottington was a nephew of Francis, Lord Cottington: he had estates in Somerset). She narrates the history of his courtship of her in Turin (where she was born) and Rome, of her resistance to him and their eventual marriage in Turin. They lived together for five months and she had a miscarriage. She had given him

£300 worth of goods and money, which he spent before leaving for England and not returning. In 1674 she travelled to England and he began a lawsuit for separation, claiming that she had already married in Italy in 1664. She says this marriage was proved null, and he knew it before he married her. The court found against him, he appealed, lost, and was ordered to pay £300 alimony. He paid one instalment of £100, then refused to pay more, and was excommunicated. He began a series of appeals, going to the king, sought protection from an aristocrat, and asked an MP to halt the proceedings. She, confronted by the pressures of a patriarchal network and in a foreign country, demanded justice. This *Case* is an illustration of the extent to which, although the woman has not herself written the document, the act of commissioning is itself an initiative and intervention.

COTTINGTON, Eliza

Eliza THIMELBY*

COTTON, Priscilla, –1664

1. Martyn; 2. Saltash (Cornwall), Plymouth; 4. Quaker; 5. Arthur Cotton (m. 1646); 6. merchant.

See Critical Appendix 3.

She wrote, with Mary COLE,* *To the priests and people of England, we discharge our consciences, and give them warning* (1655) (see Mary COLE for details of the immediate context of the writing of this text). The importance of this text is its development of the terms of the debate about women speaking. The authors define 'woman' as a biblical symbol of spiritual weakness; then (in this section of the text addressed specifically to the two ministers who visited them in prison) they turn the argument back upon the church ministers who oppose women speaking: they claim that 'you yourselves are the women, that are forbidden to speak in the church, that are become women'; 'Christ Jesus appeared to the women first, and sent them to preach the Resurrection to the Apostles, and Philip had four virgins that did prophesy' (cf. Anne CAMM,* Margaret FELL*). She was imprisoned in Exeter in 1655–6.

　　Other writings: *As I was in the prison-house* (1656); *A briefe description by way of supposition* (1659); *A visitation of love unto all people* (1661); *A testimony of truth to all Friends* (n.d.; published by Mary WESTWOOD*).

　　L. Hodgkin (*A Quaker Saint of Cornwall*, London: Longman, 1927) prints a letter from Cotton to Margaret FELL (Plymouth, 1660).

COVENTRY, Anne, Countess of, 1673–1763

1. Somerset; 2. Warwickshire; 3. genteel; 5. Thomas, Earl of Coventry; 6. genteel.

Her *The right honourable Anne, Countess of Coventry's meditations and reflections, moral and divine* was published in 1707.

COWART, Elizabeth, *fl.* ?1627–55

4. Quaker; 5. ?William Cowart, of Kendal, m. 1627.

See Margaret NEWBY,* with whom she collaborated in a letter about their experiences in the stocks in Evesham in 1655 (Besse gives her name as Courten).

COWPER, Mary, Countess, 1685–1724

1. Clavering; 2. Durham, London; 3. genteel; 5. William, Earl Cowper; 6. genteel, politician.

At the accession of George I she was a Lady of the Bedchamber to the Princess of Wales (Caroline Anspach, later queen to George II). C. S. Cowper edited the *Diary of Mary countess Cowper* (1864). It concentrates on court life between 1714 and 1720. The editor says that his text is 'taken directly from the original handwriting of Lady Cowper', adding that she 'was well-read, and of a studious disposition'.

COWPER, Sarah, 1644–1720

2. Hertfordshire.

Author of an unpublished diary for the years 1700–16.

COX, Ann, 1644–1716

1. Hinde; 2. Whitechapel (London); 4. Quaker; 5. Thomas Cox (m. 1682); 6. vintner.

She was present at Anne WHITEHEAD's* death in 1686, and signed the general testimony for her. Signed *From the womens-meeting held at the Bull-and-Mouth in London, the 16th of the 9th month, 1713. To our Friends and brethren of the six-weeks-meeting*: this concerns the need to recruit more Quakers.

CRAMOND, Lady Elizabeth

Elizabeth RICHARDSON*

CRASHAWE, Elizabeth

See Appendix III.

CRESSWELL, Lady

See Appendix III.

CROMWELL, Anna, ?1623–

2. Hertfordshire, Ramsey (Cambridge); 3. poet; 5. Henry Williams (alias Cromwell).

The only surviving child of Richard, son of Henry, Cromwell and a Mrs Jones, she married Henry Williams (who changed his name from Cromwell) of Ramsey. He was the son of the Royalist soldier Henry Cromwell. Fraser, *Cromwell* (p. 594 n.) describes Anna Cromwell as 'a passionate Royalist, who in some lines even compared Charles I to Jesus Christ' (she gives no reference for Anna Cromwell's verse, which seems not to have survived in printed form; her identification of Anna Cromwell's husband as Henry Cromwell is confusing).

CROMWELL, Elizabeth

See Appendix III.

CROUCH, Ruth, 1637–1710

1. Brown; 2. London; 4. Quaker; 5. William Crouch (m. 1659); 6. upholsterer.

Daughter of John and Ruth Brown of Wood Street, London, she was the second wife of Crouch. She bore five children between 1662 and 1677. Their home was destroyed in the Great Fire of 1666 and they moved to Devonshire House; in 1706 they moved to Palmers Green (Middx.). Stephen Crisp, an important Essex Quaker, lodged and died in their house. While she was active in the London Women's Meetings, her husband was a major figure in the national organisation of Quakers.

Signed *A tender and Christian testimony* (1685; see Mary ELSON* for details) and *A living testimony from the power and spirit of our Lord Jesus Christ* (1685; see Mary FOSTER* for details). Wrote a testimony in Ann WHITEHEAD,* *Piety . . .* (1686).

CUDWORTH, Damaris, 1658–1708

2. Cambridge, Essex; 3. professional/genteel; 5. Sir Francis Masham; 6. genteel.

Damaris was the daughter of Sir Ralph Cudworth and her husband was a widower with nine children. She knew John Norris and was taught by John Locke, who lived with the Mashams between 1691 and 1704.

Reflections upon the conduct of human life (1689). *Occasional thoughts in reference to a vertuous or Christian life* (1694; as anonymous). *Discourse concerning the love of God* (1696; this was a reply to Mary ASTELL* and John Norris, *Letters concerning* . . . . It has been attributed to Locke, was published anonymously, and translated into French in 1705).

Also correspondence with Locke.

See Greer, p. 315 f.

CULPEPPER, Anne, *fl.* 1640–56

1. Field; 2. London; 5(a) Nicholas Culpepper (m. 1640), (b) John Heydon (m. after 1656); 6(a) apothecary, astrologer, physician, millenarian, (b) astrologer.

Her 'To the Reader', in Nicholas Culpepper's *Treatise of aurum potabile* (1656), says that she has seen his reputation 'blemished and eclipsed, by the covetous and unjust forgeries of one, who . . . calls himself Nathaneal' (this being the publisher of the forgery *Culpepper's last legacy*). This forger 'to make the deceit more taking' was not ashamed 'to forge two Epistles, one in mine, and the other in my husbands name; of the penning of which, he nor I so much as dream't: And yet he impudently affirmeth in my name, that my husband layd a severe Injunction on me to publish them for the generall good, after his decease.' In fact she does say that her husband 'left seventy-nine books' in her hands, and she advertises that they can be purchased from her house. Her anger at the forger emphasises that her control of the printing is independent of male injunctions or interventions.

CUMBERLAND, Margaret Clifford, Countess of, 1560–1616

1. Russell; 2. Exeter, Brougham Castle; 3. genteel; 5. George, Earl of Cumberland; 6. genteel.

Greer refers to her epitaph for Richard Candish (1601) as 'actually engraved upon his monument in Hornsey church' and quotes it (p. 10). See *Notes and Queries*, series 7, vol. iv, p. 374.

CURTIS, Frances, *fl.* 1642–53

2. Dublin; 4. Baptist.

'Experiences' in Rogers, *Ohel* . . . (1653) (see Mary BARKER* for details). She speaks of being stripped by 'the Rebels (being abroad)' during the wars (presumably from 1641 onwards). Her husband is killed by them and she is turned out of doors with a child in her arms. She says she had a wanton youth, until she felt God's hand, for about eleven years. After her misfortunes, she claims to be heartened by the spiritual ministry of the Baptist John Rogers.

CURWEN, Alice, 1620/3–79

2. New England, Huntingdon; 4. Quaker; 5. Thomas Curwen.

A relation of the labour, travail and suffering of Alice Curwen (1680). The narrative is by Alice Curwen, but the volume also includes letters between the Curwens (some by Alice alone) and Quakers in England and the New World (see Anne BARBAR,* Elizabeth GRETTON,* Elizabeth GRIFFIN,* Mary MILLES,* Patience STORY,* Mary TYLLTON*). One of Alice Curwen's letters (an epistle for a priest at Godmanchester) says that 'in all my Travels I find no men so light and airy as you Priests are, who wear your long Robes; and by Christ's words (as you may read in the Scriptures) and by the Spirit of Truth (which God hath manifested in my particular) do I see you to be them which Christ cryed Wo against.' She was moved by stories of persecution in 1660 to travel to Boston but waited until her children were grown up (and her husband was out of gaol); though she was prepared to leave without him. They travelled widely around Boston, Rhode Island, New Jersey, Bermudas, Barbados, returning in 1677; then they made a tour of the West Country coast.

In her 'relation' she reflects on her writing: 'it was said in the secret of my Heart, *What thou has kept, write*: but I fearing said within my self, *Why should it be known?* and the answer was, *For the Encouragement of them that hereafter may put their Trust in the Lord*: and then I was made willing to write as followeth.'

D

D—, E—,

See Appendix I.

DACRES, Lady Dorothy, 1605–98
1. North; 2. Chevening (Kent), Hampshire; 3. genteel; 5(a) Richard Lennard, Baron Dacres (m. 1624/5), (b) Chaloner Chute (m. 1650); 6(a) genteel, (b) Speaker of the House of Commons.

The daughter of Sir Dudley, 3rd Lord North, she was sister-in-law of Anne NORTH.* In 1681 she exhibited a bill setting out the will of her dead husband, Chute (who died 1659), and petitioned the Lords. The petition relates to Chute's bequest of his house (The Vyne, Hants.) and lands to his son, despite his earlier agreement (1650) to a settlement on her. The previous legal battles of 1667 revived in 1680 when Chute's grandson appealed against decrees favouring Dorothy Dacres. The House of Lords decided she lost the privilege of peerage when she married a commoner. She died at Chevening.

The Lady Dacres her case (?1681).

DALE, Elizabeth, *fl.* 1623–4
2. Surrey; 3. genteel; 5. Sir Thomas Dale; 6. genteel.

In July 1623, as a widow of Thomas Dale (she was his second wife), she asked for a hearing of her claim to the goods he lost when he died; she repeated the request in May 1624. Her husband, who was knighted in 1606, was a governor of Virginia and a member of the East India Company. After his death his study and chests had been broken open by members of the Company. *A briefe of the Lady Dale's petition to the Parliament* (1624) asks that his estate confiscated by the East India Company be restored to her.

DANKS, Elizabeth, –1708
 2. Colchester; 4. Quaker; 5(a) ? — Samuel, (b) John Danks (m. 1677).

Co-author of *The captive's return, or the testimonies of John Danks, of Colchester, and Elizabeth Danks, his wife* (1680): the text attacks religious 'backsliders' (very much in the spirit of the polemics associated with Stephen Crisp's group in Colchester).

 An Elizabeth Samuel married John Danks in Colchester in 1677. We assume this was a second marriage for both of them: a John Danks married Mary Fishpoole in 1654, when he was aged 22. (Two Elizabeth Samuels were christened, in the same church, 1621 and 1627; but an age of *c.* 50 for a first marriage is very unlikely.)

D'ANVERS, Alicia, 1668–1725
 1. Clarke; 2. Oxfordshire, Northamptonshire; 5. Knightly D'Anvers (m. before 1690); 6. lawyer.

Author of *A poem upon his sacred majesty, his voyage for Holland; by way of dialogue between Belgia and Britannia* (1691); *Academia; or the humours of the University of Oxford. In burlesque verse* (1691, 1716; by 'A. D'Anvers'); and *The Oxford-Act: a poem* (1693; by 'A. D'Anvers').
 Greer has extracts, p. 376 f.

DARCIE, Lady Grace, *fl.* 1621–4
 2. Sutton (Surrey).

To the honourable assembly of the Commons house in Parliament (1624): this is a petition on behalf of her ward, Edward Darcie, to assert his (and her) rights to appoint a cleric to a living in the control of the manor of Sutton, Surrey (which belonged to her dead husband). It had fallen vacant in August 1621; but it was not her candidate, but that of Bishop Williams, who obtained the living. This act, she claimed, endangered her son's inheritance. Parliament agreed to pass an Act favouring her clerical candidate and securing her son's inheritance. This petition was one of a series directed against the corrupt practices of the Lord Keeper (another, unpublished, was from a Mrs THOMAS, 1624).

DAVIES, Lady Eleanor, 1590–1652
 1. Touchet; 2. London; 3. genteel, prophet; 5(a) Sir John Davies (m. 1609), (b) Sir Archibald Douglas; 6(a) poet and lawyer, (b) government official.

Also known as Eleanor AUDELEY, DOUGLAS, TOUCHET. See Appendix IV and Critical Appendix 2.

The daughter of George, Earl of Castlehaven, she bore a son who died young and a daughter, Lucy HASTINGS.* She first prophesied in 1625: when her husband burnt her first book of prophecies, she foretold his death within three years (he died 1626). Her second husband also burnt one of her books, and he died at communion in 1644. She predicted Buckingham's death in 1628. In 1633 she went to Amsterdam to publish a book of prophecies (foretelling the deaths of Archbishop Laud and Charles I); this book was publicly burnt in London and she was imprisoned for two years. In 1638 she desecrated the altar cloth in Lichfield cathedral, sat on the bishop's throne and called herself the Primate of England. In 1650 she employed Winstanley and other Diggers in farmwork on her estate.

She wrote more than 50 pamphlets between 1633 and 1652, among them *The restitution of prophecy* (1651; reprinted Exeter, 1978); *Amend, amend; God's kingdom is at hand* (1643); and *Elijah the Tishbites supplication* (1650).

DAVY, Sarah, ?1635–67

1. Roane; 4. Independent.

See Critical Appendix 6.

She was the author of *Heaven realiz'd or the holy pleasure of daily intimate communion with God, exemplified in a blessed soul, now in Heaven, Mrs Sarah Davy . . . Being a part of the precious reliques, written with her own hand. Stiled by her The record of my consolations, and the meditations of my heart* (1670; sold by Elizabeth CALVERT*). Includes some verse; extract in Graham.

This is a conversion narrative, published after her death. She records feelings of guilt at the death of her little brother, and says that she went away to school. On her return she was influenced by the Anglican minister Pierce, but was converted to an Independent congregation by a woman. She writes of this as though in love with the woman. The preface, by 'A. P.', is possibly by Anthony Palmer, a Baptist preacher (identified in Hobby's personal notes).

DAVYS, Mary, 1674–1732

2. Dublin, York, Cambridge; 3. coffee-house proprietor, playwright, novelist; 5. Reverend Peter Davys; 6. teacher and divine.

Mary Davys was widowed in 1698. Her comedy, *The northern heiress*, was performed at Lincoln's Inn Fields in 1716, and centres on the lives of middle-class women in York, who (as widows) enjoy their economic power. She also wrote another comedy (*The self-rival*, 1725;

unperformed), novels (the first published in 1704) and stories. A two-volume *Works* was published in 1725.

DEACONS, Prudentia, 1581–1645

2. Brussels, Cambrai; 3. nun; 4. Catholic.

She professed in 1610 at the English Benedictine Abbey at Brussels and moved to Cambrai in 1623. Translated *The mantle of the spouse* (n.d.). Information from Gillow.

DEANE, Anne, *fl.* 1661–96

2. Canterbury, Bristol; 4. ?Baptist; 5. Richard Deane; 6. secretary and treasurer for the army.

Her name is attached to a petition 'that her husband Richard, who despite his special pardon has been confined in the Canterbury Marshalsea, may be released on bond' (1661); the petition succeeded. She was in Bristol in 1670 and 1696.

DELAVAL, Lady Elizabeth, 1649–1717

1. Livingston; 2. Lincolnshire, London, Newcastle, France; 3. genteel; 4. Anglican; 5(a) Sir Robert Delaval, (b) Henry Hatcher; 6(a)/(b) genteel.

She was a maid of the Privy Chamber to Catherine of Braganza from *c.* 1663 to *c.* 1665. Her first marriage (1670) she regarded as 'putting on of shakells'. Robert was sickly and dissipated and the marriage seems to have been unhappy. In the 1670s she several times petitioned the king about lands in which she had an interest. Her second husband, Henry Hatcher (or Thatcher), was from Lincolnshire. They married in 1686. He became involved in Jacobite plots. She corresponded with James's court in exile, and seems to have fled to the continent, *c.* 1689/90, as a result of the Pewter Pot Plot. She joined the Jacobites, had access to James II and to the 'Old Pretender', and died in Rouen. Greene (see below) says that little is known of her last twenty-seven years.

Meditations of Lady Elizabeth Delaval written between 1662 and 1671, ed. D. G. Greene (Surtees Society, 1975). Extracts in Houlbrooke.

DENBIGH, Susan, Countess of, –*c.* 1655

1. Villiers; 2. Leicestershire, Oxford, Paris; 3. genteel; 4. Catholic convert; 5. William Feilding, Earl of Denbigh (m. 1607); 6. genteel.

Daughter of Sir George Villiers and Mary, Countess of Buckingham, she was a sister of James I's 'favourite', George, Duke of Buckingham. She became first Lady of the Bedchamber to HENRIETTA MARIA* at Oxford and Paris (Margaret CAVENDISH* was also one of this court-in-exile); in France she converted to Catholicism. She was a patron to the poet Richard Crashaw, and letters by her survive. She died in Cologne.

DENNE, Dorothy, ?1618–

2. Canterbury, London; 5. Roger Lufkin/Lukyn; 6. draper.

One of five daughters of Thomas Denne, MP and Recorder of Canterbury, she fell in love with William Taylor, who was in the service of her brother, Captain John Denne. Letters from her to William Taylor survive in the 'Oxinden Correspondence' (BL, Add. MSS 28.003). The letters chart their clandestine love affair, and debate the conflict between love and duty. After her marriage to Lufkin/Lukyn, a rich London draper, Taylor's mother tried to blackmail her with the letters (she was also an heiress in her own right).

See Fraser, p. 36 f. for extracts from letters.

DEW, Susanna, 1637–1707

1. Twinn; 2. London; 4. Quaker; 5. John Dew (m. 1668); 6. joiner.

Testimony in Ann WHITEHEAD,* *Piety* . . . (1686). Signed *A tender and Christian testimony* (1685; see Mary ELSON* for details) and *A living testimony from the power and spirit of our Lord Jesus Christ* (1685; see Mary FOSTER* for details).

DIGBY, Beatrice, –1658

1. Walcott; 2. Shropshire, Bedfordshire; 5(a) Sir John Dive, (b) Sir John Digby; 6(a)/(b) genteel.

Daughter of Charles Walcott of Walcott, Shropshire, her second husband became Earl of Bristol. A letter of 1621 to Sir Walter Aston is reprinted in *The Tixall letters; or the correspondence of the Aston family and their friends during the seventeenth century,* ed. A. Clifford (London & Edinburgh: Longman, Hurst, Rees, Orme & Brown, 1815), 2 vols.

DOCWRA, Ann, c. 1640–1710

2. Cambridge; 4. Quaker.

In 1683 she was involved in controversy about George Whitehead and Thomas Ellwood: she denied authorship of a passage added to *A brief discovery* (1683) which made it clear that she was attacking them. *A looking-glass for the recorder* (1682) shows a detailed knowledge of legal history and tends to suggest that she had wealth. *An epistle for love* (1683) indicates that she is over 40. *An apostate conscience exposed* (1699) was printed for Tace SOWLE.

DOGGETT, Mary

'Her book of receipts' (BL Sloane MSS). We know nothing else.

DOLE, Dorcas, –1716
1. Knight; 2. Bristol; 4. Quaker; 5. John Dole; 6. silkweaver.

Dorcas Dole married on 1 September 1667, and had four sons and a daughter, also Dorcas. She suffered for her Quakerism (1664–5, 1682–5), being imprisoned in Newgate and Bridewell, where she was treated harshly for continuing to preach and pray while in prison. Her writings include letters to Bristol magistrates and to the children who kept Bristol Friends' meetings going when all the adults were in prison. She was still living in Bristol, with her husband and daughter, in 1696. She is author of: *Once more a warning to thee, O England: but more particularly to the inhabitants of the city of Bristol* (1683, 1684). *A salutation and seasonable exhortation to children* (1683, 1700; for Tace SOWLE). *A salutation of my endeared love in God's holy fear and dread, and for the clearing of my conscience once more unto you of that city of Bristol, amongst whom my soul hath some years travelled many a dreadful exercise* (1683; with Elizabeth STIRREDGE*).

DORSET, Countess of

Anne CLIFFORD*

DOUGLAS, Eleanor

Eleanor DAVIES*

DOWDALL, Katherine, *fl. c.* 1695
2. Ireland.

To the honourable the knights . . . (Dublin, *c.* 1695). We have not been able to trace this work; it is not to be found in the location given by Wing. Dowdall was a fairly common family name in Ireland at this period, especially in Meath and Louth: Henry Dowdall was a sheriff of Meath in 1689; a Katherine Dowdall appears enrolled in the 'Decrees of Innocents' under Commonwealth rule.

DOWNER, Anne

Anne WHITEHEAD*

DOWRICHE, Anne, *fl.* **1560–89**
1. Edgcumbe; 2. Mount Edgcumbe, Honiton (Devon); 3. genteel; 5. Hugh Dowriche; 6. minister (m. 1580).

She was 'under age' in 1560, the date of her father's will. Her husband was rector of Honiton (from 1587), and she bore four children. Pollard and Redgrave give her as the author of a poem in alexandrines, *The French historie: that is, a lamentable discourse of three of the chiefe and most famous bloodie broiles that have happened in France for the gospelles of Jesus Christ* (1589). The authorship of this poem is also attributed (by Travitsky) to Anne TREFUSIS, with the implication that she is the same woman. Anne Trefusis, also of the Edgcumbe family, was, however, a niece of Anne Dowriche who married Richard Trefusis, then Ambrose Manington (MP for Launceston 1629) and died in 1638 at South Petherwyn, Cornwall.

DRAKE, Judith, *fl.* **1696–1707**
2. Cambridge.

Judith Drake wrote prefaces to the posthumous works of her brother, James Drake, a Tory pamphleteer (1667–1707); their father, Robert Drake, was an attorney of Cambridge. In one preface she speaks of her 'melancholy circumstances' and in another of being a 'retired disconsolate woman' (quotations from Ferguson, who has extracts, p. 202 f.). She is probably the author of *An essay in defence of the female sex. In which are inserted the characters of a pedant, a squire, a beau, a vertuoso, a poetaster* (published anonymously 1696; fourth edition 1721; see also Mary ASTELL*).

DREWET, Mary, –?1707
2. Cirencester; 4. Quaker; 5. Amariah Drewet.

Theophila TOWNSEND*

Amariah Drewet was her second husband; she had children by a previous marriage (also to a Quaker). She wrote *A testimony of the life, death and sufferings of Amariah Drewet* (1687) and a testimony concerning Joan VOKINS* (1691).

DUVEGERRE, Suzanne, *fl.* 1639

She translated *Admirable events, selected out of four books, written in French by Peter Comus* . . . (1639).

DYER, Mary, –1660

1. Barrett; 2. London, Boston (New England); 4. Antinomian, Quaker; 5. William Dyer; 6. milliner.

Born in London, of an Essex family, she had six children. After a trip to Boston with her husband in 1635, they moved there from London in 1643. She became friends with Anne HUTCHINSON, joining the Antinomians with her. Visited London from 1652 till 1657 and became a Quaker. On her return to New England, she went with Ann DURDEN to Boston and was arrested as a Quaker troublemaker (1657). In 1658 she was expelled from New Haven for preaching and banished from Massachusetts in 1659. She returned to Boston twice under penalty of death, and refused a last-minute chance to save her life by promising to leave the area. She was executed on Boston Common in 1660 (the penultimate Quaker executed in America).

A passage in M. Stephenson, *A call* (1660). Letters by her were reprinted in Bishop, *New England judged* (1661). (This entry draws in part on Hobby's personal notes.)

E

EBBS, Joyce, *fl.* 1661–2

2. London; 3. ?prostitute; 5. Thomas Ebbs; 6. soldier.

The last speech, confession & prayer of Joyce Ebbs, to several ministers in the presse-yard at Newgate, and at the place of execution in Smithfield Rounds on Thursday last in the forenoon . . . As also, the several passages that happened before her death; her heavie groans and shrieks in the fire, and the providing of a half sheet spread over with pitch, to shorten the time of her miserable torment. (1662)

Ebbs, whose 'place of livelyhood was in a house of wicked resort' (near Drury Lane), was executed for stabbing her husband in a quarrel (it would be tempting to conjecture her husband was her pimp, and hence the violence). She was imprisoned for ten months before execution, having initially pleaded pregnancy. The only elements of the text that can be said to be 'authored' by her are the penitent quotations that are induced in her after a period of 'spiritual advice'; these 'confessions' are, as much as the moral 'letter', an ideologically necessary part of the moral tale of a wicked woman (see Elizabeth CALDWELL*): 'wishing that she had never been born, or that she had been made any other creature than a woman, crying, "Wo, wo, wo, a weak, a woful, a wretched, and most miserable woman!"' At the lighting of the fire: "'and now thou fiery chariot, that cam'st down to fetch up Elijah, carry my poor soul to its happy hold"' . . . And so she departed this life, with three or four dolesome shrieks, when the flames of fire first seized her body.'

ECCLESTONE, Priscilla, 1627–94

2. Shoreditch, Enfield (London); 4. Seeker, Quaker; 5(a) Richard Ecclestone, (b) Thomas Hart (m. 1671); 6(a) merchant.

A son was born in 1650. A daughter, Mercy, married in 1683. A child (nameless) died in 1665, the same year as her first husband.

Co-author of a petition (*c.* 1670): see Anne WHITEHEAD,* and signatory of the 1659 tithing petition.

EDGE, Alice, *fl.* ?1665–92
2. ?Yorkshire; 5. ?Thomas Edge.

She wrote a testimony in Hannah BECKWITH,* *A true relation* . . . (1692).
If this is the wife of Thomas, she bore two children, 1665 and 1671.

EDMONDSON, Abigail, after 1697–
2. Ireland; 4. Quaker.

She signed *A testimony concerning our dear father Wm. Edmondson* (1715)
with Tryal EDMONDSON, Mary FAYLE, Eleazor and Susanna SHELDON, all
children of William (her mother was Mary EDMONDSON;* Abigail is not
mentioned in her father's will).

EDMONDSON, Mary, ?1647–1732
1. Ball; 2. Dublin; 4. Quaker; 5(a) Joshua Strangman, (b) William Edmondson (m. 1697); 6(b) farmer.

Mother of Abigail EDMONDSON* and one other child; her second husband was one of the leading Quaker organisers in Ireland.
The testimony of M.E. concerning her late husband (1715).

EDMUNDSON, Ann, ?1646–1726
2. London; 4. Quaker.

'Here are some of the words spoken by our dear friend Francis Patchett
a little before his death' in *Living words through a dying man* (1678): the
text was witnessed by Mariabella FARNBOROUGH,* elder and younger,
and Rebecca VEAL.

EDWARDS, Mary, *c.* 1635–1715
1. Surman; 2. Gloucestershire; 4. Quaker; 5. Thomas Edwards (m. 1665).

Mary Edwards preached in Shropshire and Dublin. In 1685 she, with
Esther TOWNSEND (probably the mother of Theophila TOWNSEND*), in-
terviewed Justices of Assize on behalf of prisoners in Gloucester castle.
She wrote *Her farewell* . . . (1719) and *Some brief epistles, testimonies and
counsel . . . recommended to Friends, called Quakers* (1720).

EEDES, Judith, *fl.* 1659
2. Suffolk; 4. ?Presbyterian.

A warning to all the inhabitants of the earth (1659) acknowledges the support of her minister, Robert Cade. This was presumably the same Presbyterian minister of Woodbridge, Suffolk, who supported Elizabeth WARREN;* his second period there was 1651–66.

EGERTON, Lady Bridget, –1648
1. Grey; 2. Northamptonshire; 3. genteel; 4. Anglican; 5. Rowland Egerton; 6. genteel.

The confession of . . . Lady Bridget Egerton, 1638 appears in Chetham Society Publications, vol. 83, 1870–1, as *A forme of confession grounded upon the ancient Catholique and Apostolique faith.* The editor, P. M. Grey Egerton, says that 'The composition is characterized by singular boldness . . . it was . . . courageous on the part of Bridget to venture to express, in terms so explicit, her abjuration of transubstantiation, purgatory, invocation of saints and other practices which were at that time insinuating themselves into the public worship of the reformed church.'

EGERTON, Elizabeth

Elizabeth BRACKLEY*

EGERTON, Sarah Fyge, 1669/72–1722
1. Fyge; 2. London; 3. professional; 5(a) — Field, (b) Thomas Egerton; 6(a) lawyer, (b) cleric.

Sarah Egerton claimed that she was banished from the paternal home because she wrote *The female advocate; or, an answer to a late satyr* (1686). This, which is abridged in Ferguson (p. 154 f.), is a verse reply to Robert Gould's *A late satyr* (1682). (It had a second edition, with significant changes, in 1687 and has been reprinted by the Augustan Reprint Society.) In 1703 *Poems on several occasions, together with a pastoral. By Mrs S. F.* was published (reprinted 1706): 'Emphatic feminism marks this volume . . . . There are the love poems typical, as Egerton says, of "a woman's pen", but there are also poems of praise and blame, a survey poem, and others defending ideas of Robert Boyle's and John Norris of Bemerton's' (Rothstein, pp. 186–7). 'The Emulation' says that 'From the first dawn of life unto the grave,/Poor womankind's in every state a slave', and ends 'No, we'll be wits, and then men must be fools.'

Sarah Egerton petitioned for divorce against Thomas Egerton in 1703, on grounds of cruelty. She knew Dryden, Norris and Halifax.

See Greer, p. 345 f. (including poems); Ferguson, p. 154 f.

ELESTONE, Sarah

See Appendix III.

ELIZA

See Appendix II.

ELIZABETH OF BOHEMIA, Queen, 1596–1662

1. Stuart; 2. Dunfermline, London, Prague, The Hague; 3. genteel; 4. Protestant; 5. Frederick, Elector Palatine of the Rhine; 6. genteel.

Anna HUME*

Elizabeth was daughter of Anne of Denmark and James I, and sister to Charles I. She married Frederick in 1613 and was crowned Queen of Bohemia in 1619. Frederick lost the crown in 1620, and she spent many years in exile at The Hague. At the Restoration she came to London and is buried in Westminster Abbey. She was educated in the household of Helen LIVINGSTON* and is often known as 'The Winter Queen'.

   The Letters of Elizabeth Queen of Bohemia, comp. L. M. Baker (London: Bodley Head, 1953). *The declaration and message . . .* (1652). *A true relation of the kings speech to the Lady Elizabeth, and the duke of Gloucester, the day before his death* includes 'Another relation from the Lady Elizabeths own hand' (1648).

   See *Eliza's Babes*, Appendix I. Hobby suggests (*Virtue*, p. 55) that this may have been produced at Elizabeth's court. It includes a poem 'To the Queen of Bohemia'.

   Greer prints a poem (p. 40 f.) and see Carola Oman, *Elizabeth of Bohemia* (London: Hodder & Stoughton, 1938).

ELIZABETH, Queen of England, 1533–1603

1. Tudor; 2. London; 3. monarch; 4. Anglican.

'From 1585, her speeches were deliberately and systematically copied and widely distributed, and were printed in contemporary chronicles and in separate editions' (C. Haigh, *Elizabeth I*, London: Macmillan, 1988, p. 120). Throughout the seventeenth century there were further printings of speeches, etc. by the queen (e.g. *Injunctions given by the queen's majestie*, 1641, and *Queen Elizabeth's last speech to her last Parliament*, 1642). Such printings are not antiquarian but are best seen in the context of seventeenth-century politics (see, e.g., T. Harris, *London Crowds*, Cambridge: Cambridge University Press, 1987, p. 145). Poems and translations by her can be found in modern anthologies.

'Eliza's babes'

See Appendix I.

ELLIS, Alice, –1720

1. Davy; 2. Ayrton (Yorks.); 4. Quaker; 5. William Ellis (m. 1688); 6. trade, ?weaver.

Her 'Testimony concerning her dear husband' is prefixed to *A brief account of the life etc. of William Ellis* (1710). Many letters to her husband on his travels survive: see James Backhouse (ed.), *The life and correspondence of William and Alice Ellis* (London: Charles Gilpin, 1849).

ELLIS, Sarah, 1645–95

1. Sawyer; 2. Aldersgate (London); 4. Quaker; 5. Josiah Ellis (m. 1675); 6. salesman.

Testimony for Susanna Whitrow in Joan WHITROW,* *The work of God* (1677). Signed general testimony for Anne WHITEHEAD* in *Piety . . .* (1686).

ELLWOOD, Mary, c. 1623–1708

1. Ellis; 2. Buckinghamshire, London, Kent, Sussex; 4. Quaker; 5. Thomas Ellwood (m. 1669); 6. Quaker writer.

With Margery CLIPSHAM/CLIPSON* she wrote *The spirit that works abomination and its abominable work discovered; and a faithful testimony born against it* (1685). The context is of religious fragmentation as evidenced particularly in the activities of Susanna ALDRIDGE;* the pamphlet speaks of those who have 'craftily cover'd themselves' to work subversively in meetings.

Thomas Ellwood's autobiography speaks of his marriage with Mary in 1669 as following an acquaintance of 'divers years' within Quaker circles – after which they settled in Hunger Hill (Bedfordshire). Although he speaks of finding 'those fair prints of truth and sublime virtue' in her 'to a sublime degree', he has relatively little to say about her. Women are, in fact, marginalised throughout Ellwood's text.

ELSAM, Elizabeth, –1681

2. North Collingham (Notts.); 4. Quaker; 5. Thomas Elsam.

Her two daughters were born in 1654 and 1656. She wrote a testimony which is prefixed to William Smith, *Balm from Gilead* (1675).

ELSON, Mary, c. 1623–1706
2. Wiltshire, London; 3. minister; 4. Quaker; 5. John Elson; 6. carpenter.

In 1659 Mary Elson was convinced by Anne WHITEHEAD;* from that year she and Sarah BLACKBERRY,* Rebeckah TRAVERS* and Anne WHITEHEAD worked on setting up Quaker women's meetings. The Elson house, at the sign of the Peel, became the location of one of the regular London Quaker meetings. The birth of one child is recorded in 1665.

An epistle for true love, unity and order in the church of Christ (1680; with Anne WHITEHEAD). Signed *For the King and both Houses of Parliament* (*c.* 1670; with Anne WHITEHEAD and others). *A tender and Christian testimony to young people* (1685; with others). This text asks younger Quakers to respect their elders, and addresses 'servants' that 'take Liberty as they will, being stubborn and perverse', telling them to fear the Lord. Clearly there are signs of generational and class divisions within Quakers, and Elson plays a part in insisting on unity under the leadership of the elders (see also Dorcas DOLE*). This is perhaps also the importance of the gathering of mainly older women at Anne Whitehead's death. In her testimony in WHITEHEAD, *Piety* . . . (1686) she recalls Whitehead's last testimony at the Bull and Mouth.

ELSTOB, Elizabeth, 1683–1756
2. Newcastle, Evesham, ?Canterbury, London, Worcestershire; 3. scholar, teacher.

Elizabeth's parents died when she was still an infant and she was brought up first by an uncle and then by her brother. She turned to teaching in dire financial need (*c.* 1718). From 1738 to her death, she was in the service of the Duchess of Portland, having earlier been helped by Queen Anne. She came to know eight languages and is a great figure in the development of the study of Old English, although, being a woman, she was barred from studying at Oxford and Cambridge. She edited *An English-Saxon Homily* . . . (1709, with notes and preface) and published *The rudiments of grammar for the English-Saxon tongue* . . . (1715).

Selections in Ferguson, p. 240 ff.

EMERSON, Ruth, fl. ?1646–53
2. ?Essex, Dublin; 4. Baptist.

'Experiences' in Rogers, *Ohel* . . . (1653) (see Mary BARKER* for details), 'as it came out of her own mouth in the Church at Dublin'. She speaks of being a follower of 'Mr Archer', probably the Anabaptist Thomas Archer, who was in Essex in 1646.

EMMETT, Dorothy, *fl.* 1652–3
2. Dublin; 4. Congregationalist, Baptist.

'Experiences' in Rogers, *Ohel*. . . (1653) (see Mary BARKER* for details); spiritually 'called' by John Owen who travelled from Essex as a chaplain to Cromwell's army.

'The Emulation'

See Appendix I and also Sarah Fyge EGERTON.*

ENDON, Tace, *fl.* 1688–1710
1. Davies; 2. Welshpool (Montgomeryshire/Powys); 4. Quaker; 5. Jacob Endon.

Her father, Richard Davies, was a Quaker activist in Wales. He married in 1659 and was speaking of his 'family' in 1660. She was still known as Tace Davies in 1688 (when she signed a testimony from the Montgomeryshire meeting), but in 1702, when she visited London with her father, she was Tace Endon. She wrote *A short testimony concerning my dear and loving father* (1710).

EPHELIA

See Appendix II.

EUGENIA

Mary CHUDLEIGH*

EVANS, Katherine, –1692
2. Inksbatch (Somerset), Malta; 4. Quaker; 5. John Evans; 6. property owner, minister.

Evans and Sarah CHEEVERS* travelled and wrote together: they visited Scotland in 1654. (Evans was imprisoned in Exeter in 1656.) They were stripped and whipped in Salisbury (1657) and banished from the Isle of Wight. In 1658 they went to Malta (on their way to Jerusalem), where they were imprisoned by the Inquisition for three years, returning in 1664. Later, Evans travelled to the Isle of Man and Ireland. She was in Newgate in 1682.

Their account of their imprisonment is in *This is a short relation* (1662) and *A true account* (1663; an expanded edition of the 1662 text, which tells how they were set free and narrates their visit to Tangiers on their return journey: extract in Graham). Both texts include letters to husbands and children. Evans's *A brief discovery of God's eternal truth* (1663) was printed with a pamphlet by CHEEVERS. Besse (2.399–406) prints letters and papers by them.

EVELYN, Mary jun., 1665–85
2. Surrey; 3. genteel.

Author of *Mundus muliebris: or, the ladies dressing-room unlocked and her toilette spread in burlesque etc.* (1690, 1700). The major part of this was also published, as anonymous, by Mary's father the diarist John Evelyn, under the title *A voyage to Maryland* (1690). *Mundus . . .* is sometimes attributed to John Evelyn, whose diary describes the work as 'an enumeration of the immense variety of the modes and ornaments belonging to the sex'. A manuscript miscellaneous book of meditations also survives.

   John Evelyn has little to say of Mary in his diary, but records (February 1682) that she is learning 'music of Signor Bartholomeo, and dancing of Monsieur Isaac reputed the best masters'. He does, however, write movingly of her death in March 1685, his obituary including praise of her talent as a writer.

   Greer (p. 324 ff.) has an extract from *Mundus . . .*

EVELYN, Mary sen., *c.* 1635–1708/9
1. Browne; 2. Surrey; 3. genteel; 5. John Evelyn; 6. diarist.

Mother of Mary EVELYN jun.*

'Letters of Mrs Evelyn' are in *The diary and correspondence of John Evelyn* (ed. W. Bray, London: Henry Colburn, 1850–2), vol. 4, pp. 8–48. Appendix B.2 of John Evelyn's *Life of Mrs Godolphin* (ed. H. Sampson, London: Oxford University Press, 1939) has Mary Evelyn's 'Instructions to Mrs Blague for setting up & keeping house . . . ' (1676; this is presumably Margaret BLAGGE*).

EVERARD, Margaret, *fl.* 1699
2. Chatteris, Isle of Ely; 4. Quaker (disunited); 5. John Everard; 6. preacher.

Margaret was a follower of George Keith and came to be considered unsound by Friends. She wrote *An epistle of Margaret Everard to the people called Quakers . . . shewing her dissatisfaction with the ignorance, error and uncharitableness that too much abounds among them* (1699).

EYRE, Elizabeth, *fl.* 1659–89
1. Packington; 2. Worcestershire, Rampton (Notts.); 3. genteel; 5. Anthony Eyre (m. after 1659).

Daughter of Sir John Packington of Westwood, Worcestershire, she was the second wife of Anthony Eyre, whose first wife died 1659. She bore four children, her husband dying in 1671. She wrote *A letter from a person of quality in the north* (1689).

F

FAGE, Mary, *fl.* 1637

5. Robert Fage, the younger; 6. genteel.

The Faggs (or Fages) were a genteel Sussex family, and although there were two Marys who 'fit' chronologically, there is no relevant Robert. Mary Fage wrote *Fames roule: or, the names of our dread soveraigne Lord King Charles, his royall queen Mary, and his most hopefull posterity: together with the names of the dukes, marquesses, earles . . . of . . . England, Scotland, and Ireland: anagrammatiz'd and expressed by acrostick lines on their names* (1637). A dedicatory poem by Thomas Heywood praises her 'Brave masculine spirit'.

FAIRMAN, Lydia, *fl.* 1659

4. Quaker.

A few lines given forth, and a true testimony of the way which is Christ whom the Saints enjoys who have believed in the light, and followed it into the regeneration, which they come to know through the preaching of the Gospel (1659).

FAIRMAN, Mary, *fl.* 1680–1713

1. Wilkins; 2. Southwark; 4. Quaker; 5. Robert Fairman (m. 1680); 6. brewer.

Her house was a meeting-house and she 'looked after the poor for 30 years'. She visited the workhouse and dealt with marriage and settlement problems. She is author of letters (1713) to her Monthly Meeting, reproaching them with the example of the Aldersgate Women's Meeting which regularly donated to the poor, unlike Southwark.

See Edwards, 'Women Friends of London', *JFHS*, vol. 47.

FANE, Frances

Frances ABERGAVENNY*

FANSHAW, Margaret, *fl.* **1652–3**
2. Dublin; 4. Baptist.

'Experiences' in Rogers, *Ohel* . . . (1653) (see Mary BARKER* for details). She says she heard 'Mr Fowler' preach: this could be Richard Fowler of London, or Christopher Fowler (in Reading from 1646 onwards).

FANSHAW, Mrs

See Appendix III.

FANSHAWE, Ann, 1625–80
1. Harrison; 2. London, Oxford; 3. genteel; 5. Sir Richard Fanshawe; 6. government servant.

Ann Fanshawe was instructed in French, music, singing, needlework and dancing. She travelled in France, Spain, Portugal, Ireland and the Scillies, largely because of her husband's occupation. She was the mother of fourteen children, nine of whom died before 1667. *The memoirs of Ann, Lady Fanshawe* . . . were first published in 1829 and there is a modern edition, edited by J. Loftis (Oxford: Clarendon Press, 1979), together with the memoirs of Anne HALKET.* Although her husband is largely remembered because of her memoirs, she is marginalised in *DNB*: 'See under FANSHAWE, Sir Richard'.

FARNBOROUGH, Mariabella jun., 1665–
2. London; 3. trade; 4. Quaker; 5. Peter Briggins (m. 1689); 6. tobacconist, hop-merchant.

Two daughters and a son died young (1691, 1694, 1700), but a daughter, Mariabella, survived. Like her mother (below) she witnessed testimony to Patchet (1676).

FARNBOROUGH, Mariabella sen., 1626–1708
1. Bleake; 2. Warminster (Wilts.), Stepney (London); 4. Quaker; 5. Thomas Farnborough (m. 1662).

Married in London, she bore two children, Thomas and Mariabella (1663, 1665). She was preaching in London in 1683 and acted as an emissary for the London Meeting (see Elizabeth REDFORD*). She spent much time in prison, became lame (her lameness was cured in old age), and visited the sick (with Mary ELSON*). It may be this role of medical visitor that led her to be at the deaths of some major figures:

she witnessed testimony to Francis Patchet in *Living words through a dying man* (1676) and signed the general testimonies for Anne WHITE-HEAD* (1686) and Joan VOKINS* (Reading, 1691), and possibly Alice CURWEN* (1680). She was a signatory to *A tender and Christian testimony* (1685; see Mary ELSON* for details).

FEARON, Jane, c. 1655–1737
1. Hall; 2. Little/Great Broughton (Cumberland); 3. minister; 4. Quaker; 5. Peter Fearon (m. 1693).

Author of *Universal redemption offered in Jesus Christ* (1698); *Absolute predestination not scripture: or, some questions upon a doctrine which I heard preached, 1704, to a people called Independents, at Cockermouth in Cumberland* (1705; printed and sold by Tace SOWLE; reprinted New Hampshire, 1813); and *A reply to J. Atkinson's pretended answer to Absolute predestination* (1709; printed and sold by Tace SOWLE).

FEATHERSTONE, Sarah, fl. 1673–89
2. Partney Mills (Lincs.); 3. farmer; 4. Quaker; 5(a) Joseph Featherstone, (b) Thomas Browne (m. 1684).

'There hath something lain as a weight upon my spirit for sometime' (1683, signed Sarah Featherstone) in *Living testimonies concerning the death of the righteous. Or the blessed end of Joseph Featherstone and Sarah his daughter* (1689; with Thomas Browne) and 'A brief relation of the life and death of my dear and only child, Sarah Featherstone' (1689; signed Sarah Brown). The daughter was born in 1673 (died 1688). Featherstone was prosecuted for attending Quaker meetings.

FELL, Lydia, fl. 1676–9
1. Erbury; 2. ?Wales, Barbados; 4. Quaker.

She might be the daughter of William Erbury of Wales, with a possible death-date of 1699. In 1676 she describes herself as a 'long inhabitant' of Barbados, where she suffered for her religion. *A testimony and warning given forth in the love of truth, and is for the governour, magistrates & people inhabiting on the island of Barbadoes; which is a call to turn to the Lord* (1676) warns its readers against persecuting Quakers: 'yea, the night cometh, I say, upon the children of the night'; and it describes her own punishment for disrupting, with another woman, a church service (she was 'haled along by the bell-man of the town' and imprisoned). In June 1679 she travelled to New York.

FELL, Margaret, 1614–1702
1. Askew; 2. Lancashire, London; 3. genteel; 4. Quaker; 5(a) Thomas Fell, (b) George Fox; 6(a) lawyer, (b) preacher.

See Critical Appendix 3.

Margaret Fell is sometimes known as 'the mother of Quakerism'. She was imprisoned in 1664–8 and in 1670 for holding Quaker meetings and for refusing the Oath of Allegiance. She used Swarthmore Hall for Quaker meetings. Four of her daughters were authors: see Sarah FELL,* Mary LOWER,* Margaret ROUSE,* Isabel YEAMANS.*

Margaret Fell wrote several pamphlets from 1655, including *For Manasseh Ben Israel* (1656; translated into Dutch by William Ames); *A declaration and an information from us the people of God called Quakers* (1660); and *Women's speaking justified, proved and allowed of by the Scriptures: all such as speak by the spirit and power of the Lord Jesus* (1666, 1667). This last is a contribution to the debate about women speaking (see AUDLAND,* COLE* and COTTON*). It has been reprinted in the Augustan Reprint Society 33 (1979), and there are extracts in Ferguson (p. 115 f.).

See Isabel Ross, *Margaret Fell* (London: Longman, 1949).

FELL, Sarah, 1642–1714
2. Lancashire, London; 3. genteel; 4. Quaker; 5. William Meade (m. 1681); 6. linen-draper.

She was the daughter of Margaret FELL* and established the Swarthmore Hall women's meetings. She was the only woman to manage an iron forge in the local industry. She was jailed at Dalston in 1676 (non-payment of tithes). She moved to London in 1681 at her marriage and took over the accounts of London Quaker meetings from Anne WHITE-HEAD.* She bore one son, Nathaniel, in 1684 whom she nursed herself (against the usual practice of her class). She taught herself Hebrew, the better to qualify herself as a preacher.

The household book of Sarah Fell of Swarthmore Hall 1673–1678 (ed. N. Penney, Cambridge: Cambridge University Press, 1920). *Instructions how you may order the business,* in *The Quarterly Women's meeting book* (1681); also a legal document about the lands of the manor of Osmundesley [Osmotherley] (1678).

See Ross, entry above.

FERRAR, Bathsheba, *fl.* 1630–57
1. Owen; 2. Little Gidding, London; 4. Anglican; 5. John Ferrar; 6. mercantile.

See Critical Appendix 5.

Bathsheba's one surviving letter is a painful document about her entrapment (for at least 27 years – 1630–57) in the famous religious community at Little Gidding, which had been bought for Nicholas Ferrar by his mother in 1624. Bathsheba was the second wife of John Ferrar, Nicholas (who has been called a saint) being his younger brother and the leader of the community. She had four children, one of whom died young, and there is evidence that she was kept at Little Gidding 'agaynst her will', despite her repeated threats to leave. Conflict with her deferential husband and his saintly brother centred on authority over her children and her property rights. The brothers denied her rights over a house in London left to her by her mother-in-law, and her letter appealing for her brother's help and legal advice was intercepted by them. She refused to comply with Nicholas's disciplinary methods, interrupting his reading out to her of Pauline doctrine and refusing to accept his paper of admonition. When John died in 1657, she went immediately to London, travelling in a wagon rather than waiting a week for a coach – 'for an hour longer shee would not stay'.

The letter is in B. Blackstone (ed.), *The Ferrar papers* (Cambridge: Cambridge University Press, 1938). See also Thomas Docherty, *On Modern Authority* (Brighton: Harvester, 1987), pp. 63-8.

FIENNES, Celia, 1662–1741

2. Salisbury, Bath, London; 3. genteel; 4. Presbyterian.

Celia Fiennes was of a puritan family with strong Parliamentary affiliations. She travelled widely in England, Scotland and Wales between 1687 and 1702, recording her journeys as if for publication.

See *The journeys of Celia Fiennes*, ed. C. Morris (London: Cresset Press, 1947) and *The illustrated journeys of Celia Fiennes*, ed. C. Morris (London: Macdonald, 1982).

FIGE, Sarah

Sarah Fyge EGERTON*

FINCH, Anne, Countess of Winchelsea, 1661–1720

1. Kingsmill; 2. Southampton, Kent , London; 3. genteel; 4. Anglican; 5. Heneage Finch, Earl of Winchelsea; 6. genteel, captain of halberdiers, MP.

A Royalist, Anne Finch was Maid of Honour to Mary of Modena and friend to Anne KILLIGREW.* The conflict between her support for women's active participation in the arts and her doubts about her own 'incapassity' may have led to her depression. She found country life conducive to writing: at court 'everyone would have made their remarks upon a versifying maid of honour'. She wrote:

The triumphs of love and innocence (*c.* 1688; unperformed play). *Aristomenes: or The royal shepherd* (*c.* 1690; unperformed play). *The principles of philosophy* (1692). *The prerogatives of love* (1695). *Miscellany poems written by a lady* (1713; originally as 'Ardelia').

See *The Poems*, edited by M. Reynolds (Chicago: University of Chicago Press, 1903); *Selected Poems*, edited by K. Rogers (New York: Ungar, 1979); *Selected Poems*, edited by D. Thompson (Manchester: Carcanet, 1987); and the selection in Ferguson (p. 248 ff.).

FINCH, Lady Anne

Anne CONWAY*

FISHER, Abigail, 1649–1721
1. Antrobus; 2. London; 4. Quaker; 5. Hallelujah Fisher (m. 1677); 6. mariner.

Her daughter Abigail was born in 1678. When she submitted her writings to the 'censorship' committee of Quakers, she was told 'as to what's in verse, they rather advise to have it in prose.' She died in the Friends Workhouse (London).

A testimony for Ann WHITEHEAD* in *Piety . . .* (1686), which ends in verse. *A salutation of true love to all faithful friends, brethren and sisters in the fellowship of the blessed truth* (1690). *A few lines in true love to such that frequent the meetings of the people called Quakers* (1694, 1696; for Tace SOWLE). *An epistle in the love of God* (1696; for Tace SOWLE).

FISHER, Mary, 1623–98
2. Yorkshire, Devon, Turkey, South Carolina; 3. preacher; 4. Quaker; 5(a) William Bayly (m. 1662), (b) John Cross (m. 1678); 6(a) sea-captain and minister (Baptist, Quaker).

The niece of Francis Rous, Provost of Eton, she was born near York and worked as a servant in Selby. She became active as a Quaker after Fox's visit to York in 1652. She was imprisoned in York Castle (1652) for witnessing at Selby; preaching at Pontefract produced six months imprisonment; she was whipped at Cambridge (with Elizabeth WILLIAMS) for preaching; and imprisoned in Buckinghamshire (1655). That year she visited Barbados with Anne AUSTIN, was held at and banished from

Boston, and returned to the West Indies in 1657. In 1658–60 she visited Mahomet IV in Adrianople, Turkey (with Mary PRINCE*). She bore three daughters by her first husband, married again in London and settled with her second husband in Charleston, South Carolina (*c.* 1682).

False prophets and false teachers described (1652; with Thomas Aldam, Jane HOLMES,* Elizabeth HOOTON,* Benjamin Nicholson, William Pears – 'Prisoners of the Lord at York Castle'). 'Testimony for William Bayly' (1665; at the end of Bayly's collected writings of 1676).

FLETCHER, Elizabeth, *c.* 1638–58

2. Kirby Lonsdale (Westmorland); 3. genteel, preacher; 4. Quaker.

Elizabeth Fletcher preached in Oxford with Elizabeth LEAVENS and (1655–7) in Ireland. She wrote *A few words in season to all the inhabitants of the earth . . . to leave off their wickedness . . .* (1660).

FORD, Bridget, 1636–1710

1. Gosnell; 2. Shropshire, London; 4. Quaker; 5. Philip Ford (m. 1672); 6. merchant.

Born in Shropshire, she moved to London at her marriage. Four children were born between 1676 and 1679 (one dying in infancy). She wrote a testimony in Anne WHITEHEAD,* *Piety. . .* (1686). Signed *A tender and Christian testimony* (1685; see Mary ELSON* for details).

FOSTER/FORSTER, Mary, 1619–86

1. ?Harris; 2. London; 4. Quaker; 5. Thomas Foster/Forster.

She bore eight children between 1650 and 1660, and claimed to have known Anne WHITEHEAD* since 1659 (testimony in *Piety. . .* , 1686). She was responsible for the preface to the famous anti-tithe petition *These several papers was sent to the Parliament . . . 1659. Being above seven thousand of the names of the hand-maids and daughters of the Lord . . .* (1659; printed for Mary WESTWOOD*).

Testimony for Mary HARRIS:* 'A few words of encouragement from experience' in *A declaration of the bountiful loving-kindness* (1669, reprinted 1693: the latter printed and sold by Tace SOWLE). There seems to have been an increase in testimonies written by mothers and centred on familial relationships in the 1670s (see for example work by Joan WHITROW*). From this point into the 1680s there is an apparent emphasis on the role of older women in maintaining order and unity (see the note to Mary ELSON*). Mary Foster was a central figure.

Some seasonable considerations to the young men and women (1684). *A living* *testimony from the power and spirit of our Lord Jesus Christ in our faithful women's meeting and Christian society* (1685; signed by Mary FOSTER with others: focuses on marriage and especially the roles of 'Aged Women in the Truth'). (*A modest vindication of the people called Quakers, from the aspersions of Mary Ely and Susan Everard* (*c.* 1701) is ascribed to her, but if it is a reply to Margaret EVERARD* the death-date makes her authorship impossible.)

FOWKE, Martha, *fl.* 1720

Wrote *The epistles of Clio and Strephon, being a collection of letters that passed between an English lady and an English gentleman in France . . .* (1720, 1728, 1729, 1732 – the last as *The platonic lovers*; fiction, 'By M. F.').

FOWLER, Constance, *fl.* 1630–58

1. Aston; 2. Tixall, St Thomas Priory (Staffs.); 3. genteel; 5. Walter Fowler.

Daughter of Sir Walter Aston (who married in 1607) and sister of Gertrude ASTON.* Her letters are reprinted in *The Tixall letters; or the correspondence of the Aston family and their friends during the seventeenth century*, ed. A. Clifford (London & Edinburgh: Longman, Hurst, Rees, Orme & Brown, 1815), 2 vols. Between 1636 and 1639 she wrote eight letters to her brother Herbert Aston in Madrid; she was trying to encourage his marriage to Catherine THIMELBY:* 'never creature was more fortunat then I in gaining afection from her. For I beleeve I am blest with the most perfectest and constant lover as ever women was blest with.' The letters tell of a strong female friendship and the final letter ends with a drawing of a female form around which the four last paragraphs of the letter are arranged, with the initials HA at the feet of the figure: a representation of her brother at the feet of Catherine. A later letter to her brother followed Catherine's death in 1658. *Tixall poetry*, ed. A. Clifford (London: Longman, Hurst, Rees, Orme & Brown, 1813), has a poem to Constance ASTON dating from *c.* 1630.

FOX, Margaret

Margaret FELL.*

FREEMAN, Ann-Mary, –1696

2. London, Huntingdon; 4. Quaker; 5(a) Joseph Freeman, (b) Richard Jobson (m. 1687); 6(a) mariner, (b) stapler.

A testimony in Anne WHITEHEAD,* *Piety . . .* (1686): she was educated and perhaps raised by WHITEHEAD, saying of her 'I honoured her as a Mother, and she was not only a blessing to me, but also to my Fathers

House.' She was present at WHITEHEAD's death. She moved to Huntingdon with her second husband.

FREKE, Elizabeth, 1641–1714

1. Freke; 2. Wiltshire, Cork, Norfolk; 3. genteel; 5. Percy Freke; 6. genteel.

Her family was Royalist during the Civil Wars. Her father, Raufe Freke, a Fellow of All Souls (Oxford University), educated all four of his daughters himself. Elizabeth's diary was edited by M. Carbery as *Mrs Elizabeth Freke. Her diary, 1671 to 1714* (Cork: Grey & Co., 1913). It includes an account of her son's birth after five days of agonising labour. Houlbrooke (p. 247) says that Carbery conflates the two manuscript versions of the diary ('Some few remembrances of my misfortuns {which} have attended me In my unhappy life since I were married.' – BL, Add. MSS 45718, 45719). Houlbrooke has extracts.

FRITH, Mary

See Appendix III.

FRYET, Elizabeth, –1684

2. Coggeshall (Essex); 4. Quaker; 5. John Fryet.

Testimony for William Allen in *The last words . . . of William Allen* (1680).

FURLY, Anna jun., 1649–

2. Colchester; 4. Quaker; 5(a) Peter Langley (m. 1673), (b) Thomas Gooch (m. 1709); 6(a) merchant.

Wrote a postscript to her father's *A testimony* . . . (2nd ed. 1670; see below). Moved to London at her first marriage.

FURLY, Anna sen., 1624–1715

2. Colchester; 4. Quaker; 5. John Furly; 6. merchant.

Anna Furly bore six children between 1644 and 1659. The Furlys were major Quaker figures in Colchester. She wrote a postscript to John Furly's *A testimony to the true light*, with Stephen Crisp and Anna FURLY jun.* (2nd edition 1670) and *The testimony of Anna Furly the elder, concerning our deceased friend William Allen* (1680).

FYGE, Sarah

Sarah Fyge EGERTON*

G

GAGE, Catherine, *fl.* 1680s
2. Tixall (Staffs.); 3. genteel; 5. 3rd Lord Aston; 6. genteel.

Youngest daughter of Sir Thomas Gage; her husband's first wife died in 1674 and he was in prison until 1684. She bore no children; is the possible author of some verses reprinted in *Tixall poetry,* ed. A. Clifford (London: Longman, Hurst, Rees, Orme & Brown, 1813).

GAINSBOROUGH, Katherine Noel, Countess of, after 1665–1704
1. Greville; 2. Warwickshire, Rutland; 3. genteel; 5(a) Wriothesley Baptist Noel, 2nd Earl of Gainsborough (m. 1687), (b) John Sheffield, Duke of Buckingham (m. 1699).

The eldest daughter of Fulke Greville, 5th Baron Brooke, of Beauchamps Court, Warwickshire, she bore two daughters in her first marriage and was the second wife of John Sheffield. Her text, *The respondent's case* (1693), deals with a family property dispute. The appellants were the 3rd Earl of Gainsborough and John Noel. The dispute concerns the succession of part of the estate left by the 2nd Earl, and the document, like similar 'cases' and petitions, seems to be a lawyer's text commissioned by rather than the direct work of a woman.

GARDNER, Anne, –1714
2. Kendal (Westmorland); 4. Quaker; 5(a) Richard Braythwaite, (b) Thomas Gardner (m. 1682).

Mother of Elizabeth BRAYTHWAITE,* her first husband died in 1679. She had at least one other daughter (who married in 1692). She bore twins in 1683. She died a widow. Wrote a testimony in T.C., *A brief relation* (1684).

GARGILL, Anne, ?1634–
2. Plymouth, London; 4. Catholic, Quaker, later accused of being a Ranter.

She left Plymouth in 1655 to preach in Portugal, was examined by the Inquisition and founded a congregation in Spain. The same year she was one of the first group of Quakers in Amsterdam (see Elizabeth HENDRICKS*); in Holland in 1657 she is reported to have 'laid hands on William Ames' (the translator of a text by Margaret FELL*) and to have worked to disrupt religious meetings, to 'labour utterly to destroy and to scatter'. She wrote *A brief discovery of that which is called the popish religion, with a word to the Inquisition discovering their seat of injustice and cruelty, and also a word to them who are in bondage under this deceit that upholdeth the Beast's worship* (1656) and *A warning to all the world* (1656).

GATES, Elizabeth, –1720

1. Scutcher; 2. Alton (Hants); 4. Quaker; 5. Nicholas Gates (m. 1657); 6. clothier.

She bore eleven children between 1658 and 1680 (the last one dying in infancy).

'A testimony concerning my dear husband' in *A tender invitation to all, to embrace the secret visitation of the Lord to the souls*, by Nicholas Gates (1708).

GAUNT, Elizabeth, –1685

2. London; 3. shopkeeper; 4. Anabaptist; 5. William Gaunt; 6. yeoman.

She helped John Burton, a victim of the Rye House Plot, escape to Holland. He returned with Monmouth and got a pardon after Sedgemoor by informing on her (despite the fact that she was sheltering him). She was tried for treason and when asked how she pleaded replied 'I desire to have more time to consider of it.' Henry Cornish, co-defendant, made a similar point, suggestive of a rushed trial. *The true account of the behaviour and manner of the execution of six persons* pictures her penitent in Newgate. Elizabeth Gaunt was burnt: the last woman to be executed in Britain for an explicitly political offence.

Mrs E. Gaunt's last speech, who was burnt at London, Oct. 23, 1685, as it was written by her own hand . . . (Amsterdam, 1685; in English and Dutch).

K. W. Wadsworth, 'Elizabeth Gaunt: A tercentenary', *Journal of the United Reformed Church History Society* (1968), pp. 316–20.

The gentlewoman's cabinet unlocked

See Appendix I.

The gentlewoman's delight in cookery

See Appendix I.

GETHIN, Lady Grace, 1676–97
1. Norton; 2. Somerset, Ireland; 3. genteel; 6. Sir Richard Gethin; 6. genteel.

Frances NORTON*

Misery's virtues whetstone Reliquiae Gethinanae: or, some remains of the most ingenious and excellent lady. . . (1699, 1700, 1703) is a collection of essays which were widely admired. They are, however, plagiarisms and Gethin's status as author is therefore somewhat ambiguous. Her monument is in Westminster Abbey.

GIBSON, Elizabeth, –1723
2. Bury St Edmunds; 4. Quaker; 5. ?Thomas Gibson; 6. tailor.

Testimony (1680) in *The life of Christ magnified in . . . Giles Barnardiston* (1681). Signed general testimony for Anne WHITEHEAD* in *Piety* . . . (1686).

GIFFARD, Lady Martha, 1638–1722
1. Temple; 2. Dublin, London, Moor Park (Surrey); 4. Anglican; 5. Sir Thomas Giffard; 6. genteel.

Author of *Early essays and romances. With the life and character of Sir William Temple by his sister Lady Giffard* (edited by G. C. Moore Smith, Oxford: Oxford University Press, 1930). Julia Longe (*Martha Lady Giffard. Her Life and Correspondence*, London: George Allen & Sons, 1911) says that the 'character' was published as a pamphlet in 1720 to rebut Burnet's aspersions on Temple's religious principles. Her husband died within a month of their marriage in 1701.

GILMAN, Anne, –1686
2. ?Reading; 4. Quaker; 5. ?Thomas Gilman.

She is author of *An epistle to Friends: being a tender salutation to the faithful in God everywhere. Also a letter to Charles, King of England* . . . (1662) and of *To the inhabitants of the earth* . . . (1663). The latter includes the remark 'a Love sprang up in me to the precious Seed of God, which lies hid in your earthen vessels, and in the Love was I constrained to lay pen to paper, only to shew you, how way may be made for the deliverance of this Seed.'

Also 'Wo, wo unto all you who are found eating and drinking, and rising up to play! and this is the reason that Play-houses and Bear-baitings are appointed, where you daily meet together on heaps to fulfil the lusts of the flesh.'

GODOLPHIN, Margaret

Margaret BLAGGE*

GOODENOUGH, Mary, c. 1652–92

2. Bradwell (Oxon.); 4. nonconformist.

Described as a widow living in great poverty with a daughter, 11, and son, 7. Seduced by a neighbouring baker who had provided her with foodstuffs, she became pregnant and then killed the child (the baker was married). She was arrested about ten days after delivery and imprisoned in Oxford castle. Within two months she was executed, on 7 March 1692. 'Her character amongst her neighbours was a quiet, honest, civil, harmless, poor woman; yea, religious too, before this fact.' In religion she had been a follower of Samuel Birch, nonconformist minister of Bampton, Oxfordshire; she recommends Joseph Allein's *Sure guide to heaven* to her children, telling them to 'take upon you your parts of that Baptismal Covenant which you are brought under.' This letter to her children is the customary moral/spiritual part of these murder narratives (see Elizabeth CALDWELL*). She apparently wanted to write a letter to the man who seduced her, but 'want of time prevented a letter to him' (which perhaps signifies the ideological shape of such a text).

Fair warning to murderers of infants: being an account of the tryal, codemnation and execution of Mary Goodenough at the assizes held in Oxon, in February 1691/2 together with the advice sent by her to her children, in a letter sign'd by her own hand the night before she was executed; with some reflections added upon the whole: (1692).

GOTHERSON, Dorothea, 1611–80

1. Scott; 2. Egerton (Kent); 3. landowner; 4. Protestant, Quaker; 5(a) Daniel Gotherson, (b) Joseph Hogben; 6(a) major in Cromwell's army.

She was raised as a Protestant and aligned herself with the Royalists for 10 years. She went to court to congratulate Charles II on his restoration and visited Long Island (*c.* 1680) over some complex land-dealings, in which she was being cheated and about which she petitioned the king. She told the governor of Long Island: 'that if she could make any money by the sale of her land in Kent . . . she would herself go over to New Yorke and carry an hundred and twenty families with her.'

To all that are unregenerated: a call to repentance from dead works to newness of life, by turning to the light in the conscience, which will give the knowledge of God in the face of Jesus Christ (1661; partly in verse). This is very much a 'pocket-book', advertising itself as a more genteel object than a broad-side. Its dedicatory epistle to Charles II says 'let not the King think it below him to read that which many think above me to write, in respect of my sex.'

GOULD/GOLD, Ann, ?1609–99
2. London; 4. Quaker.

Ann Gould was one of the first Quaker ministers in London (*c.* 1655). She was with Julia WESTWOOD in Northern Ireland in 1655, but, with Joanna BROWNE, was banished by Henry Cromwell. Her *An epistle to all Christian magistrates and powers in the whole Christendom, and professors and teachers, and Christians that witness the end of the law . . .* (1659) was also signed by Humphrey Bache, Daniel Baker, George Fox, Robert Hasle, and Mary WEBB*.

GRAY, Alexia (baptised Margaret), 1606–40
2. Ghent; 3. nun; 4. Catholic.

She professed at the Abbey of Immaculate Conception of the Blessed Virgin Mary, Ghent, in 1631 (having possibly left England in 1624). Her translation of *The rule of the most blessed father Saint Benedict, patriarch of all munkes* (Ghent, 1632) is dedicated to Lady Eugenia POULTON, abbess of the English monastery of St Benedict in Ghent.

GREENWAY, Francis (baptised Catherine), –1642
2. Nieuport (Belgium); 3. nun; 4. Catholic.

She may have professed in Brussels in 1622; she became abbess of the English cloister of St Francis, Nieuport, in 1637, resigning in 1639.

Translated F. Palaudanus, *A short relation of the life, virtues, and miracles of S. Elizabeth, called the Peacemaker, queen of Portugall, of the third rule of S. Francis* (Brussels, 1628; from Dutch). Information partly from Gillow.

GREENWAY, Margaret, *fl.* 1657
2. ?Berkshire; 4. Quaker; 5. ?Richard Greenway.

Parish registers for Berkshire indicate a Margaret married to a Richard

Greenway and the baptism of their child in 1654; births and marriages of Greenways are recorded by the Reading Quaker meeting, although these may all be associated with William and Anne. (A Quaker, Richard Greenway, was imprisoned for speaking in Farringdon, Berkshire, *c.* 1660.) The title of *A lamentation against the professing priest and people of Oxford and to all in the cages of unclean birds called colleges* (1657) employs a favourite Quaker image for describing academic institutions (and Oxford would be a relevant town to curse if you lived in Berkshire).

GREENWOOD, Teresa
4. Catholic.

Gillow found only a single reference to this author: in his *Portraits of the Tudor dynasty*, vol. 4, Burke apparently refers to Greenwood's *Female prisoners' sufferings for conscience-sake during Elizabeth's reign* (a black-letter text 'long out of print'). Neither Gillow nor anyone else (it seems) has been able to identify her or her text.

GREG, 'Mother', *fl.* 1682
The burgess ticket of Buckhaven . . . (Edinburgh 1682, 1689, 1695).

The National Library of Scotland has copies of the three editions mentioned above, together with two undated editions (variants of 1682). The full title of 1682 suggests a spoof: *The burgess ticket of Buckhaven, given to Alexander Bryson: within the colledge thereof, upon the 32 day of Julius Caesar, 1698 years. Suites call'd and the court lawfully fenced.* The text (full of extraordinary lists and strange inventions) supports this suggestion, and the ascription to a woman may be part of the spoof, but not necessarily.

GRETTON, Elizabeth, *fl.* 1676
2. Barbados; 4. Quaker.

A letter from Barbados (1676) in Alice CURWEN's* *A relation . . .* (1680).

GRIDLE, Mary, *fl.* 1681
2. ?Suffolk; 4. Quaker.

Testimony in *The life of Christ magnified in . . . Giles Barnardiston* (1681).

GRIFFIN, Elizabeth, *fl.* 1677
2. Barbados; 4. Quaker.

A letter to Thomas and Alice CURWEN,* from Barbados (1677), in Alice

CURWEN's *A relation* . . . (1680). There were a number of Griffins in New England and the West Indies and it is often difficult in general to trace movements in the region (for instance, an Elizabeth Griffin, daughter of John and Susanna, was born in Boston in 1656; an Elizabeth Ping married Nathaniel Griffin in 1671 in Andover, Massachusetts).

GRYMESTON, Elizabeth, before 1563–*c.* 1603

1. Bernye; 2. Norfolk; 4. Catholic; 5. Christopher Grymeston; 6. scholar and lawyer.

Elizabeth Grymeston was fined as a recusant in 1592/3. Her *Miscellanea. Meditations. Memoratives* (1604; several editions) is a counselling tract for her son, partly in verse. She was a chronic invalid.

See Hughey and Hereford, *The Library*, 4th series, vol. xv (1934).

GWIN, Anne, 1692–1715

2. Falmouth (Cornwall); 4. Quaker.

Apparently she could read at the age of 3½, learnt French and some Latin. She visited London with her father in 1712 and looked after the household while her parents went to Plymouth (she wrote them a letter about the ill health of her sister Grace). She died of an illness affecting her stomach: six months before her death she could eat only with great pain. 'Here follow some of those Scriptures which she transcribed for Matter of Meditation' contains 'some sayings of the Fathers in Relation to Maidenly Behaviour'; some transcriptions are from Plato, Socrates and Cowley, some written before she was 15. They are printed in *A memorial of Anne Gwin* (1715).

H

HACON, Catherine, *fl.* 1690

A letter to Gertrude ASTON* on the death of Winefrid THIMELBY* (1690) is reprinted in *The Tixall letters: or the correspondence of the Aston family and their friends during the seventeenth century*, ed. A. Clifford (London & Edinburgh: Longman, Hurst, Rees, Orme & Brown, 1815), 2 vols.

HALKET, Lady Anne, 1623–99

1. Murray; 2. London, Scotland; 3. genteel; 5. Sir James Halket; 6. genteel.

Anne Halket claims that both her parents were Provosts of Eton. With her lover, James Bampfyld, she rescued James, Duke of York, from Parliamentary captivity in 1648. She nursed the sick and wounded after the battle of Dunbar and – in addition to some 20 volumes in manuscript – wrote:

The autobiography of Anne, Lady Halket (Edinburgh, 1701; and there is a modern edition edited by J. Loftis: Ann FANSHAWE*). *Meditations on the twentieth and fifth psalm* (Edinburgh, 1701). *Meditations and prayers upon the first week . . .* (Edinburgh, 1701). *Meditations upon the seven gifts of the Holy Spirit* (1702). *Meditations upon Jobeshi's request* (1702).

HALL, Anne, *fl.* 1648–9

1. Wells; 2. Stoke by Nayland, Whatfield (both Suffolk); 4. Anabaptist; 5. Matthew Hall; 6. tailor.

A brief representation and discovery of the notorious falshood and dissimulation contained in a book styled The Gospel Way: being the substance of the informations, and free confessions of Anne the wife of the above-named Matthew Hall . . . (1649).

She is described as Anabaptist and the purpose of the whole text is to attack a visionary and sectarian religion. It says that Anne's parents were very 'mean' and that, 'being indisposed to labour', she attended the

Ministry of the Word, pretending 'great trouble of conscience for some years together, that she might be pitied and relieved by others'. Matthew Hall and Nicholas Ware (shoemaker) think she is possessed and exorcise her, publishing *The Gospel way* as an account of the cure. Ware marries Anne to Hall. Later, he claims that a vision says Anne will have a child in three months who will speak with tongues, but only if he has 'carnal knowledge of her'. Ware gets into bed with the Halls and Matthew thrusts 'her several times towards him, and bad her be willing'. All three go to Holland ('which they tearmed the wilderness'). When back in England (January, 1649) Anne declares everything in *The Gospel way* to be false and is rejected by husband and church. She returns to Stoke, but the inhabitants take her to a JP 'as one likely to become presently chargeable to the Town (being, as she confessed, with child)'. She gives to the JP all the information given in the text.

HAMBLY, Loveday, 1604–82

1. Billing; 2. Cornwall; 4. Quaker; 5. William Hambly; 6. farmer, genteel.

Loveday Hambly was imprisoned in Bodmin in 1658 for non-payment of tithes of geese and swine; suffered distraint of goods in 1670–1 for non-payment of tithes on several occasions. The first general meeting of local Quakers was held in her house in 1663.

A relation of the last words and departure of that ancient and memorable woman Loveday Hambly, of Trigangeeves, in the parish of Austell . . . With further testimonies concerning her life and conversation (1683). How far this is by her is not clear.

See L. Hodgkin, *A Quaker Saint of Cornwall* (London: Longman, 1927).

HAMILTON, Elizabeth, Duchess of, *c.* 1616–59

1. Maxwell; 2. Guildford, London, ?Scotland, ?The Hague; 3. genteel; 5(a) William, 2nd Duke of Hamilton, (b) Thomas Dalmahoy; 6(a) genteel, (b) MP.

She was the daughter of James Maxwell, Earl of Dirleton, and married Hamilton in 1639. She petitions for herself and four daughters against the sequestration of her husband's lands as punishment for his military support of the king (he died of wounds received at Worcester in 1651).

To the Parliament of the Common-wealth of England, the humble petition of Elizabeth dutchesse (dowager) of Hamilton and her four orphan children (1651).

HAMILTON, Margaret, Lady Dowager of Belhaven, *fl.* 1672–95

1. Hamilton; 2. Scotland; 3. genteel; 4. Protestant; 5. Sir John Hamilton (m. 1674); 6. genteel.

Unto his grace, his majesty's high commissioner, and the right honourable, the estates of Parliament (1695). This is a petition about property and inheritance, dating back to Sir Robert Hamilton of Pressnennan's purchase of the Belhaven estate in *c.* 1672. Margaret Hamilton's grandfather was Sir John Hamilton, Lord Belhaven. It was through her that his title came to her husband John when her grandfather died in 1679 (her grandfather had already agreed to this in 1675, forced by his debts). Soon after 1680 Margaret Hamilton bequeathed 12,000 marks to Elizabeth Hamilton (described as Lord Belhaven's daughter), reserving the right to dispose of it as she (Margaret) wished. After her marriage to the Viscount of Kingston, Elizabeth made over her right to the money; there followed a legal dispute between her party and Margaret Hamilton. The situation was complicated by a string of debts and bonds. Hamilton accused her opponents, in particular the laird of Garletoun, of being Catholics. She petitions to be able to summon them to a legal hearing.

HANLEY, Anne, *fl.* 1652–3
2. Dublin; 4. Baptist.

Her 'experiences' are in Rogers, *Ohel . . .* (1653) (see Mary BARKER* for details).

HARCOURT, Lady Anne, after 1602–
1. Paget; 2. Middlesex, Stanton Harcourt (Oxon.); 3. genteel; 5(a) Sir Simon Harcourt, (b) Sir William Waller; 6(a) Royalist commander, (b) Parliamentary general.

Daughter of William, Lord Paget, of West Drayton, her mother was Lettice KNOLLYS. Her parents married before 1602. She had two sons by her first marriage, a daughter by her second. Her first husband was governor of Dublin castle in 1643. Her father, brother and first husband were Royalists, her second husband a Parliamentarian. Extracts from her journal for 1649–81 are in *Harcourt Papers*, ed. E. Harcourt, vol. 1 (1880), p. 169 f. They are mainly religious, but include reflections on domestic and national affairs.

HARDING, Prudence, –1673
2. Nottingham; 4. Quaker.

She died unmarried. With Elizabeth NEWTON* she wrote *A real demonstration . . .* (1663; see NEWTON for details).

HARINGTON, Lucy, 1581–1627
3. genteel; 5. Edward Russell, Earl of Bedford; 6. genteel.

A poet and patron. Partnow (p. 133) quotes from Ann Stanford, *Women Poets in English* (Columbia: Columbia University Press, 1972). She was friend and patron of John Donne.

HARLEY, Lady Brilliana, 1600–43
1. Conway; 2. Netherlands, Herefordshire; 3. genteel; 4. puritan; 5. Sir Robert Harley; 6. genteel, MP.

Dutch by birth, she became a naturalised English person. She supported Parliament in the Civil War and was famously besieged at Brampton Bryan in July and August of 1643. She knew French and Latin. *The Letters of Lady Brilliana Harley* (ed. T. T. Lewis, Camden Society, 1854) consists of some 200 letters for the period 1625–43.

HARRIS, Mary, –1668
2. London; 4. Quaker.

A declaration of the bountifull loving-kindness of the Lord manifested to his hand-maid Mary Harris, who stood idle in the market-place, till the eleventh hour, yet then received her penny (1669, 1693) contains quotations from her. It was probably written by Mary FOSTER/FORSTER,* who signed the postscript. Mary Harris died at an early age.

HASTINGS, Lucy, –1679
1. Davies; 2. Englefield (Berks.), Ashby (Leics.); 3. genteel; 5. Ferdinando Hastings, 6th Earl of Huntingdon (m. 1623).

Lucy was daughter of Sir John and Eleanor DAVIES.* Her husband, although a commander in the Commonwealth armies, entertained the king at Ashby before and after the battle of Naseby. She bore ten children, of whom at least one died young, three of the sons being born 1630, 1632, and 1638. Greer cites a manuscript poem on the flyleaf of the Huntington Library copy of *Lachrymae Musarum* (1650) but has doubts about the ascription (Greer, pp. 9–10); the volume of poems commemorated her eldest son, Henry, who died in 1649. *The new proclamation, in answer to a letter* (1649) is usually attributed to her mother's authorship, but is in fact a defence of Lady Eleanor. (Information partly derived from Hobby manuscript notes.)

HAT, Martha, *fl.* 1641–60

1. ?Arundell; 2. Ireland; 3. ?genteel; 4. Protestant; 5. Simon Hat; 6. cavalry officer.

To the right honourable the Lords assembled in Parliament. The humble petition, and appeale of Martha Hat, alias Arundell, the oppressed widow of Cornet Simon Hat deceased. (1660)

Her husband served in the king's army in Ireland and died from wounds contracted fighting rebels between October 1641 and August 1643. They both lost their estate (valued at £4,000) to the rebels in 1641. According to Act of Parliament only those in the army who had fought in Ireland since 1649 were entitled to forfeited rebel lands. (This is presumably a reference to the Act of 1652, which ended about 10 years of insurrection: it required that any Irish proprietors who could not prove loyalty to the Commonwealth of England had to forfeit their estates. In turn members of the Cromwellian army from England were rewarded by the allocation of lands from the forfeited estates. At the Restoration in 1660 Charles II promised to respect the 1652 Act.) She claims forfeited lands as her due in payment for her husband's military service and for the provisions and money she supplied to the army in Connaught. Having attempted to sue 'known rebels' who robbed her in 1641 and again in 1646, she now claimed damages against various gentlemen and officers who obstructed the courts and prevented her obtaining justice.

We have not been able to trace her second petition *To the right honourable the Commons* (1660).

HATT, Hannah

Hannah ALLEN*

HATTON, Alice E., after 1675–

2. Kirby (Northants.); 3. genteel.

Daughter of Christopher and Frances HATTON* (see below). Roberts (p. 82, n. 54) refers to the *Hatton Correspondence*, ed. E. M. Thompson, Camden Society, n.s. 23, 1878, vol. 2, p. 245: author of a letter dating from 1700 about theatre visits (the volume contains other letters by women).

HATTON, Lady Elizabeth, 1578–1646

3. genteel; 5(a) Sir William Hatton, (b) Sir Edward Coke; 6(a) genteel, lawyer, (b) genteel.

Elizabeth Hatton inherited Corfe Castle and Hatton House from her first husband. She disliked her second husband and opposed her daughter's marriage to the mad John Villiers in 1617. Coke supported the match and Villiers stood to gain financially from it. Elizabeth took Frances from home and tried to fix a match for her with Lord Oxford. Coke dragged Frances from her mother; she got a council warrant to reclaim her daughter; Coke summoned her for kidnapping. James I encouraged a compromise and Frances returned to Hatton House, but mother and daughter continued to resist the marriage. Elizabeth was finally put under house arrest in London and Frances was 'tied to the Bedposts and whipped . . . till she consented to the Match'. Elizabeth finally separated from Coke.

A true copy of a letter from . . . (1642).

Pollock (pp. 27, 64, 81) quotes from letters by Elizabeth Hatton, giving as sources the Finch Hatton papers (Northamptonshire Record Office, MSS FH); the Hatton Finch papers (BL, Add. MSS 29550 onwards) and the family correspondence of the Hattons (Camden Society, n.s. 23, vol. II, 1878).

See L. Norsworthy, *The Lady of Bleeding Heart Yard* (London: John Murray, 1935): Norsworthy includes (Appendix II) 'the proceedinges between the Lady Eliza: Hatton and Sir Edw. Coke' (1634; a statement by her).

HATTON, Frances, –1684
1. Yelverton; 2. Norfolk, Kirby (Northants.); 3. genteel; 5. Christopher Hatton (m. 1675); 6. soldier.

Daughter of Sir Henry Yelverton of Norfolk and Susan, Baroness Grey of Ruthin, she was the second wife of Christopher Hatton. He was for a period Governor of Guernsey (where his first wife died in an explosion). Pollock (pp. 24, 56, 64, 73) quotes from letters by her to her husband: for sources, see Elizabeth HATTON.*

HATTON, Mary, after 1630–
2. Kirby (Northants.); 3. genteel.

Her mother (Elizabeth MONTAGU) died in the explosion at Cornet Castle, Guernsey (see above). Pollock (pp. 43–4) quotes from a letter by her to her brother Christopher (born 1632): for sources, see Elizabeth HATTON.*

HAWKINS, Deborah, 1665–1750
1. Gates; 2. Alton (Hants.); 4. Quaker; 5. James Hawkins (m. 1695); 6. worsted comber.

Daughter of Nicholas and Elizabeth GATES,* she bore six children between 1696 and 1705 (one of whom died in infancy). Wrote *A testimony concerning my dear father* and *Several of the sayings of my dear father* (1708).

HAWLEY, Susan (Mother Mary of the Conception), 1622–1706
2. New Brentford (Middx.), Liege; 3. nun, genteel; 4. Catholic.

She went at 19 to the Low Countries and became a novice at Tongres, moving to Liege in 1642. She led the community there from 1650, becoming (1652) the first prioress of the English Canonesses Regular of the Holy Sepulchre, abdicating in 1697.

In 1652 she circulated *A brief relation of the order and institute of the English religious women at Liege*, which advertised for ladies who wanted to join the convent and for girls who wanted to be educated.

HAY, Lucy, Countess of Carlisle, 1599–1660
1. Percy; 2. London, Petworth; 5. James Hay, Earl of Carlisle (m. 1617); 6. genteel.

She was daughter of Henry Percy, Earl of Northumberland and granddaughter of Elizabeth's favourite, the Earl of Essex. Her father opposed her marriage (not wanting her to dance 'Scottish jigs'); her husband was a favourite of Charles I. Partnow (p. 141) quotes from *Thoughts* (n.d.). She died of apoplexy.

HAYDOCK, Eleanor, –1723
1. Lowe; 2. Warrington, Penketh (Cheshire); 4. Quaker; 5. Roger Haydock (m. 1682); 6. yeoman.

She originated from Crewood Hall, Cheshire. In 1681 she visited Krisheim (Germany) and in the same year was bargaining for the sale of James Harrison's house in the event of his following Penn to New England. She was resident in Warrington in 1683 and died at Penketh. She bore five children between 1683 and 1691. Wrote *A testimony concerning her husband, Roger Haydock* (1700), which was inserted in the *Account of his death and burial*.

HAYDOCK, Eleanor, –1739
1. Shaw; 2. Penketh, Liverpool; 4. Quaker; 5. Robert Haydock (m. 1692); 6. merchant.

Born in Warrington, she seems not to be directly related to the above

Eleanor Haydock, although she comes from the same area and both husbands were of Coppull, Lancs. She bore two sons, 1701 and 1703. Wrote *A visitation of love, in the good-will of God; to the professors of the holy truth containing, lamentation over, and warning to backsliders and unfaithful* (1712; printed for the assigns of Jane SOWLE*), written from Liverpool, 1710: 'the praise shall be to her that doth well, 'tis she that delivereth girdles to the merchant, because she hath wrought willingly with her fingers, for she still riseth while it is yet dark, (to know yet more of the mind of her Lord) thus she giveth meat to her household, (to maintain life) then she giveth an early portion to her maidens.'

HAYES, Alice, 1657–1720
2. Rickmansworth (Herts.), London; 4. Quaker; 5(a) Daniel Smith, (b) — Hayes.

In 1675 she was employed as a servant; became convinced in 1680, which led to religious disagreements with her husband. She went to a church to clear the reputation of local Quakers and later was imprisoned for 13 weeks in St Albans. She bore five children by her first husband. In 1712 she moved to Tottenham and married again, but died a widow. Wrote *A legacy, or widow's mite left by A. H. to her children and others. With an account of some of her dying sayings* (1723; republished five times).

HAYNES, Elizabeth, *fl.* 1686–92
2. London; 4. Quaker; 5. ?Richard Haynes.

A daughter and son died young in 1689, another son (soon after birth) in 1692. Wrote a testimony in Anne WHITEHEAD,* *Piety* . . . (1686). (We may be confusing two Elizabeth Haynes; it was probably Elizabeth Haynes senior who wrote the testimony.)

HAYWARD, Amey, *fl.* 1699
2. Linnington.

She is said to be (in her book) from Linnington, but this seems not to exist in Britain. It may be a misprint for Limington. An Amy Hayward married William Pickford in 1730, at Wedmore, some 15 miles north of Limington, Somerset, but unless this was a second marriage, the dates do not seem very likely.

The females legacy, containing divine poems on several choice subjects (1699). This includes 'A word by way of caution to the female-sex': 'Ye female-sex, do you believe/When first the world began,/That God immortal souls did give/To you, as well as Man?'. From 'The author on her weak poems': 'do not blame her over much,/Because that she is one of such/ Which is the weaker sex,/And wanteth skill thee to correct'.

HAYWARD, Sarah, *c.* 1620–
2. Colchester; 4. Quaker (backslider).

A Sarah Hayward was christened in 1619, and another (with different parents) in 1620, both in Colchester. Author of a pamphlet attacking John Furly (Quaker) and others. This was answered by Furly in *The substance of a letter sent to the magistrates of Colchester or, A hue and cry . . .* (1666). The pamphlet says that Hayward should be detained by the magistrates until she reveals her real address. It says that 'she hath been much talked of throughout the nation, of many pranks and deceiving tricks acted by her in corners and by-places among simple people', and describes her as having 'a pretty full eye and very confident, impudent and subtile'. It also lists names she allegedly used (including COLE,* TRAVERS,* WHITEHEAD*) and places she claimed to have come from.

HAYWOOD, Eliza, ?1693–1756
1. Fowler; 2. London, Dublin; 3. actor, writer; 5. Valentine Haywood; 6. cleric.

She left her husband in 1721 and worked as a journalist, novelist, actor and playwright to support her children. See *DNB* for accusations of immorality that were made against her (as they were against BEHN* and MANLEY*). Most of her work (some 67 items) was written after 1720, but:
Love in excess, parts 1, 2 (1719; four editions by 1724; fiction). *Love in excess*, part 3 (1720; fiction). *The fair captive* (1720/1; play, performed at Lincoln's Inn Fields). Translation of Bursault, *Ten letters from a young lady of quality* (1720).

HAZZARD, Dorothy, –1674
2. Bristol; 3. grocer; 4. Independent, Baptist; 5(a) Anthony Kelly, (b) Matthew Hazzard (m. 1640); 6 (b) priest.

Dorothy and her first husband were members of a separatist group, and, despite her second husband's profession, she withdrew (in 1640) from common prayer. Her house was used by families en route for New England, and as a place in which women could give birth in order to avoid churching ceremonies in their own parishes. She was prominent in the defence of Bristol against Prince Rupert, holding the Frome gate, with some 200 women and girls, against the Royalists. She tells how the women and children were prepared to offer their bodies to 'dead' the bullets. An eyewitness of the siege speaks of Matthew Hazzard being 'violently egged on by his wife, whose Disciple the silly man is'. Her reported view on the execution of Royalist plotters was that 'it is a pity but that their children's brains should be dashed out against the stones, that no more of their race might remain on the face of the earth.' Dorothy Hazzard made a deposition against Nathaniel Fiennes's 'cowardly' surrender of Bristol, which (with other depositions) was published in the account of his trial in 1644: see Joan BATTEN* for title. There is a copy of this in the Bristol City Library. Information from *The records of a church of Christ in Bristol, 1640–1687,* ed. R. Hayden, Bristol: Bristol Record Soc., vol. 27 (1974).

HEARNE, Mary, *fl.* 1718–19
3. novelist.

The lover's week (1718) was dedicated to Delarivier MANLEY;* *The female deserters* (1719) was reprinted in 1720 as *Honour the victory; and Love the prize.* We have found no references to her in any of the standard histories of the novel. Spencer (p. 61) says that both of her epistolary novels end 'most unconventionally, with their heroines not only seduced but delighted to be so'. (She is listed in Dale Spender, *Mothers of the novel,* London: Pandora, 1986, p. 126.)

HEMSLEY/HELMSLEY, Grace

Grace BARWICK*

HENDRICKS, Elizabeth, *fl.* 1655–78
1. Cox; 2. Amsterdam; 3. preacher; 4. Quaker; 5. Pieter Hendricks; 6. buttonmaker.

She was among the first four Quakers to arrive in Amsterdam from England in 1655: the others were Hester BIDDLE,* Anne GARGIL* and Jane WILKINSON. She was married before 1671. In 1676 and 1677 she visited Princess Elizabeth of Bohemia, the second time accompanied by Elizabeth KEITH and Isabel YEAMANS.* She travelled widely in Holland and in 1678 went on a preaching tour of the Rhine with Gertrud DERIKS; she caused uproar in Krefeld and Krisheim by attempting to convert the inhabitants. The Duke of Holstein censured her for preaching in public. She wrote numerous letters and pamphlets: *Een brief aen Vrienden* (1671), *An epistle to Friends in England* (1672). (One of her letters is reprinted in J. Z. Kannegieter, *Geschiedenis van de Vroegere Quakergemeenschap te Amsterdam,* Amsterdam: Scheltema & Holkema

NV, 1971.) She also corresponded with Penn. She may have died before 1684 (when Pieter Hendricks is recorded with a different wife).

HENRIETTA MARIA, 1609–69.

2. Paris, London; 3. royal consort; 4. Catholic; 5. Charles I of England; 6. king.

A number of her letters written on political subjects were printed between 1639 and 1648. Many are reprinted in modern collections: M. Green (ed.), *Letters of queen Henrietta Maria* (1857); Charles, comte de Baillon (ed.), *Lettres de Henriette-Marie, reine d'Angleterre* (Paris, 1877). *BLC* lists printings of her speeches.

See Q. Bone, *Henrietta Maria Queen of the Cavaliers* (London: Bodley Head, 1973).

HENSHAW, Anne, *fl.* 1618–55

2. London; 5. Benjamin Henshaw; 6. genteel, captain of the city of London.

Ten children of Anne and Benjamin are listed as having been christened between 1618 and 1632, all but one of these at St Lawrence Jewry (three dying young: she refers to seven children in 1654). Payments were made to her between 1638 and 1640 totalling £3,959. 13s. *To the Parliament of the Commonwealth . . . the humble petition of A. H. late wife . . . of B. Henshaw Esquire . . .* (1654) is a claim for repayment, on behalf of herself and her children, of debts owing to her late husband. She says that *c.* £8,000 (of a debt of £12,000) is still owing by the Earl of Carlisle. In 1655 she is told she will be paid £8,000 if she reveals the whereabouts of any concealed monies or land deeds. (The text, like many of these legal documents, may not be written by her; but it is clearly written at her direction if not dictation. There are many similar cases.)

HERBERT, Lady Anne

Anne CLIFFORD*

HERRING, Anne, *fl.* 1678

5. John Herring.

The case of Anne Herring, relict of John Herring, deceased, and of Anne, Elizabeth, Mary and Sarah their daughters (1678): the petition seeks Parliament's approval for the sale of John Herring's estate in order to pay off his debts.

HEUSDE, Sarah Cornelius de, *fl.* **1660–?70**
2. Tower Hill (London); 3. physician; 5. Dr Sasbout.

Her text, *Loving reader . . . secret arts* (?1670), is an advertisement of her services and cures as a physician. She says she is 'Widow of Dr Sasbout, and Grandmother of the Doctor that had his stage upon Great Tower-Hill, and did so many cures before the Fire.' She has learned her science from her father and husband, and explains that she was taught the cures because women's illnesses needed a woman doctor: women were generally too ashamed to 'discover them unto any physician'. She specialises, among other things, in 'suffocation or rising of the mother'; 'descending or hanging out of the mother'; women and maidens 'who cannot get their natural Flux'; dropsy, leprosy, piles, pain in making water, gout, venereal disease, cancer.

HEWSON, Anne, *fl. c.* **1630–54**
2. London, Dublin; 4. Baptist; 5. Colonel Hewson; 6. soldier.

Col. Hewson embarked for Ireland in 1649, stormed Drogheda and became governor of Dublin (he had also been one of Charles I's judges and signed his death warrant, but was pardoned at the Restoration). We know that Anne Hewson travelled with her husband to Ireland in June 1654, but presumably she had crossed with him earlier too, since both of them had joined Rogers's Baptist church in Dublin (which was celebrated in *Ohel . . .*, published in 1653: see Mary BARKER*). In her 'experiences' (in *Ohel . . .*) Anne Hewson implies that she was in London in the late 1620s–early 1630s, where she was in the congregation of Culverwell, rector at Friday Street from 1628; she was also 'comforted' by Samuel Bolton of Ludgate and Southwark. The Hewsons were said to have three 'Anabaptist' sons.

HEWYTT, Mary, *fl.* **1642–60**
1. Bertie; 2. Norfolk, Chester; 3. genteel; 5(a) Dr John Hewytt, (b) Sir Abraham Shipman, (c) — Lee; 6(a) cleric, (b) governor of Chester.

Lady Mary Bertie was the daughter of Robert, 1st Earl of Lindsey (died 1642). John Hewytt, who had been Charles I's chaplain, became (after Charles's death) chaplain to Mary's brother, the current Earl. Hewytt married his employer's sister. She was his second wife, and bore two daughters (who died young) and a son. John Hewytt was involved in Royalist plots for risings against the Commonwealth. He was arrested and tried (by John Lisle) in 1658. He refused to plead and was beheaded on 8 June 1658. At the time of his arrest she was roughly handled (while pregnant) and her jewels seized. She attempted to enlist the aid of Cromwell's daughter Elizabeth CLAYPOLE in obtaining her husband's release. Her text *To the honourable the knights, cittizens and burgesses of the Commons House now assembled in Parliament. The humble petition of Dame Mary Hewytt widow, late wife of John Hewytt, Doctor in Divinity* (1658) complains about the legality of the trial. She accuses 'Oliver late pretended Protector' of setting up a court which ignored a man's birthright (John Hewytt was condemned by Lisle without jury or witnesses to his alleged treason: she asks that Lisle be brought to justice). A petition was also presented to Charles II at Breda asking for herself and her son to be put under royal protection. She later obtained a place in the Exchequer for her son, and left a legacy of £200 to her grandson. Her third husband was of Newington Butts.

HIGGES, Susan

See Appendix III.

HINCKS, Elizabeth, *fl.* 1671

2. Cornwall; 4. Quaker.

Author of *The poor widow's mite, cast into the Lord's treasury wherein are contained some reasons in the justification of the meetings of . . . Quakers . . . Written by a woman of the south, who came from the ends of the earth to hear the wisdom of him that is greater than Solomon . . . Now lest it should be counted a libel, or any should think we dare not own it in the world, I have subscribed my name* (1671; verse).

HIT-HIM-HOME, Joan

See Appendix II.

HOBY, Elizabeth, Lady Russell, 1528–1609

1. Coke; 3. genteel; 5(a) Sir Thomas Hoby, (b) Lord John Russell; 6(a) diplomat, translator, (b) genteel.

She was, at the age of 78, actively involved in a Star Chamber case, and was one of Sir Anthony Coke's four learned daughters (the others being Mildred CECIL, Katherine KILLIGREW, Anne BACON*). She translated the tract *A way of reconciliation* from French (1605; about transubstantiation), composed Latin epitaphs, inscriptions in Greek, Latin and English for the tomb of her second husband, and was a letter writer (some of these letters being to Burleigh).

HOBY, Lady Margaret, 1571–1633
1. Dakins; 2. Yorkshire; 3. genteel; 4. puritan; 5(a) Walter Devereux, (b) Thomas Sidney, (c) Sir Posthumous Hoby; 6(a)/(b)/(c) genteel.

Brought up in the Puritan household of the third Earl of Huntingdon, she is claimed as the author of the earliest-known diary by a British woman: *Diary of Lady Margaret Hoby 1599–1605*, ed. D. M. Meads (London: Routledge, 1930). Extracts in Houlbrooke.

HOLDEN, Mary, *fl.* 1688–9
2. Suffolk; 3. midwife, astrologer, physician.

The womans almanack for . . . 1688. The womans almanack for . . . 1689.
   Mary Holden sold a toothache cure, mentioned in her almanacs, 'because I see such great cruelty in them that cure by plucking out of teeth, and braking of jaw-bones in young children, that they never have any teeth in their places'. In 1689 she was still advocating the astrology of Tycho Brahe.

HOLLAND, Sister Catherine, 1635–1720
2. Norfolk, Belgium, London; 3. genteel, nun; 4. Catholic convert in 1662.

Catherine Holland's father (Sir John Holland) was a Protestant parliamentarian; her mother (Lady Sands) a Catholic. He took his daughter from his wife and educated her himself. They all went to Bruges in 1651. Catherine told her father that she wanted to become Catholic (1653) but had to return to England in 1661. Here she kept up a pretence to her father while corresponding with a nun in Bruges. She fled from London and professed in Bruges in 1664.
   At her confessor's order she wrote a conversion narrative: *How I came to change my religion* (1664). The head-note says 'Sister Catherine Holland had a satyrical sharp wit, with a high spirit', and also refers to 'her genius for poetry'. It adds that 'she so well employed her pen as to perpetuate her pious memory in this community by several pious books and Saints' lives which she translated from French and Dutch into English'. She also wrote verse and spiritual dramas.
   See C. S. Durrant, *A Link between Flemish Mystics and English Martyrs* (London: Burns, Oates & Co, 1925; this contains biographical notes and Holland's narrative, p. 271 f.). Some details from Gillow.

HOLMES, Jane, –?1681
2. Yorkshire; 4. Quaker; 5. ?John Holmes.

She wrote *False prophets and false teachers described* (1652), with Thomas

Aldam, Mary FISHER,* Elizabeth HOOTON,* Benjamin Nicholson, William Pears – 'Prisoners of the Lord at York Castle'.

Jane Holmes was preaching in Malton (Yorkshire) in 1652. She was so impressive that 'some was caused to burne a great deal of silkes and braueries and such things'. She was imprisoned in York castle the same year and fell into a 'low spiritual condition'. She was still or again in prison in 1654 (with Mary FISHER). Letters about her say that the 'wilde nature was exalted in her, aboue the seede of God' and that 'the wilde Eyrie spirit was exalted aboue the Crosse'. (Quotations from E. Manners, *Elizabeth Hooton, first Quaker woman preacher*, London: Headley Bros., 1914; *JFHS*, supplement 12.)

HOOTON, Elizabeth, c. 1600–71/2

1. ?Carrier; 2. Mansfield, Derbyshire, York, Lincoln, Massachusetts, Barbados, Jamaica; 3. preacher; 4. Baptist, Quaker; 5. Oliver Hooton; 6. farmer.

Elizabeth Hooton belonged to a Mansfield separatist group and is the earliest-known Quaker woman preacher. She was frequently in gaol in Derby, York and Cambridge (where she was whipped) for disturbing congregations and reproving priests. In 1660 she was assaulted by a Nottinghamshire minister. In 1661 she visited New England with Joan BROOKSOP* and was in Boston again in 1665 with her daughter. She was mistreated and imprisoned: when she was thrown out into the snow by the Boston authorities she was taken in by native Americans, to whom she attributed her survival. In 1671 she sailed to Barbados, then Jamaica, with Fox and others.

False prophets and false teachers described (1652), with Thomas Aldam, Mary FISHER,* Jane HOLMES,* Benjamin Nicholson, William Pears. This condemns parish churches and compulsory tithes, and says that the holy men of scripture were not scholars, but ordinary working people. *To the King and both Houses of Parliament* (1670; perhaps with Thomas Taylor). Testimony in *A short relation concerning . . . William Simpson* (1671; with William Fortescue, Oliver Hooton, George Fox). Also petitionary letters to Cromwell and Charles II.

See E. Manners, *Elizabeth Hooton, first Quaker woman preacher* (London: Headley Bros., 1914; *JFHS*, supplement 12) which includes a bibliography of her writings, a checklist of allusions to her, and quotations from her writings.

HOPPER, Elizabeth, fl. 1665–?84

1. Mahum; 2. Durham; 4. Quaker; 5(a) William Hopper (m. 1665), (b) William Wheatley (m. ?1681/4).

Fined in 1673 for non-payment of tithes, she bore a daughter the same year. She and Bridget PINDER* were the 'neighbours' who accompanied Robert Jeckell when in his last illness he wanted to travel from Newcastle-upon-Tyne to see Swarthmore. Hopper and Pinder wrote the last part of *A lively testimony to the living truth, given forth by Robert Jeckell upon his deathbed in the presence of many eye and ear witnesses whose names are subscribed* (1676), signed by Isabel YEAMANS* and others.

HOPTON, Susanna, 1627–1709

1. Harvey; 2. Herefordshire; 3. genteel; 4. Anglican, Catholic, Anglican again; 5. Richard Hopton; 6. lawyer.

Susanna Hopton was a philanthropist, and author of *Daily devotions* (1673; several editions to 1700); *Devotions in the ancient way of offices* (1700); and *An hexameron* (1717). Hickes (*Controversial Letters* 2, 1700) has her letter to Father Turberville explaining why she is rejoining the Anglican church. Hickes also edited a collection of her hymns, etc., which praises Hopton, while concealing both her sex and her identity.

HOUSMAN, H—, –1735

2. Kidderminster.

Kept an apparently unpublished religious diary for 1711–32 (Matthews).

HOWARD, Anne, Countess of Arundel, 1558–1630

1. Dacre; 2. Sussex; 3. genteel; 4. Catholic; 5. Philip Howard, Earl of Arundel; 6. genteel.

The surviving stanzas of her poem on the death of her husband appear in E. Lodge, *Illustrations of British history, biography and manners* (1791). Howard also corresponded with Mary Stuart.

HOWARD, Lady Arabella, 1655–1746

1. Alleyn; 2. Essex, Hambleton (Yorks.); 3. genteel; 4. Protestant; 5(a) Francis Thompson, (b) Lord George Howard.

Daughter and only heiress of Sir Edmund Alleyn of Hatfield, her parents were both dead by 1657. She had one child by her first marriage (he became MP for Scarborough); her second husband was a son of Henry Duke of Norfolk. She sold her estates in 1716 but her will reverted them to the Alleyn family.

Wrote (or caused to be written) *The case of Arabella Lady Howard on the behalf of her Protestant relations* and *The case of Mrs Arabella Thompson, widow* (1680). These documents appeal for exemption from a bill that prevented papists from disinheriting Protestant heirs (there seem to have been rumours that she was linked with Catholics). She inherited her parents' estates at the age of two. William Thompson, of Yorkshire, took her from the care of Sir William Dalston and, when she was seven, sought to arrange a marriage with his son, Francis. After a period in a French nunnery, she was hidden in a cottage with William's Catholic sister and, at 12, bedded with Francis. The Thompsons gained some £20,000 from this 'marriage' and Arabella was mistreated by Francis because she would not settle her estate on the Thompsons: she wished to settle this on her son, William (born 1676). Protestant relations took William away, because of rumours that he was to be taken to France and raised as a Catholic. The documents show her desire to prevent the estate going to the Thompsons, which, she said, would deprive Protestants in her own family.

HOWARD, Catherine Mary, 1683–1753
2. Brussels; 3. genteel, nun; 4. Catholic.

She was daughter of Colonel Bernard Howard (brother to dukes of Norfolk) and entered Spellekene convent, Brussels (professed 1701). She wrote 'Prayers, devotions, and spiritual exercises' (MS n.d.).

HOWARD, Mary of the Holy Cross, 1653–1735
2. London, Rouen; 3. genteel, nun; 4. Catholic.

Daughter of Sir Robert Howard and Lady Elizabeth CECIL. She was frightened at the age of 18 by Charles II's notice of her at a play, and advised to go to France to escape his attentions. She went to Paris, travelling under the name of Talbot, with Lady OSBORNE, who placed her in the Benedictine convent of Val de Grace. Howard's desire to convert to Catholicism was fiercely opposed by Osborne. She tried to enter a convent of the strictest order, the Poor Clares, in Paris, but finally went to Rouen, taking the name of Parnel. She professed in 1675 and was elected abbess (against her wishes) in 1702. The whole story, with its false names and religious rigours, places Catholic discipline as a 'solution' to sexual threat and female alienation.

   Prayers and considerations upon each article of the holy rule of the Poor Clares (n.d.). 'Brief rules for the pilgrims who tend to the celestiall Jerusalem' (MS, n.d.). Also several other similar works, some after 1720. (Information from Gillow.)

HOWGILL, Dorothy, *fl.* 1660s

2. Greyrigg (Westmorland); 4. Quaker; 5. Francis Howgill.

The sister-in-law of Mary HOWGILL,* her husband died in 1668. She wrote several unpublished letters.

HOWGILL, Mary, 1623–before 1681

2. Over Kellet (Lancs.), Kendal (Westmorland); 4. Quaker.

See Critical Appendix 5.

Daughter of Richard Howgill, she was imprisoned in Kendal (1653) for abusing Thomas Shaw (rector of Aldingham). She was in London in 1654, indicted at Lancashire Assizes (1654/5) and imprisoned in Exeter in 1656. She went to Ireland in the 1650s, but was expelled. She was sister to Francis Howgill (see above).

A remarkable letter of Mary Howgill to Oliver Cromwell, called Protector, a copy whereof was delivered by herself to his own hands some months ago, with who she had face to face a large discourse thereupon. Unto which is annexed a paper of hers directed to the inhabitants of the town of Dover (1657). Also *The vision of the Lord of Hosts faithfully declared in his own times* (1662; this is a report of a vision seen at Colchester), and letters to Fox.

HULTON, Ann, 1668–97

1. Henry; 2. Chester; 4. nonconformist; 5. John Hulton; 6. tradesman.

Sixth and youngest child of Katharine and Philip Henry, and sister to Sarah SAVAGE* and Katharine TYLSTON.* Letters to her mother and sisters survive, and fragments of her diaries. Her parents had no part in her choice of husband, though they consented to the marriage, which took place on 26 April 1688. Ann went through at least seven pregnancies before dying in childbirth (of smallpox) at the age of 29; during her first pregnancy her sister-in-law and a close friend died in childbirth, and, although she was safely delivered of a child, the baby died. Her writing, like that of her sisters, contains much reflection on childbirth and motherhood. Taken together, the scattered fragments of the sisters' letters and diaries suggest their concern to support, advise and comfort each other. Her brother Matthew wrote a memoir of her life (BL 1418 a 1) and the 1821 edition of J. B. Williams's *Memoirs of the Life and Character of Mrs Savage* includes a life of Ann Hulton.

For details of locations of surviving manuscripts, see Patricia Crawford, 'Katharine and Philip Henry and their children: a case study in family ideology', *Transactions of the Historic Society of Lancashire and Cheshire*, vol. 143, 1985.

HUMBERSTONE, Augustina, *fl.* 1718
2. Chedgrave (Norfolk), Louvain; 3. nun; 4. Catholic.

She was probably the niece of Edward and Henry Humberstone, but we know little else about her. She was a nun at St Monica, Louvain and author of an 'Account of the convent of Augustianesses at Louvain' (MS, 1718).

HUME, Anna, *fl.* before 1630–44
2. Scotland.

She translated Petrarch's *The triumphs of Love, Chastity, and Death* (1644) which she dedicated to ELIZABETH OF BOHEMIA* (reprinted in Bohn's *Petrarch by various hands*, 1859), and Latin poems by her father, David Hume of Godscroft (related to the aristocratic Humes of Wedderburn). She apparently supervised publication of his *History of the house and race of Douglas and Angus*, on which she ventured her 'whole fortune' despite the opposition (probably in the 1630s) of William Douglas, Earl of Angus (1589–1660); his father had initiated the history project. Hume's father died *c.* 1630.

Extract in Greer (p. 100 f.).

HUTCHINSON, Lucy, 1620–after 1675
1. Apsley; 2. London, Nottinghamshire, Middlesex; 3. genteel; 4. puritan; 5. Colonel Thomas Hutchinson; 6. genteel, soldier.

Lucy Hutchinson could read at the age of 4 years. Her mother had her books locked up to protect her health. Lucy knew Greek, French, Latin and Hebrew. Her *Memoirs of the life of Colonel Hutchinson* were written between 1644 and 1671 and, on publication in 1806, went through three editions in four years. The memoirs were edited by John Sutherland (Oxford: Oxford University Press) in 1973, with *The life of Mrs Lucy Hutchinson written by herself.* She also wrote two religious books for her daughter, one of which *(On the principles of the Christian religion)* was published in 1817, and she translated six books of Lucretius and part of the *Aeneid.*

Greer (p. 214 f.) includes extracts from the Lucretius and 'Verses written by Mrs Hutchinson'.

HYDE, Anne

Anne, Duchess of YORK*

I

INGAL, Ann, *fl.* 1659–70

2. Edingley, Besthorp (Notts.); 4. Quaker; 5. Thomas Ingal; 6. farmer.

She bore three children between 1659 and 1665; main signatory of *To the King and both Houses of Parliament. From the people of God called Quakers in the county of Nottingham . . . Signed by Thomas Ingal and 118 men Friends; by Ann Ingal, and 97 women Friends* (1670) and also signed *For the King and both Houses of Parliament* (*c.* 1670) with Priscilla ECCLESTONE,* Mary ELSON,* Rebeckah TRAVERS,* Anne WHITEHEAD.*

INGLIS, Esther

Esther KELLO*

IVIE, Lady Theodosia, *fl.* 1654–96

3. genteel; 5. Thomas Ivie.

In 1654 she was involved in a court case against her husband over alimony; more celebrated is the dispute with Thomas Neale in 1696 recorded as 'Lady Ivy's Trial, for great Part of Shadwell, in the County of Middlesex, June 1684' in T. B. Howell, *Cobbett's complete collection of state trials* (London: Longman, 1809–28), vol. 10.

This is a property quarrel about ownership of tenements in Radcliffe, Shadwell: her claim goes through John Stepkins to whom some of Wapping marsh was sold (drained in Henry VIII's reign). She is accused in the trial of forging a mortgage from Sir William Salkhill, and is later indicted for forging and publishing two indentures. The only text that could be said to be authored by Lady Ivie is the forged documents.

J

JAMES, Elinor, *fl.* 1675–1715

1. Bancks; 2. London; 3. printer; 4. Anglican; 5. Thomas James; 6. printer.

See Critical Appendix 7.

Elinor James worked with her husband and published her own broadsheets and pamphlets. She was in Newgate in 1689 for supporting James II and carried on the printing business after her husband's death in 1711. She is author of some thirty titles, including *Mrs James' defence of the Church of England* (1687); *An injured prince vindicated* (1688); and *May it please your most sacred majesty* (1685; on the subject of fasting).

JEFFERIES, Joyce, – *c.* 1650

2. Herefordshire, Worcestershire; 3. genteel.

Webb (see below) quotes her great nephew as saying that Joyce Jefferies became companion to Philippa, wife of Sir Thomas Conyngsby. She drew her income from her estates, annuities and moneylending.

See 'Some passages in the life and character of a lady resident in Herefordshire and Worcestershire during the Civil War . . . collected from her Account Book' (J. Webb, *Archaeologia*, vol. 37, 1857). Webb includes extracts from this account-book.

JERMYN, Lady Rebecca, *fl. c.* 1629–55

2. Rushbrooke (Suffolk); 3. genteel; 5. Sir Thomas Jermyn; 6. Treasury official.

Thomas Jermyn was trying to obtain the office of Comptroller of the Household in 1629, in 1632 he became vice-chamberlain of the Household and he was Comptroller before 1638. He lost his office in 1641.

A true state of the right and claim of Lady Jermyn to the Registers office in

Chancery (1655). Charles I had granted a position and fees in the Registrar's Office to the two sons of Sir Thomas in 1638. Sir Thomas settled all of his estate on his eldest son (Henry) and died in debt, so his widow and executrix, Lady Jermyn, was imprisoned. She says this office is the only means she has of supporting herself, and asks leave to execute it by deputy. She petitioned in March; in August 1655 it was decreed that the family had lost the right to the office, but it was recommended that they be granted subsistence for life.

JESSERSON, Susanna, *fl.* 1675

A bargain for bachelors, or The best wife in the world for a penny fairly offered to young men for directing their choice, and to maids for imitation (1675; a picture of a 'good wife').

JEVON, Rachel, ?1627–

2. Worcester; 4. Anglican.

Exultationis carmen to the king's most excellent majesty upon his most desired return (presented with her own hand, Aug. 16. 1660) (translated by her from her Latin in the same year). This is a poem of congratulation to Charles II on his Restoration: Jevon describes herself as 'The Unworthiest of His Majesties Hand-Maids'. Hobby mentions a petition of 1662 to Charles seeking a place in service to the queen (*Virtue*, p. 19): the petition is based on the loyalty to the king of her clergyman father, who withstood threats in order to keep his flock loyal; it also complains that he is without the money to maintain his children (this information derives from Hobby's personal notes). Parish registers record Rachel, daughter of Daniel and Elizabeth Jeven, christened in 1627 in Broom, Worcestershire. The family is linked with the genteel Jevens of Staffordshire.

JINNER, Sara, *fl.* 1658–64

3. astrologer.

She wrote *An almanack or prognostication* for the years 1658, 1659, 1660 and 1664. These almanacs are anti-authoritarian and they defend women; they also include medical notes, political commentary and social comment. Their position is republican: government 'hath no other foundation than the humour of the people'. They seem to be the first almanacs by a woman for women. *The womans almanack* (1659), published under the name 'Sarah Ginnor', is not by her: it is a satire which attacks Jinner and women in general.

See B. S. Capp, *Astrology and the popular press: English almanacs 1500 to 1800* (London: Faber, 1979).

JOHNSON, Ann, *fl.* 1684
2. Buckinghamshire; 3. genteel.

A letter of 1684 concerns her son's intention to be a soldier 'notwithstanding my dislike of it'. She offers to sell her plate and gold watch to raise enough money to buy him a suitable 'place' at the custom-house or with an attorney. Quoted by Pollock (p. 267), whose source is the Johnson family papers in the Bucks. Record Office (DX/827).

JOHNSON, Elizabeth, *fl.* 1695–6
2. ?London.

Author of a preface to Elizabeth SINGER's* *Poems on several occasions by Philomela* (1696) in which she says she helped persuade SINGER to publish. The preface defends women, who are 'over-rul'd by the Tyranny of the Prouder Sex'. (Information from Greer, p. 383.)

JOHNSON, Katherine, *fl.* 1639–53
3. prophet, genteel.

Her prophecy to Cromwell appears in J. Price, *The mystery and method of his majesty's happy restauration* (1680). Katherine was related to Price and spent some time in his house. The prophecy advises Cromwell to be humble, and 'as for the Scottish king (as he is called) his right here must be in peace, not by the sword.' Price says this was delivered in 1653. She had also delivered a prophecy to Charles I (in 1639–40) warning him against signing the bill to kill Strafford. Price was chaplain to Monck, and we do not know how he may have mediated Johnson's text. (A chaplain to Cromwell, Francis Johnson of Northants., had a wife Katherine; we cannot demonstrate a connection.)
See Elinor CHANNEL* for a similar case of mediation.

JONES, Sarah, *fl.* 1644–50
4. ?Congregationalist, Quaker.

The title page of the Thomason copy of her tract, *To Sion's lovers, being a golden egge, to avoid infection, or a short step into the doctrine of laying on of hands* (1644), calls her 'dyars wife'. While this could be a reference to the minister William Dyer, he was reported in Bucks. to be about to marry a wealthy heiress, Sara Ward. Furthermore Jones was still writing under that name in 1650: *This is light's appearance in the truth to all the precious dear lambs of the life dark vanished, light shines forth* (1650). There could be two women here: in 1644 the position was Congregationalist, in 1650 it was Quaker. Development between positions is possible (William Dyer became Quaker). The catalogue at Friends House, London, suggests that the author of the 1650 tract may have come from Bristol.

The epistle to *Sion's lovers* is to Dr Gouge (a member of the Assembly of Divines), recalling 'ancient acquaintance' with her and her father. She urges him to uphold the ritual of the laying on of hands. She asks rhetorically: 'Whether the Congregations be not the shee preachers to whom the command is given, to whom the promise is made, goe Preach and Baptise, observe and doe all I command you . . .', and 'Whether all the Saints shall not have honour, the power as the two edged Sword, her overseers being one with her, not Lords over her.' *This is light's appearance* stresses the divine word and censures spiritual 'in-looking'.

(We have found a Sarah Jones, eldest daughter of Hugh Jones, merchant, of London; her mother was a daughter of Thomas Hacket, a dyer; she had a brother born in 1622. A David Jones of Carmarthen reprinted Gouge's Welsh Bible.)

JOSCELINE, Elizabeth, 1592–1622

1. Brooke; 2. Cheshire, Lincoln, ?Cambridgeshire; 3. genteel; 5. Tourell Josceline; 6. genteel.

Margaret BLAGGE*

Elizabeth Josceline was brought up by her maternal grandfather (Bishop Caderton of Lincoln) who educated her in languages and history. Her *The mothers legacy to her unborn child* (?1622) had three editions by 1625, another in 1684 and one in 1852. Her *Letters* ran to five editions between 1624 and 1684, while she also left a manuscript treatise on education. She died nine days after childbirth, having expressed dread of 'that kind of death' and having already bought her own winding sheet. *The mothers legacy* . . . gives advice to her child. If a girl, she wants it taught the Bible, housewifery, writing and good works – 'other learning a woman needs not, though I admire it in those whom God hath blest with discretion yet I desire it not much in my own, having seen that sometimes women have greater portions of learning than wisdom.'

K

K—, M—

'Experiences of M.K', in Henry Walker, *Spirituall experiences, of sundry believers* (1653; Smith, p. 54).

KELLO, Esther/Hester, 1571–1624

1. Langlois; 2. France, Leith; 3. calligrapher, miniaturist, writer; 4. Huguenot; 5. Bartholomew Kello; 6. cleric.

Often known as INGLIS (=English, from maiden name), she worked for some time in Edinburgh, illustrating emblem books, and became well-known as a calligrapher. Wrote *Octonaries upon the vanitie and inconstancie of the world* (1609). Some 35 extant manuscripts are mainly religious, and many of her copies were made in imitation of printing. Her *Ecclesiastes*, 1599, includes her self-portrait (BL, Add. MS 27927).

KELSALL, Tabitha, *fl. c.* 1645–53

2. Dublin; 4. Baptist, Ranter, Fifth Monarchist.

Her 'experiences' are in Rogers, *Ohel* . . . (1653), a text based mainly around Rogers's Baptist congregation in Dublin (see also Mary BARKER*). There was a large Kelsall family in Cheshire, of which Humphrey (born 1619) had land granted him in Ireland (this often followed army service); his daughter Mary was married in 1672. It is tempting, but tenuous, to place Tabitha in this connection. She was, apparently, of 'Hobson's society' in England, but 'all the Ordinances grew dead unto me' (Paul Hobson was a Baptist lay preacher who headed a separatist congregation in London in the early 1640s, and a Baptist congregation in Newcastle-upon-Tyne in 1649–50; he was sent as a Baptist emissary to Exeter in 1646.) Kelsall also attacks Ranters, who, she says, denied the Ordinances and who lived wickedly.

KEMP, Anna, *fl.* **1658**
2. ?Gloucestershire.

A contemplation of Bassets down-hill by the most sacred adorer of the Muses Mrs A.K. (*c.* 1658). A short pastoral: 'Bassets down-hill' is near Down Ampney and Meysey Hampton in Gloucestershire.

KENT, Elizabeth Grey, Countess of

See Appendix III.

KILLAM/KILLIN, Joan, –1678
1. Aldam; 2. Balby, nr. Doncaster; 4. Quaker; 5. Thomas Killam/Killin; 6. yeoman.

Sister of Margaret KILLAM/KILLIN* (with whom she wrote a tract, see below) and Thomas Aldam. The Killam sisters and their husbands were all convinced by Fox in 1651. Joan bore two daughters in 1653 and 1655.

KILLAM/KILLIN, Margaret, –1672
1. Aldam; 2. Balby, nr. Doncaster; 4. Quaker; 5. John Killam/Killin; 6. yeoman.

Sister of Joan KILLAM/KILLIN* and Thomas Aldam. Besse describes her as 'of good education, and considerable fortune' (1.148). She bore five children between 1646 and 1656. She spoke publicly in Mansfield and Reading; visited Anne BLAYKLING in prison. In 1655 she was abused by students at Cambridge. She was imprisoned at York, Banbury, Plymouth (where in 1655 she had her feet tied under a horse's belly and her hands behind her back), Exeter and Chesterfield (1661). She wrote a tract with her sister, letters to her husband and George Fox, and *A warning from the Lord to the teachers and people of Plymouth. With a few queries to the parish teachers of this nation, that have great sums of money for teaching the people* (1655; part by Barbara PATISON*). *BLC* also lists *A short account of the barbarous sufferings* (1657).

KILLIGREW, Anne, 1660–85
2. London; 3. genteel.

Her father, Henry, was chaplain to the Duke of York and her uncle, Thomas, manager of the Theatre Royal. She was Maid of Honour to Mary of Modena. *Poems by Mrs. Anne Killigrew* was published by her father in 1686 (she died of smallpox). During her lifetime she was applauded as a portraitist, her subjects including herself and the Duke of York. She also painted Venus and Adonis, and Judith and Holofernes. Dryden wrote a famous ode on her death.

There is a reprint of her poems (New York: Scholars' Facsimiles and Reprints, 1967) and a selection in Greer, p. 299 f.

KING, Anne, 1621–after 1684

2. Buckinghamshire, Wiltshire; 5(a) John Dutton, (b) Sir Richard Howe; 6(a) genteel, MP, (b) genteel.

She was the sister of Henry King, bishop and poet. James Howell calls her 'the Tenth Muse'. She was part of the company or 'college' which gathered around Henry King and John Hales at the house of Lady Salter in Buckinghamshire in the 1650s.

Greer prints two poems (pp. 181–2): 'Under Mr. Hales Picture' which, according to Izaak Walton, accompanied Anne King's drawing of Hale, now lost; and an inscription for the monument of her sister, Dorothy HUBERT, who died in 1658 and whose monument Anne erected in 1684.

KING, Martha, 1645–1740

1. Borne; 2. Suffolk; 3. trade; 4. Quaker; 5. Thomas King (m. 1687); 6. bricklayer.

Testimony in *The last words and testimonies of and for William Allen* (1680).

Martha King seems to have been active in the Quaker movement from the age of 30 until she was very old.

KNATCHBULL, Lucy (baptised Elizabeth), 1584–1629

2. Kent, Brussels, Ghent; 3. nun; 4. Catholic.

Her 'Autobiography' is in Tobie Matthew's *Life of Lady Knatchbull*, edited by D. Knowles (London: Sheed & Ward, 1931). It was written before 1642, prepared for publication in 1651, and dedicated to Lady Mary KNATCHBULL* of the convent at Ghent. Lucy gave 'a clear account of all those things which concerned her' to Matthew, who also prints her letters to him.

Lucy Knatchbull entered a Brussels convent in 1604 and professed in 1611. In 1623 she founded a convent at Ghent and became its abbess. Her experiences strongly recall those of St Teresa. She refers to a severe crisis of faith and begs God for death, but is told 'Thou shalt not yet die, but serve me and suffer for me.' After agonies of the spirit 'When the hour was near come to an end I did smell, as I thought, the perfect savour of Violets; with which I lost all fear of the Devils.' At evensong she thinks she sees Jesus stretch out his right hand in benediction: he 'seemed to be as at the age of twelve years'.

KNATCHBULL, Mary, *fl.* 1651–8
2. Ghent; 3. nun; 4. Catholic.

CSPD, February/March 1658, contains a letter from her to Secretary Nicholas, telling him 'the world knows I am a hearty lover of his Majesty'. She was abbess of Ghent, and seemingly an important figure in the intelligence network of the exiled Royalists. In 1660 Nicholas (writing from Brussels to a Mr Lipe) copied a letter to her, in which he celebrated the probability of the king's Restoration.

KNATCHBULL, Mary, –1727
2. Ghent; 3. nun; 4. Catholic.

Grand-niece to Lucy KNATCHBULL,* she became abbess of the monastery at Ghent in 1711. Wrote 'Relation of the establishment of the Benedictine dames at Ghent' (MS, 1718). (Information from Gillow.)

KNIGHT, Mary, *fl.* 1655

'To the most honoured', a lyric set to music by Henry Lawes in his *The second book of ayres and dialogues* (1655). Lawes was connected with the Egerton family (he wrote music for Milton's *Comus*); this may perhaps imply that Mary Knight moved in the same circles.

KNOTT, Mary, ?1653–1718
1. Howard; 2. Dover; 4. Quaker; 5. John Knott (m. 1676); 6. shoemaker.

Daughter of the Kent Quaker activist and shoemaker, Luke Howard; she tells us her mother died when she was 12 – this could be Howard's first wife, Anne STEVENS, who died in 1665. John Knott was an apprentice to Howard. Mary Knott bore at least three children between 1677 and 1685, all of whom died young. She apparently died in London. Her 'testimony concerning her dear father' is in Luke Howard, *Love and truth in plainness manifested* (1704; printed by Tace SOWLE).

L

L—, Elizabeth

See Appendix I.

'A Lady of Honour'

See Appendix I.

LAMB, Barbara, *fl.* 1656–8

1. Tanner; 2. London; 4. ?Baptist; 5. Thomas Lamb (m. 1656).

A letter of August 1658 to Richard Baxter about (it seems) the religious difficulties of her Baptist husband.

LAMB, Catherine, *fl.* 1683–9

2. London; 4. ?Catholic.

Her deposition in *Remarks of A. Pulton Master in the Savoy, upon Dr. Tho. Tenison's Late Narrative* (1687) relates to a religious controversy between the Jesuit Andrew Pulton and the Anglican (and future archbishop) Thomas Tenison. After their debate (at Long Acre, London, in September 1683) there was an exchange of tracts which not only contested religious points but also the numbers of supporters present. Lamb deposed for Pulton that she saw him with only two others. Her evidence was particularly attacked by Tenison, who claimed she was not present, and likened her to the 'conjuror' Dr Lamb. This forced Lamb into print: *A full discovery of the false evidence produc'd by the papists against the most reverend and learned Dr. Tho. Tenison* (1689). This explains that the confusion about her whereabouts stemmed from a single verbal error in a statement written in her name by Pulton (which her husband said she agreed to). She confirms she was present since Tenison's 'comical schoolmaster' will remember her 'by my desiring him in the midst of his comedy, not to interrupt the conference with his several monkey tricks'. She finishes with an attack on Tenison's religion: 'I have indeed been a great zealot for your pretended Church; but the aspersive, false, and fabulous accounts I have often heard, in the most sacred places, from men of your gown, most entirely convinced me, that Truth cannot be, where studied falsehood is affectedly profest.' (Pulton's and Tenison's texts include depositions from a number of women, whom we do not list separately on the basis that we have excluded legal depositions, witnesses to wills, etc.)

LAMBERT, Lady

See Appendix III.

LANCASTER, Lydia, 1682/3–1761

1. Rawlinson; 2. Lancaster, Graithwaite, Kendal; 4. Quaker; 5. Bryan Lancaster (m. 1706).

Convinced in 1698, she travelled widely in Britain and Ireland and visited America in 1718. Her sermons were published in the eighteenth century and *Extracts from the letters of Lydia Lancaster* was published in 1840 (ed. Lydia Barclay).

LANYER, Aemilia, ?1570–1645

1. Bassani; 2. ?Kent; 3. teacher; 5. Alphonso Lanyer; 6. musician.

Aemilia Lanyer may have been of the household of Susan, Duchess of Kent, when young. Simon Forman says that she was the paramour of Henry Carey, first Lord Hunsdon. She wrote *Salve deus rex judaeorum. Containing 1. The passion of Christ; 2. Eves Apologie in defence of women; 3. The teares of the daughters of Jerusalem; 4. The salutation and sorrow of the Virgine Marie. With divers other things not unfit to be read* (1611; in *ottava rima*; the 'other things' include 'The description of Cooke-ham' in iambic pentameter).
    Greer prints 'The description . . . ' (p. 44 f.) which is an early example of the descriptive place poem.

LARCUM, Mary, –1736

1. Merrick; 2. Weston Turville (Bucks.); 4. Quaker; 5. Nicholas Larcum (m. 1686); 6. tailor.

She bore five children, of whom four died young (a daughter Anne survived). Signed 'A testimony from the Women's Meeting, concerning

Thomas Ellwood' (1713), with Mary BAKER* and Mary WHARLEY* (in *The history of the life of Thomas Ellwood*, 1714).

LATEY, Mary, 1650–1713
1. Fielder; 2. London; 4. Quaker; 5. Gilbert Latey; 6. tailor, preacher.

Mary Latey wrote *A testimony concerning my dear and well-beloved husband Gilbert Latey* (1707); she signed a general testimony for Anne WHITE-HEAD* in *Piety . . .* in 1686. She bore eleven children between 1673 and 1691, but ten of them died young.

LAWRENCE, Sarah, –1741
1. Vokins; 2. West Challow (Berks.); 4. Quaker; 5. Adam Lawrence (m. 1689); 6. yeoman.

Daughter of Joan VOKINS,* with her sisters Hannah BURGIS,* Mary LOCKEY* and Elizabeth VOKINS* she signed a testimony 'concerning our dear and tender mother, Joan Vokins' in 1691. She may have been Lawrence's second wife, and bore three children between 1691 and 1700.

LEAD, Jane, 1623–1704/9
1. Ward; 2. Norfolk, London; 3. mystic, ?bookseller; 4. Anglican, Bœhmenist, Philadelphian; 5. William Lead.

Mary BOREMAN*

Jane Lead studied Bœhme and was an associate of John Pordage. With Francis Lee she was the focus of the Philadelphian Society, which flourished between 1694 and 1703 in England, Holland and Germany. Some of her tracts were translated into Dutch and German. There are nearly twenty of these, including *The Enochian walks with God* (1694); *A fountain of gardens* (four-volume spiritual diary 1696–1701); and *The laws of paradise* (1695; for Tace SOWLE). Some of her works had new editions in the nineteenth century. In 1696 she argued that all formal worship should cease, and the 'Laws of Paradise', which she gave to Philadelphians, stressed obedience to established authority and avoidance of political commitment. She went blind in 1699 and lived in a Stepney almshouse.

LEAPER, Elizabeth, *fl.* 1686–7
2. Yorkshire; 4. Quaker; 5. ?Joshua Leaper.

'Her testimony concerning Benjamin Padley who dyed the 25th of the 6th month, 1687' in *Some fruits of a tender branch sprung from the living vine*

(1691; see Susanna PADLEY*). She speaks of how Benjamin Padley encouraged her in her journey (with her sister and Mary FROST) to visit Quakers in Cumberland. She also signed the epistle from the York Women's Meeting in 1686 (see Mary WAITE*). It is probably three daughters of hers who married between 1678 and 1682.

LEIGH, Dorothy, –?1616
1. Kemp.

Author of *The mother's blessing. Or the godly counsaille of a gentlewoman not long deceased . . . containing many good exhortations . . . for all . . . parents to leave as a legacy to their children* (1616; 15 editions by 1630; also 1707, 1718). This work includes advice on what kind of women sons should marry – 'Bear with the woman as with the weaker vessel' – and a poem 'Counsell to my children'.

L'ESTRANGE, Alice, –1656
1. Stubbe; 2. Hunstanton (Norfolk); 3. genteel; 5. Sir Hamon L'Estrange; 6. genteel.

Daughter and co-heir of Sir Richard Stubbe of Sedgeford, Norfolk, she bore four children, of whom Roger (born 1617) was the famous Royalist censor. Her husband became sheriff of Norfolk in 1609; she kept the accounts and ran the estate during his frequent absences from Hunstanton. The L'Estrange papers are held by the Norfolk and Norwich Record Office; R. W. Ketton-Cremer quotes from them in *Norfolk in the Civil War* (Norwich: Gliddon, 1969).

Letters of love and gallantry

See Appendix I.

LEVINGSTON, Anne, before 1625–
1. Caesar; 2. Hertfordshire, Hampshire; 3. genteel; 5. Thomas Levingston; 6. genteel.

Her father was from Benington, Herts.; she moved to Hampshire at her marriage. (Her grandfather, Peter Vanlore, was from Utrecht.) Her mother was dead by 1625.

The state of the case in brief. A true narrative of the case so much controverted between Mistress Anna Levingston, daughter to Sir Charles Caesar, and one of the grand-children of Sir Peter Vanlore the elder, and neece to the Lady Powel, and wife to Thomas Levingston Esquire; and John Blunt and the Lady Sterlin his wife, Sir Robert Crook and his wife, Henry Alexander alias Zinzan and his wife, and one Abraham Vandebemde, and others; concerning the estate real and personal of the Lady Powel, late wife of Sir Edward Powel both deceased; with the rise, growth, and proceedings of the differences touching the same (?1654/5).

This is a property dispute, with the woman claiming her rights. The 'narrative' was presumably commissioned rather than actually written by Levingston. Anne was accused by Mary STIRLING* of employing witchcraft in order to acquire the elderly Lady Powell's estate, and of keeping the old lady prisoner. Other pamphlets written by/in defence of the Levingstons are *Some considerations humbly proposed to the worthy members of Parliament, by Thomas Levingston Esquire, and Anne his wife* (1654) and *A true narrative of the case . . .* (1655).

LILBURNE, Elizabeth, *fl.* 1646–7

1. Dewell; 5. John Lilburne (m. 1641/2); 6. lawyer, radical.

Elizabeth Lilburne was imprisoned for distributing her husband's writings (1647) and her house in Half Moon Alley was ransacked by agents of the Stationers' Company. She was called 'Queen Bess' by some pamphleteers and worked persistently for John Lilburne's release during his various periods in prison.

To the chosen and betrusted knights, citizens and burgesses, assembled in the high and supreme court of Parliament. The humble petition of Elizabeth Lilburne, wife to the Lieut. Coll. John Lilburne, who hath been for above eleven weeks by past, most unjustly divorced from him, by the House of Lords, and their tyrannical officers, against the law of God and (as she conceives) the law of the land (1646).

See Pauline Gregg, *Free-born John* (London: Dent, 1961).

LINCOLN, Elizabeth, Countess of

Elizabeth CLINTON*

LINDLEY, Mary, 1652–

1. Thompson; 2. Malton, Yarm (Yorks.); 4. Quaker; 5. Benjamin Lindley (m. 1677).

A testimony from the yearly meeting at York (1686). She also signed the epistles from the York Women's Meetings (1686, 1688): see Mary WAITE* for details.

LINDSEY, Lady Elizabeth, 1586–1654

1. Montagu; 2. Middlesex, London; 3. genteel; 5. Robert Bertie, Earl of Lindsey.

Daughter of Lord Montagu of Boughton and mother of Mary HEWYTT;* her husband died in command of forces at the battle of Edgehill. Gibbs and *CSPD* mention letters by her: one in 1638 to her father (written from Havering), and one *c.* 1640 where she says she will not attend the 'jovial rits' of a court masque for Twelfth Night. In 1644 she was living in the Strand.

LIVINGSTON, Helen/Eleanor, Countess of Linlithgow, –1627

1. Erroll; 2. Scotland; 3. genteel; 4. Catholic; 5. Alexander Hay, Earl of Linlithgow (m. 1584); 6. genteel.

See Critical Appendix 6.

Only daughter of Andrew, Earl of Erroll, she was 'of kyn' to James VI/I; her mother died in 1570. In 1583 she had problems with the confiscation and inheritance of her father's lands. Her husband, previously Lord Livingston, received the title of Linlithgow in 1600. With him she was entrusted with the education of James VI's daughters, Princess ELIZA-BETH (later OF BOHEMIA)* and Princess Margaret. Of the five children of her own, two daughters were married in 1609 and 1612. She resisted attempts to convert her from Catholicism. In 1588 she was described as a 'malicious papist' and cited to appear before the Presbytery of Glasgow in 1594, but failed to do so. She was excommunicated in 1597, and tried before the Presbytery in 1612. Her husband died in 1622. She converted just before her death. The only known copy of *The confession and conversion of my lady of L[inlithgow]* (Edinburgh, 1629) looks like an attempt to publicise this conversion: she seems to have 'subscribed' to statements written by someone else (see facsimile reprint, privately printed, Edinburgh, 1924). A letter by her (signed Eleanor Hay) to James is printed in D. Laing (ed.), *Original letters relating to the ecclesiastical affairs of Scotland* (Edinburgh: Bannatyne Club publications 109, 1859), vol. 2, p. 464.

LOCKEY, Mary, –1693

1. Vokins; 2. West Challow, Farringdon (Berks.); 4. Quaker; 5. Edward Lockey (m. 1684); 6. shopkeeper.

Daughter of Joan VOKINS,* with her sisters Hannah BURGIS,* Sarah LAW-RENCE* and Elizabeth VOKINS* she signed a testimony 'concerning our dear and tender mother, Joan Vokins' in 1691. She bore two children in 1690 (died aged 2) and 1692.

LONG, Anne, ?1681–1711

2. London, Norfolk; 3. genteel.

Author of a poem in *Letters, poems, and tales, amorous, satyrical and gallant* (1718). She knew Swift.

LONGUEVILLE, Penelope Victoria, 1648–74
2. Buckinghamshire, Pontoise; 3. nun; 4. Catholic.

Daughter of Sir Edward Longueville of Wolverton, Buckinghamshire, she professed in 1671 at the English Benedictine monastery at Pontoise. She wrote an unpublished text of private devotions (n.d.).

LOVE, Mary, *fl.* 1647–51
2. London; 4. Presbyterian; 5. Christopher Love; 6. minister.

She bore at least two children, christened 1647 and 1648 (a first daughter died young), though some accounts say she had three and was pregnant when her husband was in prison. *CSPD* records a pass issued in December 1650 to Mary Love and Priscilla TOMSON to travel to Amsterdam, but this may not be the same woman; if it is, it may bear some relation to the events of 1651. Her husband was minister of Lawrence Jewry, London, and preacher to the garrison at Windsor (where he had a great influence on John and Anne VENN*). He was arrested and beheaded in 1651, accused of a Presbyterian plot to restore the monarchy. She stayed with him in prison in May 1651. His brother-in-law, James Winstanley, attempted to organise a large funeral, which was prohibited. The texts of Mary Love relate to this death sentence. *Love's letters, his and hers* (1651) includes four petitions from Mary Love, pleading for mercy for her husband and seeking that the death sentence be commuted to banishment (on 15 July a month's stay of execution was granted). Finally, she asked that 'her dying husband (as a Prophet from the dead) be sent to endeavour the conversion of the poor Indians, that so many souls may bless God in your behalf'. There are also moving letters to her husband. The text was reprinted as *Love's name lives: or, a publication of divers petitions presented by mistris Love to the Parliament, in behalf of her husband. With severall letters that interchangeably pass'd between them a little before his death* (1660, 1663). The publisher in 1663 says that earlier printings were private copies and inaccurate, but the texts are substantially the same (the real motive for printing being presumably politically related to the restoration of monarchy).

LOWER, Mary, *c.* 1644–1719
1. Fell; 2. Lancashire, Bristol; 4. Quaker; 5. Thomas Lower (m. 1668).

Daughter of Margaret FELL* and sister of Margaret ROUSE* and Isabel

YEAMANS.* She was the second wife of Lower, whose first wife was Elizabeth TRELAWNEY.* She and her husband were signatories to the marriage certificate of Margaret FELL and George Fox in Bristol in 1669. L. Hodgkin, *A Quaker Saint of Cornwall* (London: Longman, 1927) prints a letter by her to Margaret FELL.

LOWTHER, Lady Elizabeth, –1699

1. Hare; 2. Norfolk, Westmorland; 5(a) Woolley Leigh (m. 1638), (b) Sir John Lowther.

Daughter and co-heir of Sir John Hare of Stow Bardolph, Norfolk, she had one son (born 1639) by her first marriage. Her husband (of Addington, Surrey) married into her family's eminence and wealth; he was a Royalist who died at Oxford in 1644. In her second marriage, into the Lowther family of Westmorland (the targets of Margaret BRAIDLEY's* anger), she bore four children. She died a widow, her husband dying 1675. There are two letters from her to Williamson (later Secretary of State) in *CSPD* dated July and September 1657: they discuss her eldest son Thomas's education and travelling expenses (Williamson was his tutor).

LYNAM, Margaret, –1697

1. Ridge; 2. Derbyshire, Maryland, Pennsylvania; 4. Quaker; 5. John Lynam; 6. wheelwright.

She was preaching before 1660 in Northern Ireland; in 1661 she was in Derbyshire, where she marched with and assisted imprisoned Quakers; she was also in Derbyshire in 1677. A pamphlet she wrote in 1675 was judged unfit to be printed by Quakers. By 1681 she and her husband were in Maryland where they disputed with other Quakers: she was condemned for 'justifying herself and condemning all other Friends', and in 1682 she set up a separatist meeting (to which she was still committed in 1684). In 1691 the Lynams had moved to Pennsylvania.

Her several pamphlets include: *For the Parliament sitting at Westminster* (1659). *Extracts from letters, by Margaret Lynam, written about the year 1660 to Friends in the north of Ireland, after paying them a visit in the love of the Gospel* (n.d.). *A warning from the Lord unto all you informers, who are found fighting against God, who are as ravening wolves lying in wait, as a company of robbers* (1680).

M

M—, A—

See Appendix I.

M—, A—

'Experiences' in Samuel Petto, *The voice of the spirit* (1654; Smith, p. 41).

M—, D—

'Experiences of D.M.' in Henry Walker, *Spirituall experiences, of sundry believers* (1653; Smith, p. 44).

M—, M—

See Appendix I.

M—, R—

See Appendix I.

M—, W—

See Appendix I.

McCARTY, Margaret, Catherine and Elizabeth, *fl.* 1676–93
2. Ireland; 5. Catherine m. Paul Davys, Viscount Montcashel.

The case of the ladies Margaret, Catherine, and Elizabeth McCarty, daughters of Calaghan late Earl of Clancarty (?1700): a petition to obtain marriage portions from their father's estate. He had suddenly died in 1676, leaving them unprovided for. Their mother, without her money until 1682,

130

began to pay off debts. Then their brother Donogh forfeited the estate because of his support for James II, before portions could be paid. In 1690 the House of Lords made provision, but Parliament was prorogued; their mother petitioned the king in 1692 but there were delays in paying them (because they lived in Ireland); Queen Mary authorised payment in 1693, but before this could happen the estate passed to Lord Woodstock. Their mother died lacking means of support.

MACKETT, Ann, 1643–91

1. Howell; 2. Aldgate (London); 4. Quaker; 5. William Mackett (m. 1666); 6. coalseller.

Bore eight children between 1667 and 1681, of whom two died young. Wrote a testimony in Anne WHITEHEAD,* *Piety* . . . (1686).

MAJOR, Elizabeth, *fl.* 1630–56

2. London; 4. nonconformist.

She tells us she was brought up until the age of 15/16 by 'a godly and careful father', her mother having died in her infancy. She then spent ten years under a governess in a 'great and honorable' family before becoming 'lame' and returning to her father. She had sufficient money to pursue a cure, but spent it all and 'was much worse'. The introduction to her book of poems was written by the Independent minister Joseph Caryl (of St Magnus's, near London Bridge). Greer suggests a connection with the Hampshire Majors (though parish registers do not offer confirmation of this theory). She could more probably have been the daughter of the wealthy John Major of Blackfriars, who is recorded as unmarried in 1634 (the London link with Caryl makes this more likely). She wrote *Honey on the rod; or a comfortable contemplation for one in affliction; with sundry poems on several subjects* (1656; biblical paraphrases, essays, dialogues and verse).

MAKE-PEACE, Mary

See Appendix II.

MAKIN, Bathsua, 1600–?74

1. Reynolds; 2. Sussex, London; 3. tutor, educationalist, genteel; 5. Richard Makin (m. 1622).

Daughter of Henry Reynolds, a linguist and schoolmaster (her name 'Reginalda' is Latinised Reynolds). She taught at her father's school from 1614 onwards, and published *Musa virginea* in 1616, a collection of poems addressed to members of the royal family, written in Greek, Hebrew, French, German and Spanish. Shortly after she published *Index radiographer*, a guide to a shorthand system of her own devising (it has not survived). She was (*c.* 1641) tutor to Charles I's daughter, Elizabeth, and founded a school at Tottenham High Cross. In 1663 she called for a curriculum for girls (following the Dutch educationalist Anna Maria VAN SCHURMAN) which called for grammar, rhetoric, logic, physics, mathematics, languages (including the classics), painting and poetry. But in practice she had to modify this and revert to such subjects as dancing and music. She wrote *The malady and remedy of vexation and unjust arrests and actions* (1646; against imprisonment for debt) and *An essay to revive the antient education of gentlewomen in religion, manners, arts* (1673). (Hobby accepts the latter ascription, while noting the reasons for uncertainty, *Virtue*, pp. 200–1.)

Biographical details from Vivian Salmon, 'Bathsua Makin: a pioneer linguist and feminist in seventeenth century England' in *Neuere forschungen zur wortbildung und historiographie der linguistik: Festgabe fur Herbert E. Brekle*, ed. Brigitta Asbach-Schnitker and Johannes Roggenhofer (Tübingen: Tübinger Beiträge zur Linguistik, 1987).

MAN, Judith, *fl.* 1640

Judith Man translated John Barclay's *An epitome of the history of faire Argenis and Polyarchus* (1640). There is very little evidence to place her, but *Harleian Society*, vol. 13, p. 442 records a Judith, daughter of William Man of Lyndsell, Essex, unmarried in 1634; her grandfather was John Man, warden of Merton College, Oxford, which might indicate a suitable academic connection.

MANLEY, Delarivier, ?1663/72–1724

2. Jersey, London, Exeter; 3. genteel; 4. poet, novelist, playwright; 5. John Manley (bigamist); 6. MP.

Mary HEARNE,* Sarah PIERS*

Delarivier Manley was abandoned by her cousin-husband with an infant son. She lived (1693-4) in the household of the Duchess of CLEVELAND, and was involved in a complicated lawsuit about the Duke of Albemarle's estate. She was arrested in 1709 for her *Secret memoirs* and was involved in controversy with Steele and with Swift (who called her work at that time 'trash'). A prolific author from 1696, her works include *The adventures of Rivella* (known as *The memoirs of Mrs Manley*, 1714); *The royal mischief* (a tragedy, performed at Lincoln's Inn Fields, 1696); *The power of love* (1720, a novel). She established *The female Tatler* (which led to a brief imprisonment), helped Swift with his Tory pamphlets and, in 1711, followed him as editor of *The Examiner.*

See *The novels of . . .* (ed. P. Kostle, New York: Scholars' Facsimiles, 1971). *The royal mischief* is reprinted by Morgan; Greer (p. 396 f.) includes poems. The definitive essay on Manley is Patricia Koster, 'Delarivier Manley and the *DNB*: A cautionary tale about following black sheep, with a challenge to the cataloguers', *Eighteenth-century life*, vol. 3 (1977). For Manley's politics, see G. Needham, *Huntington Library Quarterly*, vol. 12 (1948–9).

MANNERS, Frances

Frances ABERGAVENNY*

MARKHAM, Jane, –1702

1. Elsdale; 2. Brigg (Lincs.); 4. Quaker; 5. Thomas Markham (m. 1657).

She was Thomas Markham's second wife; no children recorded. Wrote *An account of the life and death of . . . Thomas Markham* (1695; printed by Tace SOWLE).

MARROW, Elizabeth, *fl.* 1652–3

2. Cork, Dublin; 4. Baptist.

Her 'experiences' are in Rogers, *Ohel . . .* (1653) (see Mary BARKER* for details). Like Elizabeth CHAMBERS,* she says she heard Michael Briscoe preach: he was chaplain to a foot regiment in Scotland before being a minister at Walmsley, Bolton in 1648; he was stopped from preaching in 1649; was at Preston, then Blackburn from 1650 onwards. She also heard 'Dr. Sibbils' (whom we cannot identify).

MARSHALL, Hannah, *fl.* 1664–83

1. Prince; 2. Bristol, London; 3. trade; 4. Quaker; 5. Charles Marshall; 6. apothecary, medical practitioner, preacher.

Hannah Marshall was the daughter of Edward and Mary PRINCE,* and was committed to prison with her husband for attending Quaker meetings (1664; 1681). From 1664 she had two daughters, five sons; in 1683 she moved her family to London when her husband was committed to the Fleet. Her *Testimony concerning her husband, Charles Marshall,* was written in 1703 and published in 1704.

MARTEN, Mary

See Appendix III.

MARY II, Queen of England, 1662–94

1. Stuart; 2. London, The Hague; 3. queen; 4. Anglican; 5. William of Orange (William III); 6. king.

Mary was elder sister of ANNE,* who succeeded to the throne after the deaths of William and Mary, whose marriage was childless. Mary was queen regnant and, although not keen on public life, was active in it, especially in William's absences. She was fluent in French, could write Dutch, and was interested in geography and botany.

Her letters to William are in Dalrymple, *Memoirs of Great Britain and Ireland* . . . (1790 ed., vol. iii). Also *Lettres et Mémoires de Marie Reine d'Angleterre* (The Hague, 1881) and *Memoirs and Letters of Mary, Queen of England,* ed. R. Doebner (Leipzig, 1886).

See Hester Chapman, *Mary II, Queen of England* (London: Jonathan Cape, 1953).

MARTINDALL, Anne, 1659–

1. Richards; 2. Colaton (Devon), London; 4. Quaker; 5. William Martindale (m. 1679); 6. wine cooper.

Of her four children born between 1680 and 1683, two died in infancy. She wrote down some of the last words of the dying Alice CURWEN:* 'Something of Alice Curwen's testimony, which did lie upon her to declare some four dayes before she departed out of the body', in Alice CURWEN, *A relation* . . . (1680; in the two copies of this text in Friends House, this testimony is only in the unbound copy: see also Alice COBB*). She may possibly have known the Curwens from their travels in the West Country.

MASHAM, Lady Damaris

Damaris CUDWORTH*

MATERN, Rosina, *fl.* 1676–88

2. Shoreditch, Waltham Abbey, Edmonton (London); 4. Quaker; 5(a) John Matern, (b) John Bringhurst (m. 1682); 6(a) teacher, (b) printer and stationer.

Hans and Rosyna Matern were immigrants from Silesia. They appear to have moved to Waltham Abbey in 1676 after the birth of their daughter Hannah (who died aged 10 months); their names appear anglicised the next year, with the birth of their second daughter. A son was born in 1680 but died at three weeks. John Matern was usher to the schoolmaster Christopher, husband of Frances TAYLOR* (and helped him produce a language instruction book). Rosina Matern's second husband also had important connections, in that he was an apprentice to Andrew Sowle and had worked in Holland. By him she bore two children in 1683 and 1688 (one died aged five, the other stillborn), and probably moved to Whitechapel. Wrote 'I have a few lines to write concerning my dear husband', in *Testimonies for John Matern* (1680).

MEEKINGS, Margaret, 1622–92

2. Cripplegate (London); 4. Quaker; 5. John Meekings; 6. dyer.

Her daughter Elizabeth was married in 1680; she speaks of Anne WHITEHEAD* as an 'antient acquaintance'. Wrote a testimony in Anne WHITEHEAD, *Piety* . . . (1686). Signed *A tender and Christian testimony* (1685; see Mary ELSON* for details).

MEGSON, Ann, *fl.* 1652–3

2. Dublin; 4. Baptist; 5. ?John Megson.

Her 'experiences' are in Rogers, *Ohel* . . . (1653) (see Mary BARKER* for details).

MELVILL, Elizabeth, Lady Colville of Culross, –after 1631

3. genteel; 4. Presbyterian; 5. John Colville; 6. genteel.

Daughter of Sir James Melvill of Halhill. In 1598 Alexander Hume dedicated a volume of poems to her: 'I know ye delite in poesie yourselfe, and as I unfainedly confes, excelles any of your sexe in that art.' She was also famous for her religious exercises. Her *Ane godlie dreame complyit in Scotish meter by M.M. Gentlewoman in Culros, at the requeist of her freindis* (Edinburgh, Aberdeen, 1603) was reprinted numerous times up to 1892 (especially in the anglicised version of 1606): ' . . . a Calvinist tract, dealing with her vision of the hell that awaits all but God's anointed . . .' (Greer). She also left letters and a sonnet, 'My dear Brother, with courage bear the crosse', which was sent to John Welch, a Presbyterian minister imprisoned in 1605/6 for defying James's ideas about royal prerogative. (Sonnet and extracts from *Dream* . . . in Greer, p. 32 ff.)

MIDDLETON, Elizabeth, *fl.* 1637

Author of a 173-stanza poem, 'The death and passion of our Lord Jesus Christ, as it was acted by the bloody Jews, and registred by the blessed Evangelists.' This is in a manuscript volume (Bod. Don. e17) dated 1637. The volume also includes an unattributed prose Calvinist tract and part of the poem is a pastiche of the Jesuit, Robert Southwell. The entry in Greer (pp. 94–5) uses the religious nature of the volume to suggest a connection with the Middletons of Denbighshire, who were a devout Anglican family that had contacts with exiled English Catholics.

MIDDLETON, Elizabeth

See Appendix III.

MILDMAY, Lady Grace, 1522–1620

1. Sherrington; 2. Wiltshire, Northamptonshire; 3. genteel; 4. puritan; 5. Anthony Mildmay; 6. genteel.

Educated by a governess, she kept a journal from *c.* 1570 to 1617, which records thoughts on religion and married life, together with recipes and details of housekeeping. Extracts appear in R. Weighall, 'An Elizabethan Gentlewoman', *Quarterly Review*, vol. 215 (1911).

MILLES, Mary, *fl.* 1677

2. Salem, New England; 4. Quaker.

A letter from Salem (1677) to the Curwens, telling of the sufferings she and others are enduring, and of her mother and brothers being taken by Indians: in Alice CURWEN,* *A relation . . .* (1680).

MITCHELL, Mary

See Appendix III.

MOLLINEUX, Mary, *c.* 1652–95

1. Southworth; 2. Lancashire; 4. Quaker; 5. Henry Mollineux.

Mary Mollineux knew medicine, Greek and Latin, and was imprisoned in Lancaster for attending a Quaker meeting. She is the author of Latin poems to her husband, of letters and of *Fruits of retirement; or miscellaneous poems, moral and divine. To which is prefixed some account of the author* (1702). This had six editions in England and a further four in

Philadelphia. (A postscript to J. Grave's *A song of Sion* (1662) is signed M.M. but this is probably Martin Mason.)

MONCK, Mary, ?1677–1715
2. Dublin, Bath; 3. genteel; 5. George Monck.

Mary Monck taught herself Latin, Italian and Spanish. Her *Marinda. Poems and translations upon several occasions* (1716) includes versions from Tasso, Guarini, Petrarch and Quevedo. There is a poem by her on her husband in Barber's *Collection of poems by eminent ladies* (1755).

MONTAGU, Lady Mary Wortley, 1689–1762
1. Pierrepoint; 2. London, Constantinople, Nottinghamshire; 3. genteel; 5. Edward Wortley; 6. genteel.

See Critical Appendix 6.

She learnt Latin, Greek and Italian, and knew Congreve, Addison, Pope and Gay. She translated Epictetus, *Enthiridian* (?1710), published *Court Poems* (1716) and a play, *Simplicity*, which, like her nine issues of *The nonsense of commonsense*, lies outside our period. See also *Letters and works*, ed. Lord Wharncliffe (Paris, 1837) and *Complete Letters*, ed. R. Halsband (Oxford: Oxford University Press, 1965), 3 vols.

MOORE, Elizabeth, –before 1657
1. Hancock; 2. London; 4. Independent.

Sister of the printer John Hancock and member of Edmund Calamy's Independent congregation. Calamy's funeral sermon for her describes her as a poor woman, aided by her neighbours, who suffered an illness 'very long and very painful': it was breast cancer. Her own text shows she knows her scripture and uses it to deal with the pain: 'I am a sin-sick-sinner (the Lord make me more sick) I am not righteous in mine own eyes, but a Sinner'; God 'hath chastized mee less than mine iniquities deserve'. The text she selected for her own funeral sermon asks 'why doth God afflict his own children with such variety of long and great afflictions?' Her text *Mris. Moores evidences for heaven, composed and collected by her in the time of her health, for her comfort in the time of sickness* is in Edmund Calamy, *The Godly mans ark* (1657). (Hobby cites it as an example of women's work 'published posthumously by men . . . reworked by their male editors to serve their own ends': *Virtue*, p. 66.)

MOORE, Mary, *fl.* 1646–50
2. ?Northumberland; 5(a) George Muschamp, (b) Edward Moore.

Wonderfull news from the north. Or, a true relation of the sad and grievous torments, inflicted upon the bodies of three children of Mr George Muschamp, late of the county of Northumberland, by witchcraft: and how miraculously it pleased God to strengthen them, and to deliver them: as also the prosecution of the sayd witches, as by oaths, and their own confessions will appear, and by the indictment found by the jury against one of them, at the sesions of the peace held at Alnwick, the 24 day of April, 1650 (1650).

The preface, signed 'Thine, Mary Moore', says that she presents this 'with a sad heart', to show God's mercy 'for preservation of me and my children, and for delivering us from those extreame torments and miseries wherewith by Diabolicall meanes we have been afflicted'. The witchcraft ordeal lasted from 1645 to 1647: Margaret MUSCHAMP was in a trance, had tormenting fits and produced automatic writing. The witches tried to kill a child in Mary's womb, but, failing, caused its death later. The text contains verbatim reports of Margaret's speeches and the confessions of the witches. It switches on the first page from the third person ('her mother') to the first ('my neice'). Hobby thinks the text is by a man, but we disagree.

MORCOTT, Anne, *fl.* 1692

Greer (p. 23) refers to '*The Loyal Englishman's Wish* by Anne Morcott (1692), about whom we know nothing but her name'; it was a song that provided the tune for many other ballads. Greer infers a lower-class status for its author (from the use of her name).

MORDAUNT, Viscountess Elizabeth, *c.* 1632–79
1. Carey; 2. Somerset; 3. genteel; 4. Anglican; 5. John Mordaunt; 6. genteel.

Elizabeth Mordaunt had eleven children in under twenty years. Her husband was condemned to death in 1658 for his involvement in a Royalist conspiracy, but Elizabeth obtained a reprieve from Cromwell and John became Viscount Mordaunt in 1659. Clarendon calls her 'a young, beautiful lady, of a very loyal spirit and notable vivacity of wit and humour', while Evelyn refers to her as 'the most virtuous lady in the world'. *The Private diary of Elizabeth, Viscountess Mordaunt* was edited by the Earl of Roden (Duncairn, 1856).

MORDAUNT, Penelope, *fl.* 1692–9
1. Warburton; 2. Cheshire, Warwickshire; 3. genteel; 5. Sir John Mordaunt.

Daughter of Sir George Warburton of Arley, Cheshire, she bore four children. She married sometime after 1692, when John Mordaunt's first wife died. Pollock (pp. 28, 143) quotes from a letter of 1699 to her husband, about their daughter, giving as source the Mordaunt family papers in the Warwick Record Office (CR 1368).

MORE, Agnes, 1591–1655/6

2. Bampton (Oxon.), Cambrai; 3. nun; 4. Catholic.

Daughter of John More of Bampton, she went to the New English Benedictine Abbey at Cambrai and professed in 1625.

The probable translator of St Francis de Sales, *Delicious entertainment of the soule: written by the holy and most reverend Lord Francis de Sales, bishop and prince of Geneva. Translated by a Dame of our Ladies of Comfort of the Order of St Bennet in Cambray* (Douai, 1632).

The 'address' excuses faults in the work: the printer is a Walloon, the translator a woman – 'but why did shee then undertake it? wilt thou say, truely, for her private imployment and instruction; never intending more then the use of a particular cloister; though God and her superiors have otherwise disposed of it, and exposed it to the publicrk [sic] view of the world.'

She also translated the second edition of *The ruin of proper love and the building of divine love*, by Dame Jeanne of Cambrai (manuscript); part of this was transcribed by Dame Susanna PHILLIPS in 1691.

MORE, Gertrude (Grace), 1606–33

2. Cambrai; 3. nun; 4. Catholic.

Cousin to Agnes MORE,* she went with her to Douai (1623), then Cambrai; she professed in 1625.

The holy practises of a divine lover, or the sainctly ideots devotions (Paris, 1657). This series of spiritual exercises has a preface 'To my most dearlie beloved friends in Christ Jesus'. *The spiritual exercises of the most vertuous and religious Dame Gertrude More, of the holy order of St. Bennet, and English congregation of our Ladie of Comfort in Cambray* (Paris, 1658) is dedicated to her sister, Bridget More. The address 'To the reader' warns of presumption, says that the work was for her private comfort, to be seen by others 'but against my will, my superiors only excepted': they are allowed to correct it. The text seems to be a posthumous compilation.

MOREY, Dewans, c. 1644–84

4. Quaker.

Whipped for her religious beliefs in Hawkchurch, Dorset, in 1656. Wrote *A true and faithful warning from the Lord God, sounded through me, a poor despised earthen vessel, unto all the inhabitants of England who are yet in their sins* (?1665; part by Charles Bayly).

MORPETH, Mary

Mary OXLIE*

MORRIS, Mary, *fl.* 1721

2. Suffolk; 4. Quaker.

A prospect of death, a Pindaric essay (1721). She seems to have sold this herself and it was inserted in the 1746 edition of Pomfret's poems, where, however, it is attributed to Roscommon.

MORTON, Anne Douglas, Countess of, –1700

1. Hay; 2. Peebles; 3. genteel; 5. James, Earl of Morton (m. 1649); 6. genteel.

Only daughter of Sir James Hay. *The countess of Morton's daily exercise; or, a book of prayers and rules how to spend time in the service and pleasure of Almighty God* (1666; 24 eds by 1760) was written for her: 'By whose earnest desire and Religious care this Book was framed'. She is only the author in the sense she commissioned the book and her name was used to sell it.

MOSS, Elizabeth, ?1663–1702

1. Monk; 2. South Liverton (Notts.), London; 4. Quaker; 5. Thomas Moss; 6. merchant.

She provided a contribution to *A narrative . . . concerning Grace Watson* (1690) (Grace WATSON* was her stepsister). See also 'A few words written by Elizabeth Moss concerning her dear mother', in Samuel Watson, *An epistle by way of testimony* (1695). Her mother was Mary Monk/WATSON;* Elizabeth Moss was married from Samuel Watson's house; she bore four children between 1691 and 1696, all of whom died in infancy. She signed the general testimony for Anne WHITEHEAD* in *Piety . . .* (1686).

MOSS, Mary, *fl.* 1688

2. London; 4. Quaker.

Daughter of Samuel and Mary WATSON (see above). A testimony in *A memorandum . . .* (1688): Grace WATSON.*

MOSTYN, Margaret, 1625–79
2. Flintshire, Antwerp, Lierre; 3. genteel, nun; 4. Catholic.

Daughter of Sir John Mostyn of Talacre, Flint, she was born at Lehurst, Shropshire. In 1644 she went to Antwerp with her sister Elizabeth and professed in 1645. She became prioress at Lierre in 1654. Edward Bedingfield, *The life of Margaret Mostyn* (London: Burns & Oates, 1878) is based in part on her own manuscript.

The mother's blessing

See Appendix I.

MUDD, Ann, *fl.* 1670–8
2. Rickmansworth (Bucks.), ?Middlesex; 4. Quaker; 5. Thomas Mudd.

Ann Mudd was a follower of John Pennyman and her writings came to be considered unsound by Quakers. These writings include *A few lines added to a piece of John Pennyman's, beginning 'These following words'* (1670) and *A cry, a cry; a sensible cry for many months together hath been in my heart for the Quakers return out of that Egyptian darkness they have long lain in, to the grief of the souls of the righteous, and those that truly loved them* (1678).

MURRAY, Janet, *fl.* 1700

Author of the petition *Unto the lords of the council and session . . .* (Edinburgh, 1700). We have been unable to trace this text (and thus to identify its author): it is not held where Wing locates it (in the Bodleian Library, Oxford).

MYERS, Hannah, *fl.* 1721
2. Farrfield, Addingham, Craven (Yorks.); 4. Quaker.

A short testimony or account, given by George Myers and Hannah Myers, concerning their father George Myers . . . in *Spiritual Worship* (1721). George Myers was, possibly, born in 1697 (other children in the late 1680s), but we have been unable to trace Hannah Myers in Yorkshire records.

N

See Appendix I.

NELSON, Lady Theophila, 1654–1705/6

2. Broxbourne (Herts.), London; 3. genteel; 4. Catholic (convert); 5(a) Sir Kingsmill Lucy, (b) Robert Nelson (m. 1682); 6(a) (b) genteel.

Daughter of George, Earl of Berkeley, she had two children by her first marriage. She travelled in Europe between 1688 and 1691, after her first husband's death. When she converted to Catholicism in 1685 her husband remained a Protestant. Wrote *A discourse concerning a judge of controversies in matters of religion* (1686).

NEWBY, Margaret, –1657

2. Hutton (Westmorland); 4. Quaker; 5. ?Edmund Newby (m. ?1652).

Described as 'A woman of some account in the world', she was convinced in 1652 and was imprisoned at Kendal in 1653. A letter of November 1655 to Margaret FELL,* written with Elizabeth COWART,* describes their being put in the stocks at Evesham (where blocks were put between their legs to increase the pain). As a result of these injuries Newby died, having being imprisoned again, in Bewdley, on 25 December 1655.

NEWCASTLE, Margaret, Duchess of

Margaret CAVENDISH*

NEWMAN, Anne, –1685

1. Sewell; 2. Penryn, Falmouth (Cornwall); 4. Quaker; 5. John Newman (m. 1661).

She bore six children between 1665 and 1674. Wrote a testimony in *A handful after the harvest-man* (1684); the record of her death says she 'finished her testimony in peace'. She was connected with Richard and Jane SAMBLE.*

NEWMAN, Winifred, *fl.* 1658–68
2. Isle of Wight, Hampshire; 4.Quaker; 5. James Puckridge (m. 1665).

Her husband was from Romsey, Hants. Two children were born in 1667 and 1668 (the second one dying in 1671), and the deaths of two others are recorded in 1680 and 1704. Wrote with several others, *The fruits of unrighteousness and injustice brought forth by . . . the rulers in Hampshire, against the innocent people of God, called Quakers . . .* (1658). Newman was presumably a prisoner in Winchester at this time.

NEWTON, Elizabeth, –1685
2. Besthorp (Notts.); 4. Quaker; 5. William Smith (m. 1666); 6. preacher, chief constable.

Parish registers record an Elizabeth Newton christened at Sutton-in-Ashfield in 1628; another at Arnold (both in Nottinghamshire) in 1632. Besthorp seems to have been a centre of Quaker activity in Notts.
  A real demonstration of the true order in the spirit of God, and of the ground of all formality and idolatry, in William Smith, *Works* (1663; with Prudence HARDING,* John Moon, Martha PLATTS,* Hannah RECKLESS,* John Reckless, William Smith, Sarah WATSONE*). Also a testimony prefixed to William Smith, *Balm from Gilead* (1675).

NICHOLLS, Elizabeth, –1746
1. Priest; 2. Pitminster (Somerset), Dorset; 4. Quaker; 5(a) Elias Nicholls (m. 1698), (b) Samuel Bownas (m. 1722); 6(a) mercer.

Married her first husband at Taunton, bore him three children between 1698 and 1713, and moved to Dorset on her second marriage. *A testimony concerning her dear husband, Elias Nicholls, deceased* (1715) appears at the end of *Some remains of Daniel Taylor.*

NICHOLS, Bridget, *fl. c.* 1665
4. Quaker.

Wrote with Anne CLABIN* (see for details), Elizabeth NICHOLLS,* Anne WHITEHEAD* *A relation in part of what passed through a true and faithful servant and handmaid of the Lord, M. Page, when she lay upon her bed of* *sickness* (*c.* 1665). (E. NICHOLLS is not presumably the woman above.) This may be the same woman who witnessed William Dewsbury's marriage certificate in 1667.

NORFOLK, Mary, Duchess of, 1659–1705

1. Mordaunt; 2. Northamptonshire; 3. genteel; 4. Protestant; 5(a) Henry Howard, Duke of Norfolk (m. 1677), (b) Sir John Germaine (m. 1701); 6(a)/(b) genteel.

Daughter and heir of Henry, Earl of Peterborough, she became Baroness Mordaunt in 1697. In 1685 she separated from her husband and in 1700 they were legally divorced. Her texts relate to this event.

'Her grace the Dutchess of Norfolks answer to the Lords in Parliament, against a divorce' in *His grace the Duke of Norfolk's charge against the Dutchess, before the House of Lords, and the Dutchesses answer* (1692). She had been accused of committing adultery on several occasions in 1685 with John Germaine. Her text not only claims her innocence but suggests that the Duke's adultery charge is financially motivated. He had promised her £400 a year in addition to her own settlement from her father, but he never paid it; when she sued for alimony, he wrote affectionately to her. He left her in France while he returned to England to try and extract money from her family. He told her mother (in whose house in London he stayed) of his debts, and pressurised his wife to settle on him Drayton manor (to relieve his debts), which she refused to do. Later he pressed her to sell Castle Rising, which she again refused to do; she sees this action as the cause of his adultery charge. She then accused him of adultery over 10 years. She notes that the court proceedings were violent and fast. *The case of Mary Dutchess of Norfolk* (?1700) is a more detailed analysis of the legal moves during the separation and a demonstration of her innocence. She clarifies that she has paid the Duke's debts out of her own estate since separation.

NORTH, Anne, 1614–81

1. Montagu; 2. Essex, Kirtling (Cambs.); 3. genteel; 5. Sir Dudley North (m. 1632); 6. genteel.

Daughter of Sir Charles Montagu, of Cranbrook, Essex, she was a sister-in-law of Lady Dorothy DACRES* and bore 13 children. Between 1677 and 1681 wrote letters to her daughter Anne and son Francis; she was looking after three of the latter's children, whose mother died in 1678. The letters, all written from Tostock, are mostly about domestic matters: 'My dog Tagg ran mad', little Frank being put into breeches, etc. In Jan. 1680/1 she writes to Anne 'The Commet you writ of I heard of a great while ago and saw it every clear night when the other starrs appeared: it is just here as you say you saw it, with a very extraordinary long streame from it.' Around the same time she writes 'as the times are wee dare not ventur out of dores for fear of being either robbed or beaten.' Her daughter Dudleyana had a library of Oriental books.

The letters are printed in Roger North, *The Lives of the Norths*, ed. A. Jessop (1890), vol. 3.

NORTHUMBERLAND, Elizabeth Percy, Countess of, 1666–1722
3. genteel; 5(a) Henry Cavendish, Lord Ogle, (b) Charles Seymour, Duke of Somerset; 6(a)/(b) genteel.

Sole surviving heir of Josceline Percy, she and her first husband married very young (he died 1680). She then contracted to Thomas Thynne of Longleat, Wilts., who was assassinated in Pall Mall in 1682. In her second marriage (after this date) she bore 13 children (five of them died young). Wrote *Meditation and prayers* (1682; five editions by 1712).

NORTON, Lady Frances, 1640–1731
1. Freke; 2. Wiltshire; 3. genteel; 5(a) Sir George Norton, (b) Ambrose Norton, (c) William Jones; 6(b) soldier.

Frances Norton was mother of Grace GETHIN* and author of *The Applause of Virtue* (1705; religious meditations after her daughter's death) and *A miscellany of poems* (Bristol, 1714; the poems are religious).

O

OAKELEY, Anne, *fl*. ?1650s

Her couplet poem 'On a future state', with its echo of Marvell, would seem to be post-1650s. Greer quotes from it (pp. 12–13); the manuscript is at University of Nottingham Portland MS. PwV 329.

'An Ode . . . by a Young Lady'

See Appendix I.

OSBORNE, Alice, 1592–1659
2. Yorkshire, Ireland; 3. genteel; 5. Christopher Wandesford (m. 1614); 6. lord justice, Lord Lieutenant of Ireland.

Daughter of Sir Hewet Osborne of Kniveton, Yorks., she was Christopher Wandesford's second wife. She bore five children. Her husband, who accompanied Strafford to Ireland, died in 1640. *The case of the Lady Wandesford* (?late 1650s) concerns coastal land in Hampshire which was granted to Mary and William Wandesford by Charles I: she seeks permission from Parliament to encourage developers to move onto this land, since she has already spent much money on it. (William Wandesford was a brother of Christopher; a merchant tailor of London, in 1639 he was an MP of the Irish Parliament. Mary was probably the sister of George Wandesford and niece of William who founded the Old Maids Hospital, York, in 1655 and died in 1726.)

OSBORNE, Dorothy, 1627–95
2. Bedfordshire, France, Ireland, Brussels, The Hague; 3. genteel; 5. Sir William Temple; 6. politician and writer.

See Critical Appendix 5.

Dorothy met William Temple in France, having gone there with her brother at the age of 21. She is famous for her love letters to Temple; the standard edition being that of G. O. Moore Smith (Oxford: Clarendon Press, 1928) (also edited by Kenneth Parker: London: Penguin, 1988). Her family was Royalist while Temple's father supported Parliament. Both families opposed the marriage, but Dorothy refused all other suitors, including Henry Cromwell, and married Temple in 1655, after nearly seven years of courtship.

OVERTON, Mary, *fl.* 1647

1. Johnson; 2. London; 3. ?bookseller; 5. Richard Overton; 6. pamphleteer, Leveller leader.

Mary Overton was arrested in January 1647 for stitching copies of *Regall tyrannie discovered,* and 'with her tender Infant in her armes of half a yeares age, was most inhumanely and barbarously dragged headlong upon the stones through all the dirt and mire in the streets, and by the way was most unjustly reproached and vilified by their Officers'. She was brought to the bar of the House of Lords and, refusing to answer questions, was committed to Bridewell for contempt. The baby died in prison.

   To the right honourable, the knights, citizens, and burgesses, the Parliament of England, assembled at Westminster, the humble appeale and petition of Mary Overton, prisoner in Bridewell (1647) narrates this episode. The document cites Magna Carta; says she was arrested (with her brother, Thomas Johnson) because she 'would not be subject to the arbitrarie and diabolicall accustomarie proceedings of that House, to answer to Interrogatories, or to make oath against her husband or her self'; and attacks the House of Lords and the growth of arbitrary power. It is likely that she shared the house of her brother-in-law Henry Overton, the radical publisher/bookseller who was arrested earlier, and who was a neighbour and colleague of Hannah ALLEN.* See *Lords Journals,* vol. 8.

   It is possible that the petition is about her rather than by her (possibly written by her husband); that it follows the format of many legal 'cases' in being a text formed by another from the woman's narrative.

OWEN, Jane, −c. 1634

2. Godstow (Oxon.); 4. Catholic.

Her pamphlet *Antidote against purgatory* (1634) includes translation from Cardinal Bellarmine. The epistle speaks of the 'bolnes of my Sexe'. The text asks pity for 'divers well-disposed younge gentlewomen; who through the decay of their Parents state, not having sufficient portions left them to enter into Religion . . . are forced to forbeare that their most Religious inclination, and for want of meanes to take some secular Course of life, either by marriage, or otherwise.'

OXLIE, Mary, *fl.* ?1614–16
2. Morpeth (Northumberland).

The Oxleys were an important family in Morpeth: Amor Oxley (died 1609) was bailiff of Morpeth, his son Amor (born 1598) became head-master of Morpeth school in 1631. She may be one of Amor the elder's five daughters, or connected with his son's family. A poem by her in praise of William Drummond appears in the 1656 edition of his *Poems*. She was a friend of Drummond, and although her poem appeared in a posthumous edition of his works it was probably written much earlier (Greer suggests sometime soon after 1614–16). In the poem she speaks of her rustic Muse and of her own discontents, which make her verses 'muddy'.

Greer (p. 79 f.) cites Phillips in *Theatrum Poetarum* (1675) as saying that 'Mary Morpeth' (Oxlie) wrote many poems, but no others have been discovered.

P

P—, E—

See Appendix I.

P—, T—

Thomasina PENDARVES*

PACE, Mary, *fl.* **1712–57**
2. New England; 4. Quaker; 5. — Weston.

She wrote a Quaker diary for the years 1712–57, which seems not to have been published (Matthews).

PADLEY, Susanna, *fl.* **1687**
2. East Riding (Yorks.); 4. Quaker; 5. Benjamin Padley.

'This is my testimony concerning my dear husband Benjamin Padley' (1687) in *Some fruits of a tender branch sprung from the living vine* (1691). Benjamin Padley died when he was 29. There is a record of a child born in 1687.

PAGE, Ulalia

See Appendix III.

PAGET, Bridget, *fl.* **1628–39**
2. Nantwich, Amsterdam; 4. puritan; 5. John Paget; 6. non-conformist divine and author.

Bridget Paget wrote the epistle 'To the most illustrious & most excellent lady, Elizabeth, queene of Bohemia, countesse Palatine of the Rhine, &c.'

149

in John Paget, *Meditations of death* (Dort, 1639; the book consists of sermons delivered in 1628). In 1598 John Paget was in Nantwich; in 1605 he was preaching to the army; thereafter he attended the English members of the Dutch Reformed Church congregation in Amsterdam. We presume Bridget travelled with her husband; her politico-religious sympathies are clear in her address to the puritan figurehead, ELIZABETH OF BOHEMIA.*

PAKINGTON, Lady Dorothy, –1679

1. Coventry; 2. London, Worcestershire; 3. genteel; 4. Anglican; 5. Sir John Pakington; 6. genteel.

She was a Royalist, daughter of Thomas, Lord Coventry and mother of Elizabeth EYRE.* Anne FINCH* wrote of her that she 'Of each sex the two best gifts enjoy'd/The skill to write, the modesty to hide.' Fraser (p. 336) says that Pakington 'presided over a kind of Anglican salon at her house . . . in Worcestershire'. Her name is associated with *The whole duty of mankind* (1659), *The ladies calling* (1673) and several other pamphlets (1660–78) but all attributions to her have been disputed. *The whole duty* has been attributed to Richard Allestree, as has part of *The ladies calling*.

PALMER, Barbara

Barbara, Countess of CLEVELAND;* Appendix III.

PARR, Susanna, *fl.* 1635–59

2. Exeter; 4. Baptist, Presbyterian; 5. ?Christopher Parr.

She was one of the earliest members of an independent church in Exeter, formed *c.* 1650. This was probably preceded by thirteen years of child-bearing and mothering (she bore seven children between 1636 and 1649); her text speaks of her 'many Family-cares'. Initially the only woman member of her church, she tells how their minister, Lewis Stucley, always asked her to speak: 'when I was present, he himselfe would constraine me to speak my opinion of things proposed' (she presents herself as of 'stammering Tongue, slow of speech'). Her early approval of the 'Congregational way' was political: 'more liberty of Conscience, and freedome from that yoke of being servants unto Men in this Church State' (the church recognised the authority of the Fifth-Monarchist radical, Feake). Her disagreements developed out of what she saw as the undemocratic and separatist plans of Stucley: 'he desired the sisters (there being now other women added to the Church) to [approve his plans], which my selfe and some others refused, resolving that we would not act by an implicite faith'; 'fasting was perverted to carry on their own designes, and to keep the people ignorant of the occasion and ground of their fast'. Her criticisms and her increasing inclination towards a more conservative church led to her leaving the church (two years before they expelled her) together with Mary ALLEN (wife of Toby, who was opposed by Stucley). Her story exhibits an independent-thinking woman whose politics are anti-radical.

Susannas apologie against the elders. Or, a vindication of Susanna Parr; one of those two women lately excommunicated by Mr Lewis Stucley, and his church in Exeter. Composed and published by her selfe, for the clearing of her own innocency, and the satisfaction of all others (1659) (extract in Graham).

PARTRIDGE, Dorothy, *fl.* ?1694
3. midwife.

After 1700 Benjamin Harris issued almanacs under this name, falsely claiming that Dorothy was the wife of the almanac-writer John Partridge (1644–1715); his real wife was Jane KIRKHAM, whom he married as a widow in 1694. Dorothy may therefore be a pseudonym. The most plausible of the pieces attributed to her seems to be *The woman's almanack for . . . 1694, adapted to the capacity of the female sex* (1694).

PASTON, Lady Katherine, ?1578/84–1628
1. Knyvett; 2. Ashwellthorpe, Paston; 3. genteel; 5. Sir Edmund Paston; 6. genteel.

Katherine Paston acted for her husband in business matters after his illness in 1618. *The correspondence of Lady Katherine Paston, 1603–1627* was edited by Ruth Hughey for the Norfolk Record Society, vol. 14, 1941.

PATISON, Barbara, *fl.* 1656
5. Quaker.

Imprisoned in Exeter gaol for preaching in 1656. With Margaret KILLAM/KILLIN,* she wrote *A warning from the Lord* (1656).

PAVERENST, Anne
2. Germany, London; 3. physician.

A paper advertising her cures, especially suffocation or rising of the mother in women, is included in a BL compendium volume of 'Medical advertisements' (551 a. 32). The paper tells us nothing about her except that she was a 'German Gentlewoman' recently arrived in England, who was living in Holborn.

PELHAM, Lady Frances, –before 1642

1. Conway; 2. Warwickshire, Brocklesby (Lincs.); 3. genteel; 5. Sir William Pelham; 6. genteel.

Daughter of Edward, Viscount Conway's first marriage (he married again in 1614) and sister of Brilliana HARLEY.* Her father was chief of the feoffees controlling the lands of her husband's father. William Pelham was a Royalist who became sheriff of the county in 1636 (he died in 1644). She bore 12 children. Her unpublished spiritual diary, 'An expression of faith' (University of Nottingham Portland MS PwV 89), runs to twenty-seven pages and includes a history of the church, prayers and a verse description of Christian life. Its verbal echoes and conventions lead Greer (pp. 12, 29) to date it in the mid-1650s; this conflicts with our biographical suppositions (which may of course be wrong).

PENDARVES, Thomasina, 1618–

1. Newcomen; 2. Dartmouth, Abingdon; 4. Baptist; 5. John Pendarves; 6. minister.

Thomasina Pendarves's father, Thomas Newcomen, was a Parliamentary supporter in Dartmouth. Her husband, probably also from a West Country family, was a leading Baptist organiser in Abingdon and died in 1656.

'The copy of a letter, as it was sent from T.P., a friend of Mrs Elizabeth Poole, to the congregation of Saints, walking in fellowship with Mr William Kiffin': the letter is in Elizabeth POOLE,* *An alarum of war* (1649: see POOLE for details).

The letter is written from Abingdon, 6 March 1649, and is in defence of POOLE, who had been expelled from Kiffin's congregation: 'this is a time, in which mercy is required of us towards our Sister, and not such Sacrifices. If you please to send me a word of an answer, leave it with M. Calvert, at the Black Spred Eagle . . . I do not think it fit as yet, that you acquaint my husband with it, not for unlawfulnesse sake, but conveniency . . . all your care must serve the Lords designes, to bring it to my hand when my husband was not in town.' The woman's God enables her to intervene for another woman, even against her husband, in order to protect POOLE's reputation, on which her living depends: 'for you cannot be ignorant that she hath no livelihood amongst men, but what she earns by her hands; and your defaming her in this manner cannot . . . but deprive her of that, and so at last bring her blood upon you.'

For the Black Spread Eagle, see Elizabeth CALVERT,* whose shop it was; also Critical Appendix 7.

PENINGTON, Mary, *c.* 1625–82

1. Proude; 2. Sussex, Amersham (Bucks.); 3. genteel, mystic; 4. Independent, Quaker; 5(a) Sir William Springett (m. 1642), (b) Isaac Penington (m. 1654); 6(a) genteel, (b) merchant.

Born in Kent, she bore two children to her first husband, and refused to have her daughter Gulielma baptised (this daughter later married William Penn). She had one son by her second marriage, was convinced in 1656 and her house at Chalfont St Peter (Buckinghamshire) was a meeting house. Although a property-owner, she lost land when her Quaker opposition to oaths meant that she would not swear to the validity of her claim against a relative's lawsuit. In 1669 she bought a farm near Amersham and left money to establish the Chalfont Meeting.

A brief account of my exercises from childhood (1668–80, published 1797 in a pamphlet by Christopher Taylor); *Her testimony concerning her dear husband, Isaac Pennington* (1681); *Some account of the circumstances in the life of Mary Penington, from her manuscript, left for her family* (1821, 1848; this is a detailed record of her sufferings as a Quaker, and of her financial dealings); also some extant letters.

PENNYMAN, Mary

Mary BOREMAN*

PERROT, Luce, –*c.* 1679

1. Hancock; 2. London; 4. Presbyterian; 5. Robert Perrot (m. 1644, Westminster); 6. minister.

She was probably born and raised in Northamptonshire, or Huntingdonshire (her husband was born in St Ives); she married in London, then spent some time in Bedfordshire from 1647 onwards (her first child was baptised there). She bore five children between 1648 and 1660. Her husband was licensed in London in 1672, but she was almost certainly living there before this date (she speaks of hearing Thomas Jacome, rector of St Martin's Ludgate between 1647 and 1662).

An account of several observable speeches of Mrs Luce Perrot, the late wife of Mr Robert Perrot of London, minister spoken by her chiefly in the time of her sickness, and a little before her death; and taken immediately from her own mouth, though unknown to her. And now published for the comfort and benefit of her near relations, and some other of her friends (1679). This is one of those many texts where a sick woman's speeches, given spiritual authority by her physical pain, are written down and 'ordered' by a husband or minister. The text reports her conflict with Satan: ' . . . and oh says she unto me, speaking of Satan, he frighted me, he roared upon me, like a roaring ramping Lyon; he made my bones to shake, and my heart to quake and tremble within me.' She complains of 'grievous pains in my breasts', but is told that the Lamb of God 'takes away the sin of the world'.

PETITIONS

Various individual petitions are listed in the course of this volume. Here we list mass petitions (in chronological order). See Critical Appendix 4.

Severall petitions presented to the Honourable Houses of Parliament. I. The humble petition of many thousands of courtiers, citizens, gentlemen and trades-mens wives . . . concerning the staying of the Queenes intended voyage . . . (1641).

To the right honourable the house of Peers . . . the humble petition of many thousands of courtiers, citizens, gentlemen and tradesmens wives . . . (1641; looks like sub-section of *Severall petitions . . . ,* above).

A true copy of the petition of the gentlewomen, and tradesmens-wives, in and about the city of London (1641; 3 eds in 1642).

The humble petition of many hundreds of distressed women (1642).

Mercurius Philo-monarchicus (May 1649) refers to 'a sad scroul of re-membrance from the widows of the maim'd souldiery, crouded in upon them to commit a rape upon their charitable considerations; but it being a money matter, they resolved to fend off with both hands, and turn the Creatures over to a Committee in a corner.'

A modest narrative of intelligence (May 1649) refers to 'a Petition deliv-ered by the Widows of such whose Husbands have been slain in the Parliments Service, and referred to a Committee to enquire after the state of Hospitals, and what other way of relief may be hasted.' This seems to refer to the same petition as that mentioned in *Mercurius Philo-monarchicus* (above).

To the supreme authority of England the Commons . . . the humble petition of divers well-affected women (1649).

To the supreme authority of the nation, the Commons . . . the humble petition of divers well-affected persons . . . of London (1649).

To the supreme authority of this Commonwealth, the Parliament of England. The humble petition of severall wives and children of such delinquents, whose estates are propounded to be sold, as the petitioners are informed (1650).

The womens petition, to the right honourable, his excellency, the most noble and victorious Lord General Cromwell (1651), signed by E. BASSFIELD, E. COLE, K. FRESE, D. TRINKALE, who presented it to Cromwell. It speaks for 'many thousands of the poor enslaved, oppressed and distressed men and women' and concerns debtors' prisons.

To the Parliament of the Commonwealth of England: the humble petition of divers afflicted women, in behalf of M. John Lilburn prisoner in Newgate (1653) (unsigned, but often associated with Katherine CHIDLEY:* see also *Unto every individual member*, below).

Unto every individual member of Parliament, the humble representation of divers afflicted women-petitioners to the Parliament, on the behalf of Mr John Lilburn (1653): they are sad to see 'our undoubted Right of Petitioning with-held from us, having attended several days at your House-door'. There are references to Esther and Haman, and 'your Honours may be pleased to call to mind that never-to-be-forgotten deliverance obtained by the good women of England against the usurping Danes then in this Nation'.

These several papers was sent to the Parliament 1659 . . . Being above seven thousand names of the hand-maids and daughters of the Lord . . . (1659; Quaker anti-tithe petition). Mary FOSTER,* Mary WESTWOOD.* See Critical Appendix 3.

For the King, and both Houses of Parliament (1660) (a petition about the cruelty to Quakers in Merionethshire; signed by several men and 'Jane Owen widow, Joan Humphrey, Katherine Williams and others of that sex').

The royal virgine: Or, the declaration of several maydens in and about the once honourable city of London (1660; cited by T. Harris, *London Crowds . . .* Cambridge: Cambridge University Press, 1987, p. 46). According to Harris, this shows 'annoyance with the ambiguity concerning the desired political solution expressed in other petitions'. He quotes it as saying 'That the only meanes . . . to bring these nations out of bondage . . . will be that the Crown may be set upon his head whose right it is, C.R.'

To the King and both Houses of Parliament. From the people of God called Quakers in the county of Nottingham . . . Signed by Thomas Ingal and 118 men Friends; by Ann Ingal, and 97 women Friends (1670; Anne INGAL.*).

The ladies of London's petition (1684–8; both title and date seem suspicious).

PETTUS, Katherine, *fl.* 1631–54

Katherine Pettus plaintiffe, Margaret Bancroft defendent in Chancery (1654). Pettus, describing herself as a 'poore Widow', says she has been oppressed by Margaret BANCROFT and her friends for some 23 years in a Chancery suit. Bancroft was the widow of the executor of Pettus's husband's will; in order to obtain the money due to her, Pettus had Bancroft imprisoned for a year.

PHILIPS, Joan

See EPHELIA: Appendix II.

PHILIPS, Judith

See Appendix III.

PHILIPS, Katherine, 1632–64

1. Fowler; 2. London, Cardiganshire/Dyfed, Ireland; 3. trade; 4. Presbyterian; 5. James Philips; 6. government servant.

At marriage Katherine was aged 16, her husband aged 54. He was a leading Parliamentarian and she an ardent Royalist. Much of her poetry either celebrates her politics or rejoices in her love for various named women. She was called 'Matchless Orinda' and was a friend of Jeremy Taylor and Abraham Cowley. Her translation of Corneille's *Pompey* (1663) was acted in Dublin and London, and that of his *Horace* (1667) at court (the last act was by Denham). *Poems by the most deservedly admired* were published, in an unauthorised edition, in 1664, followed by authorised editions in 1667, 1669, 1678 and 1710. *Letters from Orinda to Poliarchus* was published in 1705 and 1729.

See *Selected Poems*, ed. L. I. Guiney (Cottingham, nr. Hull: J. R. Tutin, 1904) and *Minor Poets of the Caroline Period*, ed. G. Saintsbury (Oxford: Clarendon Press, 1905), vol. 1. Also P. M Souers, *The Matchless Orinda* (Harvard Studies in English 5, Cambridge, Mass., 1931). There is a selection in Ferguson (p. 103 f.) and in Greer (p. 186 f.).

PHILO-PHILIPPA

See Appendix II.

PHOENIX, Anne, *fl.* ?1631

Her *The saints legacies* was published in 1631; four reprints by 1640. An epistle says that the text is being published without the author's consent. It has been got together for private friends, but is 'published for the comfort of Gods people'.

PIERS, Lady Sarah, –1720

1. Roydon; 2. Yorkshire, Kent; 3. genteel; 5. Sir George Piers; 6. soldier.

Sarah Piers was a friend of Catherine COCKBURN* and a poet. There is an unsigned verse eulogy of Dryden by her in *The nine muses* (1700) and she contributed unsigned poems for COCKBURN'S *The unhappy penitent* (1701) and *The fatal friendship* (1698). She also has a signed poem ('George for Britain', 1714) celebrating the accession of George I.

MANLEY* suggests she may have had a lesbian relationship with Cockburn. Letters survive.

Greer includes two poems (p. 445).

PINDER, Bridget, –1684

1. Fletcher; 2. North Shields; 4. Quaker; 5. Richard Pinder (m. 1663); 6. mercer.

With Elizabeth HOPPER* she wrote the last part of *A lively testimony to the living truth, given forth by Robert Jeckell upon his deathbed in the presence of many eye and ear witnesses whose names are subscribed* (1676) (the list of signatories is headed by Isabel YEAMANS:* see her for names of the other 'witnesses' to Jeckell's dying words).

PIX, Mary, 1666–?1709

1. Griffith; 2. Nettlebed (Oxon.), London; 3. dramatist; 5. George Pix; 6. merchant tailor.

Mary Pix's only child died in 1690. She wrote poems, a novel (*The inhuman cardinal*, ?1696) and a translation from Boccaccio (*Violenta*, 1704), but was primarily a dramatist. Author of about ten plays (tragedy, comedy, farce) between 1696 and 1706, including the tragedy *Ibrahim* (1696, revived 1702, 1704, 1715), the comedy *The innocent mistress* (1697, acted by Betterton, Bracegirdle, Barry) and *The beau defeated* (1699, published as anonymous). The script of her *The deceiver deceived* was plagiarised by George Powell in 1698; thereafter, most of her plays appeared anonymously (Pearson).

The innocent mistress is reprinted by Morgan and *The Spanish wives* by Kendell. There is a facsimile edition of the *Plays of Pix and Centlivre* (Garland, 2 vols., 1982). See also Greer (p. 413 ff.).

PLATTS, Martha, –1681

2. Nottingham; 4. Quaker; 5. John Marshall (m. 1665).

Her five children were born between 1667 and 1675. She wrote with Elizabeth NEWTON* (and others) *A real demonstration* . . . (1663; for full title and details see Elizabeth NEWTON).

PLEY, Constance, *fl.* 1650s

2. Weymouth, Plymouth; 3. naval supplier; 5. Captain George Pley; 6. naval supplier.

There are many business letters by her in *CSPD* to Navy Commissioners, etc. about stock movements, contracts and imports. She probably assisted her husband in his supplies of canvas, sail cloth, etc. to the navy. He was in Weymouth in 1652–3 and also Dorchester; governor of Weymouth in 1657 and governor of Portland in 1659. A son is spoken of in 1656. Pepys often had dealings with her.

PLUMLEY, Sarah, 1638–1708
2. London; 4. Quaker; 5. ?William Plumley.

With others (all men) she was indicted for riotous assembly at Guildhall, London, in December 1684. Wrote a testimony in Anne WHITEHEAD,* *Piety* . . . (1686).

PLUMSTED, Mary, 1642–1711
1. Cutlett; 2. Tower Hill, Whitechapel (London); 4. Quaker; 5. Clement Plumsted (m. 1662); 6. ironmonger.

Her three children were born between 1663 and 1670 (the last dying in infancy). Wrote a testimony in Anne WHITEHEAD,* *Piety* . . . (1686) and signed *A tender and Christian testimony* (1685; see Mary ELSON* for details).

POCOCK, Mary, *fl.* 1649–54
2. Reading (Berks.); 4. Bœhmenist.

A follower of John Pordage, who was a visionary and student of Bœhme (with his wife, Mary Lane FREEMAN of Tenby, Worcestershire, he organised a Bœhme study-group; she believed in communal ownership of property). John Pordage was curate of St Lawrence, Reading 1644–54 (in 1669 as leader of a conventicle he met and influenced Jane LEAD*). Mary Pocock defended him before the Reading Assizes in 1654 and in her pamphlet, *The mystery of the deity in the humanity* (1649; Smith, pp. 190, 210–12).

POLWHELE, Elizabeth, *c.* ?1651–91
2. ?Devon; 3. dramatist; 5. ?Stephen Lobb; 6. cleric.

The editors of *The frolicks* . . . (below) conjecture that Elizabeth was the daughter of Theophilus Polwhele, nonconformist minister and vicar of Tiverton (Devon).

She wrote a tragedy, *The faithful virgins* (1670) which was acted at Lincoln's Inn Fields, and an unacted comedy, *The frolicks; or, the lawyer cheated*, as well as an unperformed and lost play called 'Elysium'.

The frolicks . . . has been edited by J. Milhous and R. Hume (New York: Cornell University Press, 1977). It is the first comedy written by a woman for the professional English stage. See also Morgan.

POOLE, Elizabeth, *fl.* 1648–?68
2. ?Hertfordshire; 3. prophet; 4. Baptist.

Possibly the daughter of Robert Poole, who in 1645 attacked William Kiffin for seducing his children into the Particular Baptists. On 29 December 1648 she delivered a prophecy to the General Council of the army which justified the transfer of power from king to Parliament to army. This message, effectively justifying the army's case against its political opponents, was publicised in *The manner of the deposition of Charles Stewart . . . Also the words of a woman, who pretends to have seen a vision, to the Generall Councell of the Army.* 4 Jan. 1648/9. (She is described as a woman of Hertfordshire.) Poole's own account is in *A vision: The summe of what was delivered to the Generall Councel of the Army, December 29 1648.* On her second visit to the Council (5 January) she stressed that the king's person should not be harmed. Around this time she was expelled by Kiffin's Baptist church (possibly at the instigation of members of the General Council, who now found her message less attractive). Warnings about her were sent to churches outside London, including that of Abingdon where Thomasina PENDARVES* intercepted the message. A reprint of the *Vision: An alarum of war, given to the army, and to their high court of justice (so called), revealed in a vision* . . . (1649) names William Kiffin and Thomasina's husband, John Pendarves, as Poole's enemies. Another printing of *An alarum* (1649) develops her accusations about her 'pursuit by them that are called Saints, when I was last at the generall Councell': 'It is true indeed I confessed all that was in my heart to you, when I was drunke with the indignation of the Lord . . . the which your Messengers, to render me the more odious, added, that I went about seducing.'

In 1653 she allegedly 'caused scandal by preaching her strange illuminations on several successive Sundays in Somerset-house Chapel. On 17 July only a guard of soldiers saved her from being stoned, and a week later it dispersed her congregation and ordered it to meet there no more' (A. Woolrych, *Commonwealth to Protectorate*, Oxford: Oxford University Press, 1982, p. 242). In 1668 she may have housed Elizabeth CALVERT's* secret press.

POPE, Mary, *fl.* 1644–8
2. ?Northamptonshire; 3. prophet; 4. ?Anglican.

Author of three pro-monarchist tracts, in which she claims alienation from both Presbyterians and Independents: *A treatise of magistracy, shewing the magistrate hath been, and for ever is to be the cheife officer in the Church, out of the Church, and over the Church* (1647): a plea about taxation, begun about 1644 and written down by her son; *Behold, here is a word or, an answer to the late remonstrance of the Army. And likewise, an answer to a book, cal'd the foundation of the peoples freedomes, presented to the generall counsell of officers. With a message to all covenant-breakers, whom God hates* (1648; two parts; 'to be sold by Mrs Edwards, the Book-binders widdow in the Old Baillie; and that of the Treatise of Magistracy'). Part 2 of this is *Heare, heare, heare, heare, A word or message from Heaven, to all covenant breakers (whom God hates) with all that hath committed that great sinne, that is, as the sinne of witchcraft* (1648).

She attributes the delay in finishing *A treatise* to 'extraordinary change' in the family. We may have a clue as to where she lived when she says she feels God's providence has brought the king to Holmby House (in February 1647) in Northamptonshire. Her treatise answers objections that her 'writings are non-sense': 'If they would study the Scriptures as I doe, they shall find them very good sense.' Readers should 'thinke it no dishonour to heare the Counsell of a woman, being nothing but what is according to the Word'; she asks whether the chief burden of the war 'has . . . not beene upon the middle ranks of people, that are the cheif upholders of the highest ranke, and of the lowest'. As a non-sectarian 'prophet' she forms an interesting contemporary contrast to POOLE;* her combination of monarchism and gender consciousness liken her to CAVENDISH.*

POTTER, Susanna, 1659–

1. Lay; 2. Birch, Marks Tey (Essex); 4. Quaker; 5. Thomas Potter.

Testimony concerning William Allen, in *The last words . . . of William Allen* (1680).

POWYS, Elizabeth, Marchioness

See Appendix III.

POYNTZ, Mary, *fl.* 1609

2. St Omer, Rome; 3. nun; 4. Catholic.

Companion of Mary WARD,* and one of seven women who in 1609 accompanied her from England to St Omer to set up a boarding school for the daughters of English Catholics and a day school for Belgian children. The Institute of the Blessed Virgin Mary in Rome has a copy of *Italian life* 'recently found in Rome and ascribed to Mary Poyntz', and she wrote, with Winifred WIGMORE,* *The brief relation,* a biographical sketch of Mary Ward. See Mother Pauline Parker's *The Spirit of Mary Ward* (1945), reprinted Tenbury Wells: Thomas More Books, 1963.

PRICE, Elizabeth, *c.* 1668–

2. London, Italy; 5. Charles Knollys, Earl of Banbury; 6. genteel.

The true countess of Banbury's case, relating to her marriage rightly stated in a letter to the Lord Banbury (1696).

Price, described elsewhere as a lady at the Court of St Germain, claims that 'this Defence is in some sort a Duty to your Lordship in the Right of your Wife.' The text tells of Knollys wooing her at her Pall Mall house in 1689; of their going to France to celebrate marriage (where he 'wrote letters to me your self as Countess of Banbury'); of marriage in Verona in 1692 (she reprints accounts by witnesses). Price's text aims to challenge Knollys's claim that he was already married to Elizabeth LISTER (whom he married in 1689 at the Nag's Head coffee house in Covent Garden). The Court of Delegates in January 1697 found against Price, who is said to have 'been a Player and mistress to several persons' whereas Lister has a 'good reputation' and children. It looks as if Price was exploited by Knollys, since at about the time he was meant to have married her it was legally decided that he had no right to the Earldom of Banbury, following his killing of his brother-in-law, Captain Philip Lawson, in a duel. When he was bailed in 1693 he apparently told Price that 'It would be of Service to him for me to subscribe a Paper purporting a Disclaimer of my Marriage.'

PRIMROSE, Diana, – ? *c.* 1636

2. ?France, London; 4. ?French Protestant; 5. ?Gilbert Primrose; 6. cleric.

A chaine of pearl. Or a memoriall of the peerless graces, and heroick vertues of Queene Elizabeth of glorious memory. Composed by the noble lady Diana Primrose (1630; ten couplet poems which itemise Elizabeth's religion, chastity, prudence, temperance, clemency, justice, fortitude, 'science', patience and bounty). The poem's source is Camden's *Annals of Queen Elizabeth* (published in Latin, 1615 and in French, 1624). The praise of Elizabeth I in the reign of Charles I tended to imply criticism of him (she had prestige or virtues which he lacked); in this sense the text is political. This fact makes a link between Diana and Gilbert Primrose, a minister of the French Protestant church. In 1622 a ban had been imposed on foreigners living in France, so Gilbert (who had been in Bordeaux since 1602 and saw this as a Jesuit conspiracy) came to England with his family. In October 1623 the king promised to provide for him; nothing was forthcoming, so in December Gilbert gave the king a 'Panegyric' in French and was again promised help (of which nothing came). In October 1626 he wrote a narrative stating his case, that he had been 'beneficial' to England and Scotland and that he was 'the only man of my profession in this island'. In 1634 Archbishop Laud warned him, among others, about the activities of the French and Dutch Reformed churches in London. He had become a chaplain to Charles I by 1628; he married again in 1637. The evidence for connecting Diana with Gilbert is fragmentary: Diana is not a common English name at this period; he too writes poetry to a monarch, which functions as a form of self-advertisement; they share a political outlook. Gilbert's first wife bore two sons before 1603, and two more in 1606 and 1610; she probably married c. 1600.

Dorothy BERRY* writes a poem in the same volume. Extract in Greer, p. 83 f.

PRINCE, Mary, –1679
2. Bristol, Boston, Turkey; 4. Quaker; 5. Edward Prince.

Had three daughters, one of whom was Hannah MARSHALL.* She travelled widely between 1656 and 1660: to Turkey with Mary FISHER* and Beatrice BECKLY (1657), and to Boston with Sarah GIBBONS, Dorothy WAUGH* and Mary WETHERHEAD. A sufferer in 1664, she signed the Fox/Fell marriage certificate in 1669, and in 1674 was involved in organising poor relief for Bristol Friends. There is an unpublished manuscript by her at Swarthmore, in adoration of George Fox, as well as a letter (c. 1656) praising him.

PROWSE, Anne, fl. 1590

She translated Of the marks of the children of God, and of their comforts in afflictions (1590) from the French of John Taffin. Taffin was minister in the French church at Harlem. In Prowse's address to the Countess of Warwick, she says 'because great things by reason of my sex, I may not doe, and that which I may, I ought to doe, I have according to my duetie, brought my poore basket of stones, to the strengthening of the walles of that Jerusalem.' This may possibly be Anne Vaughan, the second wife of Richard Prowse, mayor of Exeter (alive in 1589).

Q

QUARLES, Ursula, *fl.* ?1610–45

1. Woodgate; 2. ?Essex; 5. Francis Quarles (m. ?1610/13); 6. poet, chronologer of the city of London.

Ursula and Francis Quarles had 18 children, one of them at least being born in Essex (the birthplace of Francis Quarles).

A short relation of the life and death of Mr Francis Quarles, in his *Solomon's recantations* (1645). She says: 'though it had been necessary in any other, to have spoken somewhat of his writings; yet I hope it will not be expected from me, seeing that neither the judgement of my sex can be thought competent nor (if it were) would the nearness of my relation to him suffer me to praise.'

Quarles's *Judgment and mercy* (1646) was printed 'for V. Q.'.

R

R—, S—

R—, S—

See Appendix I.

RALEGH, Elizabeth, *c.* 1564–
1. Throckmorton; 3. genteel; 5. Sir Walter Ralegh; 6. explorer, courtier, writer.

She was Maid of Honour to ELIZABETH I* around 1584. Partnow (p. 145) quotes from a letter to Robert Cecil, her source being Violet Wilson, *Society women of Shakespeare's time* (London: John Lane, 1924). See also Ralegh, *Letters* (ed. E. Edwards, 1868).

RANDE, Mary

Mary CARY*

RECKLESS, Hannah, –1675
2. Nottingham; 4. Quaker; 5. John Reckless; 6. maltster, ?ironmonger.

Her four children were born between 1650 and 1658; her house was a meeting-house (and her husband was at one stage sheriff of Nottingham). With Elizabeth NEWTON* (and others) she wrote *A real demonstration . . .* (1663; see Elizabeth NEWTON for full title and details); and may also have signed *To the King and both Houses of Parliament* (1670).

REDFORD, Elizabeth, ?1646–1729
2. London; 4. Quaker.

Mariabella FARNBOROUGH* was asked to invite Redford to a meeting to receive Friends' advice after the latter had advised that Friends should not pay towards the Act relating to births, marriages and burials (the

164

money being 'to carry on Warr etc'). In December 1694 a paper by her was considered by the London Morning Meeting and 'Judged not convenient to print.' She probably travelled to the Netherlands, and William Sewel said of her that 'even though nothing could be charged against her which deserved publick censure, still, more than once in my presence she has shown such great harshness.' In 1695 John Vaughton reported that he had received copies of papers from her 'which she published beyond the seas'.

The widow's mite . . . humbly offered not impos'd; shewing by scripture when the seventh day . . . is to be kept in Christ . . . (1696). *The love of God is to gather the seasons of the earth; and the multitudes into peace* (*c.* 1690). *A warning from the Lord to the city and nation, in mercy to the people . . .* (1695). *A warning, a warning from the Lord, in mercy to the people to see if they will yet seek him . . .* (1696).

REGINALDA, Bathsua

Bathsua MAKIN*

Reports by Quaker women

See Appendix I.

RICH, Mary, Countess of Warwick, 1625–78

1. Boyle; 2. Dublin, Cork, Youghall, Leigh's Priory, London; 3. genteel; 4. puritan; 5. Charles Rich; 6. genteel.

Her courtship was opposed by her father (Richard Boyle, Earl of Cork) and she was briefly banished from home. Father and daughter were reconciled, but Mary's marriage was secret. She says she composed her autobiography in two days in 1672, and in it she describes her 'happy love-match'. By contrast, the diary which covers the last eleven years of her life reveals the marriage to have been a form of purgatory. Her texts present versions of herself for different readerships.

Rules for a holy life, Pious reflections upon several scriptures and *Occasional meditations upon sundry subjects* were published in 1686 (the latter composed from *c.* 1663). *Memoir of Lady Warwick: also her diary from A.D. 1666 to 1672* (English Monthly Tract Society, 1847; extracts). *Autobiography of Mary Countess of Warwick*, ed. T. Croker (Percy Society, 1848). Extracts from the diary are in Houlbrooke.

See Sandra Findley and Elaine Hobby, 'Seventeenth-century women's autobiography' in F. Barker (ed.), *1642: Literature and power in the seventeenth century* (Colchester: Essex University, 1981). Also

C. Fell Smith, *Mary Rich, Countess of Warwick, 1625–1678* (London: Longmans, Green & Co., 1901).

RICH, Penelope, 1562/3–after 1605

1. Devereux; 3. genteel; 5. Lord Rich; 6. genteel.

Penelope Rich was the 'model' for Sidney's *Astrophel and Stella*. Letters by her are quoted in Violet Wilson, *Society women of Shakespeare's time* (London: John Lane, 1924; Partnow, p. 126). Letters are in BL Add. MS 12500 and at Hatfield. Constable, Barnfield and John Davies of Hereford are among the poets who dedicated work to her.

RICH, Rebecca, *fl.* 1652–3

2. Dublin; 4. Baptist; 5. ?Stephen Rich; 6. naval officer.

Rebecca Rich's 'experiences' are in Rogers, *Ohel . . .* (1653) (see Mary BARKER* for details). Her husband is described as a 'captain'; the only relevant Rich we can find is Stephen (from Cheshire) who commanded ships which made the Irish crossing. She speaks of hearing Cradock preach: this may be Walter Cradock, who moved from Cardiff (where he formed an independent church in 1639) to Wrexham (possibly making a geographical link with Stephen Rich), then to London. (She could also mean Samuel Cradock: in Hertfordshire and Hampshire in 1645, and in Surrey 1652–3. The famous army radical, Nathaniel Rich, was not married to a Rebecca.)

RICHARDSON, Ann, ?1660–

2. Lincolnshire; 4. Quaker.

Testimony in Jane MARKHAM's* *An account of the life and death of . . . Thomas Markham* (1695). Letters in Swarthmore MSS 3, 101, 104. There are several Anne Richardsons in Lincolnshire: one married Gabriel Skinner in 1695; another married John Richardson in 1666 and bore three children between 1670 and 1676.

RICHARDSON, Elizabeth, *fl.* 1619–45

1. Beaumont; 2. Stoughton (Leics.), Sussex, Barking (Essex); 3. genteel; 4. Protestant; 5(a) Sir John Ashburnham; (b) Sir Thomas Richardson; 6(a) genteel, (b) Lord Chief Justice.

The eldest daughter of Sir Thomas Beaumont of Stoughton, she had five daughters by her first marriage, and was created Lady Cramond in 1628, in her second marriage (her husband as a judge could not take the title). In

1622 she set up a tomb to her mother, celebrating her as an heiress (of Farnham of Stoughton) in her own right. She also used the tomb as a memorial to her own daughter Mary, who died in 1619. This focus on the female line is apparent in her text. *A ladies legacie to her daughters. In three books* (1645) is a work written at three stages of crisis in Elizabeth Richardson's life. She began the first book at Chelsea, in rooms lent her by the Duchess of Buckingham, in 1625 after the death of her first husband; she speaks of being destitute. Book 2 was begun in Barking, after the death of her second husband in 1634. Each time she deals with her own destitution by offering the positives of education and spiritual improvement to her daughters; she turns from a tragic male world to a hopeful female one: 'however this my endeavour [for spiritual welfare] may be contemptible to many, lest being men, they misconstrue my well-meaning; yet I presume that you my daughters will not refuse your Mothers teaching (which I wish may be your ornament and a crown of glory to you).' Book 3 was written after her 'long and great fit of sicknesse'; she uses her writing to deal with this by constructing prayers for her own and others' benefit.

RICHARDSON, Elizabeth, *fl.* 1679

2. West River (Maryland); 4. Quaker.

Testimony (1679) in *A testimony concerning . . . William Coale* (1682). She was with him at his death.

RICHARDSON, Elizabeth, *fl.* 1714

2. ?Hertfordshire; 4. Quaker.

'Concerning our dear friend Thomas Ellwood' (1714; in *The history of the life of Thomas Ellwood*). She was a member of the Hunger Hill meeting (Bedfordshire). This may be the Elizabeth, daughter of William Richardson of Hitchin, who was born 1695.

ROLPH, Alice, *fl.* 1648

2. Isle of Wight, London; 5. Major Edmond Rolph; 6. shoemaker, soldier.

To the chosen and betrusted knights, citizens, and burgesses assembled in Parliament at Westminster. The humble petition of Alice Rolph, wife to Major Edmond Rolph, close prisoner at the Gate-house Westminster, etc. (1648).

Edmond Rolph was accused by Richard Osborne in June 1648 of plotting Charles I's assassination at Carisbrooke Castle. He was imprisoned in July, when his wife was prevented access to him; he was acquitted in September. (He was back on the Isle of Wight in 1649, his command strengthened in 1650.) This legal document argues that her husband was framed, accuses the Lords of tyranny in imprisoning Rolph and pleads with the Commons to stop this tyranny. In 1659 he became commissioner for sequestrations in Hertfordshire, was imprisoned in 1660 and 1663, and last heard of imprisoned in Grimsby.

RONE, Elizabeth, *fl.* 1680–8
4. ?Familist.

The description of the singers of Israel, or the Family of love, in a song of Zion (1680) is a song in defence of her religious sect against their opponents. The leader of this sect is John Taylor; she also is said, by enemies, to be a leader, of which she is proud. God's love is a concept central to the sect ('we love all both Turk and Jew'); the allusion to the Family of Love recalls a radical sect of the late 1580s. *Elizabeth Rone's short answer to Ellinor James's long preamble* (1687) is a verse attack on the Anglican position of Elinor JAMES's* *Vindication* and her support of the Test Act. Rone's position is that of a religious dissenter who is loyal to the Catholic James II (she opposes those who support religious uniformity as a means of attacking James, because that would affect her too): 'The New Church and Calvin's are alike,/When they get up, they do their Brethren strike;/They both are Persecutors.' *A reproof to those church men or ministers that refused to read the king's most gracious declaration* (1688) is another verse attack on Protestant opponents of James, this time blaming them for trying to recruit dissenters to their cause 'Tho formerly you did them stubborn call,/And in your Pulpits at them loud did baul;/Nay more than that, you Robbed many a one;/And under your oppressions made them groan.' The text was printed for her, so she presumably was fairly wealthy. *CSPD*, vol. 444:4 has an undated letter to Charles II referring to his watching a play (which may indicate again her social status): 'The players are less abominable than Baal's priests of any sort for ministers.' She asks that he hear John Taylor and Thomas Boyce, then imprisoned, dispute with the Quakers, who 'have so abused the single language with double dealing that the true people of God are almost ashamed to use it'; 'The Pope is the golden head, the Quakers the feet, part iron and part clay.'

ROUSE, Margaret, ?1633–1706
1. Fell; 2. London, Barbados; 4. Quaker; 5. John Rouse; 6. planter, Quaker preacher.

Margaret Rouse was the eldest daughter of Margaret FELL* and author of *An account of a divine visitation and blessing* (?1679). She married in 1662, and was in Bristol during Fox's visits in 1669 and 1673.

See Isabel Ross, *Margaret Fell* (London: Longmans, Green, & Co., 1949).

ROWLANDSON, Mary, –1675

1. White; 2. Lancaster (Mass.); 4. puritan; 5(a) Joseph Rowlandson, (b) Captain Samuel Talcott; 6(a) minister.

A true history of the captivity and restoration of Mrs. Mary Rowlandson . . . (1682) is the title of the London edition of her best-selling *The sovereignty and goodness of God together, with the faithfulness of his promises displayed . . .*, which appeared in 3 eds. in America the same year. It was 'Written by her own hand for her private Use' but made public at the desire of friends. Appended to her text is the last sermon of her first husband. Increase Mather seems to have encouraged her to publish her narrative, and may have written the preface.

Born in England, the daughter of wealthy proprietors of Salem, she moved to Lancaster in 1653, married three years later, and had four children, one of whom died while captive, as described in her narrative. Mary Rowlandson's husband was away when the Narrhagansets attacked and burnt Lancaster (February 1675). She and her children were taken and travelled with the Indians until May (she at one time serving as maid to a squaw). She describes much Indian brutality, but records that 'one of the Indians carried my poor wounded Babe upon a horse'. She and the children were eventually ransomed.

In *Somers Tracts*, 1800; R. K. Diebold, 'A critical edition of Mrs. Mary Rowlandson's captivity narrative', dissertation, Yale University, 1972; and K. Z. Derounian, 'The publication . . . of Mary Rowlandson's captivity narrative', *Early American Literature*, vol. 23, 1988, pp. 239-61.

RUSSELL, Lady Rachel, 1636–1723

1. Wriothesley; 2. Carmarthenshire, Hampshire, London, Hertfordshire; 3. genteel; 5(a) Francis, Lord Vaughan, (b) Lord William Russell; 6(a)/(b) genteel.

Letters of Lady Rachel Russell (1773; three editions by 1809; edited in two volumes by J. R., 1853). Also, there are letters by her in *Some account of the life . . .* (ed. M. Betty, 1819). *CSPD* July 1683 has letters from her about her husband and, on 21 July (*CSPD* 428:60), information that she arranged for Lord Russell's execution speech to be printed by the Darbys and was involved in organising its distribution. The execution of her husband, who had been a Whig leader in the Exclusion crisis, and was implicated in the Rye House Plot, made him a martyr to the Whig cause; her persistence in promoting and circulating his unrepentant last speech brought her under suspicion and surveillance.

S

SALTER, Hannah

Hannah STRANGER*

SALTONSTALL, Rosamond, 1612–

2. Yorkshire, Montgomeryshire/Powys; 4. ?Baptist; 5. Richard Price (m. *c.* 1645); 6. soldier, MP.

Baptised in Wragby (Lincolnshire), she travelled to New England with her father, the merchant Sir Richard Saltonstall (of Yorkshire), in 1630, returning in 1631. She was the second wife of Richard Price, a Fifth Monarchist captain in 1647, MP in the Barebones Parliament and commissioner for the Propagation of the Gospel in Wales. He willed his estate to Rosamond in 1671.

Author of a letter (1644) in *The Saltonstall Papers*, ed. Robert Moody (Boston: Massachusetts Historical Society, 1972), p. 136. Her letter, to her brother, is written from Warwick House (where she lived in the Earl of Warwick's family for two years) and is about spiritual beauty.

SAMBLE, Jane, *fl.* 1668–84

1. Voyse; 3. St Austell (Cornwall); 4. Quaker; 5. Richard Samble (m. 1668); 6. tailor, minister.

Originally from Creed (Cornwall), she bore six children between 1669 and 1679, three of them dying young. Wrote 'A testimony for my dear husband' in *A handful after the harvest-man* (1684). Testimony also by Anne NEWMAN* and Abigal SHEPHERD.*

SAMM, Mary, 1667–80

2. Bedfordshire; 4. Quaker.

An exhortation to all people . . . (1680): 'The following lines are what was exprest by Mary Samm.' She was the daughter of John Samm of Houghton Conquest (Bedfordshire), but was with her grandfather William Dewsbury when he was in prison in Warwick.

SANDILANDS, Mary, *fl.* 1673–96

1. Greenaway; 2. Reading; 4. Quaker; 5(a) Henry Cross, (b) Robert Sandilands (m. 1684); 6(b) former university student.

She had three children by her first marriage (between 1673 and 1679), and three by her second (between 1685 and 1690, one dying in infancy). She was a member of the Reading Women's Meeting (signing the testimony for Joan VOKINS* in 1691); but was at some stage considered unsound by Friends. She wrote *A tender salutation of endeared love, to all that sincerely believe in, and unfeignedly love our blessed Lord, and for ever to be admired saviour and adored advocate Jesus Christ. With something of Christian advice and seasonable counsel, for the encouraging of the faithful to be noble in their confessing to, and owning of their glorious captain: and to contend earnestly for the faith which was once delivered to the saints . . .* (1696).

SANSOM, Jane, *fl.* 1691–1710

1. Bunce; 2. Charney, Abingdon, Farringdon (Berks.); 4. Quaker; 5. Oliver Sansom; 6. storekeeper, minister.

'The testimony of Jane Sansom, concerning her dearly belov'd husband, Oliver Sansom' (1710; in Oliver Sansom's *Life*). She signed the general testimony from the Reading Women's Meeting for Joan VOKINS* in 1691.

SAUNDERS, Elizabeth, *fl.* 1587

3. Catholic; 4. nun.

A letter written from Rouen to Sir Francis Englefield, dated 1587, gives a detailed account of her visit to her family in England which resulted in six years' imprisonment. After the dispersal of her convent (in Rouen?) by 'heretics' she travelled to Berkshire and Hampshire, where she was arrested and interrogated under suspicion of being involved in a plot to reinstate Catholicism in England. For refusing to attend church she was imprisoned in Winchester Bridewell and accumulated fines at the rate of £20 per month. She reports her repeated arraignment at the assizes as 'spinster' ('as though by my occupation I had been a spynner') and her refusal to doff her hat. She broke prison to hear mass, was recaptured and imprisoned again, but being recalled by letter to her convent she resolved to escape. She bribed the warder's wife, who allowed her to escape via a rope over the wall. While on the run, however, she met with three priests who disapproved of her action in escaping, and who sent her back to prison to await God's deliverance. Later, convinced that in conscience she should escape, she did so again, and after help from Francis Yates and a friend of Sir Francis Walsingham she obtained a passport in the name of Elizabeth Neale.

Her letter was dictated ('I am no scrivener') and is preserved in the Englefield Correspondence at the English College, Valladolid. It is published in 'The history of Sion', *The Poor Soul's Friend,* January/February 1966, pp. 11–22. A second letter to Englefield recounting her experiences in prison survives only in a Spanish translation published by Yepez in his *Historia Particular,* a retranslation into English by Dom Adam Hamilton of Buckfast Abbey seems not to have been published.

SAVAGE, Sarah, 1664–1752

1. Henry; 2. Wrenbury Wood (Flintshire); 4. nonconformist; 5. John Savage; 6. farmer.

The third child of Katharine and Philip Henry, of Broad Oak, Sarah kept a nonconformist diary as did her father (an ejected minister), brother Matthew (minister and biblical commentator), and sisters Katharine TYLSTON* and Ann HULTON.* Only the first volume of her original diary, which she began in August 1686, survives; two eighteenth-century transcripts may represent only selections from the original entries. She was unhappy about the prospect of marriage to her 'cousin' John Savage, a widower with a young daughter, though the marriage seems to have been long and happy; they married on 23 March 1687 and her diary records her leaving home on 19 April as 'ye saddest day that ever came over my head, my heart ready to burst'. Her first diary records her distress at failing to conceive a child; eventually she had five daughters (four surviving) and one son, who died of smallpox at the age of 21. Crawford notes the introspective nature of her writing, her identification throughout her life with her family of origin, and the mutual support of the Henry women. In 1818 a descendent published a life of Sarah Savage which ran to five editions, and emphasised the piety and 'female virtue' of Sarah and her sisters.

Chester City Record Office, Diary of Sarah Savage; Bodleian, Diary of Mrs Sarah Savage from 31 May 1714 to 25 December 1723; Dr Williams's Library, Mrs Savage's Journal, Henry MS 2; also at Dr Williams's Library, Sarah Savage's commonplace book, Henry MS 3. See J. B. Williams, *Memoirs of the Life and Character of Mrs Savage,* London, 1818; Patricia Crawford, 'Katharine and Philip Henry and their children: a case study in family ideology', *Transactions of the Historic Society of Lancashire and Cheshire,* vol. 143, 1985.

SAVILLE, Katherine, 1667–1755

2. Snape, Knaresborough (Yorks.); 4. Quaker; 5. Thomas Dodson (m. 1698).

Daughter of John Saville, a joiner, of Snape. Wrote a testimony in *A true relation of the life & death of Sarah Beckwith* (1692).

SCAIFE, Issable, *fl.* 1667–86

1. Askell; 2. Blacksike, nr. Appleby (Westmorland); 4. Quaker; 5. William Scaife (m. 1667); 6. ?yeoman.

A short relation of some words and expressions that were spoken by Barbara Scaife, in the time of her sickness, a little before she parted this life . . . (1686; with William Scaife). Her daughter Barbara died aged 15 and her daughter Mary at 18; both of smallpox. The text quotes both of them.

SCARBOROW, Anne

See Appendix III.

SEARL, Margaret, *fl.* 1668–1706

2. London; 3. physician; 5. Samuel Searl; 6. physician.

She prints a document 'to certifie, that neither my father, or husband, ever instructed, or communicated this secret to any of their servants, or any apprentice whatsoever' (10 April 1706). She is protecting her sole right to practise a cure for deafness that her husband had practised for thirty-eight years and taught her to practise. (Her father is Edmund Searl.) She also claims she is still living in West Smithfield, though reported to be dead.

SEDMAN, Elizabeth, –1704

2. Scarborough (Yorks.); 4. Quaker; 5. Thomas Sedman.

Two children died early (1660), another was born 1661. She signed the *Epistle from . . . York* (1688): see Mary WAITE* for details.

SHARP, Jane, *fl.* 1671

Her *The midwives book* (1671; several editions) is the first known book of its kind by an Englishwoman. It is addressed to her fellow midwives as 'sisters' and it was published, she says, to keep midwifery in women's control. It is full of jokes at men's expense. (See the discussion in Hobby, *Virtue*, pp. 185–7).

SHARP, Joane

See Appendix III.

SHAW, Ann, –1680

2. Besthorp (Notts.); 4. Quaker; 5. Robert Shaw.

Wrote a testimony prefixed to William Smith, *Balm from Gilead* (1675), concerning him. This is also signed by Robert Shaw, Elizabeth ELSAM* and Thomas Elsam.

SHAW, Hester, *fl.* 1650–3

2. Barking (London); 3. midwife.

Author of two pamphlets, both of 1653: *Mrs Shaw's innocency restor'd, and Mr Clendon's calumny retorted, notwithstanding his late triumph; by sundry depositions, making out more than ever she by discourse or writing did positively charge upon him (in respect of the unjust detention of certain sums of money etc.)* and *A plain relation of my sufferings by that miserable combustion, which happened in Tower-Street through the unhappy firing of a great quantity of gunpowder there the 4. of January 1649* [1650] (1653).

Hester Shaw speaks of 'finding myself crouded into print with calumny and reproach' and writes 'in the plain stile of a weak woman (with all sincerity and meekness, however provoked)'. Her genteel son-in-law (Daniel Dunne) and his three children were killed in the explosion, her house blown up and her property and money scattered (she was absent, attending Lady BRENT). Some of the money was collected and deposited with the minister, Mr Clendon, but when she came to regain it, she claimed Clendon had taken some. She says she is forced into print to answer Clendon, who has abused her in an epistle to a published sermon, and to put the record straight. Her status and reputation were mobilised in her support: her friends included the Lady Mayoress and Alderman Viner; and she prints affidavits from several tradesmen and women of standing; she had, according to Clendon, 'some ability in prayer, and in speaking of matters of Religion'.

SHEPHERD, Abigal, –1719

2. Falmouth (Cornwall); 4. Quaker; 5(a) Bartholomew Shepherd, (b) Steven Richards (m. 1683).

The second wife of Richards, she bore four children between 1684 and 1688 (the first dying in infancy). Wrote a testimony in *A handful after the harvest-man* (1684), and thus connected with Richard and Jane SAMBLE.*

SHERWOOD, Ann, *fl.* 1659
2. Newport Pagnell (Bucks.); 4. Quaker.

There are letters by her to Fox (Swarthmore MSS), and five letters by her from Newport Pagnell, one of these in 1659. See *Letters to William Dewsbury and others,* ed. H. Cadbury, Friends Historical Society, 1948.

SHINKIN AP SHONE

See Appendix III.

SHIPTON, Ursula

See Appendix III.

SHIRLEY, Elizabeth, *fl.* 1611
2. ?Louvain, ?Bruges (Belgium); 3. nun; 4. Catholic.

The manuscript 'Life of mother Clement' (1611) is held at Bruges. Mother Clement was prioress of St Ursula's, Louvain (d. 1612). (Information from Gillow.)

SIDNEY, Mary, Countess of Pembroke, 1561–1621
2. Kent, Wales, Dublin, Worcestershire, Wiltshire, London; 3. poet, novelist and translator; 4. Anglican; 5. Henry Herbert, Earl of Pembroke; 6. genteel.

Mary Sidney was proficient in French and Italian, as well as knowing Latin. She was sister of Philip Sidney and patron to Spenser, Nashe, and Daniel, among others. She edited Philip Sidney's *Arcadia*: her contribution to this has often been minimised. She translated:
Garnier's *Tragedy of Antonie* (from the French, into blank verse; *c.* 1600, unpublished). Petrarch's *Trionfo della morte* (from the Italian, into terza rima; *c.* 1600, unpublished). *Psalms* (numbers 1–43 with Philip Sidney, the rest alone; modern edition by J. C. Rathmell, New York: New York University Press, 1963).
There is also an elegy for Philip Sidney: 'The doleful lay of Clorinda' (1595) and a 'Pastoral dialogue' in Davison's *Poetical rhapsody* (1602). Letters survive in British Museum MS 12506 and Salisbury MSS.
See G. F. Waller, *Mary Sidney, Countess of Pembroke,* Salzburg: Salzburg Studies in English Literature: Elizabethan and Renaissance Series, 65, 1979, and Josephine Roberts, 'Mary Sidney, Countess of Pembroke', *English Literature in the Renaissance,* 1985. Also Waller (ed.), *The Triumph of death and other unpublished and uncollected poems* (Salzburg, 1977).

SIMMONDS, Martha, 1622–65

1. Calvert; 2. Meare (Somerset), London; 3. publisher/bookseller; 4. Quaker; 5. Thomas Simmonds; 6. publisher/bookseller.

See Critical Appendix 7.

Martha was sister of the publisher/bookseller Giles Calvert (and thus sister-in-law to Elizabeth CALVERT*). Having spent some years in religious search, she was an early convert to Quakerism. She began her travelling ministry in 1655, and was imprisoned in Colchester (where she appeared in sackcloth and ashes) for her Quaker activities (1655 and 1656–7). With other Quaker women she challenged male Quaker leaders in London. Quaker historians have characterised this as a leadership struggle between James Nayler and George Fox, with the women as Nayler 'supporters'; the incident should properly be viewed as an issue about women's role within the movement, in which Nayler came to support the women against Fox. The culmination of the row came when with Nayler, Dorcas ERBURY, Hannah STRANGER* and others she staged an entry into Bristol which symbolised Christ's entry into Jerusalem. She was imprisoned there and in Bridewell and accused by Nayler's friends and enemies alike of having 'bewitched' him; Fox exploited the charge of blasphemy to disown what had become a troublesome oppositional faction. She continued, however, to interrupt Quaker meetings, and while her husband carried on publishing for the Quakers, the Calverts did not. She died, possibly on a journey to Maryland, and may have been buried among Quakers.

When the Lord Jesus came to Jerusalem . . . (1655). *A lamentation for the lost sheep of the House of Israel . . .* (1655, 1656 – the latter printed by her). *O England, thy time is come . . .* (1656; bound in with tracts by Nayler, W. T. and Hannah STRANGER*).

See K. L. Carroll, 'Martha Simmonds, a Quaker enigma', *JFHS*, vol. 53, 1 (1972); although an attempt at a sympathetic account, its language – the author uses such expressions as 'mad adoration', 'hypnotic influence' and 'unbalanced' Ranterism – denies the politics of Simmonds's argument with Foxite Quakers.

SIMPSON, Mary, c. 1617–47

2. Norwich; 4. Presbyterian.

Faith and experience: or, a short narration of the holy life and death of Mary Simpson, late of Gregories parish in the city of Norwich; who dyed anno 1647. In or about the thirtieth year of her age, after three yeares sicknesse and upwards. Containing a confession of her faith, and relation of her experience, taken from her owne mouth (1649; printed with a sermon preached at her funeral by

John Collings). She was apparently of poor parents, and 'was an Eminent preacher', not in the pulpit but by telling her experiences. The text speaks of her sense of sin: 'One time me thought my fancy in the night presented to me Sinne in a lump . . . methought I saw sin set out in a market upon a stall.' There is also her sense of her own sinfulness: 'The more understanding I had of God in that way, the more I saw of mine owne filthinesse: I saw filthinesse in the holy things of God, as performed by me.' Her account has been penned by 'a faithful friend' (presumably the radical Presbyterian Collings, who knew her for two years and who was ejected in 1660, and who also published a meditation by Anne SKELTON of Norwich, which does not seem to have survived).

SINGER, Elizabeth Rowe, 1674–1737
2. Frome, London; 3. poet; 5. Thomas Rowe (m. 1710); 6. writer.

Daughter of the dissenting minister Walter Singer, she started writing poetry at the age of 12 and learnt French and Italian at 20. She was an accomplished musician and painter. Her first poetic commission came from another nonconformist cleric, Bishop Thomas Ken. Her *Poems on several occasions by Philomela* was published in 1696, by John Dunton, with whom she had secretly corresponded since she was 19. He, a public literary figure, called her the 'richest genius of her sex'; but she rejected him when he proposed marriage. The preface to her poems is written by Elizabeth JOHNSON,* who helped persuade Singer to publish. *Miscellaneous works in prose and verse* came out in the same year. Essays and letters are also extant.

Greer (p. 383 f.) includes some of her poems.

SKEIN, Lilias, –1697
1. Gillespie; 2. Aberdeen; 4. Quaker; 5. Alexander Skein; 6. magistrate, city treasurer.

Her first three children were born between 1669 and 1676, the fourth in 1696. She wrote *A warning to the magistrates and inhabitants of Aberdeen* (in Besse, 2) and *An expostulary epistle, directed to Robert Macquare delivered some months since at his house in Rotterdam* (1679). She speaks of God doing marvellous works by 'pouring out his Spirit upon Sons and Daughters, servants and handmaids, provoking to jealousy and angering the mighty learned wise men in this generation by the foolish appearance of a company of illiterate tradesmen, who were never bred up at schools and universitys, weavers and shoe-makers, and fishers'. Her 'letter to Anna' was passed on, as a useful text, to the Princess of Bohemia in 1676 (mentioned in Kannegieter: see HENDRICKS* for bibliographical details).

SLANE, Lady Ann, *fl.* 1684–98

2. Ireland; 3. genteel; 5. Baron Slane (m. 1684); 6. genteel.

The case of Anne, wife to the late Baron Slane (1698). This is a dispute about wealth. Her husband was outlawed for high treason in 1691 (for supporting James II) and his estate passed to the Earl of Athlone, who in 1695 was confirmed by Parliament without any allowance being made to Ann. Her case aims to demonstrate that she is owed money from this estate and the argument depends on the sequence of events. She brought £6,000 to the marriage but he was under age then, so he could not fulfil his obligations. He was accused of treason before he settled money on her (and thus the money would be forfeit); but that settlement had been agreed before the treason charge: it had not been carried out at the time because he was under age. Athlone allowed her some money (but not all of it) in 1696.

SLEY, Joan, ?1623–1715/16

1. Gates; 2. Alton (Hants); 3. publican; 4. Quaker; 5. Jonathan Sley.

Testimony written at Alton, the 25th of the 3rd. month, 1708.
She seems to have followed her faith against her husband's wishes. She was fined for attending a meeting in 1664, and imprisoned, with her brother Nicholas, in Winchester gaol in 1678 (she was the sister-in-law of Elizabeth GATES*). It seems that she ran her inn, alone, for about forty years.

SMITH, Elizabeth

Elizabeth NEWTON*

SMITH, Mary, –?1689

2. York; 4. Quaker; 5. Richard Smith; 6. tanner.

Mary Smith was convinced by William Dewsbury in 1654; her husband was not a Quaker (though he did not oppose her). She was imprisoned at Middlewich (Cheshire) and York 'for no other cause then for calling upon the name of the Lord'. She wrote *These few lines are to all such as have a hand in persecuting the innocent people of God (called Quakers) . . . written: from Middlewych-house of correction in Cheshire, the 10th moneth, 1665* which is bound with *Here is another warning which was given forth some years before, to the Majestrates and Ministers (so called) of the city of York, written from Ouse-bridge the 9 day of the 7 moneth 1659*. She wrote letters to William Dewsbury in 1661–2, which speak of her imprisonment; she sends Mary

Monk (Mary WATSON*)'s love to Dewsbury (the letters are reprinted in *Letters to William Dewsbury and others*, ed. H. Cadbury, Friends Historical Society, 1948). Our conjecture about her death date is based on the record of a Mary Smith who died at Balby (one also died in 1699 at Deighton Park House).

SMITH, Rebecca

See Appendix III.

SMITH, Sarah

CHOLMLEY,* Elisabeth and Margaret

SMITH, Susanna, ?1623–93

1. Purse; 2. Pirbright, Worplesdon (Surrey); 3. trade; 4. Quaker; 5. Stephen Smith; 6. foreign merchant, writer.

'A testimony concerning her husband' (1679; in Stephen Smith, *Works*). (Her husband worked with the Levant Company in Alexandretta; he probably died in Bristol.)

SMITH, Susannah, c. 1666–

2. London, Suratt (East Indies); 4. Anglican; 5. Henry Smith (m. 1680); 6. accountant.

The case of Susannah Smith humbly represented to the right honourable Lords spiritual and temporal in Parliament assembled (?1696). This legal document gives the grounds for her divorce, which was finalised in 1696. Susannah claims cruelty and desertion: she had married in Bombay, where her parents lived, when 14; Smith, an accountant with the East India Company, was sent to England in 1684, and she was left pregnant and without maintenance. Smith married again, in London, in 1690, and Susannah obtained a divorce. She appeals now for indemnity from penalties she or her children might incur if she marries again.

SMYTH, Anne, 1605–

1. Danvers; 2. Northamptonshire; 5. Daniel Smyth; 6. curate.

The case of Anne Smyth, the wife of Daniell Smyth, one of the daughters of Sir John Danvers of Culworth in the county of Northampton kt, deceased, truly stated (1650).

This is a petition to the House of Commons. When Sir John Danvers died in 1642, he left Anne a portion of £1,000 (her mother died 1644). The petition concerns the behaviour of the executors, principally John Danvers of Chelsea (one of Charles I's judges) who suddenly removed Daniel Smyth from his living and replaced him with his own 'servant'. Anne Smyth points out that he has known her 'extreme weak and diseased condition' for twenty years, and that now she cannot provide for her small children. She attacks the executors' treatment of her husband, whom they have both deprived of his living (in Stowe) and imprisoned, and sees their actions as an attempt 'to deterre and disable your Petitioner from seeking after her right'.

SOMERSET, Elizabeth, Countess of, ?1666–1722

1. Percy; 2. London, Brussels, Petworth (Sussex); 3. genteel; 5(a) Henry, Lord Ogle, (b) Count Charles Konigsmark, (c) Charles Seymour, Duke of Somerset; 6(a)/(b)/(c) genteel.

Elizabeth Percy was married to Henry, Lord Ogle when she was 10/11 and by the age of 16 had been twice widowed. She was Mistress of the Robes to Queen ANNE.* Letters by her are in Julia Longe, *Martha Lady Giffard: Her life and correspondence* (London: George Allen & Sons, 1911).

SOMERSET, Margaret, Countess of, –1681

1. O'Brien; 2. Ireland, France, London; 3. genteel; 5(a) Edward, Marquess of Somerset, (b) Donagh Kearney; 6(a) genteel.

Also known as Margaret, Countess of WORCESTER.

Anne HENSHAW,* Katherine STONE,* for similar petitions.

Her first husband surrendered to Parliament and was committed to the Tower (1652–4). He was bailed and pensioned in 1655, his lands being restored in 1660–1. Margaret was 'found to be insane' in 1678.
To the Parliament of the Commonwealth of England, Scotland, and Ireland. The humble petition of . . . (1654): claiming rights to a fifth of property confiscated by Parliament. On her marriage to Edward in 1639 she had a portion of £20,000, but received only £400 in nine years. After four years' attendance she finds that Worcester house is still unsold, and asks to be granted that and anything else allowed.

SOPHIA AEMILIA, Queen of Denmark

See Appendix III.

SOUTHCOTE, Lady Eliza, *fl.* **1658**
1. Aston; 2. Tixall (Staffs.), Albery (Surrey); 3. genteel; 5. Sir John South-cote; 6. genteel.

Daughter of Walter, 2nd Lord Aston. A letter to her uncle, Herbert Aston, on the death of his wife in 1658 is reprinted in *The Tixall letters; or the correspondence of the Aston family and their friends during the seventeenth century,* ed. A. Clifford (London & Edinburgh: Longman, Hurst, Rees, Orme & Brown, 1815), 2 vols. A poem written to her on her wedding day is included in *Tixall poetry,* ed. A. Clifford (London: Longman, Hurst, Rees, Orme & Brown, 1813).

SOUTHWELL, Lady Anne, 1574–1636
1. Harris; 2. Devon, Ireland, London; 3. genteel; 5(a) Sir Thomas South-well, (b) Sir Henry Sibthorpe; 6(a) genteel, (b) genteel, government servant.

Lady Southwell was a poet and letter-writer. The Folger Shakespeare Library holds a manuscript volume of 'Lady Southwell's works' (1626) and Jean C. Cavanagh reproduces a brief address to Lady Ridgway which is an early 'defence of poetry' (*English Literature in the Renaissance,* vol. 14, 1984).

SOUTHWELL, Lady Elizabeth, after 1563–
1. Howard; 2. Norfolk, London; 3. genteel; 5(a) Sir Robert Southwell, (b) — Steward, Earl of Clanricard; 6(a)/(b) genteel.

Daughter of Charles Howard, Earl of Nottingham, she was Maid of Honour to ELIZABETH I* and principal Lady in Waiting to ANNE OF DENMARK.* She bore ten children (of whom five died young) to her first husband, of Woodrising, Norfolk; he died in 1599. She was granted an annuity of £200 in 1605. She may have been a lover of the Earl of Essex. 'Certaine edicts from a Parliament in Eutopia' is in the ninth edition of *The conceited news of Thomas Overbury,* ed. J. E. Savage (New York: Scholars Facsimiles and Reprints, 1968).

SOWERNAM, Ester

See Appendix II.

SOWLE, Jane, ?1631–1711
2. Clerkenwell (London); 3. printer; 4. Quaker; 5. Andrew Sowle; 6. Quaker printer.

Six children were born between 1668 and 1674, including her daughter Tace (1669) who was later to become a famous printer in her own right. She wrote a testimony in Anne WHITEHEAD,* *Piety* . . . (1686), which includes verses (she says she has known Anne WHITEHEAD for over 20 years).

SPEGHT, Rachel, *c.* 1597–

2. London; 4. puritan; 5. William Proctor (m. 1621).

Daughter of the minister and author James Speght, she had at least two children (born 1626 and 1630). Rachel Speght produced one of the earliest responses to Joseph Swetnam's misogynist *Arraignment of lewd, idle, froward and unconstant women* (1615); she wrote under her own name from a clear and articulate religious position, which marks her out from other challengers of Swetnam (such as Ester SOWERNAM and Constantia MUNDA, see Appendix II). Elements of her text (as with the others) appear in the play based on the controversy, *Swetnam the woman-hater* (1619).

A mouzell for Melastomus, the cynical bayter of, and foul mouthed barker against Evahs sex Or an apologeticall answere to that irreligious and illiterate pamphlet made by Jo. Sw. and by him intituled, The arraignment of women (1617; text in Shepherd).

Mortality's memorandum, with a dream prefixed, imaginarie in manner; real in matter (1621). This is a verse meditation on death, partly responding to her own mother's death. It is dedicated to her godmother Mary MOUNDFORD. In her Preface to it Speght attacks those who claimed her father wrote her first tract (quoted in Shepherd; extract in Greer, p. 68 f.).

Spiritual experiences . . .

See Appendix I.

STARESMORE, Sabine

See Appendix III.

STIRLING, Mary Alexander, Countess of, –?1656/7

1. Vanlore; 2. Tilehurst (Berks.), ?London; 3. genteel; 5(a) Henry Alexander (m. 1637), (b) John Blunt (m. after 1650); 6(a) genteel, (b) cavalry colonel.

Youngest daughter of Sir Peter Vanlore, of Tilehurst, she was the aunt of Anne LEVINGSTON.* She eloped with Henry Alexander (died 1650) to avoid marriage with a Mr Reade. She had three children by this marriage. Disputes about her marriage portion from her grandfather began in 1638, and grew into a long-running dispute involving various Vanlore offspring; it was continued after her death by her daughters and Blunt.

To the supream authority of the nation the Parliament . . . the humble petition of Mary Countess of Stirling (1654) and *An answer to a printed paper; entituled, Some considerations . . .* (1654).

STIRREDGE, Elizabeth, 1634–1706

1. Tayler/Tayer; 2. Thornbury (Gloucs.), Bristol, Hemel Hempstead (Herts.); 4. Quaker; 5. James Stirredge (m. 1663).

The name is also given as Sterridge/Sturge. She heard John Audland speak at a meeting in 1654; she was convinced a year later by William Dewsbury. She bore three daughters and three sons. The family seems to have been mobile: James Sterridge was in Barton Regis (1657–8), Keynsham (1663–71), Chew Magna (1683) and Hemel Hempstead from 1688 (he died in 1708). In *c.* 1670 she apparently delivered a written message of hers to Charles II. She was arrested in 1683 at a meeting in Chew Magna and imprisoned at Ilchester.

A salutation of my endeared love in God's holy fear . . . unto you of that city of Bristol (1683; with Dorcas DOLE;* four reprints). *A faithful warning to the inhabitants of England, and elsewhere* (1689; four reprints). *Strength in weakness manifest . . . in the life, various trials, and Christian testimony of . . . E.S.* (1711; four reprints).

STONE, Katherine, *fl.* 1631–55

1. Moody; 2. Wiltshire, Lincolnshire; 3. genteel; 5. John Stone.

Daughter of Sir Henry Moody of Garsdon, Wilts. (died 1632). Her husband was from High Holborn (London). She bore two sons at Skellingthorpe, Lincolnshire: Henry born 1631 (died 1693), Thomas born 1634 (died 1659). She went to law to claim her property: *To the High Court of Parliament, of the Commonwealth of England, Scotland, and Ireland. The humble petition of Katherine Stone, widdow and Henry Stone, her son* (1654/5). This is a petition for rights to one fifth of property (which had been mortgaged to them twice, the second time in 1634) confiscated by Parliament. She wants part of the manor of Skellingthorpe as her jointure, and Henry wants the rest as heir (John Stone having died in 1642). They had previously failed to claim their lands through ignorance, and act to counter an application by Nathaneal Snape and Samuel Foxley to buy them. The petition was referred to the Court of Common Pleas in 1655.

STORDY, Mary, *fl.* ?1679–92

1. ?Skelton; 2. Moorhouse (Cumberland); 4. Quaker; 5. Thomas Stordy (?m. 1679); 6. ?carpenter.

Their house was a meeting-house and they owned property. Her husband died in prison in 1684. If our identification is correct, they had a daughter and son born 1680 and 1682. She wrote a *Testimony concerning her dear husband Thomas Stordy . . . late of Cumberland* (1692).

STORY, Patience, *fl.* 1675

2. New York; 4. Quaker.

A letter from New York to the Curwens (1675), telling of Ranters disrupting meetings and of how 'when the Meeting was near ended my Husband was taken violent Sick with a Vomiting and Gripes': in Alice CURWEN,* *A relation . . .* (1680).

STOUT, Mary, ?1627–1707

1. Saunderson; 2. London, Hertfordshire; 3. servant; 4. Quaker; 5. Henry Stout (m. 1664).

Said to be 'a waiting Gentlewoman in Cromwels family', 'Oliver's wife's maid', Mary Stout was convinced in 1654 by Francis Howgill. She apparently signed the 1659 tithing petition (under the name of Sanderson). Besse says a Henry Stout was banished to Jamaica in 1664; this may not be her husband. She had one daughter. She was present at Anne WHITEHEAD's* death in 1686, and records (in her 'Testimony' in WHITEHEAD's *Piety* . . .) that she knew WHITEHEAD for 30 years. She joined with other Hertfordshire Quakers (including her husband Henry) in controversy with William Haworth, an Independent of Hertfordshire: 'Ah William Haworth' is printed at the end of John Crook and William Bayly's *Rebellion rebuked* (1673). In March 1699, a year after the murder of her daughter Sarah, she sought justice for her daughter's death (in her role as guardian of Henry Stout jun.) which Bostock Toller, the under-sheriff of Hertford, attempted to avoid hearing (for which he was fined). She was accused of making trouble: 'It hath commonly been Reported, as if the Prosecution in this Appeal, hath been purely Vexatious, Begun by a Body of Quakers, and Espoused by a Faction at Hertford': see *The Case of Mrs Mary Stout widow* (?1699; her husband died in 1695). Her biography is sometimes confused with that of a Mary SAUNDERS, who also signed the tithing petition and was among the signatories of a general testimony for WHITEHEAD in *Piety* . . . (1686).

STRANGER, Hannah, *fl.* 1656–80

2. London, ?Bristol; 4. Quaker; 5(a) John Stranger/Stringer, (b) Henry Salter (m. 1666); 6(a) combmaker.

Her tract 'Consider I beseech you how clearly the Scripture is fulfilled in our days' is one section of the text of Martha SIMMONDS,* *O England, thy time is come* . . . (1656).

Hannah Stranger was disturbing Quaker meetings in 1656 and services in Westminster Abbey in 1657. She held the reins of Nayler's horse/donkey at his entry to Bristol, and joined Martha SIMMONDS* and Dorcas ERBURY who, at his scourging, stood in imitation of the three Marys at the foot of Christ's cross. She was imprisoned in Bristol and London. In 1666, as Salter, she gave a testimony of repentance, being then received again by Friends. She bore two sons in 1667 and 1668. At a meeting on 2 November 1669 in Bristol she submitted a 'paper of contrition' for her part in Nayler's entry into Bristol. In 1671, she and Martha FISHER went to ask the king for Margaret FELL's* liberty. By 1679/80 she was a widow in Tokany (Delaware).

STRONG, Damaris, *fl.* 1654–5

2. London; 5. William Strong; 6. Independent preacher.

In *Having seen a paper printed* . . . (1655) Damaris Strong asserts her knowledge of and rights in the publication of her dead husband's work (he died 1654). The paper she refers to had suggested that *Saints communion* was an imperfect text because nobody else could understand the code in which William Strong wrote his notes: she says he printed from his notes, not from what he said in the pulpit (which meant that only those who had access to his code – such as herself – could print the authoritative text). She not only defended the care her husband took in preparing texts for publication but clarified the economic motive of those who would 'spoile mine and my childrens benefit, we might otherwise receive by those my husbands labours'. She likens her case to that of other ministers' widows. William Strong was rector of More Crichell, Dorset, in 1640, became a puritan leader in London (based at St Dunstan's 1647–50), and a member of the Assembly of Divines. She was related to the nonconformist minister, Henry Wilkinson (son of Henry Wilkinson the elder, minister at Waddesdon, Bucks., from 1601), perhaps as sister or sister-in-law.

STUART, Elizabeth

ELIZABETH OF BOHEMIA*

STUTEVILLE, Elizabeth, *fl.* 1687–97

1. Becher; 5. Charles Stuteville (m. 1687); 6. genteel.

The case of Elizabeth, the wife of Charles Stuteville Esq; and of their five children: the financial problem at issue derived from pressure by Lady Glenham (in 1682, before their marriage) to make Charles Stuteville repay debts; his mother Judith's claim in 1689 for 29 years' arrears of jointure against the estate; and his father-in-law's bill against him in 1693. Elizabeth separated from her husband in 1697 and the children went into the care of their grandfather. The text pleads that Charles Stuteville be financially provided for because the family faces ruin.

SUFFOLK, Henrietta, Countess of, 1681–1767

1. Hobart; 2. Hanover, London; 3. genteel; 5(a) Charles Howard, Earl of Suffolk, (b) George Berkeley; 6(a)/(b) genteel.

Henrietta was a mistress of George I and knew Pope and Swift. *Letters to and from Henrietta . . . and her second husband, the Hon George Berkeley from 1712 to 1767* (1824).

SUNDERLAND, Dorothy, Countess Dowager of, *c.* 1620–1715

1. Sidney; 2. Penshurst, Boundes (both Kent), London; 3. genteel; 5(a) Robert Spencer, Earl of Sunderland (m. 1639), (b) Robert Smyth (m. 1652); 6(a)/(b) genteel.

Eldest daughter of Robert Sidney, Earl of Leicester, she was Philip Sidney's niece. Her first husband died at the Battle of Edgehill, leaving her with a son and two daughters when she was about 23. She had one son by her second marriage. Her portrait was painted by Vandyke, and the poet Waller called her 'Sacharissa'. Thirteen of her letters (undated, but *c.* 1680) to her son-in-law, George Saville, and her brother, Henry Sidney, were printed by Lord John Russell (1819, bound with his *Life of Lord and Lady Russell*) and reprinted in Mrs Henry Ady, *Sacharissa* (1893).

Margaret Williamson, *Colloquial Language of the Commonwealth and Restoration* (English Association Pamphlet, 73, 1929), refers to the letters of Dorothy Sunderland to John Evelyn (BL, Add. MS 15889).

SUTCLIFFE, Alice, *fl.* 1624–34

1. Woodhows; 2. Norfolk; 5. John Sutcliffe (m. before 1624); 6. groom of the Privy Chamber.

Daughter of Luke Woodhouse/Woodhows, of Kimberley, Norfolk, her husband was from Yorkshire; she had at least one daughter, Susan. She wrote *Meditations of man's mortalitie. Or, a way to true blessedness* (1633; 'enlarged' in 1634). This is partly in verse and is dedicated to the Duchess of BUCKINGHAM and Countess of DENBIGH* (her connection with them presumably derived from her husband's service to Buckingham): she says DENBIGH has 'beene more then a Mother to mee', implying support and patronage. Her book has dedicatory verses by such as Ben Jonson, Thomas May and George Wither. There is a verse extract in Greer (p. 91 f.).

SUTTON, Katherine, *fl.* 1630–63

2. England, Holland; 3. governess, prophet; 4. ?Baptist.

The earliest part of her narrative speaks of her difficulties as a governess, wife and mother. She was asked to go as governess 'into a darck corner of the land' (?Lancashire), a place of 'many Papists' (though she converted one of the family). After marriage her religious feelings increased, following differences of opinion with her husband and loss of a child (possibly in the 1630s: she refers to the 'setting up of Altars'). God helps her to be free of her husband's house by sending someone to take over the lease. She travels abroad, loses another child and is paralysed with sickness. She dates her possession by God's Spirit and acquisition of the gift of singing and prophecy in February 1655 (the text prints her verse prophecies and hymns). (She says she 'sought the Lord 20 years . . . before I had an answer'.) She prophesies around 1658 to 'some that then were in high places' who 'were soon brought down'. She then experiences prolonged illness which she interprets as God's punishment for neglecting to make public her prophetic gift; she begins to write while God assists her in recalling thirty years' experiences (this in *c.* 1660): 'because I am an old fruitless branch, my memory failes'. She then travels to Holland but loses her writings when the ship is wrecked (this about 1662 when she notes religious persecutions). Her religion stresses justification not by good works but 'alone by a righteousness out of my self'. She likens herself to the prophet Daniel, attacks unequal division of wealth and justifies women prophesying. 'I am of a fearful timerous spirit naturally, but I find it a great help to dash Babilons brats in the first rice.'

Christian womans experiences of the glorious working of God's free grace (Rotterdam, 1663).

SYLVIA

See Appendix II.

T

TALBOT, Elizabeth

Elizabeth Grey, Countess of Kent; see Appendix III.

TATTLEWELL, Mary

See Appendix II.

TAYLOR, Elizabeth, *fl.* **1679**
2. Maryland; 4. Quaker.

Testimony (1679) in *A testimony concerning . . . William Coale* (1682). She knew him 'when he was but a lad'.

TAYLOR, Elizabeth, –1708
2. Kent; 3. genteel; 5(a) Sir Francis Wythens, (b) Sir Thomas Colepepper; 6(a) judge.

A 'Mrs Taylor' has three poems in Aphra BEHN's* *The Miscellany* (1685). Greer thinks this is probably Elizabeth Taylor and mentions other contemporary printings of these poems, as well as other poems by 'Lady Wythens'. Texts in Greer, p. 294 f.

TAYLOR, Elizabeth, –1722
1. ?Rither; 2. York; 4. Quaker; 5. John Taylor (m. ?1663).

From our women's yearly meeting held at York the 19th. and 20th. days of the fourth month, 1700 (1700; with others – see Appendix I). 'The testimony of Elizabeth Taylor, concerning John Taylor' (1710; in his *Journal*).

TAYLOR, Frances, –1696
2. Barbados, York; 4. Quaker; 5. John Taylor; 6. sugar boiler.

Their first three children were born in Barbados (1670–5), the last in York (1676) after they had travelled from Bridgetown. She signed epistles from the York Women's Meeting in 1686, 1688 and 1692 (see Mary WAITE* for details).

TAYLOR, Frances, *fl.* 1672–82

2. Edmonton (London), Pennsylvania; 4. Quaker; 5. Christopher Taylor; 6. school teacher.

Her husband (originally from Yorkshire) ran the school in which John Matern worked and they left it to George Keith when they followed Penn to Pennsylvania in 1682 (where her husband became Registrar General of the colony before he died in 1686). She bore a son Joseph in 1672 (at Waltham Abbey), and probably a daughter Mary in 1670. She wrote a preface and endpiece addressing children about morality in *A testimony to the Lord's power and blessed appearance in and amongst children* (1679). A testimony in *Testimonies for John Matern* (1680: Rosina MATERN*).

TAYLOR, Hannah, *fl.* 1685–97

2. Stafford, London; 4. Quaker.

She may have been in prison in Stafford, and is author of *A short testimony of Hannah Taylor, concerning her dear father, Thomas Taylor* (1697) (he lived in Stafford until his death in 1682). With their mother, all six of Thomas Taylor's children were supported by Margaret FELL* during his frequent spells of imprisonment; Taylor's wife moved to Stafford when he was imprisoned there. Hannah signed *A tender and Christian testimony* in 1685, which may mean that she moved to London (as did a brother and sister). Frances TAYLOR* (of Edmonton) was her aunt. (An Anne Taylor married Cornelius Bowman in London in 1696.)

TAYLOR, Mary, *fl.* 1654–1718

1. Saunders; 2. Holsworthy (Devon); 4. Presbyterian; 5. Michael Taylor (m. 1654); 6. minister.

She was daughter of Humphrey Saunders, ejected rector of Holsworthy; she had two daughters, Elizabeth and Edith. Calamy quotes a letter (dated 12 February 1718) 'rebutting Walker's suggestion that her husband would have conformed if he could have kept his living' (A. G. Matthews).

TAYLOR, Mary, *c.* 1670–

2. Edmonton, ?Pennsylvania; 4. Quaker.

She was a pupil of John Matern and probably the daughter of Frances TAYLOR* (of Edmonton). Wrote a testimony in *Testimonies for John Matern* (1680: see Rosina MATERN* for details).

THIMELBY, Catherine, –1658

2. Leicestershire, Colton (Staffs.); 3. genteel; 5. Herbert Aston; 6. genteel.

Sister-in-law of Constance FOWLER* and sister of Sir John Thimelby of Irnham, Leicestershire. She probably married around or soon after 1639. Two poems, 'Mrs Thimelby on the death of her only child' and 'To her husband on New-Years-Day, 1651' are reprinted in *Tixall poetry*, ed. A. Clifford (London: Longman, Hurst, Rees, Orme & Brown, 1813); Clifford suggests a number of other poems are also by her. Letters are reprinted in *The Tixall letters; or the correspondence of the Aston family and their friends during the seventeenth century*, ed. A. Clifford (London & Edinburgh: Longman, Hurst, Rees, Orme & Brown, 1815), 2 vols.

THIMELBY, Eliza, *fl. c.* 1669

2. Irnham (Leics.); 3. genteel; 5. — Cottington.

Niece of Catherine THIMELBY* and daughter of Sir John Thimelby; her husband was probably the nephew of Francis, Lord Cottington of Hanworth, Middx. Three letters to Herbert Aston are reprinted in *The Tixall letters; or the correspondence of the Aston family and their friends during the seventeenth century*, ed. A. Clifford (London & Edinburgh: Longman, Hurst, Rees, Orme & Brown, 1815), 2 vols. One letter (dated May 1669 by W. van Lennep in *The London Stage 1660–1800*, Illinois: Illinois University Press, 1965) talks about a woman dramatist (probably Frances BOOTHBY:* see Hobby, *Virtue*, p. 111): 'We are in expectation still of Mr Draidens play. Ther is a bold women hath oferd one; my cosen Aston can give you a better acount of her then I can . . . I shall tremble for the poor wooman exposed among the critticks. She stands need to be strongly fortified agenst them.'

THIMELBY, Winefrid, 1619–90

2. Leicestershire, Louvain; 3. nun; 4. Catholic.

She was abbess of the English Convent of Augustine nuns at Louvain, from 1668 (she professed in 1635). Her letters, written 1650–90, are reprinted in *The Tixall letters; or the correspondence of the Aston family and their friends during the seventeenth century*, ed. A. Clifford (London & Edinburgh: Longman, Hurst, Rees, Orme & Brown, 1815), 2 vols. She also wrote a manuscript volume of devotion: 'Meditations on the principal obligations of a Christian'.

THOMAS, Elizabeth, 1675–1731
2. London; 3. poet.

She began her education early, and knew Latin, mathematics and chemistry. In 1699 she began corresponding with Dryden, who thought her poems 'too good to be a Woman's'. She and her mother (with whom she lived) were beset by debts; for which she was imprisoned from 1727 to 1730. While in prison she continued literary work, collaborating on an answer to Pope's *Dunciad* (in which he had pilloried her, because she had sold some of his early letters to raise money). In some of her poetry she adopts Mary CHUDLEIGH's* critiques of marriage and women's education.

Miscellany poems on several subjects (1722, republished as *Poems on several occasions. By a lady,* 1726, 1727; including translations from French). Her later works come well after 1720. (Extracts in Greer, p. 429.)

THOMAS, Joan, *fl.* 1684

To the honourable assembly of the Commons (1684): we have been unable to locate this work.

THORNTON, Alice, 1627–1707
1. Wandesford; 2. East Newton (Yorks.), Ireland; 3. genteel; 5. William Thornton (m. 1651).

Daughter of Alice OSBORNE,* Lady Wandesford, she married William Thornton after rejecting three other suitors (one of whom planned rape), but the marriage was unhappy, though Alice said she loved her husband. In her text she speaks of her nine pregnancies and fears of childbearing.

The autobiography of Mrs Alice Thornton . . ., ed. C. Jackson (Surtees Society, vol. 62, 1875). This, according to Hobby (thesis), is a badly organised selection from Thornton's four-volume manuscript. Extracts in Houlbrooke and Graham.

THROCKMORTON, Elizabeth

Elizabeth RALEGH*

THYNNE, Joan, 1558–1612
1. Hayward; 2. Longleat (Wilts.), Westminster; 3. trade, genteel; 5. John Thynne; 6. genteel.

Joan Thynne ran the Longleat estate when her husband was at Court, he being the son of John Thynne the builder of Longleat. With the sheriff of Shropshire, she assaulted Caus castle (subject of a possession dispute between Thynnes and Staffords) and expelled Lady Stafford. She occupied and defended the castle (1591) and on the death of her husband (1604) went to live there. Joan Thynne became an entrepreneur in lead mining. Letters by her are in *Two Elizabethan women: correspondence of Joan and Maria Thynne 1575–1611*, ed. Alison Wall (Devizes: Wiltshire Record Society, vol. 38, 1983). They begin with her engagement and deal with motherhood, family problems, legal and estate affairs.

THYNNE, Maria, c. 1578–1611
1. Audley; 2. Compton Bassett, Stalbridge (Dorset), Longleat (Wilts.); 3. genteel; 5. Thomas Thynne; 6. genteel.

Maria's family (Audley/Marvin) and the Thynne family were enemies, but Maria married Thomas Thynne after one meeting (in 1594, when she was 16). The Thynnes tried to have the marriage declared invalid, but its validity was affirmed in 1601. Maria was sister to Eleanor DAVIES* and spent some time at Court. She knew Latin, and her editor (see below) says that the sisters had 'clearly received an education which made them fluent with the pen'. When John Thynne died in 1604, Maria became mistress of Longleat and abandoned earlier attempts at reconciliation with her mother-in-law, Joan THYNNE.* Her husband sat in Parliament; she ran the estate. Maria died in childbirth, leaving three sons. One of her letters to Thomas Thynne includes the remark 'Even so, being as melancholy as a red herring, and as mad as a pilchard and as proud as a piece of Aragon ling, I salute thy best beloved self.' Her letters are in Wall (see Joan THYNNE*).

TICKELL, Dorothy, fl. c. 1664–90
2. Crosthwait (Cumberland); 4. Quaker; 5. Hugh Tickell (m. c. 1664).

Her testimony, in *Some testimonies concerning the life and death of Hugh Tickell* (1690), includes a poem on her husband's death. Their house, probably near Keswick, was a Quaker meeting place.

TILLINGHAST, Mary, fl. 1678
3. ?teacher of cookery.

Rare and excellent receipts experienc'd, and taught by Mrs. Mary Tillinghast. And now printed for the use of her scholars only (1678, 1690). This is a book of cookery recipes: it is a form of advertisement of her skills (despite what the title says about the 'use of her scholars'), and thus may be compared to the advertisements by physicians which are also common at this period and which show commercial women using the availability of the new printed medium (see the discussion in Hobby, *Virtue*, p. 175 f.).

TIPPER, Elizabeth, *fl.* 1693–8

2. ?Wiltshire; 3. teacher, accountant; 4. Anglican.

The pilgrim's viaticum: or, the destitute, but not forlorn. Being a divine poem, digested from meditations upon the Holy Scripture (1698, 1699) (a collection of poems on subjects mainly religious). A prefatory poem by John Hallum says 'Phillips and Behn, whose praise fame still rehearse,/In all their works don't paralel thy verse'. The dedication to Anne, COUNTESS OF COVENTRY pleads for 'Sanctuary'. The entry in Greer (p. 422, which has extracts) uses this connection to suggest that Tipper may have been employed at a charity school supported by Lady Coventry near Badminton, Gloucestershire (though when Tipper speaks of her teaching she refers to 'ladies', which does not imply charity school pupils). One prefatory poem is by John Torbuck, rector of Ludgershall, Wilts. This could be seen to connect Tipper to Wiltshire, where parish registers record an Elizabeth Tipper, daughter of William and Elizabeth, christened in 1640 at Seend (about 23 miles from Ludgershall).

A poem on her life tells how she was a 'recluse' for five years in a country village, then moved to the city on a friend's advice. A poem to 'a young lady that desired a verse of my being servant one day, and mistress another' tells 'I teach ladies writing and accompts one day, and keep shop-books the other day, in which business I am a hired servant.' In the poem to her friend Robert Harding she takes time to praise his daugher Alicia 'that cast her pleasing eye,/To my indifferent state of poverty': 'But cease, my muse, cease, lest I now despair,/To think how I lost her, that was so dear;/Marriage, which fixes lovers in one state,/Divides us two to places separate'.

TOOVEY, Rebeckah jun., 1704–14

2. London, Croydon; 4. Quaker.

Rebeckah Toovey was sent to Rebeckah TRAFFORD's* boarding-school in Croydon. She died after what seems to have been a painful illness. Quotations from her are given in TRAFFORD's testimony and in Rebeckah and Joseph Toovey's *Brief account . . .* (below). The latter includes:

'Sweet Jesus, give me Ease/For Mercy I do crave:/And if thou wilt but give me Ease,/Then Mercy I shall have'.

TOOVEY, Rebeckah sen., 1664–1734
2. Enfield (Middx.), London; 4. Quaker; 5. Joseph Toovey; 6. cheesemonger.

She bore 14 children between 1688 and 1704; of these seven died very young and one was stillborn. She wrote *A brief account of the innocent example and pious sayings of Rebeckah Toovey, aged nine years, recommended unto children for their serious perusal* (1715; with Joseph Toovey).

TORSHELL, Elizabeth, *fl.* 1705
2. London.

Mrs Elizabeth Torshell's letter to the ordinary of Newgate, containing a particular account of the murther committed upon the body of Mr. Robert Woodcock in Chelsea-fields by Mr. Edward Jefferies, lately executed for the same (1705). Torshell had been out walking with Jefferies at the time he committed the murder. She had already been interrogated by Paul Lorrain, the ordinary of Newgate, but because she feared Jefferies would lose his life she had denied that he left her company. This text clarifies that he did leave her while he visited Woodcock (from whom he wanted to borrow money), and thus corroborates evidence by the surgeon and some 'boys'. She reveals that she had questioned him about the murder weapon; he told her that he would get one of the boys' mothers, Mrs Lambourn, to go to the queen to get him off.

TOUCHET, Eleanor
Eleanor DAVIES*

TOWNSEND, Theophila, 1656–92
2. Tetbury, Cirencester (Gloucs.); 4. Quaker; 5. Phillip Theodor Lehnmann (m. 1678).

She seems never to have used her married name nor to be known by it (which can be occasionally observed among other Quaker women). She was imprisoned in 1681 for preaching, and released in 1686. Besse prints her 'Account of proceedings against her' (1683), in which she says that she nearly died several times in prison, 'but the Lord hath raised me up and made me able to appear before you, to see whether you will do me justice or no. How do you look upon me to be a dangerous person? Do you suppose me likely to raise an Army to subvert the Government? The Law says, no Person shall be deprived of his Liberty unconvicted, and that I was never, for you have no Proof.'

A testimony concerning the life and death of Jane Whitehead concerning her sufferings, and her faithfulness . . . (1676). For WHITEHEAD, see Jane WAUGH*. *An epistle of love to Friends in the women's meetings in London, etc.* (1686, 1690). *Testimony concerning Amariah Drewet* (1687; Mary DREWET*). *A word of counsel, in the love of God to the persecuting magistrates and clergy* . . . *But chiefly to those of the city and county of Gloucester* (1687). *An epistle of tender love to all Friends* . . . (1690).

TRAFFORD, Rebeckah, *fl.* 1712–15
2. Croydon (Surrey); 3. teacher; 4. Quaker; 5. Samuel Trafford.

A son born in 1712 died the same year. She kept a boarding-school at Croydon, and wrote a 'Testimony' in *A brief account of the innocent example and pious sayings of Rebeckah Toovey* (1715; Rebeckah TOOVEY* was a pupil).

Translation of Scudery

See Appendix I.

TRAPNEL, Anna, ?1622–
2. Poplar (London); 3. trade, prophet; 4. Baptist, Fifth Monarchist.

See Critical Appendix 2.

Daughter of a shipwright, from 1642 she attended a Baptist church. In 1645 and 1647 she acted as house companion to two women (the first in Aldgate, the second in Fenchurch Street). She visited Sarah WIGHT* (a similar prophet figure) in 1647. In 1654 she travelled to Cornwall on behalf of her church, but was arrested as a vagabond and threatened with trial as a witch. A warrant for her committal to Bridewell was issued in June that year, but she was released the next month. This was the year of her first major trance, lasting twelve days. From October 1657 she entered a trance which lasted ten months. Although she used her prophecy to support the Parliamentary army, at the same time she rebuked Cromwell and was critical of religious groups such as Quakers and Ranters. Her fasting and visions had a wide audience.

The cry of a stone or a relation of something spoken in Whitehall by Anna Trapnel (1654; this is the product of a sustained oral verse prophecy uttered while waiting with others for the outcome of the hearing of Vavasour

Powell, who had claimed that the Protectorate would not last long).

A legacy for saints: being several experiences of the dealings of God with Anna Trapnel (1654) (this was printed while she was in Bridewell, to publicise her cause). *Anna Trapnel's report and plea. Or a narrative of her journey from London into Cornwall* (1654; extracts in Graham). *Strange and wonderful newes from Whitehall: or, the mighty vision proceeding from Mistris A. Trapnel . . . concerning the Government of the Commonwealth . . . and her revelations touching . . . the Lord Protector, and the army* (1654). *A voice for the king of saints* (1658; including extemporised verse). The Bodleian Library holds an untitled book of verse (1658; see Hobby, *Virtue*, p. 242). For brief extracts from her verse, see Greer (p. 175 f.).

TRAVERS, Ann, *c.* 1628/9–89

2. Hackney; 3. property-owner; 4. Quaker.

With Elizabeth COLEMAN* she wrote *The harlot's vail rent* (1669) in answer to Elizabeth ATKINSON's* *A breif and plain discovery . . .*

She became friendly with Thomas Ellwood in 1662, through her Bridewell concerns. In 1671/2 she was in charge of Quakers in Southwark prisons. She and Anne MERRICK 'provided some hot victuals, meat and a broth . . . and ordering their servants to bring it there, with bread, cheese and beer, came themselves also with it.' Signed *A living testimony* (1685, as 'Anne Travice'; see Mary FOSTER* for details).

TRAVERS, Rebeckah/Rebecca, 1609–88

1. ?Booth; 2. London; 3. preacher; 4. Baptist, Quaker; 5. William Travers; 6. tobacconist.

Rebeckah was 'sister' to Mary BOOTH,* and was convinced by Nayler, helping him when he was flogged through London. She signed the tithing petition in 1659, was imprisoned in 1670 and 1686 for preaching and was active in establishing women's meetings. At her funeral William Penn called her a mother of 'Quaker Israel'. She was the author of some dozen pamphlets, including *This is for any of that generation that are looking for the kingdom of God* (1659; printed for Mary WESTWOOD*); *A testimony concerning the light and life of Jesus* (1663); and *A testimony for God's everlasting truth* (1669; this was a tract against Robert Cobbet, with whom she linked Elizabeth ATKINSON* 'for they have joyned in one iniquity'). Her testimony for Susanna WHITROW* speaks of herself as 'a mother fearing God', and says she has experience of children dying. She signed *For the King and both Houses of Parliament* (*c.* 1670; see Anne WHITEHEAD*). Her testimony for Anne WHITEHEAD (in *Piety* . . ., 1686) says she knew her for 28 years, from before WHITEHEAD's marriage.

TRELAWNEY, Elizabeth, 1617–before 1668
2. Cornwall; 3. genteel; 4. Quaker; 5. Thomas Lower (m. after 1657).

Daughter of John Trelawney of Hall, near Fowey (he was high sheriff of Cornwall). L. Hodgkin, *A Quaker Saint of Cornwall* (London: Longman, 1927), prints a letter by her to Lady Mohun (Trelawney's mother was Elizabeth, daughter of Sir Reginald Mohun).

Triumphs of female wit
See Appendix I.

TROTTER, Catherine
Catherine COCKBURN*

TRUSWELL, Jane, 1663–?1721
1. Theaker; 2. North Collingham (Notts.), Mansfield; 4. Quaker; 5. John Truswell (m. 1686).

She was the second wife of Truswell, who died 1714. She wrote *An epistle of love and tender advice to men and women Friends, at their quarterly meeting at Mansfield, and for every particular monthly meeting in the county of Nottingham, or elsewhere* (1717).

TRYE, Mary, *fl.* 1675
1. O'Dowde; 2. London.
See Critical Appendix 4.

Mary Trye says that she learnt medicine from her father, who was in the service of Charles I, and that after his death she kept his practice going. She wrote *Medicatrix, or the woman-physician: vindicating T. O'Dowde, a chymical physician . . . against the calumnies of Henry Stubbe* (1675). Despite its formal presentation as a defence of her father, the pamphlet asserts her own knowledge of medicine and advertises her abilities.

TUFTON, Elizabeth, –1725
1. Boyle; 3. genteel; 5. Nicholas Tufton, Earl of Thanet (m. 1664).

Daughter of Richard Boyle, Earl of Burlington. Her husband, a grandson of Anne CLIFFORD,* was in France during the Civil War, and died in 1679. Pollock (p. 32) quotes from a letter by her to Cecelea Hatton, about the death of her sister, Frances Drax, in childbed. Cecelea/Cecely

Tufton was the wife of Christopher Hatton and died in the explosion at Cornet Castle, Guernsey (1675) (Frances HATTON* was his second wife); Frances Tufton, the wife of Henry Drax of Boston, Lincolnshire, died in 1665.

TURNER, Anne, *fl.* 1615

Mistris Turners farewell to all women (1615). These verses against pride are regarded by Crawford as spurious.

TURNER, Jane, *fl.* 1653

2. London, Newcastle-upon-Tyne; 4. Presbyterian, Baptist, Quaker; 5. John Turner; 6. captain.

Choice experiences of the kind dealings of God before, in and after conversion; laid down in six general heads. Together with some brief observations upon the same. Whereunto is added a description of the experience (1653; 'to be sold at Black spread-Eagle': the CALVERTS'* shop). The epistle is written by John Spilsbury. Edward Burroughs regarded the text as anti-Quaker and answered it in 1654.

She describes the text as 'the fruits of my labours written at several times in my husband's absence'; his epistle says he did not know she was writing it. She is conscious that 'I might seem to some to walk in an untrodden path, having never seen any thing written in this manner and method', but says her 'greatest discouragement' is 'from the Saints themselves'. The text narrates her movement between various religious groupings: from Anglicanism ('after the bishops were quite taken away in the beginning of the sitting of the late synod') to Presbyterianism (where 'I have seen as persecuting a spirit in them as ever I did in the former, and they did appear as bitter, if not more, against such as were called Anabaptists, than ever the bishops did against those that were called puritans'); 'it is a dangerous thing to esteem of persons above what is meet, and to be implicitly lead by them in spiritual things.' At her marriage she moved to London, where she entered a Baptist church with her husband. From here they travelled with the army and she tells of an inspirational (probably Quaker) religion, which she rejected as anarchic. She returned to Newcastle and had new religious doubts. (A Jane Briggs married John Turner in 1641 in Boldon, Durham; we cannot establish a firmer connection.)

TURRANT, Mary, *fl. c.* 1641–53

2. Dublin; 4. Baptist.

Her 'experiences' are in Rogers, *Ohel* . . . (1653) (see Mary BARKER* for details). She says she lived a godless life until she was 23. Her children were murdered by Irish rebels and her husband died of disease. She writes as an old woman.

TWYSDEN, Isabella, 1605–57

1. Saunder; 2. Surrey, London, Kent; 3. genteel; 4. Anglican; 5. Sir Roger Twysden; 6. antiquary.

The Diary of Isabella, wife of Sir Roger Twysden . . . 1645–1651 has been edited by F. W. Bennitt in the *Transactions of the Kent Archaeological Society*, vol. 51, 1939.

TYLLTON, Mary, *fl.* 1676

2. Barbados; 4. Quaker.

A letter to the Curwens from Barbados (1676) in Alice CURWEN,* *A relation* . . . (1680). Possibly she is the second wife of Peter Tilton of Windsor; she died in 1689.

TYLSTON, Katharine, 1665–1747

1. Henry; 2. Chester; 4. nonconformist; 5. John Tylston; 6. physician.

Fourth child of the ejected minister Philip Henry and his wife Katharine, and sister to Sarah SAVAGE* and Ann HULTON.* She married on 27 June 1687, and bore two sons and three daughters. The devotional journal of Katharine Tylston covers the years 1723–8 (BL, Add. MS 42,849) but earlier letters between the sisters survive.

See Patricia Crawford, 'Katharine and Philip Henry and their children: a case study in family ideology', *Transactions of the Historic Society of Lancashire and Cheshire*, vol. 143, 1985.

TYRWHIT, Lady Elizabeth, *fl.* ?1548–?82

3. genteel.

· *Morning and evening praiers, with divers psalmes, hymns, and meditations, made and set forth by the Ladie Elizabeth Tyrwhit* (1582; Partnow, p. 134). Legend has it that the book was presented to Elizabeth Tudor when she was confined in the Tower of London (before her accession) and that she wore it hanging at her girdle. Also that Tyrwhit was appointed a lady-in-waiting to Elizabeth in place of Katherine Ashley in 1548. There is no confirmation of either suggestion. Sir Robert Tyrwhitt of Kettleby, Lincolnshire (died 1581) married Elizabeth, daughter of Thomas Oxenbridge of Berkley, Hants. We do not know if this is the author (the other Elizabeths in the family seem too early).

V

VAUGHAN, Millicent

See Appendix III.

VEITCH, Marion, *fl.* 1664–89

1. Fairly; 2. Dumfries, Newcastle, Peebles; 5. William Veitch (m. 1664); 6. cleric.

She was born in Lanark; her husband was chaplain to Sir Hugh Campbell of Calder, but later ejected. In *c.* 1666, when her husband was threatened with execution, they fled Scotland with their two children (two others died in infancy). They moved to Morpeth, Northumberland; her husband was arrested in January 1680 and imprisoned. She says she was 'not in the least discouraged' while soldiers were in the house and told the arresting officer: 'I looked to a higher hand than his in this.' Later her husband escaped to Holland, where she sent her two eldest sons (a third one died). Her text says much of religious persecutions under Charles II and of friends who are tortured. 'Soon after, word came that the king was dead. When I heard it, I thought Pharaoh was dead, and I would go to God, and beg of him, that he would Spirit a Moses to lead forth the Church from under her hard bondage.' She moved to Newcastle in 1684. She was worried at this period about the possible reinstatement of Catholicism, about the particular oppression of Scotland 'my native land', and about her sons' desire to become soldiers (after 1688 they participated in colonial ventures to North America). At the end of her life she moved to Peebles and then to Dumfries. See *Memoirs of Mrs William Veitch* (Edinburgh: Committee of the General Assembly of the Free Church of Scotland, 1846).

VENABLES, Elizabeth, –1689

1. Aldersey; 2. Cheshire; 5(a) Thomas Lee, (b) Robert Venables; 6(a) genteel, (b) army, genteel.

Her autobiography appears in *Some account of General Robert Venables . . . together with the autobiographical memoranda or diary of his widow, Elizabeth Venables* (Chetham Society, vol. 83, 1870–1). It is also printed in *The narrative of General Venables* (ed. C. H. Firth, London: Historical Society of Great Britain, 1900).

VENN, Anne, ?1626–54
2. Colchester, Fulham; 4. Presbyterian.

She wrote *A wise virgins lamp burning; or Gods sweet incomes of love to a gracious soul waiting for him. Being the experiences of Mrs Anne Venn (daughter to Col. John Venn, & member of the church of Christ at Fulham:) written by her own hand, and found in her closet after her death* (1658; she was a daughter of John Venn's second marriage). The preface is by her minister, Thomas Weld, a Presbyterian based at Gateshead in 1650. The text, which she wrote secretly, is a long and detailed account of her spiritual struggles and travels (it is far less passive than Weld's preface suggests). Her religious commitment began when she was nine, and she remembers her parents going to religious meetings in 1638–9. She rejects the spiritual temptation to remain at home in contemplation rather than travelling to hear a preacher. She (and her father) were much influenced by the Presbyterian Christopher Love (husband to Mary LOVE*), chaplain to her father's regiment after 1642.

VERNON, Elizabeth, Countess of Southampton, c. 1580–after 1655
2. Shropshire, Southampton, Titchfield; 3. genteel; 5. Henry Wriothesley, 3rd Earl of Southampton; 6. genteel.

Maid of Honour to ELIZABETH I.* Her marriage was clandestine: 'Mrs. Vernon is from the Court, and lies in Essex house; some say she hath taken a venew under the girdle and swells upon it, yet she complaines not of fowle play, but sayes the Earl of Southampton will justifie it; and it is bruted, underhand, that he was latelie here fowre dayes in great secret of purpos to marry her.' (*Chamberlain's Letters Temp. Eliz.*, Camden Society, 1861, p. 18).

Letters by her are in Violet Wilson, *Society Women of Shakespeare's Time* (London: John Lane, 1924).

VOKINS, Elizabeth, *fl.* 1691
2. West Challow (Berks.); 4. Quaker.

Daughter of Joan VOKINS,* with her sisters Hannah BURGIS,* Sarah

LAWRENCE* and Mary LOCKEY,* she signed a testimony 'concerning our dear and tender mother, Joan Vokins' in 1691.

VOKINS, Joan, –1690

1. Bunce; 2. West Challow (Berks.); 3. preacher; 4. Quaker; 5. Richard Vokins.

Joan Vokins's family at first opposed her Quakerism; she had seven children (including five daughters, the youngest, Hopefull, being born in 1671). She travelled to New England in 1680–1, and visited New York, New Jersey, Rhode Island, Antigua, St Nevis, Barbados. She hastily returned from her travels when there was a threat to the organisation of the women's meeting. She was dragged out of a church in Sandwich, Kent in 1686 and visited Ireland in 1687. She lived with and fought constant ill-health and infirmity. She was highly regarded among Quakers. Among the 28 women signing a group testimony to her in 1691 (from the Reading Women's Meeting) were Mariabella FARNBOROUGH,* Mary SANDILANDS* and Jane SANSOM.* A testimony was also signed by four of her daughters, Hannah BURGIS,* Sarah LAWRENCE,* Mary LOCKEY* and Elizabeth VOKINS.* She was buried in Reading.

A loving advertisement unto all those who join together to persecute the innocent (1670); *A tender invitation unto all those that want peace with God . . .* (1687); and *God's mighty power magnified; as manifested and revealed in his faithful handmaid J. V.* (1691, ed. Oliver Sansom; reprinted Cockermouth, 1871; extracts in Graham).

W

W—, Ez—

See Appendix I.

W—, M—

'Experiences of M.W.', in Henry Walker, *Spirituall experiences, of sundry believers* (1653; Smith, p. 35).

WAILES, Isabel, –1689
1. Cowper; 2. Leeds; 4. Quaker; 5. John Wailes (m. 1665).

Two daughters were born 1666 and 1669. She was imprisoned, with her husband, for nine weeks in 1683 and her goods were distrained for tithes. Imprisoned again in 1684, for eleven weeks (in York castle, from where she writes her pamphlet).

A warning to the inhabitants of Leeds and all others in cities, towns, and villages, who have willfully been persecuting the people of the Lord, whom he hath called by his eternal spirit to magnify himself in, and to testify for truth and righteousness, and against all ungodly works, and workers thereof (1685).

WAITE, Mary, –1689
1. Smith; 2. York; 3. minister; 4. Quaker; 5. Thomas Waite (m. 1666); 6. bookbinder and seller.

Sister-in-law of Mary SMITH;* her husband acted as local agent for the distribution of Quaker texts and she 'laboured much in the ministry and in laying Friends' sufferings before such as were in authority'. She was imprisoned in 1684 in York.

A warning to all Friends who professeth the everlasting truth of God, which he hath revealed and made manifest in this his blessed day, (whether on this side, or beyond the seas) (1679; she tells of being brought 'near to the gates of death'). This was published with, and is bound after, *An epistle from the women's yearly meeting at York* (1688; both are in Augustan Society Reprints, vol. 33, 1979). She also wrote the unprinted 'The righteous shall be had in everlasting remembrance'. The epistle from York was signed by Elizabeth BECKWITH,* Judith BOULBY,* Mary LINDLEY,* Elizabeth SEDMAN,* Frances TAYLOR,* Mary WAITE, Deborah WINN,* Catherine WHITTON;* it was also published as *A testimony for the Lord and his truth* (1688). See also *A testimony from the yearly meeting at York* (1686), signed by Anna ALLENSON, Judith BOULBIE,* Margret BRECKSON, Elizabeth LEAPER,* Mary LINDLEY,* Mary MOUN, Elizabeth SIMPSON, Frances TAYLOR,* Mary WAITE, Dorothy WELLS, Catherine WITTON,* Issabella YEAMANS;* and another testimony from the York Women's Meeting in 1692 signed by Anne ALLISON, Elizabeth BECKWITH,* Judith BOULBIE,* Margaret BRACKING, Sarah ENGLISH, Grace HEMSLEY (see Grace BARWICK*), Elizabeth MOORE, Isabell MORRIS, Katherin RATLIFE, Mary WAITE, Dorothy WELLS, Deborah WINN,* Katherine WINN.*

WALKER, Elizabeth, 1623–90

1. Sadler; 2. London, Ipswich, Croydon, Fyfield (Essex); 3. trade; 5. Anthony Walker; 6. cleric.

The eldest daughter of a 'very Eminent Citizen', John Sadler, she was sent to Ipswich during the Civil Wars, married in 1650 and bore eleven children (1651–65). Anthony Walker, *The holy life of Mrs Elizabeth Walker* (1690), reprints Elizabeth's autobiographical writings, her instructions to her children and letters to friends. Anthony says 'all that's Comma'd in the Margin is transcribed verbatim, from her Writings', adding that, since she did not write for publication, the prose is simple: 'she was a plain, private Woman, and conversed only with obscure Persons of low Degree.' Therefore 'just Allowances are to be made, and too raised an Expectation ought not to be brought to the Perusal of what is offered; if it be usefull to Persons of her Level, it may suffice.' He also says 'I sometimes coming into her Chamber, when she was Writing, she would slide her Book or Papers into the Drawer of the Table on which she wrote.' She tells him 'Let me beg one promise from thee; . . . *That I would never look into the Books and Papers in that Drawer, so long as she lived.*' In contrast to her husband's construction of her and her writing, the text is articulate evidence of her experiences and contacts.

WALKER, Mary, *fl.* 1643–50

2. ?London; 5. Clement Walker; 6. Treasury official.

The case of Mrs. M. W., the wife of Clement Walker Esq. (1650). This is an appeal to the House of Commons. Her husband had settled his 'ancient inheritance', of Office of Chief Usher to the Exchequer, on her by way of jointure. When Clement was put in the Tower (in 1643), Humphrey Edwards MP procured sequestration and in 1649 entered her house, 'expelled my ancient servant, taking and keeping possession of the same'. The text claims that Clement has served Parliament, lost £10,000 to the enemy, and never had reparation; whereas Edwards had attended Charles I when he sought to arrest the Five Members, and will, if not stopped, take away her estate and jointure.

WALSINGHAM, Frances, Lady Essex, c. 1560–after 1603

5(a) Sir Philip Sidney, (b) Robert Devereux, Earl of Essex; 6(a) poet, courtier, (b) genteel.

The author of letters to her husbands and to Robert Cecil, among others (Partnow, p. 125).

WALWYN, Mary, –1725

1. Winnington; 2. Herefordshire; 5. John Walwyn (m. 1667).

The second wife of John Walwyn, she bore four children, of whom the two sons were 'idiots'. It was the rights of custody of these sons, and the inheritance that went with them, that led to her legal dispute: *The case of Mary Walwyn, widow of John Walwyn Esq; petitioner against the right honourable Charles Earl of Monmouth* (1698). Her husband was in debt and infirm in June 1684, so he made over custody of the estate and the sons to enable payment of his debts after his death. This arrangement was renewed during James II's reign, but before it could be renewed again in the new reign (after 1688), Monmouth petitioned for custody of the one son who was still alive, which he obtained (after a legal hearing) in 1690. He then tried to obtain possession of the estate, which Mary Walwyn resisted. In August 1690 'in a forcible manner' he entered her house: he forced her daughter at gunpoint to show him the son's room, kicked Mary's sister, imprisoned and carried off her son, threatened the tenants that they had to pay him rent, and promised to blow up the house if the family opposed him. Mary Walwyn pleads for relief and custody.

WANDESFORD, Elizabeth, fl. 1689–1713

2. Ireland; 5(a) Garret Foulkes, (b) George Wandesford; 6(a) soldier, (b) genteel.

An abstract of the unfortunate and unparallel case of Elizabeth Wandesford, weddow and relict of Garret Foulkes, Esq: and of her aged mother and children, who are by the faithful services and sufferings of their friends, left miserable objects of the care and bounty of this just and merciful assembly (1693).

Their property was seized some time before James II landed in Ireland and Foulkes was taken prisoner. He was released by William III and died at the battle of Aughrim (July 1691). Elizabeth claims to have lost five brothers, her husband and fortune in the king's service. She was granted a pension of £200 a year (by warrants issued in February and June 1692) and custodiam of lands, but this was blocked by land forfeitures in Ireland. She made eight journeys to England to sort out the land issue; her text asks for better treatment, and the equivalent of three years' loss of income. In February 1692 she was spoken of as Foulkes' widow, so presumably married later that year or early the next; she bore two children in her second marriage (they are mentioned in their grandmother's will of 1713). Her father-in-law (originally from Yorkshire) had his lands seized by James II's Parliament in 1689 and was in prison in 1695.

WANDESFORD, Lady

Alice OSBORNE*

WARD, Mary, 1585–1645

2. Yorkshire; 3. nun, genteel; 4. Catholic.

Of Catholic parents, and baptized 'Joan', she went to St Omer in 1606 as an out-sister of the Poor Clares, and the following year founded a convent. After visiting England she returned to St Omer to direct a boarding-school for the daughters of English Catholics. Among the 269 houses which acknowledge her as foundress are the Institute of the Blessed Virgin Mary in Rome, an educational institute for women, and foundations in Naples, Germany and Belgium. She was imprisoned on a heresy charge in Munich in 1631 and in 1637 came to England under the patronage of HENRIETTA MARIA.* She opened a school for Catholic children and in the 1640s moved to Yorkshire. She wrote an account of her travels between 1606 and 1618, and also letters to the Pope about education for women. Her innovations in education drew much opposition.

See M. Chambers, *The life of . . .*, 2 vols. (London: Burns & Oates, 1882, 1885); Mother P. Parker, *The spirit of Mary Ward* (1945, reprinted Tenbury Wells: Thomas More Books, 1963). Parker draws on much unpublished writing, including: 'The brief relation', a biographical sketch written by Mary Ward's companions Mary POYNTZ* and Winifred WIG-MORE;* fragments, notes and letters by Mary Ward herself; and the

'Sayings of Mary Ward', preserved at the Institute in Rome, and representing her spiritual teaching and advice.

See Marie B. Rowlands, 'Recusant Women 1560–1640' in Prior, 1985 (which includes details of a number of women authors of unpublished texts).

WARD, Mary

Mary MARTEN: Appendix III.

WARD, Rebecca, –1705

2. Kendal, Gateshead; 4. Quaker; 5. John Ayrey (m. 1661).

Signed the 1659 tithing petition. Spoke in Cheapside, was arrested and imprisoned in Bridewell (from a letter of 1655, Swarthmore MSS). Bore twins sometime in the 1670s and a daughter in 1674.

WARDLAW, Lady Elizabeth, 1677–1727

1. Halket; 2. Fife; 3. genteel; 5. Sir Henry Wardlaw; 6. genteel.

Todd (p. 315) sees her as 'one of the first movers of the ballad revival'. She is associated, as author or reviser, with such ballads as 'Hardyknute', 'Sir Patrick Spens' and 'Gilderay'. *BMC* lists 'Hardyknute, a fragment' (1719, 1745, 1783) under her name.

WARREN, Elizabeth, *fl.* 1645–9

2. Woodbridge (Suffolk); 3. genteel, Latin scholar; 4. Presbyterian.

Her first book *The old and good way vindicated: in a treatise wherein divers errours (both in judgment and practice, incident to these declining times) are unmasked, for the caution of humble Christians* (1645) says she is 'conscious of my mentall and Sex-deficiencie'. Despite this, she was extremely learned and used her classical and philosophical training to comment on the politico-religious situation. She attacked the growing contempt for the public ministry of the Word, and emphasised the warnings of 'godly pastours'. Although she defended the radical Henry Burton and attacked papists, her position was basically conservative. She attacked 'sectaries [who] prohibit us the publike ministry' and described women as the 'weaker sex' with Eve's 'hereditary evil', while herself producing very strongly argued learned texts: *Spiritual thrift. Or, meditations wherein humble Christians (as in a mirrour) may view the verity of their saving graces, and may see how to make a spirituall improvement of all opportunities and advantages of a pious proficiencie (or a holy growth) in grace and goodnesse. And wherein is layd open many errours incident to these declining times* (1646) contains detailed Bible commentary and reference to a range of philosophers, including Plato, Socrates, Pythagoras. In her final work, *A warning-peece from heaven, against the sins of the times, inciting us to fly from the vengeance to come. Or, mournful meditations of revealed wrath, appearing in the progresse of our sins and sorrows* (1649), she attacks the regicides and speaks of those 'in this sorrowfull kingdom, who are now in subjection to arbitrary insolence'. She was supported in publication of her works by her minister, Robert Cade, vicar of Woodbridge 1623–43.

WARWICK, Lady Mary

Mary RICH*

WATERS, Margaret, *fl.* 1670
4. Quaker.

A warning from the Lord to the inhabitants of the earth (1670).

WATSON, Grace, 1668–88
2. Knight Stainforth, nr. Settle (Yorks.); 4. Quaker.

Her sayings are quoted in *A memorandum or commemoration of some of the heavenly expressions which came from Grace Watson, daughter of Samuel Watson, which she uttered upon her bed of sickness, on the 15th and 16th, & of the 6th month, 1688. Written by her sister Elizabeth Moss, and sent to her parents* (1688). Elizabeth MOSS.*

WATSON, Mary, –before 1700
2. Knight Stainforth, nr. Settle (Yorks.); 4. Quaker; 5(a) Thomas Monk, (b) Samuel Watson (m. 1664).

With her first husband she lived at South Liverton, Nottinghamshire (although she probably spent some time in York, where she was in close contact with Mary SMITH* and was a follower of William Dewsbury). She bore Elizabeth MOSS* in her first marriage. She had four children between 1665 and 1678 in her second marriage. She was probably dead by 1700, when her husband married again. She wrote, with Samuel Watson, a testimony in *A memorandum . . .* (1688; see also Grace WATSON*).

WATSONE, Sarah, –1681
2. Nottingham; 4. Quaker; 5. Jonathan Reckless (m. 1677).

Bore three children between 1677 and 1681. Wrote, with Elizabeth NEW-
TON* and others, *A real demonstration* . . . (1653; see Elizabeth NEWTON
for details).

WAUGH, Dorothy, ?1636–

2. Hutton (Westmorland); 4. Quaker; 5. William Lotherington.

Sister to Jane WAUGH,* with whom she served in the Camm household.
She was convinced in 1652, imprisoned for preaching in Norwich
(1654), gaoled in Truro (1655) for visiting imprisoned Quakers, gaoled
in Carlisle for speaking 'against all deceit' and fitted with a scold's bridle
(1655). She went to Boston in 1656, was imprisoned in New Amsterdam
(New York) (1657) and preached with Sarah GIBBONS in Rhode Island
(1657). She walked ninety miles in winter to Salem (Massachusetts),
then to Boston, where she was imprisoned. In New England she urged
Quakers not to have children because to do so hindered work for the
Quaker cause. She wrote 'A relation' in *The Lambs defence against lies*
(1656), which describes her imprisonment in Carlisle and the experience of wearing the bridle.

WAUGH, Jane, –1674

2. Hutton (Westmorland), Somerset; 4. Quaker; 5. Thomas Whitehead
(m. 1664); 6. clothier.

Also known as Jane WHITEHEAD.

Served with her sister Dorothy in the Camm household. She was imprisoned in Cambridge (1653) and in Banbury, for testifying (1655), for
refusing the Oath of Abjuration (1658), and again in 1662. One of her
regular travelling companions was Frances RAUNCE. She bore four children between 1665 and 1670. Wrote *A true declaration* (1685) with Anne
AUDLAND* (Greaves and Zaller say she was illiterate).

WEAMYS, Anna, *fl.* 1651

*A continuation of Sir Philip Sidney's Arcadia, written by a young gentlewoman,
Mrs A. W.* (1651). The work is dedicated to Lady Anne and Lady Grace
Perpoint (Pierrepont?), daughters of the Marquess of Dorchester. Prefa-
tory poems say that the author is young, and include poems by F.
Vaughan and J. Howell: 'He [Sidney] breathes through female Organs,
yet retains/His masculine vigour in Heroick strains.'
   This is discussed by B. McCarthy, *Women writers: their contribution to the
English novel* (Cork: Cork University Press, 1944) and, briefly, by

Salzman, who is reluctant to allow Weamys any credit for the style of her continuation.

WEBB, Mary, 1617–97
2. Southwark; 4. Quaker.

Co-signatory of Ann GOULD/GOLD's* *An epistle to all Christian magistrates* (1659).

    Friends met at her house in Southwark, *c.* 1655, and she was imprisoned in Somerset in 1662. She wrote 'I being moved of the Lord doth to call unto you that are gathered together in Parliament' (1659).

WELLS, Mary, *fl.* 1684

A divine poem written by Mary Wells, who recommends it as a fit token for all young men and maids, instead of profane songs and ballads (1684, 1690; alphabetical quatrains about sin and salvation).

WEMYSS, Margaret, Countess of, 1659–1705
2. West Wemyss; 3. genteel; 5(a) Sir James Wemyss (m. 1672), (b) George Mackenzie, Earl of Cromarty (m. 1700); 6(a)/(b) genteel.

She succeeded to the peerage in her own right in July 1679, as the heir of David, Earl of Wemyss. Pollock (pp. 24, 48, 65) quotes from letters by her (in the 1690s), giving as source the Melville papers in the Scottish Record Office (GD 26).

WENTWORTH, Anne, *fl.* 1650s–77
2. Cripplegate (London); 3. prophet; 4. Baptist.

See Critical Appendix 6.

Anne Wentworth was probably married in the late 1650s. Her husband treated her violently, and she and her daughter eventually fled from home to the safety of a woman friend's house (this was *c.* 1677: see her letters in *CSPD* 1677). Her husband and his Baptist friends rejected her prophetic writing, and he refused to let her have back the papers she had left behind in her flight (one of these was *A mother's legacy to her daughter,* 1677). Her response to this mistreatment was that 'God is with me and in me while the enemy lays a horseload and a cartload of oppression on me.' She regarded her husband as 'Babylon'. In October 1677 she apparently claimed that 'Before the plague a lovely virgin appeared to her, mixing a cup, and said, Come with me and thou shalt see me pour this cup of bitterness and death on the City' (as quoted in *CSPD*). (A pass for Flanders, with Dame Susan BELASYSE, may relate to her.)

A true account of . . . (1676). *The vindication of A. W., tending to the better preparing of all people for her larger testimony . . . Also a song of triumph by the said A.W. . . . newly delivered from the captivity of Babylon* (1677; extracts in Graham). *England's spiritual pill* (?1678). *The revelation of Jesus Christ* (1679).

WENTWORTH, Lady Henrietta Maria, ?1657–86
2. Toddington (Beds.); 4. genteel.

Only daughter of Lady Philadelphia WENTWORTH.* She appeared in John Crowne's Court play, *Calisto*. A supporter and lover of James, Duke of Monmouth, she went to Holland to join him in 1684, but died in England.

The case of the Lady Maria Wentworth, (an infant) grandchild and heir of the right honourable the late Earl of Cleaveland, and daughter and heir of Thomas Wentworth deceased Humbly offered to the consideration of Parliament (1677). The Earl of Cleveland had died in 1670 leaving his estates to Lady Henrietta, but also leaving a heritage of creditors' suits. She dealt with many of these through her mother and guardian, and discharged thousands of pounds in settlement. She now petitions against the suit of Lady Anna POOLE, and asks for the protection of Parliament in keeping her estates. Like many others, the *Case* is probably a commissioned text rather than one directly written by her.

WENTWORTH, Lady Philadelphia, –1696
1. Carey; 2. Toddington (Beds.); 4. genteel; 5. Thomas Wentworth.

Daughter of Sir Frederick Carey, she was Baroness Wentworth in her own right (her husband died in 1664). *CSPD* 411: 55 (29 January, 1679) asks for an advertisement to be placed in the 'Gazette', offering a reward for anyone bringing the bookseller Tonson 'divers of her many writings' (which were lost at the time of the fire in the Temple).

WESLEY, Susannah, ?1670–1742
1. Annesley; 2 Nottinghamshire, Lincolnshire; 4. Socinian, Anglican; 5. Samuel Wesley; 6. priest, poet.

Susannah was the mother of John and Charles Wesley (and seventeen other children), and her correspondence with her sons can be found in *The works of John Wesley* (ed. F. Baker, Oxford: Oxford University Press, 1975–). See also 'Mrs Wesley's conference with her daughter' (ed. G. Rowe, *Wesley Historical Society*, vol. 3, 1898).

WESTON, Elizabeth, 1582–1612
2. London, Bohemia, Prague; 5. Johann Leon; 6. jurist and agent.

Elizabeth Weston spoke Greek, Latin, German, Italian and Czech. Her work was praised by such as Scaliger and Heinsius. *Poema . . . studio ac opera* was published in Frankfurt (1602) and *Parthenicon E.J.W., virginis nobilissimae* in Prague (?1606). *BMC* says that its copy of the latter has on its flyleaf her poetical address to the reader in manuscript and also that book one has some additional manuscript verses with her initials on them.

WESTWOOD, Mary, –1667
3. publisher; 4. Quaker.

Grace BARWICK,* Sarah BLACKBERRY,* Elizabeth CALVERT,* Priscilla COTTON,* Mary FOSTER/FORSTER,* Ann GOULD/GOLD,* PETITIONS,* Rebeckah TRAVERS.* See Critical Appendix 7.

Mary Westwood, whose identity has been at times denied or made male for no good reason, published work by Quakers from the southern counties from 1659 to 1663; and especially work by those imprisoned in Winchester. She published the women's tithing petition (1659) and may have been the author of *A testimony against tythes* (1683) but no copy of this is extant.

See M. Bell, 'Mary Westwood, Quaker publisher', *Publishing History*, vol. 23 (1988).

WEYER, Florence

See Appendix III.

WHARLEY, Mary, 1657–1726
1. Penington; 2. Amersham, Chalfont St Giles (Bucks.); 4. Quaker; 5. Daniel Wharley (m. 1686); 6. woollen draper.

Daughter of Mary PENINGTON,* she married at the famous Quaker meeting-house at Jordans and bore six children (the first two twins) between 1688 and 1702. She co-authored (with Mary BAKER* and Mary LARCUM*) 'A testimony from the Women's Meeting, concerning Thomas Ellwood' (1713) in *The history of the life of Thomas Ellwood* (1714).

WHARTON, Lady Anne, 1659–85
1. Lee; 2. Oxfordshire; 3. genteel; 5. Thomas Wharton; 6. genteel, Whig politician and rake.

The daughter of a baronet, Anne Wharton was an enormously wealthy heiress, and was brought up by the mother of her uncle, Rochester; she married a marquis. In the last years of her life she was close to Bishop Burnet. Greer says that in her lifetime, and for a few years after her death, she was 'one of the most highly esteemed women poets in England'. She wrote a blank verse tragedy about Ovid's love for Julia, 'Love's martyr, or wit above crowns'. This belongs to around 1685, but has not been acted or printed. She contributed poems to such collections as Dryden's *Miscellanies* (1694), *The Temple of Death* (1695), *Ovid's epistles by several hands* (1712) and *Tooke's Collection* (1716). Letters survive to Aphra BEHN,* Waller and her husband.

There is a selection in Greer (p. 286 f.); see also Pearson.

WHEATHILL, Anne, *fl.* 1584
3. genteel.

A handfull of holesome (though homelie) hearbs . . . (1584): a book of prayers, offering no clue as to its author's identity. She may be the daughter of Thomas Wheathill of Leicestershire (we cannot locate any other relevant Wheathills).

WHITE, Dorothy, *c.* 1630–85
2. Weymouth, London; 4. Quaker.

Dorothy White is author of some twenty titles 1659–84, often printed without date or printer's name. They include *A visitation of heavenly love unto the seed of Jacob* . . . (1660); *An alarm sounded to England's inhabitants* . . . (1661); and *Greetings of pure peace and perfect love* . . . (1662; partly in verse). *The voice of the Lord, saith, cry* (from White-lion prison, Southwark, 1662) includes 'ye Judges and Rulers stand in awe of the dreadful God, who is coming with thousands of his Angels to Judge the World, and you shall all know his power to your Everlasting Destruction, if you submit not to his Government.'

WHITE, Elizabeth, –1669
2. Caldecote (Cambs./Herts.); 5. Thomas White.

She says in her youth, for two or three years, she was 'a great lover of histories . . . and did often spend my sleeping-time in reading of them', which she comes to regret since it makes her ignore God. About three months after her marriage in 1657, God reveals her 'sad condition': 'when I have seen a spider, which of all things is most loathsome to me, I have been ready to wish my self such a one, esteeming of it to be in a far happier condition than I was.' She has many religious doubts and listens to preachers. When pregnant she became depressed, 'having a sense of my approaching danger' but she was safely delivered. The major narrative concerns her doubts, temptations, dreams: in one dream 'I thought I heard a voice saying, it would be but for a little while, and that I should die in childbed, and that the night before I dyed I should have full assurance.'

The experiences of God's gracious dealing with Mrs Elizabeth White, late wife of Mr Thomas White of Coldecot in the county of Bucks. As they were written under her own hand, and found in her closet after her decease, she dying in childbed, Decemb. 5. 1669 (Glasgow, 1696).

WHITEHEAD, Anne, 1624–86

1. Downer; 2. Oxfordshire, London, Westmorland; 3. cook, secretary; 4. Quaker; 5(a) Benjamin Greenwell, (b) George Whitehead.

For co-authors (or opponents) see Anne CLABIN,* Sarah FELL,* Sarah HAYWARD.*

Born in Oxfordshire, she was convinced in 1654 in London and then went on a preaching tour (1655–6: Hampshire, Charlbury – her birthplace, Cornwall): she was one of the earliest converts and one of the first women preachers. She returned from the Isle of Wight *c.* 1658 and was in Bristol in 1669. Her second husband was from Westmorland. She knew shorthand and arithmetic, and educated her younger sister after the death of their mother. Her first act as a Quaker was to interrupt a minister at Stepney church, which earned her time in a house of correction. She was a companion of Rebecca WARD, the itinerant preacher, in prison; was involved with Rebeckah TRAVERS* and Sarah BLACKBERRY* in setting up Quaker women's meetings; and was a major figure in London Quaker circles for many years.

For the King and both Houses of Parliament (1670; with Priscilla ECCLESTONE,* Mary ELSON,* Ann INGAL,* Rebeckah TRAVERS* and 30 others); *An epistle for true love, unity and order in the Church of Christ* . . . (1680; with Mary ELSON*); 'Some account of Anne Whitehead's early experience, as written by her near thirty years ago' (verse) in *Piety promoted by faithfulness, manifested by several testimonies concerning that true servant of God Ann Whitehead* (1686; these verses were given to Mary STOUT* when Anne Whitehead returned from the Isle of Wight). Signed *A tender and Christian testimony* (1685; see Mary ELSON* for details).

WHITEHEAD, Elizabeth, *fl.* 1647

1. ?Alcock; 2. Leamington Priors.

Author of a letter (1647) in the *Aspinwall Notarial Records from 1644 to 1651,* 32nd Report (Boston Record Commission, 1903), 101. The letter, to Thomas Alcock, seeks to discover the whereabouts of her two sons, who had been left in New Haven (USA) in the custody of Francis Hall.

WHITEHEAD, Jane

Jane WAUGH*

WHITING, Mary, 1654–76
2. Nailsea (nr. Bristol/Avon); 4. Quaker.

The source for her biography is principally her brother, John Whiting's *Early piety exemplified, in the life and death of Mary Whiting* (?1681), which also prints her two major texts: *An epistle for the meeting at Blackwell . . .* (1675; this has a postscript in verse) and *To the meetings at Clareham, Portshead, and Walton (written from London)* (1675). He mentions other letters which he does not reprint.

Her father, John Whiting, was a famous Quaker, and major Quaker figures – such as John Audland and John Camm – visited the house and heard Mary read at an early age. She was principally educated by her mother (her father died when she was about 4), but as a young child she was also cared for by her grandfather when her mother was in prison. She fasted for the first time in 1674, and began exhortations and public speaking in 1675. In this year she began to travel for her religion (visiting Gloucestershire, Wiltshire, Berkshire, Oxfordshire, Buckinghamshire), journeying about 500 miles. She visited imprisoned Quakers at Reading before arriving in London, from where she wrote an epistle (now lost). She kept a journal of the meetings she attended before she got to London.

WHITROW, Joan, *fl.* 1662–94
2. Covent Garden (London), Surrey; 4. Quaker; 5. Robert Whitrow.

Author of several pamphlets, including (as co-author) *The work of God in a dying maid* (1677): this concerns the death of her daughter Susanna WHITROW,* who died aged 15; she also mentions here her son Jason who died aged 6½; her testimony was witnessed by Anne MARTING and Susanna MEURS; *The humble address of the widow Whitrowe to King William . . .* (1689); and *The widow Whitrowe's humble thanksgiving for the king's safe return . . .* (1694).

WHITROW, Susanna, 1662–77
2. Covent Garden (London); 4. Quaker.

Her words are included in *The work of God in a dying maid* written by her parents (see above). The importance of her words is their contribution to the debate about women speaking: 'Oh! how have I been against a woman's speaking in a meeting? but now, whether it comes from man, woman or child, it is precious indeed' (see also on this Mary COLE*). Her mother's testimony rebuts suggestions that Susanna's convincement was motivated merely by being in love.

WHITTON, Katherine

Katherine WYNN*

WIGHT, Sarah, *c.* 1632–
2. London; 4. Baptist.

See Critical Appendices 2, 5, 6, 7.

The daughter of one of Henry Jessey's parishioners, Sarah Wight underwent a religious experience when 15, fasting for 76 days and being intermittently without sight or hearing. She began 'speaking' on 10 April and was visited by religious leaders, parliamentarians, members of the nobility and local tradespeople for spiritual guidance. One of these visitors was Anna TRAPNEL,* who herself fasted in June of the same year. *The exceeding riches of grace advanced by the spirit of grace* (1647), published by Hannah ALLEN and Henry Overton, is Jessey's account of her words while fasting. It reached six editions by 1652, and was republished in 1658 and 1666. *A wonderful pleasant and profitable letter written by Mrs Sarah Wight* (1656), a letter 'occasioned by the death of her brother, the troubles of her mother; but especially the workings of God in her own heart' was published by 'R. B.' without her consent, because her friends thought she would not approve publication.

WIGINGTON, Leticia, –1681
2. Ratcliffe; 4. ?Catholic.

The confession and execution of Leticia Wigington of Ratclif, who suffered at Tyburn, on Fryday the 9 h of this instant September, 1681, written by her own hand in the goal of Newgate, two days before her death, being condemned for whiping her apprentice girl to death (1681). The text combines religious confession and a circumstantial account of the evidence of her innocence. The headnote claims that her denial of guilt was prompted by

Catholic priests, and that she confessed in court after she had been in Newgate for eight months. Her case is that she had been framed by the man who committed the murder, John Sadler, and his friends. Sadler, 'a Sea-man', was a lodger in her house. She explains that she had to take in lodgers because she had been left by her husband 'who left his Ship and Living' two years before and she had to feed her three small children and two apprentices. She says she found Sadler beating the girl, and that 'when the Girl was Dead, he would have condescended to have me Bury the Girl, and he would have bought a Crape Mourning Suit and a Coffin he said this to me.' She refused to pretend the girl died a natural death and insisted Sadler be taken before a justice, but Sadler and his female companion both escaped (he through an upstairs window). She herself was arrested (in the house of the dead girl's aunt) and testified against by her apprentice, a girl aged 12.

WIGMORE, Winifred, *fl.* 1609
2. St Omer; 3. nun; 4. Catholic.

Went in 1609 with Mary POYNTZ* and Mary WARD* from England to St Omer, where with five other women they set up a community and directed a school for the daughters of English Catholics and Belgian children. With Mary POYNTZ she wrote *The brief relation*, a biographical sketch of Mary WARD which is drawn upon by Mother Pauline Parker in her *The spirit of Mary Ward*, 1945 (Tenbury Wells: Thomas More Books, 1963). It is not clear whether she later accompanied Mary Ward to Rome.

WILKS, Judith

See Appendix III.

WILMOT, Elizabeth, Countess of Rochester, –1681
1. Mallet; 2. Somerset, London, Adderbury (Oxon.); 3. genteel; 5. John Wilmot, Earl of Rochester; 6. genteel, poet.

She went to London in 1665 and two years later, against her family's wishes, married the king's favourite, Rochester. While at Adderbury she was in the company of Rochester's niece, Anne Lee, later Anne WHARTON.*

Her manuscript materials are in the library of the University of Nottingham (Portland MS PwV 31), and include poems, fragments and seventy lines of pastoral dialogue. There is confusion over the attribution of several poems which may be by her, Rochester, or 'EPHELIA',* and there may have been collaboration between her and her husband in their writing. A poem known as 'The Answer' is now attributed to her, rather than to Rochester (see Keith Walker (ed.), *The poems of John Wilmot Earl of Rochester*, Oxford: Blackwell, 1984). Greer prints versions of 'The Answer' and another poem, 'Song'.

WINCHELSEA, Anne, Countess of

Anne FINCH*

WISEMAN, Jane, *fl.* ?1680–1702

2. Oxfordshire, London; 3. servant, dramatist, ?actor; 5. — Holt; 6. vintner.

Jane Wiseman was servant to a Mr Wright of Oxfordshire and a friend of Susanna CENTLIVRE's.*

She is the author of the tragedy *Antiochus the Great* (1702) which was acted at Lincoln's Inn Fields in 1701, with Elizabeth Barry as female lead. It is reprinted by Kendell. According to Pearson, she used the profits from the play to set herself up in a tavern in Westminster. The play was revived in 1721; the plot kills off all relationships involving men, and ends with an affirmation of female friendship. Summers (*The playhouse of Pepys*, New York: Humanities Press, 1964) mentions a Mrs Wiseman as of the Duke's Company, *c.* 1680, and says she followed Mrs Betterton in the role of Roxolana in Orrery's *Mustapha* (pp. 109, 142).

WITH, Elizabeth

See Appendix III.

WOLFRESTON, Frances, 1607–77

1. Middlemore; 2. King's Norton, Statfold; 3. ?Catholic; 5. Francis Wolfreston; 6. squire.

The eldest of twenty-two children, Frances married in 1631 and had ten or eleven children of her own. Her husband, younger than herself, apparently had limited mental abilities, and the inscription on their mural tablet describes them thus: 'As different strings most harmony afford/So this unequall'd equal paire accord./Harmless disports his younger age affects/While nothing her inlarged care neglects.' She collected a large library of which she made careful disposition in her will, and many of her books were inscribed 'frances wolfreston hor bouk'.

Now dispersed, the collection included a high proportion of plays and poems, and in many cases (e.g. the 1593 *Venus and Adonis*) her copy is the only surviving one. She owned plays by Chapman, Dekker, Marlowe, Heywood and ten Shakespeare quartos; verse by Donne, Drayton, Greene, Gascoigne; and popular books of riddles and jokes, as well as works on religion and current affairs. Paul Morgan's reconstruction of her library offers unique information about the reading and interests of a woman of the land-owning class in the Midlands. Some of her books are annotated: *The good womens champion* carries her comment 'in prais of women a good one'; she added plot summaries to plays by Heywood and Ford.

See P. Morgan, 'Frances Wolfreston and "Hor Bouks": a seventeenth-century woman book collector', *The Library*, sixth series, vol. 11, 1989, pp. 197–219.

WOLLEY, Hannah, *c.* 1621–74

2. Essex, London; 3. servant, teacher; 5(a) Benjamin Wolley, (b) Francis Challinor; 6(a) teacher, (b) genteel.

Author of: *The ladies directory* (1661, 1662). *The cook's guide* (1664). *The Queen-like closet stored with all manner of rare receipts* . . . (1670; eleven editions to 1696; German version 1674). *The ladies delight . . . concerning the art of preserving and candying, both fruits and flowers* . . . (1672; translated into German in the same year). *A supplement to the Queen-like closet* (1674, 1680, 1684). This includes her autobiography. *The gentlewoman's companion* . . . (1675) and *The complete serving-maid* (1677) are both often attributed to her, but Hobby says they are not by Wolley (*Virtue*, pp. 174–5).

WOODCOCK, Jane, ?1616–86

2. London; 3. property-owner; 4. Quaker; 5. William Woodcock; 6. property-owner.

The Woodcocks' house in the Savoy was a major London meeting place for Quakers, especially those who were socially superior converts. Jane was a friend of Nayler and a letter from her to him (in Exeter gaol, 1656) was used in evidence against him at his trial: she called him 'the prophet of the Most High'. On Nayler's release, despite the fact that he was avoided by many Quakers, the Woodcocks allowed him to hold a meeting at their house. Jane was connected with Elizabeth CALVERT.* After her husband's death in 1667, she and Martha FISHER carried out extensive building schemes between the Savoy gates in the Strand, using

William's property and some surrounding houses. She was active in women's meetings. Her letter to Nayler is quoted in *State Trials*.

WOODFORDE, Mary, –1730

1. Norton; 2. Binstead (Hants); 5. Samuel Woodforde; 6. Anglican priest, poet.

'Mary Woodforde's book, 1684–1690: a domestic diary' in *Woodforde Papers and Diaries*, ed. D. H. Woodforde (London: Peter Davies, 1932). Extracts in Houlbrooke. She records domestic events and political changes: Monmouth's rising is 'horrid treason'; she hopes William will 'reign in righteousness'.

WOOLLEY, Mary, 1630–1710

2. Bishopsgate (London); 4. Quaker; 5. Ezekiel Woolley; 6. broadweaver.

Two sons were born, 1668 and 1670. She wrote a testimony in Anne WHITEHEAD,* *Piety* . . . (1686).

WORCESTER, Margaret

Margaret SOMERSET*

WORSOPP, Elizabeth, *fl.* 1653

1. Greenway; 2. Berkshire.

A brief reply to the narration of Don Pantaleon Sa. (1653): see Frances CLARK.*

WORTLEY, Mary

Mary Wortley MONTAGU*

WROTH, Lady Mary, ?1586–*c*.1652

1. Sidney; 2. Essex, London, Netherlands, Kent; 3. genteel, novelist; 5. Sir Robert Wroth; 6. genteel, landowner.

Mary Wroth was active in the court of James I and, according to Ben Jonson, 'unworthily married to a jealous husband'. He dedicated *The Alchemist* to her and Wither called her 'Arts sweet lover'. She is known for *The Countess of Montgomery's Urania* (1621), a volume which was seen as satirical by some at court and so withdrawn by the author. Her *Poems* have been edited by Josephine Roberts (Baton Rouge: Louisiana State

University Press, 1983). A sonnet sequence (*Pamphilia to Amphilanthus*) is appended to *Urania*, while Greer mentions two versions of a pastoral, *Love's victories*. As a widow she had children by William Herbert, Earl of Pembroke.

See Greer (p. 61 f. including a selection of sonnets) and Salzman, pp. 138–44.

WYAT, Hester, *fl.* 1600s

Greer (pp. 5–6) cites 'A poem made by [a frie]nd of mine in answere to one who askt w[hy s]he wrotte' as typical of the products of 'lonely young' women who wrote verse.

WYNDHAM, Anne, 1632–98

1. Gerard; 2. Trent (Somerset); 3. genteel; 5. Francis Wyndham; 6. colonel, governor of Dunster castle.

Daughter and co-heir of Thomas Gerard; through her his estate passed to Francis Wyndham, by whom she had three sons. *Claustrum regale reseratum or the king's concealment at Trent* (1667) tells of and celebrates Charles II's escape (after the battle of Worcester), and Francis Wyndham's part in organising it. Francis was asked, 'by especial command from His Majesty' (soon after 1660), to write an account, but the title-page credits 'A. W.'. When the volume was presented to the king it 'was laid up in his Royal Cabinet, there to rest for some time'. It may be that Francis wrote the main text, and Anne the dedicatory epistle. There is, on the other hand, an attempt to present the book as Anne's. This may be connected with her petition in May 1667 which appeals for a pension in her own right for helping the king. (Her husband had received £1,000 at the Restoration and others who had helped the king had petitioned in 1664 for money.) The book stresses the role of the Wyndhams, paying particular attention to the women: when Francis told his wife and mother that the king was coming to them, 'The relation he gave them, did not (through the weakness of their sex) bring upon them any womanish passion, but surprized with joy, they most cheerfully resolve (without the least shew of fear) to hazard all, for the safety of the King.' The focus on Francis's mother is important because she had been nurse to Charles II when he was Prince of Wales. It looks as if the book, which had been ignored for six years, was published to coincide with Anne's appeal; and that she made an appeal separately from her husband in order, presumably, to supplement the family income.

WYNN, Deborah, ?1645–1727

1. Kitching; 2. Bradford; 4. Quaker; 5. John Wynn (m. 1668); 6. clothier.

Four children were born between 1670 and 1686 (two died in infancy), one being Deborah BELL.* She signed epistles from the York Women's Meeting in 1688 and 1692 (see Mary WAITE* for details) and wrote 'The testimony of Deborah Wynne concerning her husband' (1699) in *The memory of the just . . . John Wynn* (1715).

WYNN, Katherine, *fl.* 1670–92

2. Melmerbury, Snape (Yorks.); 4. Quaker; 5(a) Robert Whitton, (b) Stephen Wynn (m. 1688); 6(b) artisan.

She was fined in 1670–1 for Quaker activities. She wrote *An epistle to Friends everywhere: to be distinctly read in their meetings when assembled together in the fear of the Lord by a friend of truth, and a lover of righteousness* (1681); signed epistles from the York Women's Meeting in 1686, 1688 and 1692 (see Mary WAITE* for details); wrote a testimony for Robert Lodge in *Several living testimonies given forth by divers Friends* (1691) and a testimony for Sarah BECKWITH (1692; see Hannah BECKWITH*).

WYTHENS, Lady

Elizabeth TAYLOR*

Υ

YARBRUGH, Lady Henrietta Maria, 1694–1776
1. Blagge; 2. Yorkshire, London; 3. genteel; 5. Sir John Vanbrugh; 6. dramatist and architect.

C. B. Robinson mentions *My Lady Yarbrugh's Book of Meditations* in his *History of the Priory and Peculiar of Snaith* (1861) but this seems to be lost. She was great-aunt to Margaret BLAGGE.*

YEAMANS, Isabel, ?1637–1704
1. Fell; 2. Bristol, London; 4. Quaker; 5(a) William Yeamans (m. 1664), (b) Abraham Morrice (m. 1689); 6(b) silk merchant.

The daughter of Margaret FELL,* she bore four children in her first marriage. She was persecuted for her faith in 1664; signed the Fox/FELL marriage certificate in 1669 and in the 1670s was active in the Bristol Women's Meeting: in 1671 she was involved in a dispute with the Men's Meeting, which objected to the women's wishes to meet monthly. William Yeamans died in 1674; in 1677 Isabel was in Holland where she visited the Princess of Bohemia with Elizabeth HENDRICKS* and Elizabeth KEITH. She lived in many places, including London and Stockton-on-Tees, between 1680 and 1690 (her second husband was from Lincoln).

She wrote *An invitation of love* (1679) and was the main signatory to *A lively testimony to the living truth, given forth by Robert Jeckell upon his deathbed. In the presence of many eye and ear witnesses whose names are subscribed* (1676). Among the witnesses were Rachel FELL, Sarah FELL* and Susanna FELL (her sisters), Elizabeth HOPPER*, Agnes ORMANDY and Bridget PINDER* (who wrote the final description of Jeckell's death).

See Isabel Ross, *Margaret Fell* (London: Longman, 1949).

YORK, Anne Hyde, Duchess of, 1637–71
2. London, Breda; 3. genteel; 4. (finally) Catholic; 5. James, Duke of York (James II); 6. king.

Anne Hyde married James secretly in September 1660. She was a patron to Lely and had eight children of whom only Anne and Mary survived infancy. *DNB* refers to her written 'portrait' of the Princess of Orange and says that she began a narrative of her husband's career.

A copy of a letter written by the late Duchess of York (1671). *Reasons of her leaving the communion* (1670). *Copies of two papers . . .* (1686, 1687). *A copy of a paper* (1682).

'A Young Lady'

See Appendix I.

Z

ZINSPENNINCK, Judith, –1664

2. Amsterdam, Colchester; 3. minister; 4. Quaker; 5. Jacob Sewell.

Her paternal grandfather was a Brownist emigrant from Kidderminster to Holland. Judith herself was influential as a minister among early Quaker converts, first in Amsterdam and later in Colchester. It is not clear whether she wrote in English and Dutch, or only in Dutch. English versions of her writing were certainly popular among English Friends. She died in Amsterdam.

Ein ernstige Berispinge (A serious reproof to the teachers of the Flemish Baptists congregation, and the members thereof), 1660, was written with William Ames. *Some worthy proverbs left behind by Judith Zinspenninck, to be read in the congregation of the Saints*, 1663, was translated by William Caton and dated from Colchester, 2 June. Her son, William Sewell, provided a preface to her *Eenige Schriften en Zend-Brieven*, published in Amsterdam in 1684; and what may be the same text in English, *An epistle to the friends of truth*, is inserted in Sewell's *History . . . of Quakers*, 1722, which mentions others of her works.

Appendix I
Anonymous texts

Advice to the women and maidens of London, by one of that sex (**1678**)

Also in Stephen Monteage, *Debtor and creditor*, 1682.

'Anonymous business diary of a midwife' ?1696 or *c.* 1719

Rawlinson MS D1141; Fraser, p. 441.

'Aphra Behn's circle'

Greer, p. 21 ff.

B—, M—

The ladies cabinet enlarged and opened (1654).

CSPD

CSPD 1668 (251: 199) has reference to a description by a woman of her Christian training and experience.

CSPD June 30, 1666 (160: 120) refers to a letter from York by a female preacher: 'A woman in the country pretending the gift of prophecy has been before Lord Fauconberg, but was not sent to gaol.'

CSPD June 30, 1666 (160: 104) refers to a letter from a woman to the king, telling him what his subjects think of him; but this may be a forgery.

D—, E— [?Elizabeth Davies]

Two sonnets prefacing William Fowler's translation of Petrarch (1587). See *Works of William Fowler*, ed. H. W. Meikle (Edinburgh: Scottish Text Society, 1914).

'Eliza's babes'

See Hobby, *Virtue*, pp. 55–9, 75, 159, 185.

'The Emulation'

Greer, p. 309 f.

The gentlewoman's cabinet unlocked **(1673, 1675, 1686)**

The gentlewoman's delight in cookery **(?1690)**

L—, Elizabeth

Short remains of a dead gentlewoman (?1690).

A Lady of Honour

See Greer, p. 439.

Letters of love and gallantry **(1693)**

'. . . all written by ladies', allegedly including Catherine COCKBURN.*

M—, A—

Queen Elizabeth closet of physical secrets (1652, 1656). *A rich closet of physical secrets* (1652, 1653). *The cook's New Years gift, cookery refined, or the Lady, gentlewoman and servant-maid's companion* (n.d.).

M—, M— (M—Marsin)

The womens advocate (1683, 1687). Crawford notes that if 'M. M.' = M. Marsin sixteen other works should be added, but the name 'Marsin' looks like a pseudonym.

M—, R—

The mothers counsellor, live within compasse. Being the last will and testament to her dearest daughter (1630; Partnow, p. 130; Crawford doubts).

M—, W—

The queen's closet opened (1665; 15 editions by 1698).

The mother's blessing (1685)

N—, M—

Her play *The faithful general,* 1706, performed at the Haymarket, is an adaptation of Beaumont and Fletcher's *The loyal subject.* The author calls it her 'first Essay' in drama, and refers to herself as an 'anti-Sappho'. She complains of scenes being cut by the actors. For more on the play, see J. Pearson, *The Prostituted Muse*, 1988.

'An ode . . . by a Young Lady' (1694–5)

Poem on the death of Queen Mary.

P—, E—

CSPD (1672) refers to a 60 line broadsheet 'On his royal highness' expedition against the Dutch, by Mrs E. P.' It begins 'Proud Hogen Mogens, we will make you bow,/Have at you, greasy butterboxes, now'.

R—, M—

The mother's counsell (?1630; Crawford queries the ascription of this to a woman).

R—, S—

A tender visitation of love to professors and profane, but especially to the inhabitants of the town of Weymouth. Being written from the breathings of life, by a hand-maid of the Lord, S.R. (1661).

Reports by Quaker women

From our half-years meeting in Dublin (1691). *From our yearly meeting at York* (1690). *From our women's meeting held at York* (1692). *From our women's yearly meeting held at York* (1698). *From our women's yearly meeting held at York* (1700).

Spiritual experiences of sundry believers. Held forth by them at several solemne meetings, and conferences (1653)

Translation of Scudery's *Manzini* **(1654, 1655)**

Triumphs of female wit, in some Pindaric odes **(1683)**

W—, Ez—

The answere of a mother, unto her seduced sonnes letter (Amsterdam, 1627; a dialogue between a Protestant mother and Catholic son).

'A Young Lady'

See ARIADNE, Appendix II.

The unnatural mother (1698; see Greer, p. 370 f.).

Appendix II
Pseudonymous and possibly pseudonymous texts

Where there is an asterisk against a name a full entry will be found in the body of the text.

ANGER,* Jane

ARIADNE

She ventures and he wins (1696), a comedy, was performed at Lincoln's Inn Fields in 1695; it was 'Written by a young lady', and was the first play to be performed by Betterton's new company, with Anne Bracegirdle in male disguise and Elizabeth Barry as the virtuous wife.

The unnatural mother, the scene in the kingdom of Spain, 1698, was performed at Lincoln's Inn Fields in 1697; it, too, was 'Written by a young lady' – 'Nor shall you know, harsh men, at whom you rail'. Todd feels this is probably by 'Ariadne', but Pearson has doubts.

CONSTANTIA MUNDA

Ester SOWERNAM,* Rachel SPEGHT*

The worming of a mad dog; or a sop for Cerberus (1617). Shepherd suspects 'Munda' is a man. He feels that the author's use of Juvenal makes it unlikely that a woman is writing and offers evidence that suggests that the printer, Purslowe, manufactured a pamphlet debate for commercial reasons. SPEGHT, however, assumes that *The worming . . .* is by a woman.

ELIZA

See Greer, p. 141 ff.

EPHELIA

The suggestion that Ephelia is Joan 'Phillips', and her identification as the only daughter of Katherine Philips, is widespread but unfounded: Katherine Philips' daughter was named after her mother (see Greer for a detailed discussion of Ephelia's possible identity).

Female poems on several occasions, written by Ephelia (1679, 1682) includes 'love poems to shepherds', acrostics and poems by Rochester, Scroope etc. (Rothstein, p. 173). 'The royal-pair of coxcombs' (an unpublished comedy; lost except for prologue; 1678) was to be 'Acted at a Dancing School'. Prologue in Greer, p. 275. *Advice to his Grace* (1681; broadside verses rebuking the Duke of Monmouth).

Greer prints several poems, including one addressed to Aphra Behn.

EUGENIA

Mary CHUDLEIGH*

HIT-HIM-HOME, Joan

Mary TATTLEWELL, Mary MAKE-PEACE

LOVE,* Mary

MAKE-PEACE, Mary, and HIT-HIM-HOME, Joan

Divers Crabtree lectures (1639). Shepherd says that these form part of a phoney pamphlet controversy set up by John Taylor and the printer John Okes. See Mary TATTLEWELL for a similar case.

PHILO-PHILIPPA

See Greer, p. 204 f.

SOWERNAM, Ester

Rachel SPEGHT,* CONSTANTIA MUNDA

The name 'Sowernam' is obviously a pseudonym, punning on 'Swetnam', and using the biblical Esther, defender of her nation. Shepherd sees no reason to believe that the author of *Ester hath hang'd Haman . . .* is necessarily a man, and notes that SPEGHT thinks of 'her' as a woman.

Ester hath hang'd Haman: or an answere to a lewd pamphlet, entituled The arraignment of women With the arraignment of lewd, idle, froward, and unconstant men, and husbands (1617). This is one of at least four replies to Joseph Swetnam's misogynist pamphlet *The arraignment* . . . , the others being by CONSTANTIA MUNDA, Rachel SPEGHT and Daniel Tuvil.

SYLVIA

Sylvia's revenge . . . (1688). *Sylvia's complaint* . . . (1688).

TATTLEWELL, Mary and/HIT-HIM-HOME, Joan

See Mary MAKE-PEACE.

The women's sharp revenge (1640). The fake text probably by John Taylor.

Appendix III

False ascriptions; cases where ascription has been doubted

ASTELL,* Mary

AUBERT,* Isabella

BECK, Sarah, – ?1680
2. Westmorland; 4. Quaker; 5. John Beck.

She has been seen as the author of *A certain and true relation . . .* (1680) but Hobby says the text is by a man (*Virtue*, pp. 230, 246).

BECKWITH,* Elizabeth

BECKWITH,* Hannah

BLEMING, Jone

The new prayers for K. William and Q. Mary, and prosperity to their arms both by sea and land, against the French king. Used by the people called Quakers (1693) consists of two prayers, one 'against the French king or other foreign enemies', the other 'for the perpetual happiness of our most gracious king and queen'. It is almost certainly a satirical fake. The religious language is nonsensical ('We have sinned, O Lord, with our Fathers'), prayers were not used by Quakers, nor was this language. The 'loyal' prayer says: 'They shal fall, and be overcome, but we couragiously will presist' and 'suppress their open and secret Enemies both by Sea and Land'; it is deliberately unclear who 'we' are. Presumably this is a Jacobite text opposed both to William and Mary and to Quakerism. The name of the author is meant to sound Dutch, and, if pronounced that way, becomes the English word 'blaming'.

234

BOULBIE,* Judith

BRADMORE, Sarah

Mrs Sarah Bradmores prophecy of the wonders that will happen, anno dom. 1687 Also what will be the effects of the whales coming up the river of Thames, and continued the 4th. and 5th. of August, anno. dom. 1686 (1686).
  This seems to be a fake: the prophecy is:

> According to the constellations of the stars which I converse with, there will happen (anno 1687) a great rot amongst the quack doctors, but they will not be half so much pitty'd, as if it had hapned in Rumney Marsh, for the honest can spare them, and those as are not, will have no cause to lament, for they oftner kill than cure.

It is mainly (in its two pages) concerned with quack doctors 'and now and then a female spirit appears, and immediately vanisheth'.

> So hoping you do not expect a prophecy from me, who so much contemns them and their art, I rather did it for two reasons. 1st That the wise as well as the ignorant might avoid the rock of deceit, if not, I cannot help it. The 2d. is, I will assure you it's very hard times, and I wanted money; so taking my leave till the coming up of the next whale, I remain a true and loyal subject to His Majesty etc. SB.

CAREW/CAREY,* Clementine

CAREW/CAREY,* Elizabeth

CARLETON,* Mary

CELLIER,* Elizabeth

CHUDLEIGH,* Mary

CLARK,* Margaret

CLEVELAND, Barbara Palmer, Countess of, 1640–1709
1. Villiers; 3. genteel; 4. Catholic convert; 5(a) Roger Palmer, later Earl of Castlemaine, (b) 'beau' Fielding (marriage annulled as bigamous).

Barbara Palmer was mistress to Charles II from *c.* 1659 and had five children by him in as many years. Her sons by Charles were created dukes of Cleveland, Grafton, Northumberland. Her name is associated with *The gracious answer of the most illustrious lady of pleasure, the countess of Castlem . . . To the poor whores petition* (1668). See Harris, *London Crowds . . .*, p. 84 f.: this text exists in two substantially different versions and is almost certainly not by her.

CRASHAWE, Elizabeth, *c.* 1596–1620

1. Skinner; 5. William Crashawe; 6. poet, religious writer.

Stepmother of Richard Crashawe. She is sometimes given as author of *The honour of virtue, or the monument erected by the sorowfull husband . . . to the immemorial memory of . . . Mrs Elizabeth Crashawe . . .* (verse; 1620), but there is no evidence that she created her own monument.

CRESSWELL, Lady

Elizabeth CELLIER*

A letter from . . . to Madam Cellier (1680). Pollard and Redgrave say that 'Lady Cresswell is a pseudonym', while *DNB* has an entry for 'Madam Cresswell' – 'a notorious courtesan and procuress'. The prologue to Thomas Otway's *Venice preserved* has the line 'Match him at Mother Creswold's if you can', and a note to the Mermaid edition claims that this 'notorious procuress kept up an extensive correspondence with spies and emissaries, by whom she was informed of "the rising beauties in different parts of the kingdom".'

CROMWELL, Elizabeth

The court and kitchen . . . (1664; Hobby, *Virtue*, lists as male work).

CUDWORTH,* Damaris

CURWEN,* Alice

D'ANVERS,* Alicia

DRAKE,* Judith

ELESTONE, Sarah, ?1632–78

2. Southwark; 5. Thomas Elestone; 6. felt-maker.

The last speech and confession of Sarah Elestone at the place of execution: who was burned for killing her husband April 24. 1678 (1678). Of all these 'last confession'/'criminal woman' tracts, this one has the least amount of 'text' from the woman: there are about 5 lines in all, with such quotations as 'O Lord for Jesus sake let this be my last burning'. It is most clearly a male-authored text about a woman (consistently seen as the only guilty party).

EVELYN,* Mary jun.

FANSHAW, Mrs

Mrs Fanshaw was the illegitimate daughter of Charles II and Lucy Walters. In 1681 a broadsheet came out satirically recounting a 'cure' by her on Jonathan Trott, supposedly the son of a poor woman who sold fruit in Covent Garden. This – *A true and wonderful account of a cure of the king's evil, by Mrs F., sister to his grace, the duke of Monmouth* – was a counter to *His grace the duke of Monmouth honoured in his progress in the West of England in an account of a most extraordinary cure of the King's Evil* (1680). This information largely from B. Little, *The Monmouth Episode* (London: Werner Laurie, 1956).

FRITH, Mary, 1584–1659
2. London; 3. trade, pickpocket, forger, highway person.

Mary Frith wore men's clothing and was sentenced to public penance at Paul's Cross (1612). She is the central character in Dekker and Middleton's *The roaring girl*. The text associated with her is *The life . . . of Mrs M.F., commonly called Mal Cutpurse* (1662), but there is no reason to believe that she wrote this (especially since it refers to her as dead).

GETHIN,* Grace

HASTINGS,* Lucy

HIGGES, Susan
2. ?Buckinghamshire, ?Worcestershire.

The sorowfull complaint of Susan Higges, who for twenty years, maintained herselfe by robberies on the highway side (ballad of c. 1630), ? = *A true relation of one S. Higges dwelling in Risborrow, a town in Bucks., and how she lived 20 yeares by robbing on the highways* (ballad, *c.* 1635). (There is a Risbury in Worcestershire; and the ballad is *about* her, although 'I' is used.)

KENT, Elizabeth Grey, Countess of, 1581–1651

1. Talbot; 3. genteel; 5(a) Henry Grey, Earl of Kent, (b) ?John Selden; 6(a) genteel, (b) scholar.

Elizabeth Grey was granddaughter of Bess of Hardwick and patron to Selden and Samuel Butler. *A choice manuall, of rare and select secrets in physick and chyrurgery* . . . had sixteen editions between its publication in 1653 and 1687. Several of these editions were by Gert DAWSON and one was 'to be sold' by Margaret SHEARS. *A true gentlewoman's delight* (1653) reached nineteen editions by 1687, and one of these (1671) was for Margaret SHEARS. Hobby, however, says that these texts are by William Jarvis (*Virtue*, pp. 238, 248).

LAMBERT, Lady

This is presumably the wife of John Lambert, the Parliamentary soldier. According to *DNB* she was renowned for her pride and satirised in Tatham's play *The Rump* and in Aphra BEHN's* *The Roundheads*. The text associated with her name, *To his Excellency General Monck* (1660) is a satire.

MAKIN,* Bathsua

MARTEN,* Mary

Also known as Mary WARD.

Coll. Henry Marten's familiar letters to his lady of delight. Also her kinde returns. [W]ith his rivall R. Pettingalls heroical epistles (1662).

The publisher's epistle to Mary Ward includes: 'Sparrows are for Lesbia, and the Epistles, most of them salacious, ought to flutter to the breasts of such a Lady, who knew how to chirp to the Bird, or Martin that presented them . . . Mary is not Mary now, but shall stand upon a Ward, or Guard, which you will, of future Chastity.' The text begins with Henry Marten's letter about the execution of Charles I, and includes Mary Marten's letter to Pettingall, as well as 'A Letter written by Marten's Lady upon a distast taken against the Lady B–, suspecting Martens too much familiarity.' The publication is probably a fake. Henry Marten (1602–80) was a wit, a regicide and a republican, and was imprisoned for life after the Restoration. The invention of false wives or lovers to satirise famous men was a fairly common device.

MIDDLETON, Elizabeth

Thomas (p. 123) mentions *A full and true narrative of one Elizabeth Middleton*, but there is no reason to believe that this is by her.

MITCHELL, Mary

This is what Mary saw – She dwelt at Brightemstone in Sussex, and laid down the body in Aberden in Scotland, in a good condition, after she had travelled far in that land, on truth's account . . . (1708). This, however, may well be spurious: there are eighteenth-century chapbooks about Mary Mitchell, a 'scourged apprentice'.

MORRIS,* Mary

OWEN,* Jane

PAGE, Ulalia

The lamentation of Masters Pages wife of Plimmouth, who being enforced by her parents to wed him against her will, did most wickedly consent to his murther, for the love of George Strangwidge; for which fate she suffered death at Barnstable in Devonshire. Written by her owne hand a little before her death. To the tune of Fortrune my foe (?1640). This ballad envisages her and Strangwidge dying together and moralises against rebellious wives. It is accompanied by a 'lamentation' of Strangwidge, in the same form, and the ballad appears in the Roxburghe and Bagford collections.

PAKINGTON,* Dorothy

PARTRIDGE,* Dorothy

PHILIPS, Judith

The brideling, sadling and ryding, of a rich churle in Hampshire, by one Judith Philips. With a true discourse of her vnwomanly vsing of a trype wife (1595).

POWYS, Elizabeth, Marchioness
1. Meadows; 2. Suffolk, Shropshire; 3. genteel; 5. Sir Thomas Powys; 6. genteel, lawyer.

Sometimes given as author of part of a ballad 'Upon the Popish Plot', but Greer (p. 22) sees no reason to accept the attribution.

PRIMROSE,* Diana

SCARBOROW, Anne

A looking-glass for maids (1655, ?1670). Crawford doubts the authorship of this; Hobby lists as male work (*Virtue*, pp. 241, 248).

SHARP, Joane

Named as author of a couplet poem which makes up chapter 8 of Ester SOWERNAM's tract (see Appendix II). Shepherd (p. 115 f.) argues that this is 'a poem cobbled together from the existing contents of the pamphlet', probably as 'a make-weight appended to an otherwise unfinished pamphlet'. The name may be a pseudonym.

SHINKIN AP SHONE

Her prognostication for . . . 1654 . . . As also a true storie of the beginning of the Welsh-men (1653). Crawford has doubts about the authorship of this; Hobby lists as male work (*Virtue*, pp. 241, 249).

SHIPTON, Ursula

A dozen prophecies, between 1641 and 1685, have been attributed to her. *DNB* suggests that 'in all likelihood' Shipton is a 'wholly mythical personage'; Hobby gives *Mother Shipton's Christmas carols* as male work (*Virtue*, pp. 241, 249). Salzman lists *The strange and wonderful history of Mother Shipton* (anon.; 1688).

SMITH, Rebecca

The foundation of true preaching (1687). An incorrect ascription by Wing.

SOPHIA AEMILIA, Queen of Denmark

The queen of Denmark's letter (1651). The letter apparently congratulates Charles II on his 'magnanimity' after his escape from England, and adds 'he is not worthy to be a king over others, that is not a king over himself'. This is a somewhat ambiguous remark, and indeed the monarchism transforms into anti-monarchism in the text. At the end it says that 'Divine providence . . . hath mutated the English nation . . . from a Monarchical to a popular Estate'. It ends with an appeal for the release of Major General Massey from the Tower. These features, combined with the apparent non-existence of its stated author, make it look like a mock-letter.

STARESMORE, Sabine

The author of *The unlawfulnes of reading in prayer* . . . is sometimes regarded as a woman, but Sabine occurs as a male name in the seventeenth century, and our reading of the text indicates that the author is male.

TURNER, Anne*

VAUGHAN, Millicent, *fl.* ?1599–1624
2. ?Wiltshire; 5. Walter Vaughan.

To the right honourable the Lords spirituall and temporall in Parliament assembled. The humble petition of Erasmus Record and Millicent Vaughan widow the administratrix of the goods, chattels and debts of Walter Vaughan deceased (?1624). The petition is mainly concerned with establishing Edward Record's claim to the manor of Castle Camps in Cambridgeshire. Record and Walter Vaughan were creditors of William Winnie. Despite legal decisions allocating the manor to Record and Vaughan, financial arrangements by other interested parties deprived them of it. The case began in 1599; Record was 72 when he wrote his text. Millicent Vaughan figures only in the title, as if merely to add weight to Record's own suit (the text of this petition is very similar to that of a petition in Record's name alone, *To the most honourable assemblie of the Commons House of Parliament*).

WESTWOOD,* Mary

WEYER, Florence

Florence is a male name in the seventeenth century, and a reading of *The honesty and true zeal of the King's witnesses* indicates it is written by a man.

WILKS, Judith

The confession of Mrs Judith Wilks the queens midwife; with the full account of her running away by night; and going into France (1689). This looks like a spoof.

WITH, Elizabeth

Elizabeth fools warning, being a true and most perfect relation of all that has happened to her since her marriage. Being a caveat for all young women to marry with old men (1659). This is verse printed in black-letter; its language and assumptions about gender do not suggest a woman author.

WOLLEY,* Hannah

WYNDHAM,* Anne

Appendix IV

An extract from Lady Eleanor Davies

This extract and the accompanying notes reflect the difficulties involved in editing a seventeenth-century text. For further discussion of the content see Critical Appendix 2.

THE RESTITUTION OF PROPHECY THAT BURIED TALENT TO BE REVIVED, 1651

Farther giving to understand, had advertiz'd him what befel immediately afore, signed with *Whitehals Powder mischance*. Bidden to shake of their dust,[1] that have but *ears* for a shew:[2] How in the same moneth *October*, &c. about the same hour at *Night, &c.* wherein delivered to *His Excellency*[3] by her a *Book*, Entituled, *Babylons Hand-writing*, bearing date *Anno* 1633.[4] Printed beyond Sea;[5] by the same token with *Specticles*[6] put on, read by him. That *watch word* superscribed, *Is a candle to be put under a Bed, &c.*[7] (useless and unsafe) He that hath Ear hear this *Piece.*[8] *Contents* of the said Book (*Dan. 5*)[9] contained in a sheet of *Paper*, sometime served on the late *K.C.* after his return from *Scotland*, *Anno* 33. Crowned, &c.[10] concluded with *Charls* Be, from his name, attended with his Riotous *Lords, Belshazer* the last (to wit) *Beheaded, &c.*[11] to beware his *Banquetting Houses salutation*;[12] *Great Babylons* exchanged *Feast*, into such confusion, instead of *kissing hands*, stampt a *hand writing*, subscribed, Great B*ritains Lamentation Mourning* and *Wo.*[13]

VVhereupon like his *killing* and *slaying Decree, Dan. 2. &c.*[14] She to *appear* and *answer* forthwith,[15] as by that *Babylonian* reference annext, Signed *Sydney, Mountagne*,[16] for *presuming* to *prefer* and *imprint, That detestable,* &c. *An. Dom.* 1633. *October*,[17] *Whitehals* no petty Trespass.

pp. 26–8

(All Bible references are to the Authorized version.)

1. Christ's instructions to his disciples: 'And whosoever shall not receive you, nor hear your words, when ye depart out of that house or city, shake off the dust of your feet' (Matt. 10:14; also Mark 6:11, Luke 9:5).

2. 'He that hath ears to hear, let him hear' (Matt. 11:15; repeated a number of times throughout Matt., Mark and Luke).

3. Cromwell, then (1651) Lord General.

4. Presumably this is the title of one of the books with whose illegal publication she was charged in 1633; it seems not to have survived. *Babylons Hand-writing* refers to Dan. 5, in which writing appears on the wall during Belshazzar's feast, and is later interpreted by Daniel: 'Mene Mene Tekel Upharsin' is interpreted as 'God hath numbered thy kingdom, and finished it . . .'.

5. Lady Eleanor arranged the publication of her prophecies, a number being printed in Amsterdam.

6. Cromwell's biographers make no mention of his wearing reading glasses.

7. 'Is a candle brought to be put under a bushel, or under a bed? and not to be set on a candlestick?' (Mark 4:21; also Matt. 5:15, Luke 8:16, 11:33. Sometimes given as 'light' under a bushel). Lady Eleanor's practical comment, that it is 'useless and unsafe', adds a material dimension to the spiritual!

8. See note 2 above.

9. Dan. 5 has the story of Belshazzar's feast, the writing on the wall (see note 4 above) and Daniel's interpretation; verse 20 tells of deposing Nebuchadnezzar, Belshazzar's father.

10. Charles I visited Scotland in 1633 and was crowned King of Scotland on 18 June, attended by bishops in surplices.

11. After the coronation Charles gave a banquet for the Scots nobility at which, notoriously, the Highland lairds drank copiously and hurled their glasses to the floor after each of many loyal toasts. Thus Lady Eleanor uses the idea of feasting and mentions specifically the 'Riotous *Lords*' to elaborate the identification of Charles with Belshazzar who 'made a great feast to a thousand of his lords, and drank wine before the thousand' (Dan. 5:1). In 1649, two years before *The restitution of prophecy* . . . , Charles was beheaded.

12. The warning to beware the '*Banquetting Houses salutation*' was presumably part of the prophecy contained in Lady Eleanor's book of 1633 and addressed to Charles.

13. *Great Britains lamentation mourning and wo* may have been the title of one of the pamphlets for which she was prosecuted in 1633; no trace of it survives, however.

14. Dan. 2 has Nebuchadnezzar's order to destroy the wise men of Babylon: 'And the decree went forth that the wise *men* should be slain; and they sought Daniel and his fellow to be slain' (Dan. 2:13). Again, Charles is identified with the King of Babylon, and Eleanor's own persecution by Charles is seen, figurally, as that of Daniel. Although it is nowhere in this passage stated directly, Eleanor *is* Daniel the prophet.

15. Eleanor appeared before the Court of High Commission in October 1633 and was found guilty of printing books illegally in Amsterdam and 'of the interpretation of the new laws and some of the prophets' (*CSPD* 1633, 248:65). She was fined £3,000 and committed close prisoner to the Gatehouse. Her books were burnt in public at Paul's Cross, but one of 29 pages survives in the State Papers (see *CSPD* 1633, 255:19) and includes her anagrammatical identification of herself with Daniel (her maiden name, Eleanor Avdeley, is printed backwards and rendered into REVEALE O DANIEL).

16. Presumably the two signatories to the warrant for her arrest in 1633; 'Mountagne' is perhaps Richard Montague, the Laudian Bishop of Chichester.

17. *That detestable, &c.* may be the title of another of her lost (i.e. burnt) pamphlets.

Critical appendices

INTRODUCTION

The immense range of kinds of writing by women is obvious. The audience for that writing was equally diverse: from the domestic (the women themselves, their children, their families, friends and husbands) through very particular groups (local communities, congregations, inhabitants of specified towns, MPs, government officials) to a wider public. The material circumstances in which they did their writing varied enormously too, and to begin to understand how, why and what any of these women were writing we need to look to the specifics of age, social status, education, religion and occupation. In examining women's published writing, we need also to look at the status – low, for much of our period – of printing itself, and the ways in which a woman's words, spoken or written, might be shaped by the intermediaries between producer and printed text: transcriber, amanuensis, editor, printer, publisher and bookseller. In these brief essays we draw on material from the dictionary entries, adding some material not amenable to inclusion there, in order to highlight what, out of all the diversity, seem to us to be the most striking aspects of women's writing in the period and those in most urgent need of further attention. Our choice of topics is determined by our experience of working on the dictionary, by our own particular politics and critical interests. The dictionary will, we hope, provide other people with other starting points, and the way in which we here attempt to read *across* the entries will demonstrate both a way of using the material it contains, and raise questions about the meaning of the words 'writing' and 'woman' in the seventeenth century which are of wider application.

Twentieth-century readers cannot hope to understand what women wrote in the seventeenth century without some knowledge of the society in which those women lived and tried to make sense of their lives. While it is beyond our scope to offer an analysis of the construction of gender in that society,[1] we begin by pointing to some particular aspects of being 'woman' then, before proceeding to a discussion of some of the writings themselves and the implications of reading them.

The inferior status of all women to men in seventeenth-century England was enshrined in law. For most of her life, a woman was legally under the control of a man: her father, step-father, brother or husband. In London, with its own trade customs, wives could in some circumstances contract business agreements in their own right, even though they were excluded from positions of power within trade and craft guilds; in the rest of the country, economic independence could be achieved only by widows. The powerlessness and consequent vulnerability of women under 'civil subjection' to their husbands are spelt out in *The law's resolutions of women's rights*, a work sympathetic to the position of women and not published until forty years after it was written; and power over the wife's body, property and actions was of course sanctioned by religion as well as law, St Peter's injunction to wives – 'be ye in subjection to obey your own husbands' – neatly providing the basis for a spiritual subjection to complement the civil.[2] Recent work on patterns of remarriage among women in trade suggests that as the century wore on fewer widows remarried, which might indicate that avoidance of remarriage – and retention of legal and economic independence – was becoming, at least for more prosperous tradeswomen, a possible option.[3]

The absence of any plea for female suffrage in the seventeenth century suggests that their legal status was not a focus for women's political demands.[4] But that women *were* politically active is clear. In the early part of the century women participated in political demonstrations – notably in the fen and enclosure riots – and in the 1640s and 1650s that involvement seems to have increased. Petitions and demonstrations organised by women are recorded throughout these two decades, and women were involved in the preparations for war, the building of fortifications and the defence of towns. Women were particularly active as preachers and missionaries, and in the Leveller demonstrations. The prominence of women in the political and religious changes of the mid-century is obvious from their vilification by opponents: women petitioners were mocked as 'The Meek-hearted Congregation of Oyster-wives, the Civill-Sisterhood of Oranges and Lemmons, and likewise the Mealymouth'd Muttonmongers wives', and individual women, like Mrs Attaway the tub-preacher, were personally abused and their sexual habits publicly debated.[5] (The responses of misogynists, it will be noted, change little over the centuries.) Such women persisted in claiming their right to speak, using as justification their own reading of scriptures, or voicing their common concern with men in the political development of the country. The view that the Civil War and the rise of the sects heralded new freedoms for women needs some modification, however, given the way in which the freedom of speech and action won by women in the early years was withdrawn once such movements were either suppressed, like the Levellers, or established and institutionalised, like the Quakers. The seizure of class power enacted by the sects did present opportunities for women's involvement in political and religious action, though the entrance of women into religious action and debate was happening long before the Civil War, as is obvious from the writings of Elizabethan puritan women. The puritan emphasis on individual faith gave validity to women's own spiritual experiences, and women participated in the new kinds of social organisation developed by congregations which operated collectively, voting to admit members and to elect ministers. Women were thus both ideologically and materially enabled to speak, preach, write, travel and take part in actions. A series of women was both applauded and condemned for 'unwomanly' behaviour: the visionaries and prophets Lady Eleanor Davies, Anna Trapnel and Elizabeth Poole; the preachers Mrs Attaway and Katherine Chidley; the Quakers Martha Simmonds and Dorcas Erbury. The proportion of female members of the sects is reckoned to be high; estimates have been made as high as 75 per cent for the gathered churches and 50 per cent among Quakers, and certainly women were prominent among the many Quakers who were assaulted, imprisoned and fined.[6]

1. WOMEN'S WRITING BEFORE 1640

The number of women writers we have been able to identify in the period 1580–1639 is relatively small: between 1580 and 1599 nine women had their work published, and between 1600 and 1639 another twenty-six. In other words, around 9 per cent of all the women who had their work printed during our period as a whole were writing before 1639.[1] In the sixteenth century, of course, the conditions of printing and censorship as well as the status of writing were different from those operating later in the seventeenth century; in particular, the publication of writing by those associated with the court was by circulation in manuscript rather than by printing, which was of low status. Most pre-1640 women writers were aristocratic or had connections with the nobility and the work they published represents the accomplishments peculiar to the 'learned woman'.[2] Just as Queen Elizabeth herself was noted for her education in classics, modern languages and verse composition, a number of women (encouraged usually by fathers) acquired learning in those areas and exercised their abilities as translators and poets. Elizabeth Arnold, Lady Ann Bacon, Suzanne Duvegerre, Lady Elizabeth Hoby, Anne Prowse, Bathsua Makin and Mary Sidney all displayed their skill as linguists and translators; and translations of the lives of saints and of other religious works occupied Catholic women such as Alexia Grey and the nuns Catherine Greenway and Agnes More. The handful of texts by women printed between 1580 and 1599 gives a misleading impression about the amount of writing actually produced by women: the low status of print affected attitudes to publication, and manuscript collections no doubt contain many more texts by women as yet never printed. A number of letters and journals have been discovered and published: Lady Grace Mildmay's journal for 1570–1617 was published in 1911; Lady Margaret Hoby's diary for 1599–1605 was published in 1930; and recently the letters of Joan and Maria Thynne, covering the period 1576–1611, have been printed. Yet more posthumously printed writing by women is not immediately identifiable as such, hidden as it is in volumes of family papers such as those of the Verneys and the Barringtons.[3]

Appeals by women to other women as patrons or protectors are frequent in the published writing of this period: dedications, prefaces and dedicatory sonnets addressed to other women make an explicit request for protection against men and the world in general. If the 'courtly' address to a noblewoman is a convention learnt from male writers, the stress on the common sex of author and dedicatee suggests that the convention is put to a specific use by women. Aemilia Lanyer makes multiple dedications of her work to women: to the Queen, to the Queen's ladies and to the Countess of Cumberland; Dorothy Leigh appeals to Princess Elizabeth to be 'protectress' of her book; Anne Prowse has an address to the Countess of Warwick; Alice Sutcliffe dedicates her *Meditations of man's mortalitie* to the Duchess of Buckingham and the Countess of Denbigh, asking for their protection against 'mocking Ishmaels' and remarking 'it being, I know not usuall for a Woman to doe such things'.

Catholic writers make a point of disclaiming any personal pride or ambition which their publications might imply: Agnes More's *Delicious entertainments of the soule* was written 'never intending more then the use of a particular cloister; though God and her superiours have otherwise disposed of it, & exposed it to the publicrk [sic] view of the world.' Twenty-five years later Gertrude More, another nun whose work was published abroad and presumably imported illegally into England, stresses similarly that her intention in writing was for her private comfort, to be seen by others 'but against my wil, my superiors only excepted'; her work appears in print at the insistence of those superiors and corrected by them. For any woman, it seems, the act of publication requires justification; for nuns, whose lives embodied the extreme of female submission and humility, publication can be justified only as an act of obedience to male superiors in the church.

Acknowledgement of the writer's status as woman runs through the published writing of this earlier period, and alongside it the need for sometimes elaborate justification. The conventional nature of such womanly apologies is revealed when occasionally a writer refuses to comply. Elizabeth Carew/Carey in her translation of Perron writes:

> I will not make vse of that worne-out forme of saying, I printed it against my will, mooued by the importunitie of Friends: I was mooued to it by my beleefe, that it might make those English that understand not French, where-of there are maine, euen in our vniversities, reade Perron.

Anne Prowse finds justification, paradoxically, in her sense of her own womanhood, disqualified from larger action:

> because great things by reason of my sex, I may not doo, and that which I may, I ought to doo, I have according to my duetie, brought my poore basket of stones to the strengthening of the walles of that Jerusalem.

Here, since writing is within her capabilities, it can be presented as a duty. A view of writing as duty, and a less apologetic tone, may be due to Prowse's likely position as a puritan.[4] The puritan insistence on the relationship between individual and God implicitly absolved the writer from charges of unnatural presumption by placing responsibility with the highest authority – the deity. Coupled with the experience, for some women, of leading prayer meetings and joining in theological debate, puritanism may have offered material and ideological conditions in which women writers could adopt a less hesitant stance than other, non-puritan writers. That puritan-ism could give women an experience of action and an ideologically co-herent basis for moving into print is borne out by the remarkable boom in women's writing fostered by the radical sects after 1640.

It is rare, however, for a woman writing in the early part of the period to make little or no reference to her sex. Jane Anger, writing in defence of women, uses both her sex and her name to good effect, insisting that she was provoked to reply to the misogynist author of *Book: his surfeit in love,* and excusing her 'presumption' in writing 'because it was Anger that did write it'. Whatever the topic of her writing, a woman has to justify her action: Diana Primrose writes in order to praise Elizabeth I (and to criticise Charles by implication) and embedded in Primrose's text are Dorothy Berry's lines in praise of Primrose; Elizabeth Josceline, like Dorothy Leigh, addresses her children and offers them moral, spiritual and practical guid-ance. Disclaimers, apologies and excuses for writing abound; as writers these women reveal, in their use of the dedication as literary display, their own vulnerability to attack as exceptions to the rule of female submission; and except in the 'defence of women' pamphlets there is no attempt to argue against the imposition of that rule. Given the operation of such a convention of apology, it is perhaps not surprising that among these liter-ate and for the most part privileged women there is also displayed a mis-trust of women's learning. Elizabeth Josceline, for example, despite her own education, is not in favour of her daughter's learning, 'having seen that sometimes women have greater portions of learning than wisdom'. Decades later, Margaret Cavendish's writing displays the same self-consciousness and at times the same disparagement of women's abilities. When she remarks on 'women breeding up women; one fool breeding up another; and as long as that custom lasts, there is no hope of amendment', it is difficult to see whether she is echoing conventional male thinking about women teachers or offering an analysis which demonstrates that the 'foolishness' attributed to women is the result of their lack of education, and in particular the lack of competent female teachers.[5]

2. AFTER 1640: THE PROPHETS

A glance through the dictionary immediately demonstrates how much more writing by women was published during and after the revolution (the Civil War and the Interregnum). What is particularly striking is that a large proportion of that writing came from women of a lower social status than the predominantly aristocratic and genteel writers of the preceding sixty years, and much of it was the product of women inspired by their commitment to the radical puritan movement. About a third of our writers were Quakers, and between them the other puritan groups – Presbyterians, Baptists, Independents, Fifth Monarchists, Muggletonians, Seekers, Ranters, Familists, Brownists and 'millenarians' – form a sizeable minority of 9 to 10 per cent. It is important to note, however, that our information about social class and religious affiliation may well be misleading, in part because of its incompleteness: for example, we do not know the religious affiliation of about half the women in the dictionary. We might reasonably ask what a declaration of religious affiliation (or the lack of such a declaration) might mean. Women writing out of their commitment to a particular sect, or in specific opposition to the established church, will declare their position; the 'not knowns' may well be largely made up of more or less committed adherents to the Church of England, their writing springing from activity other than the religious. Quakers in particular are probably disproportionately represented here: the decision made by Quakers in 1672 to collect and preserve their own writings means that their texts survive in greater numbers than those of other sects which had no such policy. For all sectarian writers, participation in the social organisation of the sect was a central factor enabling their writing, and their explicit statement of their religious position, which renders them more 'visible' than their numbers perhaps warrant, is itself an important factor in our understanding of how and why women published their work. The contribution of Quakerism in particular to the enabling of women's writing (and writing by women of lower, 'unlearned' classes) needs examination, and will be discussed at more length below.

The apparent upsurge in the number of publications by women after 1640 is not so striking if we consider the developments in printing generally.

It is clear that print was more available and accessible after that date. Charles I had used the courts of Star Chamber and the High Commission to restrict and punish the publication of opposition literature, both secular and religious; their abolition by the Long Parliament in 1641 removed the tight controls on the press which had reached a peak with the 1637 Star Chamber Decree. At the same time the Stationers' Company, the guild to which all printers and traders in books had to belong and which controlled rights to print, was weakened as a controlling agency by a series of internal challenges for power, particularly from booksellers who resented the Company's mono- polies and campaigned for democratic rights in Company elections. A sur- plus of freed apprentices in the trade meant that there was a flood of printers eager to set up businesses and willing to print illegally to earn a living. In the early 1640s Parliament, despite its awareness of the dangers of a 'free' press, had in practice little impact on control. By 1643 there was chaos in the trade, with for the first time no restriction on the numbers of printers, apprentices and presses at work; piracies were frequent, and fewer printers and publishers were complying with the law by entering copies in the Stationers' Register (a procedure designed to secure the publishers' legal right to print, but used as a means of control by the Company, which could refuse entry to unlicensed and 'offensive' books). The freedom to print and publish which exploded in those years was not easy to reverse, and despite successive attempts by Parliament, the army, Cromwell as Protector and the restored Charles II to force through various measures of control, the pro- cesses of production could never again be contained and controlled as they were before 1640.[1]

In this explosion of printed material, women's writing remained a tiny proportion. Elaine Hobby estimates texts by women in the period 1649–88 to have constituted only ½ to 1 per cent of the total output of the presses. (Even today, with feminist presses devoted to the production of books by women, women's writing constitutes only around 20 per cent of all publica- tions.[2]) The range of topics, genres and concerns represented in the writ- ing of these women is more diverse than in the earlier period. Elaine Hobby's *Virtue* provides a much-needed survey of women's writing in the later seventeenth century, and it is not our intention to provide here a 'potted version' of her full and detailed analysis of kinds of writing. Rather, what we aim to do is to draw out some of the similarities and differences between the two (unequal) halves of our period, and to point to areas where a great deal more work could usefully be done. The division at 1640 is not a simple chronological break, but a response to the political change occurring then.

One of the central problems about reading women's writing of this period is exactly that: the *reading* of it. One way of confronting the diffi- culties of reading women of the period is to concentrate on what has been characterised as the most 'unreadable' form of writing by women: the prophecy. Its dismissal by historians as the product of 'hysterics' needs inspection, too: the use of the concept 'hysteric' accepts the fact of utterance, while devaluing it as a shapeless form of speech and writing. Prophecy is not simply a phenomenon confined to the Interregnum: Elinor Channel, Lady Eleanor Davies and Jane Hawkins (whose verse prophecies of 1629, though noted by a curate, seem not to have survived) were active as prophets before 1640, and prophecy did not end with the Restoration: as late as the 1670s and 1680s Anne Wentworth and Dorothy White were still prophesying. Nevertheless, it was during the middle decades of the century that, largely within the wider development of women's activity as preachers in sectarian churches, women prophets moved (or were moved) into print. Not only were women prophets published, but they also found a ready market; at least for their contemporaries and co-religionists, these women's works were not 'unreadable', but popular. If we can find ways of reading the words of Anna Trapnel, Elinor Channel, Elizabeth Poole, Lady Eleanor and others without recourse to the old labels of 'hysterical' and 'eccentric', we might be able properly to value prophetic writing as one of the ways in which women could move, unapologetically, into print. To give an example of the kind of writing involved, here is an extract from Lady Eleanor's *The restitution of prophecy* . . . , published in 1651 and written while she was a prisoner in the Fleet, a gaol by the river housing chiefly debtors:

> Farther giving to understand, had advertiz'd him what befel immediately afore, signed with *Whitehals Powder mischance*. Bidden to shake of their dust, that have but *ears* for a shew: How in the same moneth *October*, &c. about the same hour at *Night*, *&c.* wherein delivered to *His Excellency* by her a *Book*, Entituled, *Babylons Hand-writing*, bearing date *Anno* 1633. Printed beyond Sea; by the same token with *Specticles* put on, read by him. That *watch word* superscribed, *Is a candle to be put under a Bed*, *&c.* (useless and unsafe) He that hath Ear hear this *Piece. Contents* of the said Book (*Dan. 5*) contained in a sheet of *Paper*, sometime served on the late K.*C.* after his return from *Scotland*, *Anno* 33. Crowned, &c. concluded with *Charls* Be, from his name, attended with his Riotous *Lords*, *Belshazer* the last (to wit) *Beheaded*, *&c.* to beware his *Banquetting Houses salutation; Great Babylons* exchanged *Feast*, into such confusion, instead of *kissing hands*, stampt a *hand writing*, subscribed, Great B*ritains Lamentation Mourning* and *Wo.*
>
> VVhereupon like his *killing* and *slaying Decree, Dan. 2. &c.* She to *appear* and *answer* forthwith, as by that *Babylonian* reference annext, Signed *Sydney, Mountagne,* for *presuming* to *prefer* and *imprint, That detestable,* &c. *An. Dom.* 1633. *October, Whitehals* no petty Trespass.
>
> (pp. 26–8)

Lady Eleanor's style appears 'difficult' for two main reasons. First, the reader requires a detailed knowledge of the Bible, and there are at least nine phrases in this brief extract which echo Bible passages. Lady Eleanor was immersed in the language of the Bible, especially that of the prophetic books, and assumes the same immersion on the part of her reader: only occasionally, as twice here, does she refer the reader to the Bible directly. It should be noted that, despite the problems the biblical language poses for readers today, this was an immensely democratic way of writing: the Bible was, after all, the one book with which the majority of people, even those of little or no education, were familiar either through their own reading or through the medium of sermons. The second 'difficulty' is that both the text itself and the voice of Lady Eleanor, its writer, are shifting and unstable. The passage conflates two experiences seen as figural: her recent approach to Cromwell, in 1651, and her earlier written warnings to Charles I, which led to her arrest and imprisonment. In describing Cromwell's reception of her work (he puts on his *Specticles* to read it) she recalls the event of her earlier warning to the King, which he ignored to his cost (*'Belshazer* the last (to wit) *Beheaded'*). Within the shifting frame of the narrative, which is governed not by chronology but by figural relationships between Eleanor's own experience, political events, and biblical history, the 'I' of the narrator hardly ever appears. The first person has disappeared completely, and when the writer describes herself it is as 'her' and 'She', observed externally by herself as writer. Her 'real self' remains, for the most part, unspoken yet insistent: in fact she *is* Daniel the prophet, interpreting the writing on the wall for the benefit of kings and rulers, and like Daniel subject to the '*killing* and *slaying Decree*' of Nebuchadnezzar. Her voice as writer is unnamed, unfixed, allowing free play between the narrative and prophetic modes and accommodating, too, the startlingly practical: hiding candles under beds (Mark 4:21) is, she remarks in passing, 'useless and unsafe'. Here the languages of the material world and of the scriptures are merged.

To remark on the difficulties of the text is not, however, to confirm that they are indeed so obscure as to be unreclaimable. If a hundredth of the amount of careful editorial exposition expended on the works of Shakespeare were devoted to these texts, they would indeed be 'readable', and to demonstrate the point we append on pp. 243–4 a full annotation of this passage for the interested reader. Readability depends not on the transparency of language, but on the shared conventions of writer and reader. The privileging/disprivileging of particular languages is a social and political concern. Hence, the dismissal of these texts as 'obscure' and 'hysterical' by historians such as Keith Thomas works to preserve a certain sort of canonical literature, excluding Lady Eleanor's writing and denying its politics. Lady Eleanor's arrest in 1633 was a result of her open criticism of Laud and Charles I (Belshazzar), and of the Court and London society (Babylon). Her construction of herself as a type of the prophet Daniel gave a power to her writing which the Court of High Commission could not

stomach. In October 1633 she was fined £3,000 and committed close prisoner to the Gatehouse for her interpretation of the prophets printed
illegally in Amsterdam ('Printed beyond Sea'). A pamphlet collected in
the State Papers and presumably used in evidence against her expounds
several chapters from the book of Daniel, employing millenarian numerol-
ogy and the famous anagram of her name (Eleanor Avdeley=Reveale O
Daniel). The shifting, referential and figural style of her writing was not too
difficult for the Court to read, and to punish.[3] The response of pro-
monarchist prophet Mary Pope to objections that her 'writings are non-
sense' is instructive: 'If they would study the Scriptures as I doe, they shall
finde them very good sense.'

The apparent instability in the figure of the narrator or writer is not
confined to prophetic writing. Other women's texts display shifts from first
to third person, for example. Mary Moore in her *Wonderfull news from the
north: or a true relation of the sad and grievous torments inflicted upon the bodies of
three children of Mr. George Muschamp* . . . switches between first and third
persons; so confusing are her uses of 'I' and 'she' that it is not immediately
apparent that she is narrating her own and her family's experiences, and
only after careful reading can the relationships between the writer and the
other people she describes be untangled. In our sense, Mary Moore has no
stated and defined character – she is dispersed across the text in shifting
relations with others.[4]

Recent work on Elizabethan and Jacobean drama offers one way of
understanding the construction of these works as 'unreadable'. It has recently been argued that the drama displays a decentred view of the self,
which has been distorted and obscured by liberal humanist literary theory
which privileges the unitary subject, the single subject-position. Catherine
Belsey remarks on the implications for seventeenth-century women viewing
or reading the plays:

> The subject of liberal humanism claims to be the unified, autonomous author
> of his or her own choices (moral, electoral and consumer), and the source
> and origin of speech. Women in Britain for most of the sixteenth and seven-
> teenth centuries were not fully any of these things . . . A discursive instability
> in the texts about women has the effect of withholding from women readers
> any single position which they can identify as theirs.[5]

It is precisely the lack of a single unified subject position, identified by
Belsey in relation to texts *about* women, that characterises the 'difficult'
prophetic texts *by* women. This is not to suggest that other, less 'difficult',
texts by women of the period are more coherent – indeed, it would be our
contention that the 'single' subject position is only achieved by a deliberate
and exclusive reading – but the multiplicity of subject-positions is inscribed
particularly rawly in these texts, and renders them incapable of 'sense' for
a readership which assumes a unitary subject. The same features have

recently been noted in the writing of some male prophets, and the time has come for a serious inspection of these styles of writing.[6] It may be that the styles of speaking and writing used by prophets are throwbacks to earlier modes (compare the Elizabethan drama which is more 'de-centred' than Jacobean, or the styles of the Marprelate tracts in the 1580s). There may be in the prophets a strong resistance to the development of a 'unified' discourse which is allied to bourgeois patriarchy. The genuine difficulty for twentieth-century readers, unlikely to be steeped in, or even familiar with, the language and imagery of the Bible, must not be underestimated; but a more crucial impediment is the way in which the literary canon, because of its emphasis on the 'individual' subject-position, necessarily excludes such works as 'faulty'; even in the current wave of anthologising these 'problem' texts have been excluded. Were reprints available – and the need is pressing – it is our belief that students of literature familiar with new critical theories might find this kind of writing fascinating, rather than 'unreadable'.[7]

The construction of Lady Eleanor by historians (she has largely been ignored by literary critics) as an isolated eccentric is a telling example of what the failure to read these shifting, complex texts can lead to. Lady Eleanor is different from most of the other women prophets in terms of her social position, and her social prominence and connection with notable men of the period have at least led to some attention being paid to her; prophets of a lower social order can be more easily discarded. Her position and wealth presumably contributed to her confidence and to her prolific writing. Certainly she had the means to arrange the printing of her work in Amsterdam, and her publications were worrying enough to the authorities to have attracted repeated fines, imprisonment, the burning of her books and her own exile. Keith Thomas, in *Religion and the Decline of Magic*, relegated her to the genus 'eccentric aristocrat', but she was clearly neither alone nor isolated in her actions, being accompanied, for example, in her protest at Lichfield cathedral by like-minded women friends. Thomas was content to question her sanity, dismissing as 'ecstatic and utterly obscure' her complex writing which presumably, because it is 'unreadable', he has not tried to make sense of.[8]

That such texts were both read and understood in their own time is undeniable: the popularity of the prophetic writings in particular, their suppression or attempted suppression by church and state, and the vilification of their authors are testimony enough. Elinor Channel, Anna Trapnel, Elizabeth Poole and Hester Biddle addressed their words to the rulers of the nation. Trapnel, a supporter of the Welsh preacher Vavasour Powell, describes in *The cry of a stone* her singing and fasting while at Whitehall, awaiting the outcome of Powell's summons to the Council. The implications of her visions and prophecies alarmed the authorities, and her visit to the Southwest led to her arrest on the grounds that she was provoking rebellion. Her letters to her home congregation while incarcerated in Plymouth are printed in *A legacy for saints*. Lists of visitors to Anna Trapnel and Sarah Wight during their lengthy fasts indicate the seriousness with which Parliamentary and Independent leaders viewed their words. Visitors to Trapnel included a member of Council, several MPs, and the Independent preachers associated with the church at Allhallows the Great, including John Simpson, William Greenhill, Henry Jessey and Christopher Feake: a group of preachers which became increasingly disenchanted with Cromwell, some of them moving towards Fifth Monarchism as a religious/ political alternative. Sarah Wight's visitors were numerous, including Trapnel herself, religious leaders such as Jessey, Cradock, Simpson and Lockyer, members of the nobility, politicians and a variety of local tradespeople, one of whom was Hannah Allen, the bookseller who published Jessey's account of Sarah Wight's visionary utterances.[9]

What marks the activity of these prophets and visionaries, and of other sectarian writers, is a clearly stated sense of community, an interconnected group of preachers, writers and readers, and a social shift in the status of the writers. These women, unlike the majority of pre-1640 writers, were not aristocrats, though many of them attracted the support and attention of sections of the nobility and gentry. Trapnel was the daughter of a shipwright of Poplar in Stepney, and identifies herself primarily as a member of Simpson's Allhallows congregation. Sarah Wight, though her origins are less certain, seems to have come from the same 'middling' trade background as many members of the London gathered churches. Elizabeth Poole earned her living with her own hands, and Thomasina Pendarves's defence of her was necessary if she were to find work and survive. Across the spectrum of puritan women's writing, from the prophets, preachers such as Katherine Chidley, itinerating Quakers such as Martha Simmonds, Elizabeth Hooton and many more, to the women engaged in theological debate – Priscilla Cotton, Mary Cole, Sarah Blackberry, Rebeckah Travers– and those whose writing is a public testament of their spiritual progress, a shift in the social status of writing women is apparent. After 1640 the publications of women of professional and trading families outweigh those of aristocrats, and it is the speaking and writing of these women which draws the attention of the authorities as constituting a threat to order. The categories of 'private' and 'public' prove to be a false distinction: all these kinds of writing, including the apparently 'personal' spiritual autobiography, are the products of engagement in public church practices, and the majority of the sectarian women whose names we record as writers were, primarily, church activists whose writing was part of that work.

Yet the question of class in seventeenth-century women's writing has as yet escaped attention. The repeated refusal of historians and literary critics to engage with the 'unreadable' words of these women, leaving out of account the large body of sectarian women's writing (or, where it is noticed, to dismiss it as the 'obscure' and 'hysterical' product of crazed individuals) demands our attention and action. In taking space here to foreground, out of all post-1640 writing, the work of women prophets in particular and, more widely, that of puritan women in general, we want to suggest that the recent interest in women's writing in the later period, concentrating on Behn, Cavendish, a non-lesbian Philips, Astell and others, constructs women's writing very narrowly, searching as it does for the nearest female equivalent of men, 'readable' writers of the genres constructed by a male literary criticism – poetry, drama and prose fiction. As well as denying the range of women's writing (in terms of content, form, and the religion, politics and class of the writer) the chimerical search for proto-feminist 'good' writers avoids questioning the very notions of genre, 'readability' and 'good writing' which attention to the full range of women's writing must confront.

We hope that the record in this dictionary of so many women writing in ways disqualified as 'literature' by the literary canon will at least make it impossible for their existence to be denied, and for an analysis which includes class, religion and politics to be avoided any longer. It is the intention of the essays which follow to point to specific areas in which that analysis can begin to be developed.

3. QUAKER WOMEN WRITERS

More than one third of the writers included in this dictionary were Quakers.[1] We have already noted that the policy of Quakers to preserve their own writings may account for the apparently disproportionate numbers of Quaker texts which survive; their survival does not necessarily mean that women of other sects wrote less, but only that their work has disappeared. The very fact that so many Quaker texts have survived, however, gives us an opportunity to investigate the connections between Quakerism and women's writing and publishing, and these texts raise issues which may be of relevance to sectarian women's writing more generally. Many extant Quaker pamphlets and books are to be found not in the British Library nor other national academic collections, but in Friends House in London: we owe much to the care and diligence with which Friends have collected their own historical documents, and to their generosity in allowing access to them. Yet, despite their high rate of survival, few Quaker women's texts are available to the reader in anthologies or reprints. Moira Ferguson, in *First Feminists*, reprints an extract from Margaret Fell's *Women's speaking justified* . . . (a text already available in full as a reprint) and Janet Todd includes only six Quaker women in her *A Dictionary of British and American Women Writers*, one of whom is again Margaret Fell.[2] Todd makes clear the representative function of her selection:

> The many Quaker pamphleteers who are omitted, for example, are of great interest to a student of family or piety, but the points they make are repeated by the writers who are included, and the general circumstances (particular ones are usually hidden) are duplicated again and again.[3]

The sheer effort of each individual woman's entry into print is thus obscured. But all Quaker pamphlets are *not* the same, and their interest is hardly limited to 'a student of family or piety'; the language of family and piety is demonstrably a necessary strategy for the discussion of many other things.[4] Quaker women wrote proclamations, prophetic judgments, autobiography, polemics, doctrinal disputes (with other Quakers, Baptists, Anglicans and other sects), accounts of sufferings, appeals for toleration, addresses to and criticisms of political leaders, epistles, verses, testimonies and memoirs. Far from being centred on 'family', these writers often left their husbands and families in order to travel as itinerating ministers and missionaries; far from unproblematically affirming 'piety', they interrupted church services, engaged in the theatrical acting out of public 'signs', spent long periods in prison, suffered persecution at home and abroad, took sides in inter-Quaker factions, campaigned for religious and political change, and organised systems of social welfare and education. A representation of Quaker women writers as all broadly similar, all concerned with 'family or piety', not only misrepresents the texts themselves, but denies the material agency of these very active women.

Engagement with the *real* breadth and diversity of Quaker production radically alters our view of those few Quaker women reproduced in our culture as 'representative'. Fell's *Women's speaking justified* . . . , for example, with its concessions to Fox's fear of unruly women disrupting the post-Restoration Quaker orthodoxy, is very different from the earlier, tougher tracts on women's right to speak, such as those by Anne Audland and Priscilla Cotton and Mary Cole, issued in 1655. Cotton and Cole's *To the priests* . . . , in particular, is fascinating for its recognition of 'woman' as construct; their definition of 'woman' as a signifier of spiritual weakness in the Bible allows them, daringly, to assign the term 'woman' to their male opponents and to reject it for themselves:

> Women must not speak in a Church, whereas it is not spoke onely of a Female, for we are all one both male and female in Christ Jesus, but it's weakness that is the woman by the Scriptures forbidden, for else thou puttest the Scriptures at a difference in themselves, as still its thy practice out of thy ignorance; for the Scriptures do say, that all the Church may prophesie one by one, and that women were in the Church, as well as men, do thou judge . . . Indeed, you yourselves are the women, that are forbidden to speak in the

Church, that are become women; for two of your Priests came to speak with us; and when they could not bear sound reproof and wholesome Doctrine, that did concern them, they railed on us with filthy speeches, as no other can they give to us, that deal plainly and singly with them, and so ran from us.

Both Fox himself in *The vvoman learning in silence* . . . (1656) and Fell in *Women's speaking justified* . . . (1666) attempt to limit the freedom of women's speech claimed by the earlier writers; while upholding the principle they manage to justify exclusions, neatly disqualifying from speaking the women whom Fox found troublesome. Fox calls them those 'not led by the Spirit of God', describing them as 'in the disobedience as Eve was, and so goes into tatlings and goes out of truth as Iesabel did'. (The opposition of truth and tattling, i.e. gossiping, is an interesting one, and recurs in these pamphlets.) Women should speak only 'in the obedience to the power & spirit which does not bring to usurpe, over the man, as the disobedience doth'. Similarly, Fell excludes 'the Jezebel, and the Woman, the false Church, the great Whore, and tatling women, and busie-bodies, which are forbidden to Preach, which have a long time spoke and tatled, which are forbidden to speak by the True Church, which Christ is the Head of' and later restates the exclusion: 'but the Apostle permits not tatlers, busie-bodies, and such as usurp authority over the Man, would not have Christ Reign, nor speak neither in the Male nor Female'.[5] The common threads here are clear: the use of 'Jezebel' (a term applied by Quakers to Elizabeth Calvert when she attended Mary Boreman's 'wedding'[6]) and 'Whore' (used by early radical Quaker women of those opposed to reform), and the repeated reference to the usurpation of male authority.

Fox, himself presumably the voice of the 'True Church', and Fell were concerned to set limits to women's speaking in order to win the struggle then going on within Quakerism. The activity of Martha Simmonds, Dorcas Erbury, Hannah Stranger, Judy Crouch and a woman known only as Mildred, all of them supported by James Nayler, was seen by Fox as an attack on his own authority and that of the male activists in London. That it is Margaret Fell's statement on women's speaking that has been reprinted and anthologised is ironic: Fox won the argument in part by mobilising Fell and other women against the more radical women, and as Quakerism developed under his dominant leadership it shed as less 'respectable' elements the uncomfortably vocal women who had opposed him. The selective anthologising which offers Fell as in some way representative, privileges the conservative and leaves out of account that bolder, radical stance (both politically and linguistically) offered by other writers. The marginalisation of the voices of Audland, Cotton and Cole, Simmonds, the early Travers, Dorothy White and a number of other early activists was effected in the late seventeenth century by 'respectable' Foxite Quakers for political as well as religious reasons; it is high time for the texts of these 'forgotten' Quaker women to be reread, and for their intervention in the history of women's speaking and writing to be inspected.[7]

What was it about Quakerism, of all the Civil War sects, that led so many women to write and to publish their writing? The answer may lie in the conjunction between the early acceptance of women's activity, ministry and prophecy which characterised several of the sects and the Quakers' particular readiness to exploit print to further their cause. Printing was an important medium of communication for the Quaker movement from its earliest days in the 1650s. Surviving letters between Friends point to the distribution of pamphlets as an integral part of Quaker meetings, and Northern Friends in particular financed publications by collections and personal donations. Quakers seized any opportunity to address a wide public (nobility, tradespeople, judiciary, professionals, artisans) by speaking at markets, fairs and court hearings, and accompanied their speaking with the free distribution of pamphlets. The many itinerating Quakers carried with them leaflets and pamphlets which they distributed in towns they passed through, and consignments of pamphlets were sent to the regions and accompanied missions abroad. The first recorded appearance of Quakers in London was in the persons of two women who had a paper by Fox printed, which they then dispersed in the streets. Records of arrests and imprisonments demonstrate the frequency with which Quakers were involved in distributing 'seditious' literature, and it seems to have been a regular practice for magistrates to search Quakers for any printed material they might be carrying. The coming of a sect whose first converts were mostly female, in a society in which women were associated both with demonstrations and with the distributive branch of the printing trade (as hawkers, street sellers and ballad-singers) may in part account for the central role of women in all these activities.[8]

Runyon's analysis of Quaker writing shows that in the years 1658–63 there was a peak in Quaker output, and that the type of writing published by Quakers changed over time: in the early years most frequent were proclamations and prophecies addressed to non-Quakers, doctrinal disputes and responses to attacks, appeals to government and political leaders, and works designed to accompany missionary work abroad. Later, autobiographical works and an increasing number of memorials, testimonies and collected works were published. At particular times of stress, especially from 1658 to the mid-sixties, records of sufferings and epistles to Quakers became more numerous. Although we have attempted no analysis of women's writing as detailed as Runyon's is for all Quaker writing, it seems that the pattern of writing by Quaker women is part of the general pattern he identifies, and the prominence of particular forms of writing at particular times varies among women in much the same way.[9]

A common feature of all Quaker writing is that frequently it is a communal act. An extreme (and therefore untypical) example is the women's tithing petition *These several papers was sent to the Parliament the twentieth day of the fifth moneth, 1659* . . . which consists of separate petitions, each with its own preamble, sent in from different regions. The separate addresses identify different concerns: the abolition of tithes is the theme which runs throughout, but individual areas make their own demands, for example for the abolition of the universities. The preface is signed by Mary Foster/ Forster, but attribution of the rest of the petition's demands is impossible, the appended signatories numbering 'above seven thousand of the names of the hand-maids and daughters of the Lord'. The petition was also published by a woman, Mary Westwood.[10] More usual is collaboration by pairs or local groups of women: *To the priests and people of England* . . . was written by Priscilla Cotton and Mary Cole while they were imprisoned together in Exeter. Imprisoned Quakers frequently produced joint pamphlets: a group of prisoners at York castle, including Mary Fisher, Jane Holmes and Elizabeth Hooton, in 1652 worked together on *False prophets and false teachers described*; *Fruits of unrighteousness and injustice* . . . , whose authors include Winifred Newman, was the product of prisoners at Winchester. A number of other multiple-authored texts may well spring from collaborative writing during imprisonment. Later, when the system of meetings was formally established, epistles from one region to another often bear several names. Pairs of women who travelled together sometimes wrote jointly: Katherine Evans and Sarah Cheevers wrote collaborative accounts of their imprisonments, sufferings and travels to Malta; Mary Elson and Anne Whitehead, instrumental in the setting up of women's meetings in London, collaborated similarly; Margaret Newby and Elizabeth Cowart together wrote to Margaret Fell describing their experience of the stocks at Evesham; Bridget Pinder and Elizabeth Hopper in 1676, and Bridget Nichols and Elizabeth Nicholls, Anne Whitehead and Anne Clabin in 1665, produced accounts of events of which they were eyewitnesses.

In many of these cases of collaborative writing it is impossible to allocate primary responsibility for the text, though in some the text is divided into separate sections which appear over different sets of initials. The compilers of the British Museum Catalogue, Wing and other indexers have 'solved' the problem by entering the works under a male name where one is available. The consequence of cataloguing and indexing conventions, which are geared to single authorship and which require decisions (often badly informed) about 'main author', is obvious: women writers tend to disappear, and the extent to which Quaker women in particular engaged in collaborative writing is obscured. We are grateful for Smith's *A Descriptive Catalogue of Friends' Books* . . . which is remarkable for its careful treatment of multiple authors, and has enabled us to identify women writers rendered invisible by other major indexes. In general, though, the assumptions of indexers are founded on a critical tradition which centres on the author as individual, and the low status of multiple-authored texts is not confined to women's writing: witness the editorial gymnastics of scholars attempting to prove the consistency (and therefore single-authorship) of *Dr. Faustus*, the desire to break down the Beaumont–Fletcher canon, and the neglect of products such as Jonson–Chapman–Marston's *Eastward ho!*. Literary criticism finds recalcitrant the very writing which was, in its production, an organisational and social event. Inasmuch as Quaker women's role in collaborative texts is demoted as part of this screening out of messily multiple-authored texts, their work too is hidden. Yet to arrive at any analysis of the connections between Quakerism and the wider practices of women's writing, this kind of activity needs to be taken into account.

What is particularly exciting about Quaker women writers is that, despite the difficulties of access via standard bibliographical tools, so much material does survive and, with persistence, can be identified. This means that there exists a large body of women's writing which can be studied not only to develop an understanding of how Quaker women came both to write and to publish, but also to investigate how, over several decades, Quaker women's writing changes its forms and concerns. It seems clear that Quakerism offered particular opportunities for women to act and to write as part of that action; what also needs to be addressed is the extent to which Quakerism itself dictated or limited the forms of those writings. We know from Runyon's analysis that by the late 1670s and for the rest of the century one of the most prominent forms of Quaker writing was the memorial volume, and this period too saw the beginnings of the regular issue of volumes of collected works. Women's writing seems to conform to this development: whereas the first decade of Quakerism saw the publication of women's prophetic declamations, doctrinal disputes, exhortations, political appeals and records of sufferings, later women's writing is often hidden as prefaces, testimonies or contributions to the memorial volumes issued to honour the first generation of respected Friends, recently dead. The development of this new genre of writing, still collaborative, but within which women's writing is much less visible, needs to be considered as part of the wider development of Quakerism from sect to 'church-type' religion. One of the results of the institution of hierarchical meetings and tighter organisational structures was the separation of male policy meetings from women's meetings dealing with fundraising and social welfare. Women who in the 1650s and 1660s had been active as itinerating ministers, interrupting meetings, preaching and prophesying, had by the 1670s become the mainstays of the women's meetings, concentrating on education, poor relief and prison visiting. Most of the 'troublesome' women of the earlier decades had by now either left Quakerism, emigrated to America, or died, and it seems likely that in opposing and eventually seeing off the dissident women, the 'respectable' women were able to gain support from more conservative Quakers for the development of their own style of women's meetings. In investigating women's writing, we need to examine the interconnection between the changes in women's social role, from prophet to carer, and the changes in the organisational structure which were beginning to regulate publishing. In the earlier period Quaker publishing, like preaching, had been enthusiastic and *ad hoc*, unsystematic, locally financed and organised; Fox's imposition (as critics saw it) of unity and hierarchy eventually led to the establishment of what was in effect a board of censorship.[11] The extent to which women may have been affected by this 'in house' censorship is discussed on p. 286 below.

The material exists, much of it in the library of Friends House in London, for a close examination of Quaker women and writing in the second half of the seventeenth century. Questions which we can only raise on the basis of our own, limited, reading of some of the texts need exploring further, so that we can begin to see how the specifics of religious, political and social conditions provide opportunities for different kinds of writing by women at different times. What seems to be a cycle of women's early active involvement in a new movement at its inception, their initial enjoyment of greater opportunities, and their gradual exclusion or containment as the movement becomes formalised or institutionalised, occurs not only in seventeenth-century Quakerism but in religious sects in other periods. Moreover, it is not confined to religious movements, and it has been demonstrated that a similar cycle of free participation followed by exclusion accompanied the rise of history as an academic subject.[12] By attending to the many as yet *un*anthologised Quaker women writers we can examine such a process in detail, and refuse the separation of political struggle from literature which the elevation of Margaret Fell as 'representative' Quaker woman attempts.

4. PETITIONS

Although petitions by individual women appear throughout the period, it is the burst of mass petitioning by women in the 1640s and 1650s which has attracted most attention. Patricia Higgins has surveyed the work of women petitioners, and has pointed to activities related to petitioning: women as demonstrators, supporters of 'the cause' through fundraising and speaking, workers on buildings and fortifications, couriers, spies, and distributors of printed matter.[1] The effect of this mobilisation of all classes of women in protesting against Parliament's policies, and in particular in support of Lilburne and the Levellers, can be measured by the misogynist reaction: 'fishwife' and 'oysterwife' became terms of abuse at this time;

Parliament suggested that these women petitioners would be better employed at home washing dishes; and joke pseudo-petitions appeared in print. Henry Neville wrote spoofs on female parliaments (*The ladies parliament* and *The ladies, a second time, assembled*, 1647; *The commonwealth of ladies*, 1650) and Royalist parodies of the petitions appeared: *A remonstrance of the shee-citizens of London*, 1647 and *The ladies remonstrance*, 1659.[2]

The women whose actions were met with such sustained hostility seem to have accepted their own inferior legal status and to have made no claim for their own democratic rights. When Leveller women were told that the House 'could not take cognizance of their petition . . . they being women, and many of them wives, so that the Lawe took no notice of them', the women's response was not to argue the rights of *all* women to speak, but 'that they were not all wives'.[3] In doing so they both indicate how Parliament took refuge in written laws, and refuse the linguistic (and political) position allocated them by those laws. The numbers of women involved, if accurate, are impressive: the Leveller petition of April 1649 was signed by 10,000 women; that of July 1653 for the release of Lilburne had 6,000 signatures. Despite the sneers and jokes the women activists persisted and developed their argument that they had an equal interest in religion and in the political future of the Commonwealth: 'Have we not an equal interest with the men of this Nation.'[4] By 1653 the wave of women's petitioning was almost over; the huge Quaker women's petition against tithes, *These several papers* . . . , of 1659, marks the brief renewal of radical hopes during the turmoil of that year's changing administrations. Throughout the Interregnum, petitioning was an aspect of specifically radical and sectarian women's political activity. Few examples of genuine petitions by Royalist women survive: *To the supreme authority of the Commonwealth* (1650) is an appeal to consider the plight of the dependants of those who, as delinquents, had had their property confiscated; and *The royal virgine . . .* (1660) supports the restoration of the monarchy.

Mass petitions obviously present insuperable problems for a literary criticism which looks for authors rather than agents of delivery. While it is reasonable to assume, for example, that the preacher and writer Katherine Chidley, who led the deputation of women appealing for Lilburne's release in 1653, had a hand in the composition of the petition they presented, as well as being the likely author of the challenge to patriarchy embodied in the petition of May 1649, in other cases speculation is fruitless.[5] As is usual in cases of multiple or disputed authorship involving women, the suggestion has been made that the petitions were written by men. This neatly displaces the problem of authorship while firmly constructing women in their role as silly sheep led astray by the cunning of male leaders who manipulate them. Thus Antonia Fraser, writing of the April 1649 petition for Lilburne's release, tells us that 'whatever the public indignation of these furies [sic: i.e. the women who presented it], *The petition of women* was a considered document; it is likely that Lilburne had a strong hand in its production.'[6] No *evidence* is offered for Lilburne's supposed authorship, and by characterising them as 'furies' Fraser offers us a view of the women as frenzied transgressors rather than political activists. (The 'furies', by the way, had persisted for three days before they were allowed into the lobby, and their only violent action seems to have been their seizing of Cromwell's cloak to prevent his avoiding them; the soldiers who attempted to keep them out, on the other hand, jeered and threw squibs at them.) In characterising the women thus, the 'considered' tone of the document can only be explained as the product of the cooler head of a man. In fact, if the language of these mass petitions is compared with that of petitions presented by *individual* women such as Elizabeth Lilburne, it is the individual petitions, with their elaborate and Latinate language, which seem more likely to have been written by men. Assuming on the evidence of this dictionary that women could both think and write, and valuing petitions as texts launched into the political sphere by women, we prefer to claim petitions signed by women and presented by women as texts written by women, until evidence to the contrary is offered. For that reason we have placed a list of women's mass petitions in the main body of the dictionary, under the heading 'Petitions'.

Apart from the anonymous mass petitions, confined largely to the Interregnum, the seventeenth century also saw individual women petitioning Parliament on behalf of themselves and their families. Interestingly, the peak of individual petitioning occurs also during the period of the Interregnum, though in the 1650s rather than the 1640s.[7] The pre-1640 petitions often relate to disputes about property; and questions of property rights, family estates, inheritance and position remain common themes throughout the period. Not surprisingly, the sequestrations of the Commonwealth period led to argument and appeal, and it was often the women in Royalist families who acted as 'solicitors' on their absent husbands' behalf.[8] Women made appeals both to the sequestration committees in the counties and to Parliament itself. The petitions by, for example, Anne Henshaw, Katherine Stone and Margaret Somerset, Countess of Worcester, all in 1654, are claims of this kind. Again, 'authorship' is a problem: the legalistic form of the petition may well have been written up by a male lawyer, on the instruction of the woman petitioner, and the apparently direct and personal, specifically *female* appeal may well be the result of collaboration between female employer and male legal hand. To identify in these petitions a strong sense of personal grievance and a specifically *female* voice is to ignore the legal–social circumstances which produce a particular expression of 'woman'; an expression which may have little to do with the *realities* of 'woman' outside the petition in which it is constructed.

One of the determinants for the *publication* of such petitions may have been the delay and expense of the legal system. The case of Mary Blaithwaite demonstrates both the frustrating slowness of the formal process and the motive for publication. Her case had been referred by the Lords on 10 March 1648 and was then neglected because of the dissolution of Parliament. In 1654 she waited for eighteen weeks in London for her petition to be read (no small expense and inconvenience for a single mother whose children were left at home, 250 miles away in Cumberland). *The complaint of Mary Blaithwaite widdow* . . . prints her petition, an account of her persecution by Royalists in Cumberland, a warrant issued against her in 1644 for dispersing parliamentarian pamphlets, and an appeal to the reader. Its very publication (or the news that she intended to publish) presumably speeded the process: on 11 May 1654 her petition was presented, and Thomason dates his copy of the pamphlet as having been purchased on 19 May.[9] Her story of continued persecution and harassment, imprisonment with her husband and his resulting death, and her approaches to individual parliamentarians, expresses fully her sense of frustration with a Parliament, her support for which has led to her widowhood and poverty. The renewal of her efforts for justice in 1654 seems to be directly related to Cromwell's appointment as Protector, and the pamphlet is presented as a last ditch attempt to reach his attention:

> hoping hereby I [*sic*] by some hand, mouth, or pen, this my complaint may come to the eare of that great man, who hath taken upon him the Protection of the Commonwealth . . . to stirr him up to come forth and here the Widdowes complaint, and give reliefe unto mee and my fatherlesse children.

The spate of individual petitioning around this time may well owe something to Cromwell's new position as Protector and to his image as benevolent patriarch: a man sympathetic to the claims of distressed wives and widows, regardless of their political allegiance. The connection between power structures and the forms of writing becomes clear at this point: Cromwell's promotion of the image of 'personal rule' encourages/enables the redeployment of a language and form, inherited from pre-1640, through which to address patriarchal power.

The very form of the individual petition, usually 'the humble petition of . . .', with its stress on the humility of the petitioner, requires an excessively deferential style of writing. Mass petitions, determined by communal social and political action, use language which is both confident and, sometimes, socially as well as physically threatening: the Leveller petitioners of 1653 reminded MPs that if their petition was refused, they 'had husbands and friends' who 'wore Swords'; and Quaker petitioners were prepared to call down the vengeance of God on those who refused to listen to their demands.[10] Individual petitions, however, are very different objects, and arise out of the (powerless) individual's personal circumstances. An individual petitioner, concerned perhaps for the well-being of her family, appeals to male power for justice or mercy by refusing challenging modes of address, choosing rather to recognise and play along with her social role. The necessity of constructing a sense of her own plight – perhaps even a sense of her self – out of the terms socially available has its positive side for the woman petitioner: her adoption of the role of supplicant implies an obligation, on the part of those petitioned, of reciprocal charity. Susannah Bastwick, petitioning as a 'distressed widow' on behalf of herself and her children, thus adopts the stance of 'poor woman': 'your petitioner being a woman [is] no way able to follow nor manage so weighty a course'.[11] In fact, she was extremely well off, and her husband had died many years previously; but in the feudal contract within which individual petitions operate, she has to keep her side of the 'bargain' out of which her request might be granted. Mary Blaithwaite combines this (requisite) deferential acknowledgement of her status as woman with a clear determination to be heard: she writes that she is 'forced after much Labour in vaine, and many a weary step, to no purpose, to make myself a foole in Print'. Interestingly, her text is not given the status of work, being here defined *not* as 'Labour', but as 'foolery' consequent upon labour's failure to produce results. For individual women petitioners such as these, being 'forced' into print is justification for an action whose boldness might otherwise belie their presentation of themselves as humble and deferential. They exhibit the vulnerability, emotional expressiveness, and attachment to private concerns associated with womanhood, identifying themselves as creatures who have been 'forced', while at the same time demanding that they be heard. The contradictions of being 'woman' are creatively mobilised, so that their status as women is simultaneously expressed and subverted. More work on petitions might establish whether, as seems likely, much of the language of deference was conscious role-playing, recognised on both sides (petitioner and recipient) as a necessary part of the negotiation.

This hypothesis about the expression/subversion of the image of 'woman' can be tested at this point by looking at one particular woman's case. A number of narratives survive which were designed to state the 'case' of a woman or her family in an appeal for a justice otherwise unobtainable. The narratives of the Levingston–Stirling dispute; Elizabeth Lilburne's *The case* . . . against William Carr; Hester Shaw's *Mrs. Shaw's innocency restor'd* . . . and *A plain relation of my sufferings* . . .; Damaris Strong's *Having seen a paper printed* . . .; and Mary Trye's vindication of her father are all appeals of this kind.[12] Trye's *Medicatrix, or the woman-physician* . . . is a defence of her father, Thomas O'Dowde, 'against the calumnies and abusive reflections of Henry Stubbe a Physician at Warwick'. The text itself is a remarkable mixture of learned dispute, testament and life of her dead father. Trye presents herself as fulfilling her father's dying wish that his medicines should not die with him; trained by him, she continued his practice 'more out of charity then my private Interest' and on her arrival in London she read Stubbe's opposition to the Royal Society which was coupled with aspersions of her father. As his only child and custodian of his skills she was compelled to vindicate his honour. But although Trye adopts the position of being forced into print against her own character and inclinations, her text can also be read as self-advertisement. For as well as her chronicle of her father's work, she offers her own recipes and cures, and 'The Author's opinion of learning'; as well as refuting Stubbe, she challenges him in a postscript to a dispute and a competition in the curing of diseases (going so far as to allow Stubbe odds); and she ends with advertisements of both her father's remedies and her own, including remedies for 'diseases attending women'. The strong elements of biography and autobiography, the open self-advertisement, and the very title *Medicatrix, or the woman-physician*, suggest that the formal defence of a father's reputation (in which she conforms to her correct social role) offers a framework (justifiable because 'naturally' she is 'forced' to write, and is, after all, only expressing her 'private' affections) for a woman to write of herself, her talents and her aspirations as a physician. In doing so, Trye reconstructs her identity, finding a way both of expressing those qualities of vulnerability and personal, familial affection associated with womanhood, and of subverting such norms of womanhood by displaying her competence as debater and physician. There is a similar 'doubleness' in several of these kinds of texts: Hester Shaw, for example, is concerned both with an appeal for justice, wanting her money returned by the clergyman who has appropriated it, and with a defence of her reputation as a midwife; Damaris Strong is concerned to defend her late husband's reputation as a theologian, but also to assert her ownership of his publications.

While it is possible to make a distinction between mass petitions as cooperative interventions in politics, and single-authored petitions as more circumscribed by the dictates of the feudal contract which generated the form, there are, nevertheless, a few petitions by individual authors which address questions of national politics. Mary Blaithwaite's publication, for example, indirectly exposes the injustices and delays of Parliament's handling of her case, and articulates questions about the individual's difficulties in obtaining justice in that society. Very few single-authored petitions, however, directly address the national politics of the time. *The petition of the Jewes* . . . (1649), addressed to Fairfax and the Council of War by Johanna Cartwright and her son Ebenezer, asks that the banishment of Jews be revoked so that they 'may again be received and permitted to trade and dwell amongst you in this Land, as now they do in the Nether-lands' (where both of them lived). The necessary participation of the Jews in the Second

Coming is made explicit, and the petition had already been favourably received on 5 January by Fairfax. The importance of the readmission of Jews was being stressed by millenarian preachers and a number of works appeared at this time identifying American Indians as descendants of the tribes of Israel, lobbying for the propagation of the Gospel in America, and pressing for the readmission of the Jews into England as a way of completing the last stage of the Dispersion of Jews, which millenarians argued was a prerequisite to the Fifth Monarchy, Christ's rule on earth.[13] Henry Jessey's *Of the conversion of five thousand and nine hundred East-Indians* . . . (1650), Edward Winslow's *The glorious progress of the Gospel amongst the Indians* . . . (1649) and Manasseh ben Israel's *The hope of Israel* . . . (1650), all of them published by Hannah Allen, mark a wave of concern. The topicality of the readmission of Jews both reflects the urgency of the millenarian programme (John Archer, for example, had predicted that the conversion of the Jews would take place in 1650 or 1656) and looks to the Netherlands as an example of a state whose religious toleration leads to economic prosperity.[14] The publication of Johanna Cartwright's petition was not in furtherance of her obtaining a hearing – the petition had already been favourably received – but was perhaps designed both to swell a growing public interest in the issue and to widen public pressure for change. The campaign succeeded only partially: the incorporation of the Gospel Society on 29 July 1649 established propagation of the gospel in America; but while Cromwell proved tolerant of the resettlement of some Jews at an individual level, and later met Manasseh ben Israel to confer on the matter, readmission never became a reality. The issue remained a contentious one, and most of Margaret Fell's early pamphlets address it, some of them being translated into Hebrew.

Grace Barwick's *To all present rulers* . . . (1659), while not formally a petition, might also usefully be considered in this context: it constitutes a specific appeal to the rulers of the country, and to Lambert in particular. Again, the situation is urgent, and its publication relates to the hopes and frustrations of a turbulent year in national politics. Grace Barwick, a Quaker, travelled 150 miles from her home in Yorkshire with an urgent message from God to the rulers of the nation. The title of the pamphlet implies some uncertainty as to who really were the 'rulers' at the time of publication; and the heading of its second section, 'To John Lambert, and the rest of the Officers', suggests that it was published around the time of the army coup in October. Barwick appeals to Lambert (in whose regiment her husband had served) to abolish tithes while there is an opportunity. Interestingly, the voice of the woman has a political value as expressive of enduring truth, set against the changeability of governments and titles: 'for it is truth and freedomme and just judgement and mercy, that good men seekes after, and it is these things that will please the Nation. It is not the changings of Governments into new titles and names.' The urgency of her message is explicit: 'so now it is brought to yoour dore that you may doe something while time is in your hands, for time is pretious.' For both Johanna Cartwright and Grace Barwick, the desire for political solutions to urgent religious problems seems to have been what impelled them into print.

No doubt many more petitions by women exist in manuscript form and these need to be found and examined. *Commons Journals*, for example, list many petitions which were presented but which apparently were never printed, and the *CSPD* notes many which are preserved in the Public Record Office. More of these texts must be found and examined if the model we have here developed is to be properly tested. In petitions, and in the similar texts in which women state their 'case', we see the stance of submissive woman both embraced and subverted; it is in these texts that women can be seen to be energetically remaking their female 'selves', negotiating their identity, and revaluing their status as speakers and writers. These 'marginal' writings speak to and of both national politics and the politics of gender, and must have therefore a central place in the study of seventeenth-century women's writing.

5. LETTERS

Letter-writing was (and is?) perhaps the commonest form of writing for women. Masses of letters by women survive, unpublished and largely unread, and the women whose names we have included in the dictionary as letter-writers are probably only a small proportion of those which a systematic search of manuscript sources would reveal. Few letters by women were published in the seventeenth century, though some collections have been printed subsequently. To have any sense of the body of letters written by women is therefore virtually impossible. But it is our contention that the relegation of 'letters' to the margins of literary study works to exclude a particularly rich area of women's writing, and probably the form of writing most practised by women throughout our period. If we comply with the generic bases of the literary tradition, we must conclude that since relatively few women wrote plays, poetry and fiction, there were not many women writers. If, on the other hand, we start by looking at what women actually wrote, we notice that many, many women – of all classes, trades, religions, families – wrote letters. At one level, we have then to rethink the activity that is denoted as writing, and to realise that for most of the time our model of writing has been built on assumptions about writing for publication. A reopening of definitions of writing, and a rereading of the huge and scattered mass of letters, in manuscript and in print, despite all its difficulties, would open up a rich area for the study of women's handling of language. The whole business of publishing letters needs attention in order to establish how the letter is transformed from private object of use into public commodity. Our intention in this essay is to draw on the limited information we have gathered to suggest both the importance of investigating letter-writing among women, and a possible theoretical approach.

Most of the women who wrote (and write) letters probably did not think of themselves as 'writers'. Their writing was part of their involvement in trade or business activity, in the managing of land or estates, or in the requirements of family life. Letter-writing was production for someone else, outside the market of literary writing, and not even for the sake of the existence of the letter itself. Letters had jobs to do, were part of the labour of being a woman. The writing of private letters could be chore or pleasure; but it was open to women untrained, as most were, in the skills of rhetoric and Latin, and its functional and private character perhaps made it a more agreeable form in which to risk revealing what women often felt to be their inferior spelling and grammar. When Dorothy Osborne remarks: 'All letters, methinks, should be as free and easy as one's discourse, not studied as an oration, nor made up of hard words like a charm',[1] she is both criticising male self-conscious rhetoric in letters and finding, in the writing of letters, a form of writing through which she can lay claim to her own language as suitable. Women's consciousness of their own exclusion from training in rhetoric and classics was undoubtedly an obstacle for those wanting to be writers in the public sense (see Margaret Cavendish's remarks on the skills required for the writing of history, quoted below, p. 279); private letters, at least, provided a space in which women's 'free and easy' language might be developed. The private letter enacts women's habituation to the 'private' domain, but simultaneously provides a frame within which women's language can take control. (For all her disclaimers, Osborne's placing of 'methinks', above, is rhetorically poised.)

The period is marked by a growing awareness of the letter's potential as a literary form to be exploited. The period after 1660 was that of the property-owning individual. As writing itself became commodity and élite literature legitimated private thought as its subject matter, the letter written for private use was drawn into the market and the fictional letter was invented. In 1724 we find Lady Mary Wortley Montagu writing, perhaps only half in self-mockery,

> The last pleasure that fell in my way was Madame de Sévigné's letters; very pretty they are, but I assert without the least vanity, mine will be full as entertaining forty years hence. I advise you, therefore, to put none of them to the use of waste-paper.[2]

Here, as well as the recognition of letter as pleasure, is the acknowledgement that the letter is not a transparent object serving particular and present needs, but a new form of commodity; the need for irony in the last sentence suggests a self-consciousness about making the point.

Relatively few letters by women were published during the seventeenth century. The only woman who seems to have written letters specifically for collection and publication in her own lifetime is Margaret Cavendish, whose *CCXI Sociable letters* and *Philosophical letters* appeared in 1664. Arguably, though, these are not autobiographical letters at all, but a fictional exploitation of the form of the letter as a vehicle for lively writing on a variety of topics. Other publications of letters in the period are posthumous, such as the collection of Mary Boreman Pennyman's letters and papers published in 1701–2, and Susanna Hopton's letter printed in *Controversial letters* (1710). Some contemporary publications, advertised as 'true copies' of letters by women, are of dubious authenticity, the publication of invented letters being one mode of intervention in current political controversies. Like the petition and the 'true confession' of the female criminal, the letter might be used by male writers: satire providing a very different kind of 'pleasure' from that identified by Lady Mary.

Of the few letters by women published during their lifetimes, some are rather different in kind from the letter as private object of use, standing aside from what has been so far described as a process of commodification. Mary Howgill's *A remarkable letter . . . to Oliver Cromwell, called Protector . . .* (1657), like many Quaker appeals, addresses and admonitions to rulers, is an open letter published with specific political intent; its publication was an extension of a woman's agency as campaigner rather than an entry into the market for commercial reasons. Here, the letter is an object of use, an extension of particular action, rather than a literary artefact. The same is true of a number of 'epistles' written by Quakers and other sectarians, often to their home congregations: their being printed was merely a way of easing the laboriousness of making multiple copies by hand, and speeding the otherwise slow process of circulation among regional groups.

Sectarian groups were capable, however, of using the private letters of women and their expressive form for their own purposes, and in the collection and publication of, for example, Anna Trapnel's letters in *A legacy for saints . . .* we see the use – by others – of the woman's private letter. Another example is Sarah Wight's *A wonderful pleasant and profitable letter . . .* published in 1656 and, as the text makes clear, printed without the author's permission. Sarah Wight was the woman whose fasting and religious utterances were recorded in the popular *The exceeding riches of grace . . .* of 1647, and it seems likely that the publication of her letter was an attempt by publisher or co-religionists to capitalise on the already established best seller. Like *The exceeding riches . . .* , her published letter is intended 'for the use of the afflicted'; in both cases her appearance in print was engineered by others. The letter was, we are told, 'Occasioned by the death of her brother, the troubles of her mother; but especially the working of God in her own heart'; it was made ready for the press by 'R.B.', who dedicated it to Lady Fleetwood. The editor includes 'Some apology to Mrs. Sarah Wight, touching the printing of her letter without her knowledge or consent', the excuse being that her friends considered the letter worthy of publication, but thought that she would refuse any such suggestion. The 'friends' thus stand as intermediaries between the personal and the public uses of the letter. (The use of women's writing made by ministers in particular, and the relationships between ministers and publishers, would be worth exploring more generally; for Henry Jessey's use of Sarah Wight's words in *The exceeding riches . . .* , see p. 284 below.) Here we see an instance of the causes which impelled the 'private' form into publication, the object of personal use into commodity; an instance, moreover, which arises from the members of an independent church whose members were predominantly property-owning individuals.

It is later historians, not literary critics, who have valued women's letters enough to seek to print them, and it is to historians that we owe the availability of a number of collections. Many letters written by women will be found among the published family papers of, for example, the Verneys, the Conways, the Ferrars, the Knyvetts and the Barringtons.[3] Unpublished collections in archives around the country probably hold many more letters by women, 'hidden' among family and estate papers.[4] As well as family collections, volumes of letters by individual women have been published in the nineteenth and twentieth centuries, and again it is historians who have made the material accessible. It will be our argument, however, that the historian as editor, with a tendency to read letters as if they offered a transparent 'truth' or 'personality', distorts the material itself. The process of cultural reproduction, involving the commodification we have sketched above, necessarily implicates the historian as part of that process. This is an important issue, since most readers of women's writing will choose the convenience of modern reprints rather than travel to see manuscript originals; and to make explicit the operations of modern editors we turn to an examination of a particular example, the letters of Dorothy Osborne.

The first publication of any of Dorothy Osborne's letters was in 1836, when Thomas Courtenay appended forty-two extracts from the letters to his *Memoirs of the life, works, and correspondence of Sir William Temple*. Macaulay, reviewing the *Life* for *The Edinburgh Review*, expressed interest in the fragmentary letters:

> We only wish that there were twice as many. Very little indeed of the diplomatic correspondence of that generation is so well worth reading. . . . The mutual relations of the two sexes seem to us to be at least as important as the mutual relations of any two Governments in the world . . .[5]

Parry, the editor of the first edition of the complete letters, was led from Macaulay's review to Courtenay's appendix, and himself wrote an article on Dorothy Osborne in 1886. He was then approached by an unnamed person who offered him transcripts of the original letters, together with the results of his or her own research. (It would be interesting to know the identity of this person who, judging by Parry's remarks about 'modesty', may have wished to remain nameless because of her sex.) In his edition of the letters, Parry modernised spelling, punctuation and paragraphing, arranging the letters and providing an interwoven commentary. Reviews of Parry's work remarked on his 'real service to English literature', compared Osborne's letters (favourably) with the writing of Lucy Hutchinson and Ann Fanshawe, commented on the value of the letters as documents of social history, and praised their style. Attention was drawn to their qualities of 'charm' and 'womanly sympathy'; they were judged as 'worthy of George Eliot or Jane Welsh Carlyle'; and, highest of praises, they were recognised as useful for 'the mothers and daughters of England' as 'an example of all that makes nations strong, men brave, and homes happy'.[6]

Several important points arise from the way in which Osborne's letters came to be published and valued. First, they were originally published, in part only, as an appendix to the life of a male. This is a common feature of the publication of women's letters. The correspondence with their sons of Lady Ann Bacon at the beginning of our period and Susannah Wesley at the end was similarly published as part of books about their male recipients, in Spedding's *Works of Francis Bacon* and Baker's *Works of John Wesley* respectively. The insertion of writing by women into the collected works of men, and its publication in biographies of men, has paradoxically both preserved women's writing (in its 'natural' place as serving men's interest) and simultaneously hidden its existence. The terms of the survival of women's writing thus construct its meaning as peripheral and dependent. The consequence for our sense of women's activity as writers, when much of that writing is fragmented and subsumed in the works of and by men, is obvious: with writing so scattered, so difficult to find (even for those of us looking for it), women's writing is perceived as a sporadic and subsidiary activity, and the writing itself seems fragmentary and unsustained. We have not only to find these works (a practical problem) but also to attend to the conceptual problem of de-'naturalising' them, restoring them as *work by* women and refusing their valuation as speaking for and to men.

Secondly, the process of editing itself changes texts, reconstructing their meaning and rewriting the style and tone of what was written. Not surprisingly, in an age when orthography was far from standardised, women's writing was even less orthodox than the writing of men. The ways in which editorial practice – the correction of 'quaint' mistakes, alterations in punctuation and layout – might alter texts were questions which nineteenth-century editors (and many twentieth-century ones) neither perceived nor addressed. Thus, in the case of Parry's edition of Osborne's letters, the reviewer in *Truth* could remark 'What most surprised me in these charming letters . . . is the modernness of their style, sentiment and humour. You can hardly believe you are reading letters written in Cromwell's day, so different is their tone and style from those of the rugged, harsh, involved letters of most of her Commonwealth contemporaries.' The *New York Times* critic's comparison with George Eliot and Jane Carlyle attests a similar 'modernity', by which Osborne is deracinated, separated from her contemporaries, and rewritten as a charming model for a Victorian ideology of empire and family – which by the 1880s was increasingly under pressure from demands for women's rights within the family and the state.

Parry's success in editing (i.e. rewriting) Osborne is attested by the critical reception of the book. The only comparisons made are with other *women* writers, and only Hutchinson and Fanshawe are cited from among her contemporaries. This is perhaps understandable: how many women's letters from the period have been published, in their own right, even now? Not to be compared with male writers, she is placed alongside the few known women writers, despite wide differences in time, form, style and content. As *woman* she is hijacked for the ideological purposes of a cultural élite whose interests lie in the promotion of a particular view of woman and family: she is thus claimed both as an example of womanhood and as the positive antithesis of her 'rugged, harsh' Commonwealth contemporaries. As *writer* she is conceived according to the needs of late nineteenth-century English society: 'interesting' for her information as social history ('those social domestic trivialities'), displaying an 'extraordinary merit' which allows her into the margins of English literature. In the end, she remains, as do many other women writers rewritten by later editors, an oddity, an aberration, a charming freak.[7] While the publication in our own century of more women's letters has done something to alleviate the isolation in which these women have been constructed, the very circumstances of their printing – often by local history societies, edited from an interest in social and political history – have unwittingly rewritten the texts as 'true' and transparent. In particular, the emphasis has been on aristocratic women, those whose husbands were political figures, whose families were of political importance, or whose estates and connections are of special interest to the historian. Thus Brilliana Harley's letters (published by the Camden Society in 1854) vividly report her defence of Brampton Bryan in 1643; Lady Katherine Paston's correspondence (Norfolk Record Society, 1941) adds a further element to the reconstruction of a family history through letters; more recently, the Wiltshire Record Society has printed the Elizabethan correspondence of Joan and Maria Thynne. We have made no attempt to trawl the indexes of voluminous family papers to include entries on every Verney or Paston woman whose letters are there included, believing that alerting the reader to the existence of those volumes and giving references to them is adequate. On the other hand, we have included entries for women whose writing survives in only one or two letters, which would otherwise be difficult to locate. Among these are letters which exemplify the subtlety and diversity of women's use of language.

Elizabeth Calvert's letter to Jane Woodcock, for example, demonstrates a very knowing manipulation of language and tone. Calvert wrote from prison, to her friend, ostensibly in frank explanation of the actions which led to her imprisonment. But she is also addressing indirectly the authorities who, as she rightly suspected, would intercept the letter. The writing is an accomplished performance of wronged innocence by a woman who, as we know from her career, was unashamedly guilty of seditious publishing; in her one letter we can begin to grasp the contradictions of women's social position, where agency is both denied and demonstrated. Another single letter that raises a host of questions is that of Bathsheba Ferrar, printed in Blackstone's *Ferrar papers*. The focus of Blackstone's volume is Nicholas Ferrar, founder of the religious community at Little Gidding noted for its piety, harmony and co-operative style of living. Bathsheba's letter, inserted among those of the male members of the community, cracks open the otherwise smooth veneer of pious harmony, and shows an energy in her struggle with language which springs from desperation. Her letter survives only because it was (like Elizabeth Calvert's) intercepted; John Ferrar both prevented it reaching its destination and passed it over to the 'leader' of the community, Nicholas Ferrar. The hurried, trapped tone of the letter tells much about the lives of the 'Sisters' whom Ferrar made part of his religious project; the jumbled reported speech it contains speaks of the despair which Ferrar's surface pieties in *his* letters hides:

> For Saith Nicholas may not a man doe wth his owne what he listeth wthout asking his wifes good will for what power hath the wife of any thinge whilest her husband doth Live not the Cote of my Backe is not myne owne but my husbands he Saith.

The slippage from 'wifes' to 'my' indicates the personal cost of Nicholas Ferrar's Pauline doctrine for a woman in that community; *his* language invades hers, and the split between social role and personal identity is inscribed in grammatical syntax which mingles first and third person. The repeated negatives show grammar under attack from the weight of prohibition heaped upon the woman. The letter challenges historians' and theologians' projection of Nicholas Ferrar and his (*his*) community as caring and saintly; it is hardly surprising that John Ferrar, who intercepted it, annotates the letter as 'Slander'.[8]

Writing like this needs to be read; finding it remains, however, a problem.

We have indicated that women's letters can be found in works by or about the men with whom they were associated. More difficult of access is the much larger body of material which remains in manuscript. The collection of State Papers at the Public Record Office, for example, contains numerous letters by women, and sometimes series of letters sustained over several years. Their variety is enormous: Constance Pley, for example, wrote letters to the Navy Officers over a number of years, and seems to have been in charge of a substantial business concerned with supplying the Navy and the import of goods. The collection contains letters by sectarian women like Hester Biddle and Anne Wentworth. The latter's prophetic letters to the king include an apology for her 'bad English . . . being it is a woman who hath no help of man': an acknowledgement, incidentally, of the relationship between language and social formation, refuting the idea that language is somehow autonomous and available to all. Secretaries of State intercepted letters from Quakers such as Mary Penington and letters thought to be seditious, such as that from Ann Blow to the Mayor of Chester and another, anonymous, letter from a woman telling the king exactly what his subjects think of him, his taxes and his war. Lady Rachel Russell's letters about her husband, and Aphra Behn's increasingly desperate letters from Antwerp – repeating information she had gathered, requesting aid and money, and testifying to her increasing sickness – are also here. The publication of abstracts of the documents (as the *CSPD*) provides an indispensable finding aid; but, as so often with indexes of any kind, it is hardly satisfactory as far as women are concerned. Whereas letters by men are usually abstracted fully whatever the content (endless instructions to tailors, notes about buying furniture, instructions to servants to send venison pasties to influential friends), women's letters are treated more briefly and dismissively. A letter from Albania Vane to Anne Hutchinson is thus abstracted as 'Gossip about private friends', while gossip in men's letters, elevated by the term 'private news', is recorded at length. Thus even an apparently detailed secondary source proves unsatisfactory because of the assumptions about women informing its compilation in the nineteenth century, and only a sight of the original letter (involving a trip to London and obtaining permission to use the institution's archives) can determine what a woman wrote.[9]

We have tried by including women writers of letters in the dictionary, and by this discussion, to draw attention to a form of writing practised frequently by women regardless of age, social status, religion or politics. Much has been made by critics of the development of epistolary fiction of the late seventeenth century; and, within that, women's contribution to 'the beginnings of the English novel' has been noticed.[10] The importance of reading women's letters in the way we have attempted it is that thereby we can not only recognise this development as part of a commodification of literature but also explore the effects of this commodification on gender relations and the discourses in which gender is inscribed.

6. MEN AS 'GATEKEEPERS'

Recent studies of contemporary women's writing and of the practices of publishers and review journals have identified the power of men as 'keepers of the gate', guardians of access not only to the institutions of study but also to those of publishing.[1] How easily such a concept can be transferred to the seventeenth century is debatable: more detailed work on the practices of women printers and publishers might, at least, complicate the picture, but so far there is no demonstrable correlation between women's interests as members of the book trade and the promotion of writing by women.[2] This might point to the split between the kinds of work in each case, one directed at a market, and the other, for the most part, not. In looking at why and how women came both to write and to publish, however, the effects of male power and control in the areas of education, publishing, and indeed at every stage of the production of women's writing, are evident.

The attitudes of fathers and male guardians were often crucial for women's acquisition of literacy and learning; we know little or nothing of their mothers' support, and women's recorded gratitude to fathers, reflecting the power of male heads of families, may be an acknowledgement of paternal power in matters educational rather than a denial of any encouragement by their mothers. The part played by mothers in supporting their daughters' acquisition of skills and learning needs to be explored. What we do know is that a number of women who developed skills and acquired knowledge of the classics, mathematics, astronomy, languages and the sciences benefited from having genteel/professional fathers who actively supported this kind of education for their daughters, or brothers from whom they could learn at second-hand. Women such as Ann Baynard, Elizabeth Elstob, Elizabeth Freke, Elizabeth Hoby, Anna Hume, Elizabeth Josceline, Bathsua Makin, Mary Sidney and Mary Trye were encouraged in their learning by men, and a number of women were accepted into male circles of scholarly friendship. Mary Blagge, Lady Anne Conway, Damaris Cudworth, Mary Davys, Sarah Fyge Egerton, Mary Evelyn, Anne Finch, Lady Mary Wortley Montagu, Katherine Philips, Mary Sidney and Lady Mary Wroth are among those whose male friends took seriously their intellectual capacities and achievements, including their writing. This is not to deny that circles of female friendship might be vitally important to these women: Thomasina Pendarves helped Elizabeth Poole; it was a woman friend of Anne Wentworth's who sheltered her from her husband's violence and urged her publication; and among sectarian writers the support of women co-religionists was particularly important. But acceptance and promotion by men, particularly when it came to publication, could be a crucial factor.[3]

The admission of some women into chiefly aristocratic literary circles need not imply, however, that they were always regarded then (or have been regarded since) as intellectual equals of men. Margaret Cavendish's attendance at Royal Society experiments, for example, was fiercely debated, and no official invitation was offered.[4] Moreover, whatever the status of these women among their contemporaries, many of them have been persistently characterised by literary historians as facilitators of male works, dispensers of intellectual 'tea and sympathy', rather than as thinkers and writers in their own right. The commodification of 'author' in our literary tradition works to obscure and deny the collaborative. Only recently, for example, has there been any interest in discovering Mary Sidney's share in work which for centuries has been attributed to her brother; her work as co-author, editor, writer and translator has been ignored or debased as the work of a helpmate, a kind of seventeenth-century unpaid secretary.[5] The benefits of participation in learned (male) society can hardly have been simple or direct, and there are enough examples in these pages of women educated (trained?) by husbands and fathers to be, in effect, unpaid and unacknowledged research assistants for us to view the occasional exercise of benevolent male patronage in the field of education as a mixed blessing. Anna Hume, for instance, translated her father's Latin poems and supervised his publications; this servicing of a male author must have been both spur and hindrance to her own writing.

Despite their learning and literacy, women frequently call attention to their 'bad English'. Hester Shaw says that she writes 'in the plain stile of a weak woman' and Elizabeth Warren is 'conscious of my mentall and Sex-deficiencie' despite her obvious Latin scholarship. Such remarks occur even in the writing of the most well-educated and fluent women writers such as Margaret Cavendish, who in the preface to her husband's life resolves, 'to write, in a natural plain style, without Latin sentences, moral instructions, politick designs, feigned orations, or envious and malicious exclamations'.[6] At one level she may be acknowledging, defensively, the irreparable inadequacies in her own education: although she is well-placed to write and publish (she has support from her husband, the wealth to publish her own works, and the leisure and confidence to write from a position of social superiority) she is still constructed as writer by the prevailing economic and social power relations. But in marking out her difference of style, against a background of male history writing which she is unequipped to emulate, she does more than defend her own inability to write 'Latin sentences': in claiming a 'plain style' for herself, she offers a critique of the male style, linking 'Latin sentences' and 'malicious exclamations' as the characteristics of male historians. The claim to 'plain style' and 'bad English' made by a number of women may indicate not merely defensiveness, but a refusal of male styles which marks out women writers as different – and separate – from men.

The power of men to help or hinder is most obvious, of course, when exercised in opposition to women's writing. Sarah Fyge Egerton's poem *The female advocate . . .* was apparently the cause of her banishment from home and estrangement from her father. Elizabeth Avery's brother opposed her writing for publication, mobilising the full weight of the family, including the memory of her dead father, against her: 'your printing of a Book, beyond the custom of your Sex, doth rankly smell.' Elizabeth Walker's habit of hiding her papers whenever her husband entered the room, and her extraction of a promise from him not to look at her writing while she lived, suggest that she was well aware of the low opinion of her style which, as her editor, he later displayed. Anne Wentworth's husband went so far as to steal her papers, and a letter written in her support and appealing for their return indicates what has been lost:

1. A book with a white parchment cover. The Epistle to the Lady Tyddle. The title, *A mother's legacy to her daughter*, dated 22 Sept., 1677.
2. A little book with a painted red cover having 8 or 9 titles with a prayer of faith to show my wrestling with God till I prevailed.
3. A paper of verses dated 22 Sept.

Anne Wentworth fled for her life from her husband, taking her child with her into hiding. Her friends attest that 'There is some other and greater thing than private differences between her and her husband, that has raised such a storm against her and exposed her to such unmerciful usage and oppression.' It was in fact her prophetic writing which led not only to her being battered by her husband, but also to her rejection by family, friends and Baptist congregation. What is clear from the letters is that the 'fraud and force' of the husband were focused, in the absence of the wife, on her writings. Her fears were that he and his co-religionists would not only suppress and revile, but also burn her work.[7]

Freedom from the influence of male family members, whether benevolent or antagonistic, may well have been a contributory factor in the development of several prolific women writers towards the end of the century, when writing as marketable commodity became an option. The writing careers of Aphra Behn, Mary Astell, Delarivier Manley, Susanna Centlivre, Eliza Haywood and Catherine Trotter were possible both because of the growing commercial value of writing, and perhaps because each benefited from periods of freedom from dependence on fathers and husbands. It would be misleading, however, to suggest that these women were entirely free from male control: male power was, of course, exercised through the market itself. The connection between commercialism and economic independence is important here: the determination to achieve economic independence arises out of the existing condition of the market, the exchange value of writing. There is no need, however, to retreat to a kind of Thatcherite romanticism and propose the struggle for economic independence as a prerequisite for the production of art; economic independence for women in the seventeenth century, as for women now, usually meant poverty, and the struggle to make a living must have deflected as many women from writing as it spurred on to write more. Bathsua Makin might well have written more had she not been burdened by debt; Elizabeth Elstob's pioneering Anglo-Saxon scholarship turned to 'a life of disappointment' when her need to make a living necessitated her working as a school teacher; the combined effects of childbearing and poverty clearly prevented Catherine Trotter from continuing her writing career.[8] The fact that so many women did write, despite glaring inequalities in education, unsympathetic (or, at best, indifferent) fathers and husbands, the pressures of poverty, and the exhaustion of childbearing and childrearing, is itself a cause for celebration; but we cannot ignore the fact that few women managed to overcome the material conditions of their lives and that many more were prevented from writing at all.

When it comes to the issue of publication by women, it can be seen that men could act as 'gatekeepers' to devastating effect. They were, of course, implicated in the wider social conventions and pressures which made women reluctant to expose themselves as 'fools in print'. The list of works included in Appendix I, II as anonymous or pseudonymous works by women needs investigation; men, too, wrote anonymously, sometimes out of fear of political persecution, but the reasons for the adoption of such a strategy by women need to be addressed. The protection of modesty and reputation may have been only one of several reasons why women refused to name themselves in print. Such texts, of course, have little status in an author-centred literary tradition, and the impossibility of identifying many of these women in terms of biography places their work on the margins of that tradition. Much more specific, though, is the part played by men in relation to the actual processes of publication. Women's texts 'helped' into print by men reveal the marks of male control, and the existence of such control needs to be taken into account when we read them.

One of the ways in which men might control women's entrance into print was as printers and publishers. Printers, with an eye to commercial opportunity, might encourage pamphlet debates and engineer their continuation. Jane Anger's pamphlet was probably solicited by the printer Thomas Orwin, who wanted to publish a 'reply' to another publication of his (now lost, entitled *Book: his surfeit in love*) which picked up the anti-woman stance of Lyly's *Euphues*, recently (in 1587) reprinted. The appearance of *Jane Anger: her protection for women* . . . in 1589 was part of Orwin's deliberate provocation of a pamphlet controversy. Ester Sowernam's *Ester hath hang'd Haman* . . . , which appeared thirty years later, seems similarly to have been 'set up' by a printer as a 'reply' to his own reprint of Swetnam's *Arraignment of lewd, idle, froward and unconstant women*. The engineering of pamphlet debates, especially those dealing in the relations between the sexes, resulted not only in printers approaching women to write for them, but also in male pamphleteers masquerading as women: *The women's sharp revenge* by 'Mary Tattlewell and Joan Hit-him-home' was the product of a male author (John Taylor) and a printer (John Okes) setting up another round of the gender debate following a reprinting of Swetnam in 1637.[9] The setting up of pamphlet debates about women was not new in the 1580s. Edward Gosynhill wrote on both sides of the debate in the 1540s, and the interest in the idea of women speaking out goes back at least as far as Chaucer's Wife of Bath. But while Gosynhill was writing 'for' women he saw no need to appear as a woman: what is new is the valuing of the idea of a woman speaking out in women's defence, and the 'faking' of a female authorial persona by Taylor and Okes suggests a new value being placed on the idea of women speaking and on the authority of what is spoken by them.

If printers found women's words (and sometimes pretended women's words) useful for commercial reasons, men with political or religious axes to grind found them useful as propaganda. Some women's words achieved the prestige (and permanence) of print because they served a particular religious movement or sect; but this could also lead to the words being manipulated and appropriated by the men whose interests were involved. We have already noted that Catholic writers might publish in obedience to their superiors, and there are examples from many denominations of ministers encouraging or organising the publication of women's work. The interposition of male editorial hands between women's words as spoken or written and the final printed version suggests – for a literary tradition which centres on author, 'author'ity and authenticity – a range of problems. *The confession and conversion of my lady of L[inlithgow]*, 1629, must have been a coup for the Presbyterians in Scotland. Helen Livingston, Countess of Linlithgow, was a (notoriously) staunch Catholic related to James VI; the placing of the king's daughters in her household for their education aroused great controversy. The leaders of the Reformed Kirk pursued her as 'a malicious Papist' and their hounding of her, despite her protection by James, was in part successful: after repeated attempts to prosecute her, and to convert her, she was excommunicated in 1597 and there were renewed attempts to remove the princesses from her care. In 1612, with James now in England, she was tried before the Presbytery, but remained unshaken in her faith.[10] Her conversion, close to her death in 1627, must have represented a huge success for the Presbyterians after so many years of struggle, and their desire to publicise it presumably lies behind this publication. The narrative presented as her conversion, however, seems to consist of notes of her conversation arranged (and perhaps augmented) by someone else. The 'confession' itself refers to her throughout in the third person, and the 'conversion' is made up of numbered statements of renunciation, a more conversational section in which she speaks of being in her old age and of hoping to hear 100 sermons before dying in the true Kirk, and a psalm and a prayer. The text ends:

> This profession of faith, meditations, prayers and prayses, as they were most joyfullie, and constantlie uttered, and declared before many honorable men and women: so were they most heartilie sealed and subscryved by the right religious, most noble, and truely wise Lady, the 25. of Maij. Finis.

Author-centred literary criticism has no place for a text such as this: it records, in the main, what appears to be a pre-prepared conversion service read at the bedside of a sick and elderly woman who 'subscryved' it. Little of it reads like direct speech, still less writing, 'by' the woman herself. Though the whole text is presented as 'her' confession and conversion, the little that may be attributable to the woman herself is difficult to unpick. In refusing to discard this text as not 'by' Helen Livingston, we wish to draw attention not only to the limitations of author-centred criticism, but also to the way in which a 'woman's text' could be used as a controlling mechanism by offering its readers a version of her life which satisfactorily normalises and neutralises the challenge posed by her actions. In Livingston's case, as in many others, the juxtaposition in entries of information about the woman's life with a text which substantially misrepresents that life, exposes the text as a denial, rather than an expression, of experience. We came across many women (often among the Quakers and other sectarians) whose lives were exciting and eventful, but noticed that the texts produced by these women excluded much of that experience. The texts seem to have been created in order to contain, to deal with, these otherwise unruly women. Notable amongst these texts are the 'confessions' of criminal women.[11] The degree to which a woman is present as 'author' is, in a sense, beside the point. Whether we look at Helen Livingston, who is hardly 'author' at all, or at Elinor Channel, who is presented more fully as originator of the text by Arise Evans, the minister who actually controls it, we have to attend to a dislocation between life and text. The text itself marks the terms of the woman's entrance into culture.

Less extreme cases than that of Helen Livingston are not necessarily more straightforward. How much, for example, of Bessie Clarkson's text is in any sense 'hers', and how much of it is the text of her amanuensis, her minister William Livingstone? The same question arises where a text purports to record a woman's dying sayings: in the cases of Loveday Hambly and Alice Hayes, whose text are we reading? Susanna Hopton's letter to Fr. Turberville, explaining her reconversion to Anglicanism, was published by Hickes in his *Controversial letters*; can we rule out the possibility of editorial interference by a man who, in publishing a collection in praise of Hopton, took pains to hide both her sex and her identity?

Sarah Wight's two publications were both accomplished without her knowledge. The account of her experiences and sayings published as *The exceeding riches of grace . . .* was put together by the minister Henry Jessey, who visited her regularly during her long fast and kept a diary of her physical state and her visionary utterances. He wrote down her 'Soliloquies' as she spoke them (herself unaware that anyone was listening) and drew on the memories of her mother and maid for further information. Jessey, along with the publishers Hannah Allen and Henry Overton, must have spotted the potential of Sarah Wight's experience as a narrative of interest to the radical sectarian community in London of which they were part. They entered the title in the Stationers' Register on 20 May 1649, at the point when Sarah Wight's death seemed imminent, and presumably they were ready to publish at that stage; in fact, she began to recover and publication was held back until after 16 July. Jessey's preface makes it clear that the first part of the account was being printed while the second part (the recovery) was still being enacted. Her recovery gave an added twist to the publication, which could now promote her as living evidence of a miracle as well as an exemplar of God's grace. The text was popular enough to merit three more editions, and that very popularity may have been the reason for the publication, in 1656, of her *A wonderful and pleasant . . . letter . . .* Although the letter is more clearly 'her' text, written by her to a friend, it was published without her permission, possibly as an attempt by minister or publisher to cash in on her earlier fame.[12] Editorial activity by the 'friend' who had it published is not explicit in the letter, but cannot be discounted. In what sense, then, is Sarah Wight an 'author' at all? Once again, an author-centred literary practice would regard such writing as not 'mainstream'; a judgment which serves not only to exclude another woman's voice from the canon of literature, but also to evade questions about the treatment of women writers which might expose the defensive male ideologies of scholarship. By including Sarah Wight as a writer, we want not to deny that texts such as hers ('hers') present difficulties, but to suggest that we need to develop a literary practice which can address these very problems. If orthodox literary history and criticism have nothing to say about such texts – beyond justifying ignoring them – then literary history and criticism need changing.

The intervention of ministers extends to many of the devotional writings and spiritual autobiographies of the period, and in particular to those published posthumously. Sarah Davy's *Heaven realiz'd* . . . , sold by Elizabeth Calvert, includes a first person spiritual autobiography and a number of verses; a crucial event in the narrative is her meeting and falling in love with a member of an Independent congregation – a woman. The 'publisher' (i.e. editor), 'A.P.', seems to have shaped and ordered the material, but the extent of A.P.'s intervention (and the possible omission of material) cannot be determined from the text itself. *Conversion exemplified* . . . , another posthumously published conversion narrative also sold by Elizabeth Calvert, is anonymous; its subject, 'a gracious gentlewoman now in glory', dictated the account to 'her dearest friend' who is unnamed. The only name mentioned in the 'Epistle to the reader' is that of Mr. Caryl (presumably Joseph Caryl), the minister who visited the 'gentlewoman' before she died; his part in the publication is not described, but it would seem likely that whether or not he was the 'friend' who wrote down the account he may have had a hand in getting it printed. Again, there is a strong possibility of male intervention, and in relation to texts such as these terms like 'authorship' and 'authenticity' (which locate value in individual expression and creation) become unstable, uncertain, and in the end of little use.

The influence of ministers on the publication of women's writing pervades all denominations, though it may have been stronger in some religious groups than in others. The control of male Quakers over what was published by Friends after 1672 was, for example, particularly effective. Whereas in the early Quaker period access to printing was organised locally by enthusiastic individuals, the post-Restoration establishment of a hierarchical organisation led to close co-ordination and centralised supervision. In the 1650s women such as Priscilla Cotton, Mary Cole, Rebeckah Travers and Martha Simmonds wrote and published as and when they chose. Sometimes women unused to theological debate turned to preachers for help, as Fox's journal records:

> Elizabeth Trelauny [*sic*] of Plymouth beinge convinct a baronetts daughter: the preists was in a great rage concerninge her & other great persons and professors (her kindred) & beinge a wise & tender woman in ye feare of God shee sent her letters to mee: & I aunswered the preists & if shee coulde owne ym shee might sett her hande to ym & give ym to ye preists which she did: & shee grew soe in ye power & spiritt (& wisedome) of God yt shee coulde aunswer ye wisest preist & professor of ym all.[13]

Turning to Fox and other male leaders to help with writing became, for some writers, a regular submission to them of manuscripts for approval: Dorothy White is recorded as sending a paper for Fox or Howgill to look at before its being printed.[14] The formalisation of centralised control over printing was eventually established by the appointment of a committee to supervise the press in 1672, and by the setting up of the Second Day

Morning Meeting the following year to deal with the financing, publication and distribution of Quaker books. Accusations of censorship were made by Friends resistant to the changes; Francis Bugg wrote to the Meeting in 1683:

> although any may affirm and say they are moved by the Lord to write a message, epistle or warning to a nation or people, yet say you by your practice, they ought to acquieze in your adding diminishing and altering ye same.[15]

No work has yet been done to establish how this may have affected, perhaps disproportionately, women Friends, whose early enthusiasm, enactments of signs and wonders, and opposition to the increasingly male leadership and its organisational reforms tended to alienate them from Fox; a thorough search of the Meeting's surviving records would be useful. But by the 1670s, many of those early women Friends opposed to Fox were no longer active as Quakers; the women who stayed, perhaps more conservative, grasped the opportunities for separate women's organisation which Fox's re-modelled Society of Friends afforded them in the establishment of Women's Meetings, and it is they who had to comply with the new controls on publishing. It is perhaps not difficult to guess the consequences for women of submission to a male editorial board. How many women were put off writing entirely by the new, formalised process we cannot know; but women who did submit manuscripts certainly faced criticism. Abigail Fisher, for example, was told by the Meeting that 'as to what's in verse, they rather advise to have it in prose'. Judith Boulbie repeatedly ran into difficulties in getting her work approved: her *A warning* . . . was considered unsafe to print 'without some alterations or amendments' and, although it was amended, 14 months later the Meeting still found it 'not mete to print'. Her paper written just after the 1688 Revolution was rejected because 'severall severe ancient pphesys applyed to England' were 'too generall & absolute'. As O'Malley remarks, 'the prophetic religio-political spirit which marked the early years of the movement was stamped on frequently' by the committee; and, inasmuch as many women Friends were in the forefront of that early wave, we can assume that women were among those stamped on.[16] Quaker control was not, of course, absolute, and the Meeting may have supervised only about 40 per cent of all Quaker books (though the minutes do not record all the publications which were passed without comment). Nevertheless, the rejection of about 20 per cent of the manuscripts known to have been submitted suggests the scale of the Meeting's intervention, and further study might indicate what proportion of those texts was by women.

The intervention of men as 'gatekeepers' is not confined to the seventeenth century. Women's writing of the period has continued to be used and abused, reprinted and distorted, well beyond their own time. In 1714 Steele used about 100 pages of Mary Astell's *A serious proposal . . .* in *The ladies library* without attribution; John Evelyn's anonymous publication of Mary Evelyn's work after her death has led to confusion about authorship and to frequent misattribution of the daughter's work to the father. Anonymous publication has often enabled later critics to attribute women's work to men with little fear of contradiction. Damaris Cudworth's *A discourse concerning the love of God,* published anonymously in 1696, was attributed to Locke; and the question whether or not Dorothy Pakington was author of the books variously attributed to Dr Henry Hammond (in the seventeenth century) and Richard Allestree (in the nineteenth) is, in the end, unresolved.

If we accept that publishing in the seventeenth century was at least as male-dominated as it is now (which seems likely), and add to that the fact that the operations of historians, literary critics, bibliographers and indexers have had a tendency to screen out women, then the cumulative effect of male controllers of women's writing is inescapable. Can there have been any women whose writings were unaffected by male control? We could point, perhaps, to women such as Elinor James and Martha Simmonds whose involvement in printing and publishing respectively would have given them the knowledge and opportunity to oversee the printing of their own texts; and aristocrats such as Lady Eleanor and Margaret Cavendish who could at least finance their own publications from a position of relative social confidence (though, interestingly, both were isolated, and felt themselves so, by their social equals). But although their material circumstances provided these women with a more direct access to print as one way of circumventing the 'keepers of the gate', like all other writers of their time they wrote and were read, then as now, in a society whose ideas about the status both of writing and of gender were male constructs. In different ways and at different times they all inscribe within their writing the tensions of the contradiction out of which they wrote: that of being both 'writer' and 'woman'.

7. WOMEN IN THE BOOK TRADE

The focus of our attention in the dictionary has been women as writers, but the active involvement of women in the material production of books, as printers, publishers and booksellers, must not be overlooked. In dictionary entries we have noted, where we have such information, the publication of women's writing by women working in the book trade, in the belief that the connections between women as writers and women as producers and sellers of books merit further exploration.

The participation of women in the book trade has been largely ignored by the trade's historians. Not surprisingly, perhaps, when they are noticed

such women are relegated to footnotes and parentheses within descrip-
tions of what is assumed to have been a male occupation. Recent work,
however, indicates not merely a few female exceptions to an otherwise male
trade, but a more common day-to-day involvement by women at a number
of levels.[1] Reliance on the records of the Stationers' Company, the 'official'
face of book trade history, is misleading: women were excluded from position and power within the Company, and it is usually the names of the male
members of book trade families which appear in Company records. The
Company did, however, concede a number of valuable rights to women:
stationers' widows, for example, were allowed to bind apprentices and to
hold shares in the Company's copyright monopoly, the English Stock.
From the late 1660s there was a growing tendency for girls to be bound
apprentices: in 1666 Joanna Nye became the first girl to be formally ap-
prenticed in the trade, to an engraver.[2] Despite their exclusion from office-
holding in the Company, women could exercise a measure of economic
power; printers' widows in particular were in a strong position at a time
when the number of presses was legally limited and growing numbers of
journeyman printers with no presses of their own were looking for work.

Throughout the century women are found entering copies in the
Stationers' Register; taking, transferring and freeing apprentices; being investigated, harassed, fined and imprisoned by the authorities for illegal or
'seditious' activities; and entering into trade partnerships. The chaos in the
book trade during and after the Civil War benefited women as well as men
printers, publishers and booksellers, and of the 300 or so women identified
as connected with the trade during our period, most were active after
1640.[3]

As well as radical and opposition publishers like Elizabeth Calvert, Hannah Allen, Anna Brewster, Joan Darby, Jane Curtis and the two Eleanor
Smiths, there were prolific and well-established women printers, such as
Gertrude Dawson and the great Quaker printer, Tace Sowle. Most of these
women had a family link with the trade (Mary Westwood, another Quaker
publisher, seems an exception here) and they were usually wives, widows or
daughters of printers or booksellers. The majority appear in records and
on title-pages only after the deaths of the men whom they succeeded, and
many of their working lives are completely blank except for brief periods of
documented activity occurring in the spaces between and after marriages.
Whether or not a woman was active in the business during the man's
lifetime, it is his name which appears in imprints and in records. Only
when a man is rendered inactive, temporarily (by flight from London to
evade creditors, or by imprisonment) or permanently (by his death), does
the woman's name appear in transactions. This sporadic appearance of
women's names creates obvious difficulties for anyone trying to trace their
activity over time; nevertheless it has been possible to establish, for some

women, convincing evidence of their development of and participation in businesses over several decades, and there is no reason to believe that these women are exceptional, except in the degree to which evidence about them has survived.

Some of the women included in the dictionary as authors were themselves active in the book trade. Elizabeth Alkin, more popularly known as 'Parliament Joan', was the most effective of Cromwell's agents in his campaign to clean up the Royalist press in 1650. References to her in newspapers of the time are numerous. One of her favourite methods was to flush out Royalist editors and sympathisers by peddling anti-government papers herself. As well as securing information about Royalist presses, she published two short-lived government papers, and a pseudo-royalist paper, *Mercurius Scoticus*, which she probably used to trap unwary Royalist customers. Payments to her for specific discoveries and for 'good service' appear in the State Papers from November 1651 until the following year, when she seems to have become short of cash. The success of her attack on the Royalist press presumably left her without employment, for in 1653 she was petitioning for a place as a nurse, and she was later paid for nursing sick and wounded seamen in Dover. Book trade historians who notice her have dwelt on a hostile description of her as a 'fat woman . . . about fifty', and have assumed (though with no supporting evidence) that the newspapers appearing in her name were in fact edited by a man.[4]

Elinor James, the wife of a prosperous printer, wrote prolifically about politics and current affairs, supporting James II and the established church. Not surprisingly, such a confident pamphleteer was considered eccentric, and attacked both on the grounds of politics and of gender: Dunton refers to her as 'that She-State-Politician' and Nichols notes her as 'a very extraordinary character, a mixture of benevolence and madness'.[5] Her *Advice to all printers in general* . . . , concerned with reforming the current practice of boarding for apprentices, attests both her knowledge of, and involvement in, the day-to-day running of the trade, which she clearly enjoyed: 'I have been in the element of Printing above forty years, and I have a great love for it.' Not one to avoid controversy, she had a tablet erected in St Bene't, Paul's Wharf, inscribed with the amounts of money she had given her children since her husband's death, and the dates on which the gifts were made, 'to prevent scandal'. A portrait of her shows her holding a copy of her own *A vindication of the Church of England*.

Mary Overton played an active part in the radical sectarian publishing network, and in 1647 suffered imprisonment after being caught stitching an illegal pamphlet, *Regall tyrannie discovered*. Her violent arrest led to a miscarriage. A likely associate of hers was Elizabeth Lilburne, who was also implicated in the distribution of Leveller pamphlets, and was arrested the same year for dispersing her husband's writings. As well as working for John

Lilburne's release, Elizabeth lived with him in Newgate, bore ten children (five of whom died young) and after Lilburne's death she was given a small allowance by Cromwell. Women were involved, too, at the very edges of the trade, as distributors of printed material: Mary Blaithwaite was punished for distributing pro-Parliamentary pamphlets in Cumberland. Martha Simmonds, anathematised by 'respectable' Quakers for her opposition to Fox and for her alleged evil influence over James Nayler, was part of a family network of publishers. She was sister of Giles Calvert who, with Elizabeth Calvert, ran a prolific radical publishing business at the sign of the Black Spread Eagle; and she was the wife of Thomas Simmonds, whose bookshop at the Bull and Mouth became a centre for London Quakers. Interestingly, Martha Simmonds' own pamphlets were published by her brother, rather than by her Quaker publisher husband; and when she was herself ostracised by Quakers it was the Calverts who withdrew from Quaker publishing, while Thomas Simmonds replaced them as the main Quaker publisher. When Martha was arrested after the 'blasphemous' entry into Bristol with Nayler, Hannah Stranger and Dorcas Erbury, a letter was found on her from her husband, in which he pleaded with her to give up her mission, suggesting that, like the Levellers whom Cromwell had suppressed by force at Burford, she and Nayler were doomed to failure:

> Dear heart my love is to thee . . . but this I could not but write, to warn you that you stand single to the Lord, and not believe every spirit. Your work is soon come to an end; part of the Army that fell at Burford was your figure.[6]

It seems, from her choice of publisher for her own work, that she drew support from the Calverts who shared her politics, rather than from her husband, who regarded her as an extremist.

What becomes apparent after tracing some of these women *across* entries, both as writers and as publishers or printers, is the existence of networks of common interest and acquaintance within particular (often sectarian) groups. Thus Mary Westwood, while remaining a mystery in terms of her own biography, appears elsewhere in these pages as the publisher of a number of works by Quaker women: Grace Barwick, Sarah Blackberry, Margaret Fell, Rebeckah Travers, Priscilla Cotton and Mary Cole. Her publication of these and other (male) Quaker authors suggests that she was operating an illegal trade, serving local groups of Friends, particularly in the Southwest of England. In particular, her association through publishing with the prophetic and enthusiastic early Quakers, several of whom later became 'dissidents' as far as the growing Quaker orthodoxy was concerned, may explain her absence from Quaker records: like Nayler and Martha Simmonds, she may have been deliberately excluded from Fox's version of the movement's early history.[7] Elizabeth Calvert, publishing for two decades alongside her husband and independently, as a widow, for another, is similarly connected with a number of women authors. While her imprint appears on few works by women, the inclusion of both Sarah Davy's *Heaven realiz'd* . . . and the anonymous *Conversion exemplified* . . . in her advertised stock lists in the early 1670s suggests that her business was an outlet for, among other nonconformist works, puritan women's spiritual autobiography.[8] Elizabeth Calvert carried on the trade in opposition literature after the imprisonments and trials of male radical publishers which effectively wiped out the ring of male 'Confederates' who had persisted after the Restoration. Both her husband and elder son died as a result of their imprisonments, and between 1661 and 1664 she herself was arrested four times, spending several months in prison and at least four months on the run. Thereafter, in debt from legal expenses and with her shop and stock destroyed in the Great Fire of 1666, she continued the business from new premises and continued, too, her 'under the counter' trade in illegal pamphlets. In the following years she was arrested three more times, was informed against, had books seized in London and in Bristol, ran a secret press in Southwark (at the house of Elizabeth Poole) which was found and dismantled by the Stationers' Company, and was eventually brought to trial in 1671. Her friends and associates included women sympathetic to the Simmonds–Nayler faction within Quakerism, and the association of the Calverts with radical causes remained steady. In 1649–50 they had introduced Laurence Clarkson to the Ranters; years later, in 1671, Elizabeth Calvert was a guest at the 'wedding' of Mary Boreman and John Pennyman. A letter to Margaret Fell from a London Quaker reporting the event indicates in its description of her as 'Jesebell' that there had been no rapprochement between her and orthodox Quakers.[9]

Networks of common religious and political interest uniting publishers and writers can sometimes be identified by attention to the names in imprints. Occasionally, a text itself can be revealing: it is clear, for example, from *The exceeding riches of grace* . . . that one of its publishers, Hannah Allen, was herself a visitor to Sarah Wight during the latter's extended fast. The appearance of Hannah Allen's name on a list of visitors which includes ministers, Parliamentary leaders and army officers both confirms Hannah Allen's involvement in the Independent congregation led by Henry Jessey, with whom she was associated in a number of other publications, and points to a community of interest between publisher and 'author'. Reconstruction of Hannah Allen's publishing career, and of her deliberate development of a publishing policy centred on Independency, republicanism and the radical wing which developed into Fifth Monarchism, affords a new basis for reading Sarah Wight's text, and argues that, like Jessey, who transcribed Sarah Wight's words, the publisher had a personal connection with the woman whose spiritual crisis she both witnessed and saw into print.[10]

A woman whose printing career is overdue for investigation, in terms of its importance within the book trade generally, and specifically for its contribution to Quakerism, is Tace Sowle, whose name appears on many Quaker works towards the end of our period. Her output includes work by Elizabeth Bathurst, Barbara Blaugdone, Jane Fearon and Abigail Fisher, and she printed the first part of *Piety promoted* . . . Tace Sowle was the daughter of the first 'official' Quaker printer, Andrew Sowle, and was herself freed by the Stationers' Company (i.e. given the 'freedom' of the Company, enabling her to print in her own right) in 1695, having taken over her father's business in Shoreditch four years earlier when he lost his sight. The business expanded quickly under her management: in 1694 she moved to the Bible in Leadenhall Street, where Meeting House and Quaker bookshop seem to have been combined in the same building. Her name appears in 205 imprints between 1693 and 1700 alone. After 1706 when she married a hosier, Thomas Raylton, the business passed nominally to her mother, Jane, who died in 1711; thereafter it passed to Jane's 'assigns'. But Tace Sowle was printing again, under her own name, and from her husband's address, at least as early as 1722, and from 1735 until her death in 1749 she printed in partnership with a relative, Luke Hinde, who was her executor and seems to have succeeded her.[11] Tace Sowle was a practical printer as well as a business manager, and Dunton testifies to her skill: 'She is both a Printer as well as a Bookseller and the Daughter of one; and understands her trade very well, being a good Compositor herself.'[12] As well as printing, she took an active part in Quaker affairs as a member of the London Women's Meeting. Her sister Elizabeth was also in the trade, though not in England: she married her father's apprentice, William Bradford, in 1685, and they emigrated to America where they set up presses in Pennsylvania and later in New York.

In drawing attention to some of the women whose names appear in imprints as printers, publishers and booksellers, we must not ignore the role of women in other branches of the trade, both legal and illegal. In the latter half of the seventeenth century women were hawkers of papers and pamphlets in the streets, and 'mercuries' who organised the wholesale distribution of newspapers. Both were risky occupations, as records of fines, whippings and imprisonments testify.[13] Women were drawn into distribution both by economic necessity and by religious and political conviction. The first distribution of Quaker pamphlets in London was effected by two women, and among the Fifth Monarchists there seems to have been a women's group which undertook the distribution of propaganda. Notes of a Fifth Monarchist meeting record that:

> the declarations be left with the sisters, that meet together, to be sent into the countries, all opportunityes after wee are gon; and to be delivered to the

churches and meetings in this citty, and published to all upon the 6th day of the weeke.[14]

The existence of a women's group within an organisation persistently characterised by historians as male (in books entitled *The Fifth Monarchy men*) is itself worthy of note; moreover, women's groups may well have been a feature of a number of radical sects.[15] Certainly, pairs of women preaching and travelling together are a feature of the early Quakers, pre-dating the formalised women's meetings set up after the Restoration; and the prophet Anna Trapnel reports meeting with her sisters before setting off on her mission to Cornwall.[16] In the 1670s there was an informal network of women handling the stitching and small-scale distribution of opposition pamphlets in London.[17] Countless women were involved at all levels of the trade, from the open trade activities of Elizabeth Calvert and Tace Sowle to the pyramid organisations set up (legally) by the newspaper distributor Mrs Andrews and (illegally) by the opposition printers and publishers Joan Darby and Anna Brewster; at a more humble level there were the regular hawkers and the women who, like Mary Blaithwaite and Isabel Buttery, got involved in distribution perhaps only once, because of a particular political or religious belief.

Much more work on women's activity in the book trade is still to be done. As yet there is no obvious correlation between women publishers and women writers, but the few established links between them are suggestive. Women's writing constituted so small a percentage of printed output that it is hardly surprising that no woman publisher or printer appears to have produced a relatively large proportion of women's texts; it would hardly have made financial sense for a woman to have set herself up as a seventeenth-century equivalent of Virago, Sheba or Women's Press. It is, however, important for our understanding of women as writers that the role of women as material producers of books should be investigated. The synthesis of what have until now been separate enquiries – one into women's history in the book trade, and the other into women writers – could prove especially fruitful in increasing our as yet piecemeal information about women working together, and could end the gap between 'book as object' and 'author's text' which is constructed by a literary study which ignores the processes of production. Problematising the word 'author', we have used the form of biographical dictionary in order to unpick it, exposing its limitations by insisting, through these critical appendices, on the reading of entries across/ alongside each other. But our intention is to attack not simply the form, but the critical values and procedures on which it relies; values and procedures which work to eliminate women's writing and which must, therefore, be abandoned. Now.

NOTES

(The place of publication is London unless otherwise stated.)

Introduction

1. See Linda Woodbridge, *Women and the English Renaissance*, Brighton: Harvester, 1987.
2. I Pet. 3:1; quoted in the Elizabethan *Homily on Matrimony*. For extracts from the homily and from *The law's resolutions . . .* , *1632*, see Simon Shepherd, *The Women's Sharp Revenge*, Fourth Estate, 1985, pp. 25–7.
3. Barbara J. Todd, 'The remarrying widow: a stereotype reconsidered' in Mary Prior (ed.), *Women in English Society 1500–1800*, Methuen, 1985.
4. Even the Levellers, most far-reaching in their demands for the extension of the franchise, seem not to have envisaged extending the vote to labouring men, let alone women.
5. Patricia Higgins 'The reactions of women, with special reference to women petitioners', in B. Manning (ed.), *Politics, Religion and the English Civil War*, Edward Arnold, 1973; for Mrs. Attaway, see T. Edwards, *Gangraena*, 1646: i, Appendix, pp. 120–3; ii, pp. 10–11, 101; iii, pp. 26–7, 188.
6. R. T. Vann, *The Social Development of English Quakerism 1655–1755*, Cambridge (Mass.): Harvard University Press, 1969; but Cross argues that women did not necessarily dominate congregations: Claire Cross, ' "He-goats before the flocks": a note on the part played by women in the founding of some civil war churches' in *Studies in Church History*, vol. 8, 1972, pp. 195–202.

1. Women's writing before 1640

1. Of the women writers we have found for the early period, i.e. before 1640, just over one third had their works published during that time.
2. 'Learned woman' is, of course, itself a mobile historical construction. We use it here in its early modern sense.
3. See entries for publication details, except for Barringtons (*Barrington Family Letters, 1628–1632*, A. Searle (ed.), Camden Society, 4th ser., vol. 28, 1983) and Verneys (*Letters and Papers of the Verney Family, Down to the End of the Year 1639*, John Bruce (ed.), Camden Society, 1853; Frances P. Verney, *Memoirs of the Verney Family during the Civil War*, 4 vols., 1892).
4. 'Address to The Countesse of Warwicke' in *Of the markes of the children of God . . .* , trs., 1590.
5. Quoted in Antonia Fraser, *The Weaker Vessel*, Weidenfeld & Nicolson, 1984, p. 327.

2. After 1640: the prophets

1. F. S. Siebert, *Freedom of the Press in England 1476–1776: The rise and decline of government control*, Urbana: University of Illinois Press, 1965; C. Blagden, *The Stationers' Company: A history 1403–1959*, Allen & Unwin, 1960, chronicles the internal wrangles of the Company.
2. Hobby, thesis; L. Spender, *Intruders on the Rights of Men*, Pandora, 1983.

3. For her arrest and imprisonment in 1633, see *CSPD* 248: 65, 93; 250:16; 255:19.

4. Hobby suggests that Moore's text is by a man, attempting to 'take on' the persona of the woman, but failing grammatically. For another example of 'shifting' subject positions, see Bathsheba Ferrar's letter (p. 276 below).

5. Catherine Belsey, *The Subject of Tragedy: Identity and difference in Renaissance drama*, Methuen, 1985, p. 149.

6. See N. Smith, *Perfection Proclaimed: Language and literature in English radical religion 1640–1660*, Oxford: Clarendon, 1989.

7. Moira Ferguson's anthology excludes prophetic writings; Greer's includes a mere 34 lines of Trapnel's verse.

8. K. Thomas, *Religion and the Decline of Magic*, Harmondsworth: Penguin, 1978, pp. 162–3. Thomas describes Lady Eleanor's staging of a protest against the Church of England thus: 'she went berserk in Lichfield Cathedral'. His muddle is exemplified when he remarks 'Yet, though undoubtedly linked to a hysterical temperament, her eccentricity is probably best regarded as a response to the social obstacles with which she had to contend'.

9. See p. 284 below for Sarah Wight.

3. Quaker women writers

1. We include more than 200 Quaker women writers, and it is likely that we have missed many whose writing is 'embedded' in testimonies and collections of Quaker writing.

2. Fell's text was reprinted in 1980 by Mosher Book and Tract Committee, New England Yearly Meeting of Friends, Amherst, Massachusetts. Todd's other five Quaker writers are Boulbie, Docwra, Travers, Hooton and Pennyman (Boreman).

3. Todd, p. xix.

4. Hobby, *Virtue*, ch. 2.

5. It is interesting that while Cotton and Cole's pamphlet was published by Giles Calvert, brother of Martha Simmonds, the Fox pamphlet was published by Martha's husband, Thomas, who seems to have distanced himself from the demands and actions of his wife and her women friends.

6. Swarthmore MSS, I.57; see p. 291 below.

7. See M. Bell, 'Mary Westwood, Quaker publisher', *Publishing History*, vol. 23, 1988, pp. 5–66 for fuller discussion of the struggle within Quakerism.

8. *ibid.*; T. P. O'Malley, 'The press and Quakerism 1653–1659', *JFHS*, vol. 54, 1979, pp. 169–84. The association of women with the distribution of pamphlets is a long one.

9. D. Runyon, 'Types of Quaker writings by year 1650–1699', in H. Barbour and A. Roberts, *Early Quaker Writings*, Grand Rapids: Eerdman's, 1973.

10. See Critical appendix 7.

11. For developments in Quakerism, see A. Lloyd, *Quaker Social History 1669–1738*, 1950, esp. ch. 11, 'The Quaker press'; L. M. Wright, *The Literary Life of the Early Friends 1650–1725*, New York: Columbia University Studies in English and Comparative Literature, 1932, esp. ch. 6, 'The distribution of literature'.

12. M. French, *Beyond Power: On women, men and morals*, Cape, 1985, p. 176; Joan Thirsk's 'Foreword', p. 17 and note, in *Women in English Society 1500–1800*, M. Prior (ed.), Methuen, 1985.

4. Petitions

1. Patricia Higgins, *op. cit.*
2. Hobby, thesis.
3. July 1653 petition for the release of Lilburne; see Higgins.
4. Higgins, p. 217.
5. For Chidley, see E. M. Williams, 'Women preachers in the civil war', *Journal of Modern History*, vol. 1, 1929, pp. 561–9.
6. Fraser, p. 239; the *title* given is wrong: properly, *To the supreme . . . of divers well-affected women.*
7. Individual petitioning also peaked in the 1690s.
8. See Fraser, chapter 11, 'A soliciting temper', which gives examples from Verney, Twysden and Knyvett families; and Hobby, thesis, for Stone, Henshaw and the Countess of Worcester i.e. Margaret Somerset.
9. The petition was presented on 11 May 1654, *CSPD* 71:61.
10. Quoted in Fraser, p. 240.
11. Women in the book trade often adopted the 'poor woman' stance to avoid prosecution; for discussion of the legal advantages of this role for women publishers, see M. Bell, 'Women publishers of puritan literature in the mid-seventeenth century: three case studies', unpublished Ph.D. thesis, Loughborough University of Technology, 1987.
12. Anne Levingston, *A true narrative of the case . . .* , 1654 and *The state of the case in brief . . .* , 1654; Mary Alexander, Countess of Stirling, *To the supream authority of the nation the Parliament of the Common-wealth of England*, 1654; Damaris Strong, *Having seen a paper printed . . .* , 1655; Mary Trye, *Medicatrix, or the woman-physician . . .* , 1675.
13. C. Roth, *A History of the Jews in England*, 3rd ed., Oxford: Clarendon, 1964.
14 John Archer, *The personal reign of Christ upon earth . . .* , 1642, published by Hannah Allen's first husband, Benjamin. The link between advocacy of toleration and free trade, with the Netherlands as the model, continued: see, for example, Josiah Child, *Brief observations concerning trade, and interest of money*, published by Elizabeth Calvert in 1668.

5. Letters

1. Letter to Sir William Temple, Oct. 1653.
2. Letter to Lady Mar, 1724.
3. For the Conways and Ferrars, see dictionary entries; see also *Letters and Papers of the Verney Family, Down to the End of the Year 1639*, John Bruce (ed.), Camden Society, 1853; Frances P. Verney, *Memoirs of the Verney Family during the Civil War*, 4 vols., 1892; *Knyvett Letters, 1620–1644*, B. Schofield (ed.), Norfolk Record Society, 1949; *Barrington Family Letters, 1628–1632*, A. Searle (ed.), Camden Society, 4th ser., 1983.
4. For extracts from manuscript materials and details of their locations see Linda Pollock, *A Lasting Relationship: Parents and children over three centuries*, Fourth Estate, 1987 and Ralph Houlbrooke, *English Family Life 1576–1716*, Oxford: Blackwell, 1988.
5. Quoted in E. A. Parry, *Letters from Dorothy Osborne to Sir William Temple 1652–54*, London and Edinburgh: Griffith & Farran, 1888, Introduction.
6. 'Extracts from reviews', appended to Parry, *op. cit.*, 'new and cheaper ed. with portraits', 1888?.

7. 'Extracts from reviews' in Parry, *op. cit.*

8. T. Docherty, *On Modern Authority: The theory and condition of writing 1500 to the present day*, Brighton: Harvester, 1987, pp. 63–8, discusses Bathsheba's isolation within the Little Gidding community, and the way in which her claim for parental and property rights conflicted with the Pauline patriarchal community: 'In Bathsheba Owen we see the beginnings of some kind of proto-feminist assumption of authority in historical action.' Her letter is printed in *The Ferrar Papers*, B. Blackstone (ed.), Cambridge: Cambridge University Press, 1938, pp. 288–9.

9. Letters to and from Constance Pley throughout 1665; a letter from 'Ester' Biddle in Bridewell (*CSPD* 1664/5, 103:75, 17 Oct.); letters by Anne Wentworth (*CSPD* 1677, 395:82, 84; 397:103, 104); a letter from Mary Penington (*CSPD* 1670, 441:70, 14 May); letter from Ann Blow (*CSPD* 1666, 175:86, 18 Oct.); letters from Rachel, Lady Russell from July 1683 onwards; and from Aphra Behn from 16 August 1666 (*CSPD* 167:160) onwards.

10. See, for example, Jane Spencer, *The Rise of the Woman Novelist from Aphra Behn to Jane Austen*, Oxford: Blackwell, 1986; despite attention to changing conditions in the late seventeenth century, both in the status of women and in the markets for literature, the connection between letters as objects of use and letters as 'literature' is not explored.

6. Men as 'gatekeepers'

1. 'Gatekeeping' is the 'Systematic use of processes of selection and censorship to ensure perpetuation of male views of the world. For example, publishers have an effective gatekeeping system which has helped to ensure that women's understandings of the world do not receive wide circulation in print' (C. Kramarae and P. A. Treichler, *A Feminist Dictionary*, Pandora, 1985). For discussion of the term see chapter 1 of L. Spender, *Intruders on the Rights of Men*, Pandora, 1983.

2. See Critical appendix 7.

3. See p. 291 below for discussion of groups of women.

4. Hobby, *Virtue*, p. 196 and note.

5. For a revaluation of Mary Sidney, see Gary Waller, *Mary Sidney, Countess of Pembroke*, Salzburg, 1979; and Waller's briefer survey in his *English Poetry of the Sixteenth Century*, Longman, 1986.

6. Margaret Cavendish, *The life of William Cavendish Duke of Newcastle . . .*, C. H. Firth (ed.), p. xli. Margaret Cavendish, perhaps uniquely, was a woman whose writing has overshadowed that of her husband: G. L. Anzilotti complains that encyclopaedias treat the Duke as an afterthought ('the Duke of Newcastle, husband of the whimsical Duchess'). Such a reversal of the usual state of affairs, while no less distorted than that we complain of, is perhaps the exception that proves the rule. (G. L. Anzilotti, *An English 'Prince': Newcastle's Machiavellian political guide to Charles II*, Biblioteca di Letteratura e Arte' 3, Pisa: Giardini Editore e Stampatori, 1988.

7. *CSPD* Oct. 1677, 397:103, 4. See Hobby, *Virtue*, pp. 49–53.

8. Elstob, letter to George Ballard; for more on Elstob, see Moira Ferguson, *First feminists . . .* and Ada Wallas, *Before the Bluestockings*, Allen & Unwin, 1929.

9. S. Shepherd, *The Women's Sharp Revenge*, Fourth Estate, 1985.

10. Information from introduction to facsimile of *The confession and conversion of my Lady C. of L.*, G. P. Johnston (ed.), Edinburgh: privately printed, 1924.

11. The (often fake) criminal woman's 'confession' is a genre that would bear further investigation; see, for example, Carleton, Higges, Mitchell, Page and Wilks.
12. M. Bell, 'Women publishers of puritan literature in the mid-seventeenth century', unpublished Ph.D. thesis, Loughborough University of Technology, 1987.
13. *The Journal of George Fox*, N. Penney (ed.), 2 vols., Cambridge, 1911: vol. 1, p. 237.
14. W. C. Braithwaite, *The Beginnings of Quakerism*, Macmillan, 1912, p. 304.
15. T. P. O'Malley, ' "Defying the powers and tempering the spirit." A review of Quaker control over their publications 1672–1689', in *Journal of Ecclesiastical History*, vol. 33, 1982, pp. 72–88.
16. *ibid.*

7. Women in the book trade

1. M. Bell, 'Women publishers of puritan literature in the mid-seventeenth century: three case studies', unpublished Ph.D. thesis, Loughborough University of Technology, 1987.
2. *ibid.*; in the eighteenth century, female apprentices within the trade were in fact bound to milliners and haberdashers: M. Hunt, 'Hawkers, bawlers and mercuries: women and the London press in the early enlightenment', in *Women and History*, vol. 9, 1984, pp. 41–68.
3. M. Bell, 'A dictionary of women in the London book trade, 1540–1730', unpublished Master of Library Studies dissertation, Loughborough University of Technology, 1983.
4. Many references to Elizabeth Alkin appear in *CSPD* between 28 Nov. 1651 and 11 May 1655; see also J. Frank, *The Beginnings of the English Newspaper 1620–1660*, Cambridge, Mass.: Harvard University Press, 1961.
5. J. Dunton, *The Life and Errors of John Dunton, Citizen of London*, 1818; J. Nichols, *Literary Anecdotes of the Eighteenth Century*, 2nd ed. rev., 1812–15.
6. Letter from Thomas to Martha Simmonds, quoted more fully in K. L. Carroll, 'Martha Simmonds, a Quaker enigma', *JFHS*, vol. 53, 1, 1972, pp. 31–52.
7. M. Bell, 'Mary Westwood, Quaker publisher', in *Publishing History*, vol. 23, 1988, pp. 5–66.
8. List of 'Books printed, and to be sold by Elizabeth Calvert . . .' at end of Samuel Petto's *The difference between the old and new covenant stated*, 1674.
9. Ellis Hookes to Margaret (Fell) Fox, London 21 8th (i.e. Oct.) 1671, Swarthmore MSS, I.57.
10. M. Bell, 'Hannah Allen and the development of a puritan publishing business, 1646–51' in *Publishing History*, vol. 26, 1989, pp. 5–66.
11. Bell, dissertation.
12. Dunton, *op. cit.*
13. Hunt, *op. cit.*
14. W. C. Braithwaite, *The Beginnings of Quakerism*, Macmillan, 1912, p. 157; T. Birch, *A Collection of the State Papers of John Thurloe*, 1742, vol. 6, p. 187.
15. L. F. Brown, *The Political Activities of the Baptists and Fifth Monarchy Men in England during the Interregnum*, Washington: Oxford University Press, 1912; B. S. Capp, *The Fifth Monarchy Men: A study in seventeenth-century English millenarianism*, Totowa: Rowman & Littlefield, 1972. Neither account has anything to say about the organised activity of women, beyond noticing Mary Cary as a writer.
16. *Anna Trapnel's report and plea . . .*
17. *CSPD* 1675/6, 374: 261, 281 (10 and 12 November).